THE WESTMINSTER CONFESSION OF FAITH

A Study Guide for the 21st Century

ROWLAND S. WARD

The Westminster Confession of Faith: A Study Guide

Fourth Edition

For information contact:

Tulip Publishing, PO Box 3150, Lansvale, NSW, Australia 2166

www.tulippublishing.com.au

Book and Cover design by Tulip Publishing

Cover Image: Westminster Abbey

PAPERBACK ISBN: 978-1-922584-01-4

HARDBACK ISBN: 978-1-922584-03-8

DIGITAL ISBN: 978-1-922584-02-1

NATIONAL LIBRARY OF AUSTRALIA

A catalogue record for this work is available from the National Library of Australia

10 9 8 7 6 5 4 3 2 1

"Rowland Ward's *The Westminster Confession of Faith: A Study Guide* has, in its various editions, been a constant and indispensable companion to me for a quarter century as I have taught the Westminster Standards in the seminary and church. There is really no modern commentary like it. If you have Robert Shaw, A.A. Hodge, Chad Van Dixhoorn, and Rowland Ward on the Confession, you really have the core library you need to unlock and apply the riches of the Confession's articulation of the Christian faith. I am thrilled that a new edition is coming back into print. Dr. Ward continues to improve an already superb and supremely helpful resource. The concision and accuracy of the theological background and summary that Ward provides, as well as the balance and insight of his historical and theological assessments, make this a "go to" volume for people who want to know what the Assembly intended in their formulations. I have pointed pastors, professors and students to this book for 25 years, and I will be recommending this edition in the years to come."

Dr. Ligon Duncan

Chancellor/CEO of Reformed Theological Seminary and the John E. Richards Professor of Systematic and Historical Theology.

"While older commentaries on the Confession are standard, there is a freshness about Rowland Ward's Study Guide that appeals immediately. Its information is up-to-date, and takes account of modern formulation of biblical doctrines. It is also designed as a study guide, which makes it suitable for group use as well as for individuals. Anyone looking for a good introduction and reliable guide to the Confession should get this book."

Dr. Allan M. Harman

Research Professor of Old Testament, Presbyterian Theological College, Melbourne, Australia.

"In the rapidly changing times in which we live, it is more important than ever that Christians are catechized in the whole counsel of God. And there is surely no better way of doing this than studying the great creeds and confessions of the past. Yet often these documents can seem alien and obscure to the contemporary mind. That is why it is so useful to have reliable guides to their teaching. Rowland Ward is one such, and this book is the fruit of a lifetime of believing and teaching biblical truth as summarized in the Westminster Confession of Faith. A great tool for personal and group study, and a sound handbook for ministers."

Dr. Carl Trueman

Professor of Biblical & Religious Studies at Grove City College, Pennsylvania.

"When our church's Adult Sunday School class did a series on the Westminster Confession of Faith a couple of years ago we did this in conversation with a couple of handpicked resources that aided us in our study. Dr. Rowland Ward's *The Westminster Confession of Faith: A Study Guide*, with its modernized text and brief yet precise commentary, was one of the resources that we constantly engaged with and learned from throughout the the two years of our study. Drawing upon scripture, tradition, and history, Dr. Ward explains the doctrines behind the text succintly and plainly without sacrificing theological accuracy and pastoral warmth. This excellent study, now made even better with fresh updates, is perfect for equipping classes, Bible study groups, or even for personal study. I commend it to pastors and to their churches everywhere."

James Bryner Chu

Minister of Pilgrim Community Church, Quezon City, Philippines.

"Dr. Rowland Ward is a well-known theologian who is particularly conversant with Reformed theology and confessionalism. His revised version of *The Westminster Confession of Faith: A Study Guide* is a pleasing gift to all lovers of biblical truth who are looking for a fresh but familiar statement of the Christian faith in the midst of pressing theological challenges. I am glad to recommend this book as a timely and readable guide to those essential truths in the Westminster Confession of Faith that form the basis of vital Christian witness and experience."

Peter Hastie

Principal, Presbyterian Theological College, Melbourne, Australia.

"The Westminster Confession of Faith may be venerable, but it's by no means outdated. There are compelling reasons for studying the Confession of Faith today, and Rowland Ward's excellent Study Guide is second to none in providing help for that healthy exercise. In an age of obsessive individualism, subjectivism and shallow thinking, the Confession provides clear, balanced and Bible-based direction in doctrine and life. Dr. Ward writes clearly, and with compelling brevity and wise moderation. He is concerned to address the issues and questions that face the churches today – and has wisely updated the Confession's language without altering its substance. Highly recommended, not just for students and church leaders, but for all thoughtful Christians."

Dr. John Nicholls

Former CEO of the London City Mission (2005–13), Board Member of the World Reformed Fellowship, Retired Minister of the Free Church of Scotland.

"There are several very useful study guides to the Westminster Confession of Faith currently available, but Rowland Ward's volume stands apart. Dr. Ward combines an acute theological mind and a warm pastoral heart, both of which contribute to this updated version of his widely used study of the Confession. The Westminster Divines, with their deep biblical knowledge and reverent submission to the Scriptures, produced one of the greatest summaries of doctrine in the history of the Christian Church. Most readers, however, need help to mine these riches, and that is where this study guide comes into its own. Dr. Ward has a thorough grasp of the debates in the Assembly which lie behind the text of the Confession and makes good use of this knowledge to expound each chapter of the Confession. He knows too that these truths are to be lived out and so doctrine is applied with wisdom and grace. All in all, this is an excellent resource both for personal study and also for the instruction of those who want to understand and be transformed by the Word of God."

Dr. David McKay

Professor of Systematic Theology, Ethics and Apologetics at the Reformed Theological College, Belfast, and minister of Shaftesbury Square Reformed Presbyterian Church, Belfast.

To the memory of Rev. James Forbes (1813–1851), the first Christian minister settled in such a capacity in Melbourne. Minister of Scots Church 1838–1846 and founder of the Free Presbyterian Church of Victoria [since 1953 incorporated into the Presbyterian Church of Eastern Australia—the parallel body in New South Wales], as well as other public institutions, he was a man of integrity and energy, abundant in labours.

On 7 March 1991 the James Forbes' School of Theology was inaugurated in conjunction with the Knox Congregation, which was still one but worshipping in three locations. This book contains the lectures, duly revised, given on Thursday evenings between August 1991 and November 1992 in the Knox building in Wantirna.

In issuing this new edition I also dedicate it to the people of the Melbourne PCEA congregations, and particularly to the Knox Congregation of which I was minister 1987–2012. Thank you, brothers and sisters, for your encouragement in the things of the Lord.

CONTENTS

Introduction 1
Dates and Events 6
Scripture and Confession 9

Exposition of the Confession

Part 1: The Foundations of Christian Truth

God's Revelation

Scripture's Nature & Necessity 13
Scripture's Authority & Perfection 29
The Use of Scripture 39

God and his purposes

God's Being & Blessedness 51
God's Trinitarian Life 57
God's Eternal Plan 71
Creation 89
Providence 103
Sin in the Human Race 109
God's Covenant with Man 113
Christ the Mediator 127

Part 2: The Application of Redemption

The human setting

Human Freedom 137

God's grace

God's Effective Call 145

Justification 153

Adoption 163

Sanctification 167

The response to grace

Saving Faith 171

Repentance Leading to Life 177

Good Works 183

The Perseverance of the Saints 189

Assurance of Grace and Salvation 193

Part 3: The Christian Life

The laws of God and man

The Divine Laws 199

God's Moral Law 207

Christian Liberty & Liberty of Conscience 213

Religious Worship 221

The Sabbath or Rest Day 231

Lawful Oaths & Vows 243

Civil Government 249

Marriage & Divorce 257

The Christian Church

The Church 269

The Communion of the Saints 283

The Sacraments in General 287
Baptism 293
The Lord's Supper 301
Church Discipline 309
Synods and Councils 315

The Christian hope

The State of the Dead & the Resurrection 319
The Last Judgment & Eternal State 325
Addendum: Note re Unfulfilled Prophecy 329

Additonal Chapters:

The additional chapters inserted by the major American Presbyterian Churches have a logical place at this point and therefore have been included for interest and because of their intrinsic value:

The Holy Spirit 337
The Gospel Call 339

Appendix

Subscription to the Confession in History

Scotland 342
Ireland 347
America 349
A Draft Modern Subscription 353

Selected Bibliography 357
Index of Names 371
Index of Prooftexts 375
Index to the Confession of Faith and Larger Catechism 391

INTRODUCTION

In 1643 the English Parliament called for an assembly of 'learned, godly and judicious Divines' [=theologians] to meet in London in order to advise it on matters of worship, doctrine, church government and discipline. Over a period of several years the resultant assembly drew up a number of important documents. The meetings formally commenced on Saturday July 1, 1643 in Henry VII's Chapel at Westminster, and in September 1643 highly influential Commissioners from the Church of Scotland were added. The documents produced included the Westminster Confession and two catechisms—Larger and Shorter.

On August 27, 1647 the Church of Scotland adopted the Westminster Confession 'as to the truth of the matter' and as 'most agreeable to the word of God, and in nothing contrary to the received doctrine, worship, discipline and government of this Kirk' (but with a qualification on 31:2). In 1846 the Free Church of Scotland disavowed that intolerant or persecuting principles are a proper part of a fair interpretation of the Confession, and it is the Confession as thus adopted and understood that is expounded in these pages. However, note has been taken of changes and additions to the text in American Presbyterian churches. Further, some account of the history of subscription in different churches has been given in an Appendix. So conservative Presbyterians world-wide should find this work of service.

Of course, the Westminster Confession is not a sectional creed since it has commended itself as an excellent statement of Christian truth to all who accept the authority of Scripture. With some changes, mainly on church-state issues and the sacraments, Congregationalists (via the *Savoy Declaration of 1658*) and Baptists (via the *Second London Confession of 1677/1689*) have held the same doctrines, and the teaching is in line with the *Thirty-nine Articles*, the nominal creed of the Anglican Church. If the Confession seems to express a minority position today it is more because of the weakness in the doctrinal interest and understanding of the modern church than from any defect in the Confession.

Text

For the purpose of study, a careful verbal modernisation of the text of the Confession has been incorporated in these notes. It is based on the critical text collated by Dr. S. W. Carruthers in 1937 and the text edited by John Bower and published by Reformation Heritage Books in 2020. The modernisation aims to retain the precision and majesty of the original and has been well received since its publication in 1996. As well as serving as a commentary for those with the original text, it will be easier to follow for newcomers to the study of the Confession. *Subscribers adhere to the doctrine expressed by the words rather than the mere words themselves, and no doctrinal changes have been introduced.*

Soon after Carruthers' text was published a manuscript in Cornelius Burges' hand (known as the Braye manuscript) was located. Edited by Carruthers it was published by the Presbyterian Church in England in 1946. Carruthers already knew its readings from the first of the three printed editions prepared for the Assembly, but now claimed the Braye manuscript was 'a more accurate text than has ever yet appeared', effectively shifting ground from his 1937 edition (see its page 19). The 1946 text was adopted by the Orthodox Presbyterian Church in 1956 and the Presbyterian Church in America in 1973. There are eleven or more changes commonly noted from the final edition supervised by the Assembly. The principal variations in the Braye manuscript are not of great moment and are as follows. At 3.4 (omitting is before so), at 6.2: *parts and* faculties rather than the reverse; at 7.3: *eternal* inserted before the last *life*; at 8.7: *acts* not *acteth*; at 10.4: *laws* not *law*; at 13.1: *once* inserted before *effectually*; at 15.3: read *it is* rather than *is it*; at 16.6: omit *Yet* before *notwithstanding*; at 23.4: *or* replaced *and* in '*and* other dues'; at 24.4 *by* the Word rather than *in*; and in 26.3: *propriety* replaced *property*. Only the last of these survives in Bower's critical text. This is also the case in Carruthers' 1937 text. The really significant differences in the Bower text are in regard to punctuation and to the nearly 2,800 proof text verses appended to the third printed edition as ordered by the English Parliament where 21 substantive corrections have been made.

In Bower's edition we have the final accurate text as supervised by the Assembly of Divines ignoring editions subsequently published. The Assembly's supervision was tighter than usual and extended to punctuation, capitalisation and spelling, which were commonly a matter of the printer's preference, and of course do not necessarily represent modern conventions. The differences between the Carruthers and Bower texts are minor and mainly in punctuation. There are of course a number of editions in print that have errors of various kinds so it is very helpful to have Bower's golden standard.

The Scripture texts given are designed to illustrate the scripturalness of the statements in the Confession, and they should be looked up and carefully considered. The Assembly was rather reluctant to include the texts, and only added them from an overall consideration of Scripture at the insistence of the English Parliament *after* the Confession had been completed. The edition approved by the Scottish Parliament in 1690 does not have the texts. Nevertheless, they can be of real service. Although there have been improvements in the selected texts in some editions of the Confession in North America, *the texts cited here are those included in the Assembly's final text* as established by John Bower unless otherwise indicated.

Commentary

The text of the Confession and basic format remains the same as earlier editions. The whole text has been reviewed, some quotations and questions added and the bibliography updated. Attention has been given to recent discussions on aspects of the Confession arising from the magisterial work of Dr. Chad Van Dixhoorn on the minutes and papers of the Assembly of Divines and other scholars' work in early Reformed theology (especially 2.1; 3.2; 3.6).

Some of the chapters of the Confession have been broken into two or more sections for ease of use in study groups. Even so, some chapters of this book provide too much material for one study session, and users should take the material at a pace appropriate for the purposes in view. The Select Bibliography has also been revised to take account of recent material.

This study guide is meant for a wide audience of Christians who want a balanced understanding of the Christian faith as understood in the Reformed tradition. My hope remains that it will be a helpful text not only for students in the affluent West, but for those in the developing world who have only a few books. May the Lord use this guide for his glory in the edifying of his people.

Rowland S. Ward

February 2021

'A creed, a system of doctrine is a necessity. It is a necessity of thought. It is a necessity of character. It is a necessity of instruction. It is a necessity of fellowship and co-operation. A cogent system of doctrine is an intellectual and educational necessity. If the Church would edify her people, unify and mobilise them, she must educate them after a thorough manner in her creed. Some are not of this way of thinking, they decry creeds; they demand a creedless Christianity, a religion without a theology. This demand has been called pious nonsense. Leave off the pious—call it simply nonsense. To say of a man that he has no creed is tantamount to saying that he has no intelligence and no character.'

J. B. Green[1]

'Whilst a short simple composition like the Apostles' Creed may express the Christian joy of discovery, it cannot adequately express the Christian passion for truth.'

Principal-emeritus Clement Graham (1919–2007),
Free Church of Scotland College, Edinburgh.

THE VOW TAKEN BY MEMBERS OF THE ASSEMBLY

I A.B. do seriously promise and vow, in the presence of Almighty GOD, that in this Assembly, whereof I am a member, I will maintain nothing in point of doctrine, but what I believe to be most agreeable to the word of GOD; nor in point of discipline, but what may make most for GOD'S glory, and the peace and good of this church.

1. *A Harmony of the Westminster Presbyterian Standards with Explanatory Notes* (Collins World, 1976), 7.

DATES AND EVENTS IN THE HISTORY OF THE WESTMINSTER ASSEMBLY OF DIVINES

1643

June 12	Ordinance passed by Parliament for calling an Assembly
July 1	The Assembly meets.
July 8	The Assembly forms its three Committees.
July 12	Revision of the Thirty-nine Articles begins.
Sept 25	The Solemn League and Covenant subscribed.
Oct 12	End of Revision of the Thirty-nine Articles.
Oct 17	Church Government under discussion.

1644

May 24	Report and debate on Directory for Public Worship.
Aug 20	First appointment of Committee re 'Confession of Faith.'
Nov 8	Form of Presbyterial Church Government sent to Parliament.

1645

Jan 3	Directory for Public Worship passes House of Commons.
Jan 23	Resolution of House of Commons supporting Presbyterianism.
Feb 3	Directory for Public Worship approved by Church of Scotland.
Feb 7	Catechism Committee to be augmented.
Feb 10	Form of Presbyterial Church Government approved by Church of Scotland
May 12	Small Confession Committee reports.
July 7	Directory for Church Government sent to Parliament
July 11	Confession of Faith Committee divided into three.
Sept 12	Rous' Psalms as revised approved by Assembly.

1646

Oct 9	House of Commons requires proof-texts with Confession.
Dec 4	Text of Confession completed.

1647

Apr 29	Confession with Scripture proofs presented to Parliament.
Aug 27	Confession adopted by Church of Scotland.
Oct 15	Larger Catechism completed.
Nov 25	Shorter Catechism presented to House of Commons.

1648

Apr 14	Catechisms with Scripture citations presented to Parliament.
Jul 2	Larger Catechism approved by the Church of Scotland.
Jul 28	Shorter Catechism approved by the Church of Scotland.

1649

Jan 30	Execution of Charles I at Whitehall.
Feb 7	Confession ratified by Scottish Parliament.
Feb 22	Last numbered session.

1652

Mar 25	Assembly record ends (for previous 3 years a Committee for examining Ministers).

1653	Concluded (minutes lost)

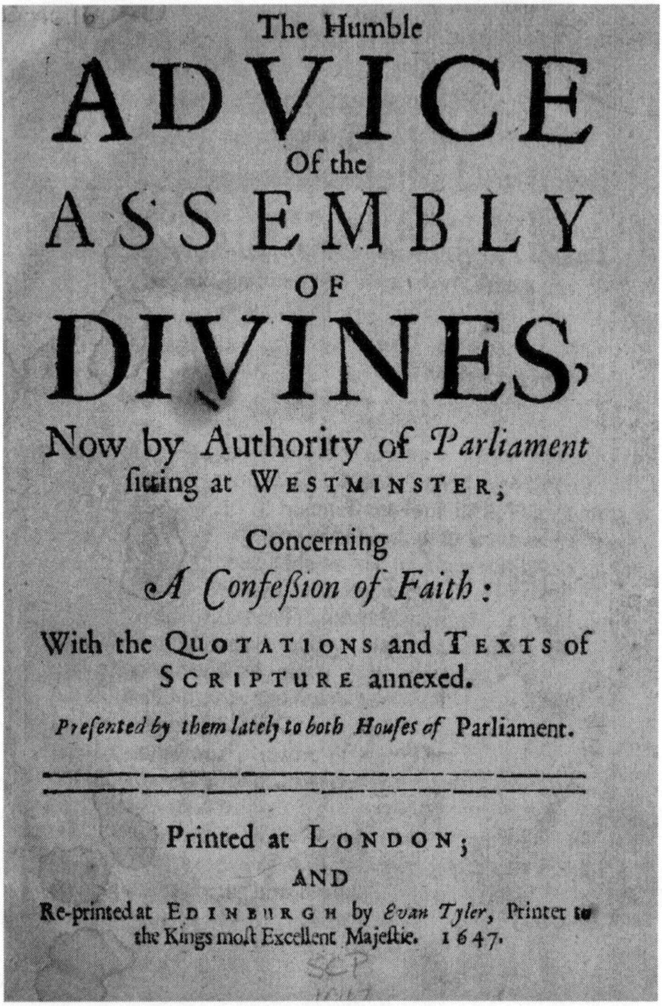

The Humble
ADVICE
Of the
ASSEMBLY
OF
DIVINES,
Now by Authority of *Parliament* sitting at WESTMINSTER;
Concerning
A Confession of Faith:
With the QUOTATIONS and TEXTS of SCRIPTURE annexed.
Presented by them lately to both Houses of Parliament.

Printed at LONDON;
AND
Re-printed at EDINBURGH by *Evan Tyler*, Printer to the Kings most Excellent Majestie. 1647.

The original title page. The Minutes describe the document as 'the Confession of Faith' by which name it was known in Scotland, where it was adopted with certain qualifications in 1647. The original title reflects the point made in WCF 31:5. The English Parliament published it in 1648 with some alterations on church and state issues under the title, 'Articles of Christian religion...' In 1660 it was declared to be the 'Public Confession of the Church of England' by the 'Rump Parliament' but was almost at once abandoned following the restoration of the monarchy the same year.

SCRIPTURE AND CONFESSION

In the early years of the Christian Church it was enough to assert belief in some major truths of the Scriptures. Yet a brief confession, such as 'Jesus is Lord', has many implications. As differences arose among those who claimed loyalty to Christ and the Scriptures, it was necessary to set out some of these implications at length.

In early Christian centuries there was much dispute concerning the person of Christ and his relationship to the Father and the Holy Spirit. The orthodox of the time set out their understanding in a form we sum up as the doctrine of the Trinity. In the 16th century Reformation the issues included the relationship of Scripture and church tradition, the nature of justification, and the nature of the church and the sacraments. Protestants made statements on such issues, protesting against the denial of Scripture as the primary and ultimate standard. In the early 17th century there was controversy over God's grace and salvation leading to the Calvinistic statements of the Synod of Dort 1618/19.

While the Roman Catholic Church produced its decrees and sought submission to them on the authority of the Church, Protestants produced creeds but insisted on the primacy of Scripture, not Church or pope. Many Confessions were produced in the different lands to which the Reformation spread. The Westminster Confession of 1646/47 comes at the virtual close of the creed-writing age among Protestants. This accounts in part for it being really the high—water mark of Protestant creedal composition.

The primacy of Scripture is to be respected in Christ's Church. Elders and ministers are not to be chiefly specialists in Canon Law, resisting examination of the Word of God by a mere citation of the Confession of Faith. They *are* to be capable teachers of the Word of God, for it is to such that Christ has committed the affairs of his Church. The past cannot be ignored but the Gospel must be confessed in the present.

Hence, the FIRST function of a Confession of Faith is to make sure that Scripture is our primary standard in all matters of faith and conduct.
We make that claim in the very first question addressed to candidates for office! This question is commonly along the lines: '*Do you believe the Scriptures of the Old and New Testaments to be the Word of God and the only rule of faith and practice?*' Thus a truly Scriptural Confession derives its authority from the Scriptures, not the other way around. The placement of the subject of Scripture as Chapter 1 in the Westminster Confession reminds us of this in a striking way. Also important is the way in which the Confession drives us back to the Scriptures in any controversy (1:8–10).

A SECOND function of a Confession of Faith is to provide a rallying point for those of like mind concerning the main teachings of Scripture.
A Church with a Confession of Faith is saying that individualistic interpretation of the Bible is not right. It is within the community of faith that we learn and confess together as Christians. A Confession will probably become more full in the light of fresh disputes or heresies that require a response, although it can never be a kind of definitive commentary on every passage of Scripture. Its explanations, however good and correct, are not inspired as Scripture is. Indeed, it is always open to revision and restatement in the light of Scripture as the primary standard.

A THIRD function of a Confession of Faith is to serve as a public statement of the faith of the people of God, and to instruct in the faith.
A Confession of Faith will be carefully expressed but it should not be in old-fashioned language lest it fail to be an adequate public statement and means of instruction. Its coverage is not all the small points of debate in the theological schools, but the grand and clearly revealed truths in the Bible, which it seeks to commend to others. Scriptural Confessions and catechisms form excellent devotional manuals and should be used as such.

A FOURTH function of a Confession of Faith is to be a solemn bond for the office-bearers of the Church.
Their subscription to such a form of sound words provides a bond of fellowship and co-operation. The terms of subscription must recognise the primary authority of Scripture as the rule of faith. And the vow must be taken sincerely (WCF 22:4), therefore also the meaning of the Confession must be clear.

A Confession produced by a meeting of many minds and/or formally adopted by the Church is likely to have greater authority than the opinion of an individual. Office-bearers need to be particularly careful not to elevate personal opinions on subsidiary issues to greater importance than the teachings expressed in the Confession. The Confession sets out the highway; preoccupation with the side-tracks is not helpful.

The Roman Church made its appeal to Scripture and tradition including decrees of Councils. Canon Law was the rule of faith not the Scriptures. The Confession forbids us to make Synods or Councils the rule of faith, and this is a uniform principle of our Reformed tradition (eg. *Belgic Confession* Art 7; *Second Helvetic Confession* Ch II). Thus the productions of the Westminster Assembly cannot be regarded as the *rule* of faith, but they may be and ought to be a *help* to faith (WCF31.4).

True, appealing to Scripture against the Confession in any significant way does involve 'abandonment of the communion of which the Confession is the bond'.2 Yet even here, any judicial proceeding should emphasise the Scripture basis of the doctrine rejected. That will honour the Confession, because that will honour Scripture!

A FIFTH function of a Confession is to form the basis of the trust on which Church property is held.

If these trusts do not give any power of change at all, to that extent they may not conform to the inherent power of the Church to formulate her Confession, subject to Holy Scripture, as set out above.3 On the other hand, those who seek change have often done so with a view to modifying adversely the essential doctrine of the Confession, rather than making it an even closer representation of the teaching of Scripture. If there is a genuine unanimity on the scripturalness of proposed changes, there should be no problem.

FOR DISCUSSION

1. What is a creed?
2. All truth is important but are some truths more important than others? Consider 1 Cor.15:1ff.
3. Is there a basis in Scripture for a form of sound words, faithful sayings? Consider 1 Tim. 1:15–16; 1 Tim. 4:9; 2 Tim. 1:13; Rom. 10:9–10; 1 Cor.11:23f; Luke 12:8–9.
4. What are some ways the Confession and Catechisms can be of help in your Christian life?
5. Recall the five points made in this section.

---

1. John Macpherson, *The Confession of Faith* (T. & T. Clark, 1882), 2.
2. Note this point in *Constitutional Catechism of the Free Church of Scotland* (1847) Q.44 & fn.

CHAPTER 1
1–3: SCRIPTURE'S NATURE AND NECESSITY

ANALYSIS ***WCF 1:1–3***

1. Revelation

a. General or natural revelation
- true but now inadequate

b. Special revelation
- necessary due to sin
- a variety of ways
- now committed to writing
  - i. to preserve the truth
  - ii. to comfort the church
- former ways have ceased

2 & 3. What Scripture is

a. positively, inspired books — OT/NT
b. negatively, not uninspired writings
c. purpose: to be rule of faith and life

The first chapter of the Confession of Faith is widely admired as one of the best statements of a doctrine ever written. Most Protestant creeds had begun with the subject of God, but Westminster follows the First and Second Helvetic Confessions (1536/66) and the Irish Articles (1615) in giving Scripture the first place. Indeed, all differences about God among men ultimately go back to differences about Scripture. In other words, Scripture is the ultimate foundation of theology, and it is fitting to begin with it.

Although the inspiration of Scripture was not as such an issue between the Church of Rome and Protestants at the time of the Reformation, in actual fact there was and still is a great deal of difference between the two on the doctrine of Scripture. These differences were very much in mind when Chapter 1 was written.

- Rome held that special revelation was necessary, but that it was not necessary for it to be in written form.
- Although Rome recognised Scripture as genuine and divine, generally her apologists held that the church could manage without it. The writers of Scripture were not regarded as under a divine direction to write, but wrote merely because the circumstances of the time suggested that it was expedient.
- Always Rome had in view support for her traditions, unwritten teachings and the authority of the Pope. Thus Rome not only cast doubt on the necessity of Scripture but accepted some extra books (the Old Testament Apocrypha) at the Council of Trent in 1546.

FIVE POINTS ABOUT SCRIPTURE IN THE CONFESSION

B*iblical, not Biblicist in approach.* The WCF does not look simply for a text on which to pin a doctrine but considers the unified teaching of Scripture. It acknowledges over against the Anabaptists the validity of good and necessary consequences of Scripture statements [WCF 1:6]. The nearly 2,800 verses appended to the Confession are rooted in an exegetical tradition rather than being isolated proof texts.

L*iteral, not literalistic in interpretation.* By literal we mean that we are to interpret each part according to its literary form and its intended place in the unfolding of the drama of salvation according to God's covenant purpose [WCF 7]. Literalistic interpretation leads to making such a radical distinction between Israel and the church that the intention of God's covenant with Israel to provide a preparatory portrayal of the realities that come in Christ and the new covenant is missed.

E*vangelical not rationalistic or mystical reception of the word of God.* The Confession recognizes that humans have true knowledge by the light of nature. It also acknowledges Scripture has many good arguments supporting its Divine character. Nevertheless, the Confession insists that a *saving* knowledge is the work of the Spirit *by* and *with* the word [WCF 1:5; cf 14:1–2]. So it rejects a merely rational approach, and also mystical experience not informed by Scripture. In WCF 1:10 the words 'the Holy Spirit speaking in the Scriptures' also remind us that Scripture is no bare word but living and active in the Spirit's hands.

Sole sufficiency of Scripture as the rule of faith. The WCF rejects anything additional to Scripture in matters of faith and worship [WCF 20:2]. In asserting that God's former ways of revealing his will have ceased [WCF 1:1] the Confession simply spells out what is fundamental to the entire Reformed position. Any question of non-canonical 'revelations' today is really a matter more properly discussed under the heading of guidance or assurance. New revelation for the church is not being given today.

Truthfulness of Scripture as the fully inerrant or verbally inspired word of God.
Part of the 1974 'Chicago Statement on Biblical Inerrancy' states fairly: "We deny that it is proper to evaluate Scripture according to standards of truth and error that are alien to its usage or purpose. We further deny that inerrancy is negated by Biblical phenomena such as lack of modern technical precision, irregularities of grammar or spelling, observational descriptions of nature, the reporting of falsehoods, the use of hyperbole and round numbers, the topical arrangement of material, variant selections of material in parallel accounts, or the use of free citations." [Art. XIII]

1.1 The Word of God and Scripture

Although the human conscience and the works of creation and providence so clearly show the goodness, wisdom and power of God, that human beings are without excuse,[1] they are not sufficient to give that knowledge of God, and of his will, which is necessary for salvation.[2] Therefore it pleased the Lord at different times and in various ways to reveal himself, and to declare his will to his church.[3] Afterwards, for the better preservation and propagation of the truth, and for the more sure establishment and comfort of the church against the corruption of the human heart, and the malice of Satan and of the world, God was pleased to commit this revelation of himself and his will wholly to written form.[4] Accordingly, the Holy Scripture is now essential,[5] for God's former ways of revealing his will to his people have ceased.[6]

1. Rom. 2:14,15; Rom. 1:19–20; Psalm 19:1–3; Rom. 1:32 with 2.1.
2. 1 Cor.1:21; 1 Cor.2:13–14. 3. Heb. 1:1
4. Prov. 22:19–21; Luke 1:3–4; Rom. 15:4; Matt. 4:4,7,10; Isa. 8:19–20.
5. 2 Tim. 3:15; 2 Pet. 1:19. 6. Heb. 1:1–2.

The fundamental reality is the God is Creator and we are creatures and therefore accountable. We know ourselves to be so but seek to suppress the truth and to express ourselves in evil ways that are a fruit of our sinful rebellion. This natural or general revelation (as it is called) is a reality for all humans and the illustrative texts in Romans speak powerfully to it. Of course once a transcendent purpose is abandoned one is left to construct reality for oneself and in our world of many choices my autonomy is fundamental. In our modern society this has come to the point where identity is found in freedom to be what I want and specifically, sex has replaced gender as the key identity marker in the general society as traditional ideas of community have declined. Whatever would restrict the sexual expression of the individual must be swept aside as harmful, including traditional marriage, and traditional church teaching is stigmatised as homophobic, and hurtful. The LBGTQI movement and the rise of radical transgenderism follows. Romans speaks realistically in the first century of our era and still today. The importance of understanding natural or general revelation is therefore vital not so as to abuse individuals but to ensure we bring the truth to bear which diagnoses the plight of man but brings the message of the powerful grace of God through the special revelation God has given to his rebellious creatures.

Scripture arises from the saving work of God in history. In the Old Testament period God revealed himself and his will in many different ways—dreams, visions, angelic visitations etc. In the time of Moses (c.1400 BC) much was given in written form, and subsequent prophets called the people back to faithfulness to God's word through Moses. In doing so they gave oral teaching and later there was much written revelation too. The essence of both unwritten and written revelation is the will of God made known, the teaching of God which for good reasons God now brings to us solely in written form, the former ways of revealing himself and his will having ceased. Thus, the church may be older than the Scripture (the written word) but it is not older than the word of God preached by apostles and prophets who, indeed, are the church's foundation (Eph. 2:20). The word of God is now to be found only in sacred Scripture. Similarly, WLC 3: 'The Holy Scriptures *are the Word of God, the only rule of faith and obedience*.' Notice the formulation of WSC 2: 'The word of God *which is contained in the Scriptures …*' The contrast is not between parts of Scripture only some of which are the word of God, but between the word of God in *unwritten* form and the word of God in *written* form: the words define the location of the word of God. God is the god of words but also saving deeds in his Son, but appeal to Christ, the Word of God (John 1), to the detriment of the Scripture is illegitimate since God is its ultimate author.

Orthodox Protestants hold that it was God's intention that his word be reduced to writing, doubtless because of a written form being more effective in preserving the truth. In regard to the Old Testament we see this intention in several ways but we will limit ourselves to the New Testament witness:

- Writing to the Church at Rome Paul says: 'For everything written in the past was written to teach us, so that through endurance and the encouragement of the Scriptures we might have hope' (Rom. 15:4).
- To a chiefly Gentile church at Corinth Paul draws teaching from the Old Testament history affirming: 'These things happened to them as examples and were written down as warnings for us, on whom the fulfillment of the ages has come' (1 Cor.10:11).

If the Old Testament was given by God with us in mind, as these quotations show, how much more the New Testament! Indeed, the New Testament era is one in which the word of God again is being put into written form. Thus, Peter classes Paul's writings with 'the other Scriptures' (2 Pet. 3:16).

If we accept Augustine's dictum: 'The New is in the Old concealed, the Old is in the New revealed'[4] we can see that the New completes the Old and gives us a completed canon of faith.

At the same time we must not under-estimate the New Testament warnings of apostasy, and the signs of this already in the first century (cf. Revelation 2 and 3). This underscores the importance of the word of God in written form and warns against making even early teaching or practices not warranted by Scripture a rule for ourselves.

The word of God is the highest authority and by its very nature judges all other authorities. Accordingly, God's people are warned about adding to or subtracting from the word of God (Deut. 4:2; Rev. 22:18–19). We could lawfully add to the Bible only if we had further words from God given for this purpose. Rome cannot provide words from God undoubtedly going back to Christ and his apostles, and so resorts to claiming a supposedly infallible authority over Scripture to prevent its proper authority over the church.

God did not have to put his revelation in written form, but once he had determined to do so and to cease other methods (by angels, dreams, personal communications etc.), the Scripture is essential. Note that the Bible is not a history of revelations but is itself the revelation of God and his will for us. In short, everything now revealed for our guidance is written. The Old Testament was written with New Testament believers, even of Gentile background, such as those at Rome and Corinth, in view (Rom. 15:4; 1 Cor. 10:11). The same principle applies to the NT Scriptures.

4. Augustine (AD 354–430) was bishop of Hippo in North Africa, and one of the greatest thinkers in the history of the Christian church.

THOUGHTS FROM OTHER MINDS

'The idea that all human beings are of equal worth is rooted in the idea that all human beings are made in the image of God. The problem with expressive individualism is not its emphasis on the dignity or individual value of every human being. That is what undergirded the fight against slavery in the nineteenth century and the civil rights movement of the 1950s and 1960s. Rather, it is the fact that expressive individualism has detached these concepts of individual dignity and value from any kind of grounding in a sacred order.'

Carl R. Trueman[5]

'The heavenly Father, who instructs his people as the head of a family (Deut. 8:5), taught the church, when it was still young and childish, by the spoken word, the most simple form of revelation. Then, as it began to mature and was established under the law in its early youth, he taught both by the spoken word, because of continuing childishness, and by writing, because of the beginnings of maturity, until the apostles' time. But when the church had reached adulthood, under the gospel, he wanted it to be satisfied with the most perfect form of revelation, that is, the written light.'

Francis Turretin (1623–1687)[6]

FOR DISCUSSION

1. How is it that there are different religions if humans are God's creatures?
2. What is the position of those who have natural (i.e. general) revelation only?
3. 'The church existed before the New Testament therefore Scripture is subject to the Church.' Refute this claim.

5. *The Rise and Triumph of the Modern Self* (Crossway, 2020), 387.
6. *Institutes of Elenctic Theology*, ed. James T. Dennison, Jr., trans. George Musgrave Giger (P&R Publishing, 1992), 1:57.

1.2 What books form part of Scripture?

Under the name of Holy Scripture, or the word of God written, are now comprised all the books of the Old and New Testaments, namely,

THE OLD TESTAMENT

Genesis	1 Kings	Ecclesiastes	Obadiah
Exodus	2 Kings	Song of Songs	Jonah
Leviticus	1 Chronicles	Isaiah	Micah
Numbers	2 Chronicles	Jeremiah	Nahum
Deuteronomy	Ezra	Lamentations	Habakkuk
Joshua	Nehemiah	Ezekiel	Zephaniah
Judges	Esther	Daniel	Haggai
Ruth	Job	Hosea	Zechariah
I Samuel	Psalms	Joel	Malachi
II Samuel	Proverbs	Amos	

THE NEW TESTAMENT

The Gospels:	Galatians	Epistle of James
Matthew	Ephesians	1 Peter
Mark	Philippians	2 Peter
Luke	Colossians	1 John
John	1 Thessalonians	2 John
The Acts of the Apostles	2 Thessalonians	3 John
	1 Timothy	Jude
Paul's Epistles:	2 Timothy	Revelation
to the Romans	Titus	
1 Corinthians	Philemon	
2 Corinthians	Epistle to the Hebrews	

All of these are given by inspiration of God to be the rule of faith and life.[7]

7. Luke 16:29,31; Eph. 2:20; Rev. 22:18,18; 2 Tim. 3:16.

The last sentence, 'All which are given by inspiration of God, to be the rule of faith and life' (1646 text) is not a definition of inspiration as if inspiration extends only to matters of faith and life and not to matters of fact and history. Rather it is an assertion of the inspiration of all the 66 books, so that they are 'the word of God written' and thus not 'human writings' [WCF 1:3] as are uninspired books. Hence also the statement that God is their 'author' [WCF 1:4] and that they are 'immediately inspired by God' [WCF 1:8], possessing 'entire perfection' and 'infallible truth' [WCF 1:5].

The modern term 'inerrancy' is not used. However, although this term is sometimes today associated with an extreme literalism and a preoccupation with seeking to prove Scripture by rational arguments, there is no doubt that the complete reliability of Scripture in all it affirms is taught by the Confession. The term 'inerrant', correctly understood, is an appropriate description. Of course, the Bible is given primarily in order that we might know what to believe concerning God and what duty God requires of man (WSC 3). This fact must not be lost sight of by an exaggerated use of Scripture to answer those questions which are outside its purpose. Nor should the occasional obscurities or difficulties in parts of Scripture lead to scepticism about the whole but to humility.

The Scripture canon

The word 'canon' means 'rule' or 'standard.' The canon of Scripture is therefore the list of books that are the rule of Christian teaching.

Old Testament

The canon includes the Old Testament (contrary to some Anabaptists in Reformation times and, in practice, many people today). The Jews had a canon of faith that was the same as the Protestant canon of faith although some of the books are in a different order. With the discovery of the Dead Sea Scrolls in 1947 and later, we now have pre-Christian copies of part or all of every Old Testament book except Esther. Before these discoveries the oldest copy was dated about AD 850.

Arguments for the Protestant canon include:

- Philo the Jewish philosopher (20BC-AD40) never once quotes from the Apocrypha.
- Josephus the Jewish historian (AD30–100) specifically identifies the 22 books that are equivalent to the Protestant canon of 39 books (*Antiquities, Against Apion* 1:8).
- The Jews acknowledged the cessation of prophecy with Malachi ca.400BC.
- Christ's division of Scripture (Luke 24:44) into the three classes accepted by the Jews (the Law, the Prophets and the Psalms) endorses the Jewish canon.
- To the Jews were committed 'the very words of God' (Romans 3:2) and Christians receive these oracles from them.

We could illustrate the way the Old Testament books fit together as follows:

1. Covenant Foundation (Genesis to Deuteronomy)

The lead up to and inauguration of the covenant at Sinai. The Old Testament writings begin with Moses ca 1450 BC. He may have used earlier records, while his own work received some editing subsequently (eg. Gen. 14:14, cf. Judges 18:29, an event dated perhaps 400 years later). Certainly Moses did not record the circumstances of his own death (Deut. 34), while phrases like 'to this day' (Gen. 35:4; Deut. 34:5–6) indicate a gap between the time of the event and the publishing of the book in its current form.

2. Covenant History (Joshua to Esther)

Showing continuity of God's covenant faithfulness. Joshua to 2 Kings cover the period from about 1400 BC to 560 BC in more or less chronological sequence. 1 and 2 Chronicles recapitulates the history from Adam to

Cyrus in terms appropriate to covenant renewal in the time of Ezra. Esther is set in Persia about 460 BC, and Ezra and Nehemiah a little later in Judah.

3. Covenant Living (Job to Song of Solomon)

Common issues of life for God's people in every age. Job teaches that true wisdom is to trust and obey, not to speculate. Psalms is the songs of the covenant, the Bible in miniature. Proverbs gives practical instruction in covenant living. Ecclesiastes shows the emptiness of life outside God's gracious covenant. Song of Songs shows the beauty and pleasure of married love, leading to appreciation of God's covenant as a love bond between God and Israel, Christ and his Church.

4. Covenant Messengers (Isaiah to Malachi)

The prophets point back to Moses, but also point forward to changes in the future with a new and better covenant bringing about God's purpose to bless all the nations. The following table gives a general view.

Major prophets from the division of the Kingdom c.931 BC

Date	***Judah***	***Israel***
900–875		Elijah
875–850		
850–825		Elisha
825–800		
800–775		
775–750		Amos, Hosea, Jonah
750–725	Isaiah, Micah	*Assyrian Captivity*
725–700		
700–675		
675–650		
650–625	Zephaniah	
625–600	Jeremiah, Habakkuk, Joel(?), Nahum	

Notes:
Isaiah's ministry 740–700; Jeremiah's ministry 626–c.587 BC.

Nahum, c. 614 BC predicts conquest of Assyria by Babylonians.

600–575	Obadiah(?), Ezekiel, Daniel	Ezekiel's ministry 593–573; Daniel's for many decades to c.537 BC Jerusalem destroyed by the Babylonians 586 BC. Babylonians conquered by Persians, 539. Cyrus allows return 538 BC. Rebuilt temple dedicated 516 BC.
575–550		
550–525		
525–500		
500–475		
475–450		
450–425	Malachi	

God instituted prophecy in Israel (Deut. 18:14–22), but only from around 800 BC do we have prophets writing extended books. The prophets were not innovators but guardians of God's covenant. They often speak in language drawn from the existing institutions in Israel to predict the reality of which these were a shadow: a greater temple, an expanded Israel, etc. The underlying redemptive covenant must interpret the language. The order in our common Bibles lists the large books first in chronological order (with Lamentations attached to Jeremiah). The 12 smaller books follow, but the chronology of these is not in every case clear. The last is Malachi, and then there is a silence of over 400 years until John the Baptist.

New Testament

The periods of the New Covenant writings*			
James	45	Early Years	**Church**
Galatians	49		**Founded**
1 Thessalonians	51	First	
2 Thessalonians	51	Pauline	
1 Corinthians	52	Period	
2 Corinthians	55		

* Some dates involve conjecture. It is usual for Mark, which is supposed to represent the preaching of Peter, to be regarded as the earliest Gospel.

Romans	57		
Matthew	58	First	
Luke	60	Gospels	

Colossians	60	Central	**Church**
Philemon	60	Pauline	**Established**
Ephesians	61	Period	
Philippians	61	(in prison)	
Acts	63		
Hebrews	64		
1 Peter	64		

1 Timothy	64	Paul's	**Closing**
Titus	64	Legacy	**Period**
2 Timothy	67		
2 Peter	67	Peter's	
Mark	68	Legacy	
Jude	70	Jude's	
		Legacy	
John	85		
1 John	90	John's	
2 John	90	Legacy	
3 John	90		
Revelation	95		

FOR DISCUSSION

1. Can you state the difference between revelation, inspiration and illumination?
2. Does inspiration mean that every part of Scripture is equally important?

1.3 The Apocrypha

The books commonly called 'Apocrypha' are not divinely inspired and so are not part of the canon of the Scripture. Therefore they do not have authority in the church of God, and are only to be regarded and used in the same way as other merely human writings.[8]

8. Luke 24:27,44; Rom. 3:2; 2 Pet. 1:21.

Old Testament Apocrypha

The apocryphal (= hidden) books were written in Greek and composed during the period between Malachi (c.400 BC) and the New Testament, and mainly in the 200 years before Jesus' birth. The Apocrypha bears plain marks that it cannot have God as its author, since nothing can be a rule for faith which contradicts existing revelation, or in other ways lacks the marks of inspiration such as truthfulness. Indeed, one of the best of the apocryphal books (1 Maccabees c.110 BC) admits that there was no true prophet in Israel at the time (9:27;14:41), while 2 Maccabees 15:38 reads in a way no prophet wrote: 'If it [my book] is found well written and aptly composed, that is what I myself hoped for; if cheap and mediocre, I could only do my best' (cf. 2:23–27). The preface to Ecclesiasticus (Ben Sirach) shows the author was simply trying to help people understand the Old Testament. Other aspects of the content are inconsistent with Divine authorship.

The Jews did not accept the Apocrypha as canon for faith, but the Christian church used the Greek translation of the Old Testament (the Septuagint or LXX, dating from c.200 BC). Some copies of this translation included the Apocrypha. Hence there grew up in the Christian Church a *canon* of faith (our Bible) and a canon of books read for *edification*, but not used to establish any doctrine (the Apocrypha).

The influence of Augustine (354–430) in the 4th century in approving the apocryphal books ultimately overcame the influence of those who rejected them, such as Jerome (c.345–420), the Bible translator. In 1546 the Roman Catholic Council of Trent included most (not all) the apocryphal books as part of the canon of faith. Early Protestants maintained the earlier position, distinguishing a canon of faith and a canon of edifying books not to be used to establish doctrine, hence even the first edition of the King James Bible (1611) included the apocryphal books. The Westminster Confession's statement reflects the clarity and consistency attained through the debate with Rome.

New Testament Apocrypha

As early as the second century Irenaeus (AD ca.130–200) of Lyons, a missionary bishop and opponent of Gnosticism, complains that there are numerous spurious gospels. They are often called *pseudepigrapha* because they falsely claim to be by some prominent person so as to gain credence. Today about 50 are known, but most only by title or brief reference. They show an interest in filling in 'gaps' in Scripture, particularly about Jesus' early life, although the *Gospel of Peter* gives an (outlandish) actual description of Jesus' resurrection. Some reflect Gnostic doctrines, such as the *Gospel of Mary* (which makes Jesus and Mary Magdalene to be very close), and the gospels of Thomas and Philip, which were among the books discovered at Nag Hammadi in 1945/46. The *Gospel of Thomas* gives 114 alleged sayings of Jesus stressing perfection through avoidance of sex and a life of asceticism, while the *Gospel of Philip* has 127 paragraphs which put quite a stress on sacraments. There are also a few apocryphal epistles and other writings like the *Apocalypse of Peter*. The so-called *Gospel of Barnabas* is late. It exists only in a 16th century Italian manuscript and is a pro-Islamic writing. It was probably written by a recent Italian convert to Islam. This would account for why it is not fully consistent with the Qur'an, whilst 12 times purporting to predict the coming of Muhammed.

Most of the New Testament apocrypha originated in the second century, some in orthodox circles and some in heretical circles. Some became part of popular devotion and had a significant influence in the 13th to 15th centuries. Others from heretical sources passed into relative obscurity until rediscovered in the modern period. Some of the Gnostic writings have been employed recently to further the interest in hidden knowledge which characterised the Gnostic movement. An example is Dan Brown's *The Da Vinci Code* (2003), which many readers mistakenly suppose is factual in its references to early Christianity. As one has said, 'The rubbish of the second century is still rubbish.' Anyone who compares the apocryphal writings with the New Testament writings will be convinced that the latter are superior in every way.

FOR DISCUSSION

1. Find out the names of the Old Testament Apocryphal books. Why do you think Rome found it convenient to accept most of them?
2. How do we know the apocryphal books are not part of Scripture?

CHAPTER 1
4–7: SCRIPTURE'S AUTHORITY AND PERFECTON

ANALYSIS *WCF 1:4–7*

4. The authority of Scripture
a. derived from Author
b. not given authority by others

5. Why Scripture is believed
a. a rational basis — but inadequate of itself for spiritual understanding
b. the Spirit's witness is based on yet transcends rational grounds

6. The sufficiency of Scripture
a. adequate for the purpose for which it has been given
b. not to be added to

7. The sufficiency of Scripture
a. clear on matters essential to salvation
b. ordinary people can understand sufficiently

The Church of Rome sought to maintain its authority in several ways by teaching that:

- the word of God, both written and unwritten, was deposited with her;
- the chief reason we accept Scripture as divine is because of the testimony of the church; and
- it is not necessary or safe for the Scripture to be read by all the faithful except under careful guidance.

These are the issues dealt with by the Confession at this point.

1.4 The authority of Scripture

The authority of the Holy Scripture does not depend on human testimony or a church's witness but entirely on God its author, who is truth itself. Therefore Holy Scripture is to be received, believed and obeyed because it is the word of God.[9]

9. 2 Pet. 1:19,21; 2 Tim. 3:16; 1 Jn. 5:9; 1 Thess. 2:13.

The view of the Church of Rome is expressed popularly in John O'Brien's *The Faith of Millions*: 'The declaration of the Catholic Church that the books of the New Testament are all inspired by God constitutes the *sole* authority for the universal belief of both Catholics and Protestants in their inspired character'[1] (emphasis his). But against this the truth must be that God's word bears *his* authority and in the nature of the case no higher or more compelling testimony to it is possible. As God's word it possesses authority over the thoughts and acts of all, whether or not they believe.

If we are to accept the inspiration of the Scriptures because the church tells us so, how do we know that the church is right? If the Roman Catholic responds that the church has been given infallibility on such matters, we ask for the evidence. If Scripture texts are quoted, such as Matthew 16:18—'You are Peter and on this rock I will build my church,' then we have a circular argument. For before using such texts one must decide if they are part of the word of God and, if so, what their correct meaning is. And the Scripture suggests a different meaning than Rome assigns, and history confirms that the infallibility claimed has not been given. The Church Fathers held five different opinions as to the meaning of Matthew 16:18–19: seventeen Fathers held the rock was Peter, eight that it was the Apostles represented by Peter, forty-four that it was the faith which Peter confessed, sixteen that the rock was Christ,

1. John O'Brien, *The Faith of Millions* (Our Sunday Visitor, 1962), 174.

while OriGen. and others that it was the whole body of the faithful. Some Fathers give different interpretations in different places.[2]

At root the true Roman Catholic places the authority of the hierarchy above all the evidences of reason and history. Consider the meek submission of virtually all the prelates to the *Decree on Papal Infallibility* of 1870, despite the biblical and historical arguments urged against it by the majority of the Council before the final vote was taken (largely by an Italian rump). One sees the same principle in cults like the Watchtower Society (Jehovah's Witnesses), the Mormons or the Exclusive Brethren. In these groups, the Governing Body, the Chief Apostle or the 'spiritual men' are the basis of authority and Scripture is understood according to the official interpretations, even if inconsistent with previous rulings or contradictory to clear statements in Scripture.

FOR DISCUSSION

1. What is the role of the church in deciding on the books that form part of the canon or rule of faith?
2. What is the difference between the faith of a person who accepts the Scriptures simply because the church accepts them, and the basis of acceptance in WCF 1.4?

2. See C. B. Moss, *The Old Catholic Movement: Its Origin and History* (SPCK, 1948), 6–7.

1.5 Why Christians believe Scripture

We may be brought by the witness of the church to have the highest respect for Holy Scripture.[10] The heavenly character of its content, the powerful effects of its teaching, the majesty of its style, the agreement of all its parts, the fact that throughout it gives all glory to God, the full disclosure it gives of the only way of salvation, its many other incomparable excellencies, and its entire perfection: all these supply abundant evidence that Scripture is the word of God. Nevertheless, our full persuasion and assurance of its infallible truth and divine authority results from the inward work of the Holy Spirit bearing witness by and with the word in our hearts.[11]

10. 1 Tim. 3:15.
11. 1 Jn. 2:20,27; Jn 16:13,14; 1 Cor. 2:10–12; Isa. 59:21.

If we ask, 'How can sinful people be brought to full conviction of and practical obedience to the infallible truth and divine authority of Scripture?' the answer is that faith in Scripture as God-breathed is not irrational; many reasons for faith can be offered since the qualities of Scripture are consistent with its divine authorship. Still, such arguments—and we could add archaeology to those listed in the Confession—cannot give us *saving* knowledge and true assurance. Faith is not bare intellectual assent but a spiritual grace (see WCF 14:1) which God gives by the working of his Holy Spirit. Yet the Spirit does not act independently of the word of God, but *by* and *with* it (contra the 'inner light' teaching of the Society of Friends in the 17th century or some 'charismatics' today). So a saving understanding does not contradict a rational understanding.

Note that the necessity of the Spirit's work does not mean believers are *inspired*; rather, they are *illumined* by the Spirit to receive the testimony of Holy Scripture in a saving way. Not all believers are equally illumined nor do they all have equal knowledge, hence the Holy Spirit's testimony does not eliminate all disagreement on some matters of lesser importance revealed in Scripture (cf. WCF 14:2,3). The role of the church is not to place herself above the word of God on which, indeed, she is founded

(Eph. 2:20), but to be the servant of Christ. She should guard Scripture, draw attention to its qualities, make plain its meaning, and submit to its authority as the word of Christ.

THOUGHTS FROM OTHER MINDS

'But even if anyone clears God's Sacred Word from man's evil speaking, he will not at once imprint upon their hearts that certainty which piety requires. . . . For as God alone is a fit witness of himself in his Word, so also the Word will not find acceptance in men's hearts before it is sealed by the inward testimony of the Spirit. The same Spirit, therefore, who has spoken through the mouths of the prophets must penetrate into our hearts to persuade us that they faithfully proclaimed what has been divinely commanded.'

John Calvin (1509–1564)[3]

FOR DISCUSSION

1. What value have the proofs of Scripture's divine origin?
2. Why is the inward testimony of the Spirit necessary to a saving understanding of Scripture?
3. "The two pillars of true faith in Scripture as God's Word are the objective witness and the internal testimony." (Professor John Murray, (1898–1975). Discuss this statement in the light of WCF 1:5.

3. *Institutes of the Christian Religion*, 1.7.4 (Battles' edition cited).

1.6 The sufficiency of Scripture

The whole counsel of God concerning all things necessary for his own glory, and for our salvation, faith and life, is either expressly stated in Scripture, or by good and necessary reasoning may be deduced from Scripture. Nothing, whether new revelations of the Spirit or human traditions, is ever to be added to Scripture.[12] Nevertheless, we acknowledge the inward illumination of the Spirit of God to be necessary for the saving understanding of the things that are revealed in the word.[13] We also acknowledge that there are some circumstances concerning the worship of God and the government of the church, circumstances common to human actions and societies, which are to be ordered by natural intelligence and Christian prudence, but always in line with the general rules of God's word.[14]

10. 2 Tim. 3:15–17; Gal. 1:8–9; 2 Thess. 2:2.
11. Jn. 6:45; 1 Cor. 2:9,10,12.
12. 1 Cor. 11:13,14; 1 Cor.14:26,40.

This section asserts that Scripture is the sufficient and only rule over against those who place church traditions above or on a level with Scripture (eg. Rome), or those who claim new revelations (as did some of the Anabaptist sects then, and some now). Contrary to those who insist that explicit words for every practice are needed and hence, for example, reject baptism of believers' infants or the change of the day of rest from Saturday to Sunday, we confess the validity of the good and necessary implications of, and deductions from, Scripture statements.

The word of God, being superior to every other word, is not to be added to or subtracted from. This is the message of passages like Deuteronomy 4:2 and Revelation 22:18. Our attitude to God's word should be one in which we do not supplement or take away from the meaning they have. With the completion of the Book of Revelation we are to look for no further addition or supplement to the Bible. Scripture is an organic revelation gradually unfolding the promise of God until its complete disclosure in God's Son and the new covenant of which he is mediator. Nothing is to be added.

Jesus is more than a prophet. He is God the eternal Son, God's final Word to humanity; not just a messenger but the Message. Purported 'revelations', which claim to surpass or correct the revelation of which Jesus Christ is the fulfillment, cannot be accepted. Thus we read:

'In the past God spoke to our forefathers through the prophets at many times and in various ways, but in these last days he has spoken to us by his Son, whom he appointed heir of all things, and through whom he made the universe. The Son is the radiance of God's glory and the exact representation of his being, sustaining all things by his powerful word. After he had provided purification for sins, he sat down at the right hand of the Majesty in heaven' (Hebrews 1:1–3). 'Jesus has been found worthy of greater honour than Moses, just as the builder of a house has greater honour than the house itself...Moses was faithful as a servant in all God's house...but Christ is faithful as a son over God's house' (Hebrews 3:3–6).

Two examples contradicting the sufficiency of Scripture:

1. The **Qur'an** [=Recitation] allegedly given directly by God to Muhammed (AD c.570-c.632) over 23 years contains 114 suras or chapters. They are arranged generally in descending order of length, rather than chronologically. The Qur'an professes to believe in the Bible, to confirm it, and to present Muhammed as the last prophet to humankind. Yet its teaching is inconsistent with the Bible, and its claims that the Bible has been corrupted involve contradiction with the Qur'an's claim that the Bible is God's word. If the corruption claimed relates to the text of the Bible, the claim is not correct since the copyists' errors do not corrupt the message of Scripture. If the corruption alleged relates to the interpretation of the Bible, of course one agrees misinterpretation has occurred. Yet, when one

gets down to it, it appears rather Muhammed has misinterpreted the Bible, sometimes through the influence of Christian and Jewish misinterpretation on him. We plead simply a readiness to look fairly at Scripture.

Authoritative alongside the Qur'an are the Hadith [=Sayings], various collections of sayings mostly ascribed to Muhammed himself, and there are different school of interpretation of these. The hadith are very important in establishing Islamic teaching and practice and there are also widely varying cultural practices in Islamic communities, so Islam in far from monolithic.

2. The **Book of Mormon** (1830) is an account of two groups of people. The Jaredites are said to have come to America before the time of Abraham (ca. 2000 BC). After the invasion of Israel by Nebuchadnezzar about 600 BC they were followed by Israelites who became known as Nephites and Lamanites. The Jaredites had died out by this time, and the Israelites had almost died out by AD 350, with some of the indigenous peoples of North and South America being their only remnant. Mormon, the last of the early Mormon prophets, abridged the records of his people, imprinting them on golden plates and burying them in what is now New York State. In 1827 God permitted Joseph Smith (1805–44) to recover and supernaturally translate them, after which an angel took them away. The resultant Book of Mormon (published 1830) is said to contain 'the fullness of the everlasting Gospel' and to enable the restoration of the true church, since all existing churches were apostate and 'an abomination in God's sight'. Although 'righteous' persons in other churches can be saved, the highest heaven can be achieved only through the ordinances of the *Church of Jesus Christ of Latter-day Saints* administered either in this life or by proxy after death. Led

by a person who is regarded as Prophet, Seer and Revelator, the Mormon Church has other inspired writings, such as Doctrine and Covenants, which are the source of many of its distinctive teachings. Careful historical investigation is fatal to the Mormon claims. More to the point, the Mormon claims are utterly inconsistent with the teaching of the Bible.

An example somewhat compromising the sufficiency of Scripture:

The writings of Mrs Ellen White (1827–1915), a founder of the Seventh-day Adventist Church in 1863, are in major respects different from the other two noted above which are not Christian in any orthodox sense. Indeed, much of what Mrs White wrote, often culled from others, is Christian and edifying. However, in official SDA teaching, she is claimed to have a Biblically-prophesied role, with her writings given by 'the Spirit of Prophecy' to the end-time church, so she is much more than a gifted teacher.

Reason is not the basis of Christian doctrine, but sound thinking is a proper means for finding out what God has revealed. Indeed, some matters are to be ordered by the light of nature and by Christian prudence subject to the general rules of the word. We cannot claim a course of action to be God's will if it opposes these principles.

FOR DISCUSSION

1. Can you give examples of 'circumstances common to human actions and societies' that relate to worship and church government? [WCF 21 and WCF 30 respectively set out Biblical principles of worship and church government.]
2. Should a Christian today say, 'The Lord has told me...'?
3. Distinguish the 'inward illumination of the Spirit' from inspiration.

1.7 The clarity of Scripture

All things in Scripture are not equally plain in themselves, nor equally clear to all.[15] However, those things that are necessary to know, believe and observe for salvation, are so clearly stated and explained in one place of Scripture or another, that the uneducated person as well as the scholar can sufficiently understand them by appropriate use of the ordinary means.[16]

15. 2 Pet. 3:16.
16. Psalm 119:105,130.

The Roman Church not only claims that sacred tradition plus Holy Scripture makes up the word of God which is entrusted to the church, but asserts, in the language of the Second Vatican Council: 'But the task of giving an authentic interpretation of the word of God, whether in its written form or in the form of Tradition, has been entrusted to the living teaching office of the Church alone.... It is for the bishops ... suitably to instruct the faithful ... in the correct use of the divine books ... by giving them translations of the sacred texts which are equipped with necessary and really adequate explanations'.[4]

The true Protestant teaching is that, while not all parts of Scripture are equally clear, the Scripture can be given to those who are not scholars as well as those who are, and that the central truths are clear enough for any who apply ordinary methods. 'The main things are the plain things.' Of course some will abuse and twist Scripture (note 2 Peter 3:16), but short of applying physical coercion, this is inevitable, even on Rome's theory. It is, of course, notorious that members of the Church of Rome are not generally familiar with Bible content, while true Protestants promote the use of the Bible at every opportunity.

FOR DISCUSSION

1. What is 'an appropriate use of the ordinary means'?
2. What is the role of those who have made a special study of Scripture? Do we need such 'experts'? (Compare Eph. 4:7–16)
3. What should be our attitude when we come to a text like 1 Corinthians 15:29 or Revelation 20?

4. *Dei Verbum: Dogmatic Constitution on Divine Revelation* (1965); cf. *Catechism of the Catholic Church*, 1994 #85.

CHAPTER 1

8–10: THE USE OF SCRIPTURE

ANALYSIS *WCF 1:8–10*

8. The transmission of Scripture

a. inspiration in Hebrew and Greek
   - special providence preserves
   - purity of text
     ie. no doctrine lost
       what mistake is in one manuscript is corrected in another
   - final appeal to Hebrew and Greek

b. translations to be made
   - in common language
   - are sufficient for purposes stated

9. The interpretation of Scripture

a. Scripture interprets Scripture
b. grounded in the grammatical meaning

10. The final authority of Scripture

a. through it the Spirit speaks

On the basis of the origin and characteristics of Scripture set out in the earlier sections, we now have several fundamental statements of Biblical principle. We should remember, when reading these sections, such facts as the following:

1. Rome exploited the existence of various readings in the Hebrew and Greek manuscripts with a view to exalting the Latin Vulgate translation and furthering her claim to be the infallible depository of truth, the infallible interpreter of Scripture, and the final court of appeal in controversies.

2. In 1546 the Roman Catholic *Council of Trent* declared the Latin Vulgate to be the 'authentic' text, and 'that no one is to dare, or presume to reject it under any pretext whatsoever.' Actually, the allegedly 'authentic text' was not issued until 1590 by authority of Pope Sixtus V. Two years later Pope Clement VIII issued a fresh edition with some 2,000 changes!
3. The fourth rule of the *Index* concerning prohibited books, sanctioned by Pope Pius IV in 1564, forbade any Roman Catholic to read or have in his possession a copy of the Bible in the vernacular without a written licence from the bishop or inquisitor, which licence was only to be given under strict conditions. Any person having a Bible without permission was not to be granted absolution until the Bible was given up to the bishop. Violation of this rule was declared to be a mortal sin. In Pope Leo XII's 1824 Encyclical Letter, this regulation was reaffirmed and the Protestant Bible was condemned as 'the gospel of the devil' and as 'deadly pastures.' The Letter further stated that 'if the sacred Scriptures be indiscriminately read, more evil than good would arise from it.'

Of recent years some more definite encouragement has been given to study of the Scriptures by the Roman Church, and for this we should be thankful. Even so, a discretion and control over a privilege God has freely granted is maintained (see also comments on WCF 1:7).

1.8 The transmission of Scripture and translations

The Old Testament in Hebrew (which was the native language of the people of God of old), and the New Testament in Greek (which, at the time it was written, was the language most generally known among the nations), are immediately inspired by God. By his special care and providence, God has preserved them in purity ever since, so that they are authoritative,[17] and in all religious controversies are the church's final court of appeal.[18] All the people of God have a right to and interest in the Scriptures, and are commanded to read and search them in the fear of God.[19] But as the Hebrew and Greek are not known to all God's people, the Scriptures are to be translated into the common language of every nation to which they are brought.[20] In this way the word of God may be abundant in the life of each believer, who may worship God in an acceptable manner[21] and, through endurance in faith and the comfort of the Scriptures, have hope.[22]

17. Matt. 5:18. 18. Isa. 8:20; Acts 15:15; John 5:39,46.
19. John 5:39. 20. 1 Cor.14:6,9,11,12,24,27,28.
21. Col. 3:16. 22. Rom. 15:4.

Notice that the Scriptures are said to be *immediately* inspired by God—this points to the autographs as the very word of God. They were given in the common language of those who first received them.[1] Concerning the transmission of these Scriptures to us, a special providential care (not a miraculous intervention) is asserted, and this has resulted in the Scriptures being 'kept pure in all ages' (1646 text) so that full authority is retained.

It has been suggested by some that 'kept pure in all ages' means that the Westminster Divines did not accept that any variations from the common Hebrew and Greek texts used in their time were valid. A few advocate this position because they want to undermine the high view of Scripture taught in the Confession by associating it with ignorance on the part of the Divines, but this is an absurd claim. Others fear that the confidence of believers in the Bibles they have will be undermined if variant readings are admitted. It is a position often associated with asserting that the text behind the King James Bible (1611) is the 'pure' text. Some even make extravagant claims for the KJV as if it is without any mistake or error – quite contrary to the Translators own comments in their lengthy *Preface* found in library editions.

1. Daniel 2:4b-7:28 is in Aramaic, the language of the nations at that time.

However, the Westminster Divines, like the earlier Reformers, were well aware that they did not have the autographs but only copies of the Hebrew and Greek manuscripts, and they were well aware of diversity in these due to the frequent errors in the hand copying of books that was the norm until Gutenberg introduced printing by movable type in 1450. The Reformers accepted the common principle of scholars of manuscripts: 'What mistake is in one copy is corrected in another.' Their ultimate appeal was to the copies preserved in God's providence duly compared and evaluated. As God's providence extends to *all* events, there is no justification for excluding consideration of *all* the manuscript evidence preserved for us. For the past 200 years scholars, often not Christian believers, have pored over the text. In the very small number of places where there is any real question of which reading is to be preferred, there is no effect on the certainty of any Christian doctrine, regardless of which reading is preferred.

Until 1947 the oldest Hebrew text we had was dated around AD 850, but since the discovery of the Dead Sea Scrolls we have manuscripts of almost all the Old Testament books dating from around 100 BC. For all ordinary purposes these manuscripts are the same as those underlying our common Bibles. For the New Testament we now have close to 6,000 manuscripts, most being fragments, drawn from widely different locations. It is possible to classify the copies into families according to the distinctive readings that developed in different early centres. In areas where Greek continued in church use there are more manuscripts but other Greek manuscripts from areas that subsequently chiefly used Latin or Syriac or which, like Alexandria, were overrun by Islam, need also to be considered. With such an abundance of evidence there are tens of thousands of variations but most fall into the category of spelling mistakes and other trivia, and so are not really variant readings at all.

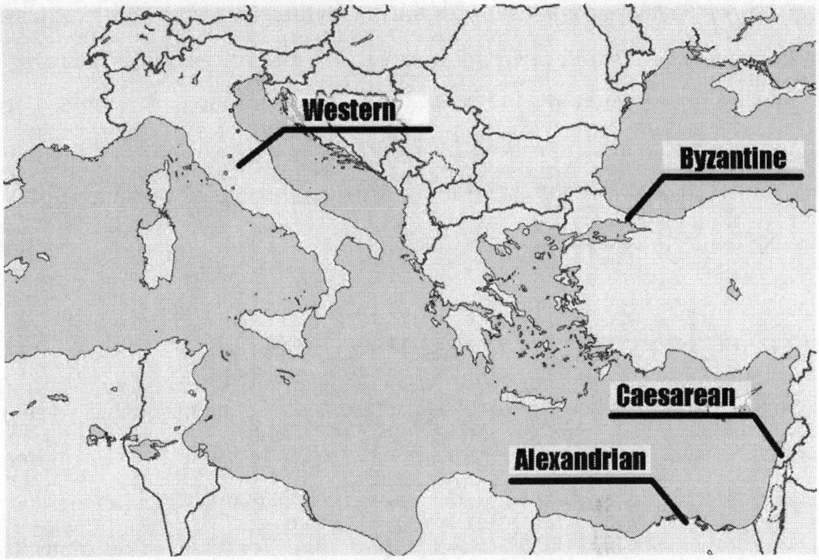

In the 1890s, through archaeological discovery of old letters and bills from New Testament times, it became crystal clear that the New Testament was written in Koiné or Common Greek rather than the Classical Greek of scholars. This gave impetus to the very important work of producing translations in modern language. As Scripture is perfect (WCF 1:6) and clear on essential truth (WCF 1:7), translations suffice for everyday purposes of ordinary Christians. Although not inspired as to the very words yet, as to the truth and substance of the teaching, faith finds adequate foundation through an honest translation, just as it does through faithful preaching (John 7:17; 1 Peter 1:25).

The stress on the *duty* of making translations in the 'vulgar' or common language reflects the Protestant conviction that a personal, vital and constant contact with the word of God is characteristic of true piety. Translations ought to be from the Hebrew and Greek and in a form of the language capable of being understood as to its basic content by the ordinary or common person. According to their lengthy *Preface* the translators of the King James Version of 1611 aimed to be understood by the 'very vulgar', that is, those with minimal education. Similarly, Luther's was not the first Bible in German, but it was the first in a German that could be appreciated readily by ordinary Germans. It is desirable that the translation work be done by believing scholars, who are sensitive to Biblical theology, but orthodox faith does not automatically supply deficiencies in scholarship.

THOUGHTS FROM OTHER MINDS

'The Scriptures are not so tied to these first languages that they cannot and ought not to be translated into other languages for common use in the church. But among interpreters, neither the seventy who turned them into Greek, nor Jerome, nor any other such held the office of a prophet; they were not free from errors in interpretation. Hence no versions are fully authentic except as they express the sources, by which they are also to be weighed. Neither is there any authority on earth whereby any version may be made absolutely authentic. God's providence in preserving the sources is notable and glorious, for neither have they wholly perished nor have they been injured by the loss of any book or blemished by any serious defect—though today not one of the earlier versions remains intact.'

William Ames (1576–1633)[2]

'First then, it is granted that the individual autographs of Moses, the prophets and the apostles, are in all probability, and as to all that we know, utterly perished and lost out of the world....

Secondly, For the Scriptures of the New Testament, it doth not appear that the autographs of the several writers of it were ever gathered together into one volume ... the first transcribers of the original copies, and those who in succeeding ages have done the like work from them, ... we say not, as is vainly charged by Morinus and Capellus, that they were all or any of them 'infallible and divinely inspired,' so

2. *The Marrow of Theology*, 1.34.27–31.

that it was impossible for them in anything to mistake. It is known, it is granted, that failings have been amongst them, and that various lections [readings] have from thence arisen. . . .

Thirdly, We add that *the whole Scripture*, entire as given out from God, without any loss, is preserved in the copies of the originals yet remaining. . . . In them all, we say, is every letter and tittle of the word. These copies we say, are the rule, standard, and touchstone of all translations, ancient or modern, by which they in all things are to be examined, tried, corrected, amended; and themselves only by themselves.'

John Owen (1616–1683)[3]

'It has often been said, and rightly, that not one word in a thousand of the Greek text of the New Testament is open to serious doubt, and that there is no place in either Testament where uncertainty about the text raises a question of doctrinal substance.

Also, it is often said, and surely rightly again, that no honest translation of the Bible has ever been so bad that God's life-giving message could not reach men through it. Nonetheless, human mistakes in translation and transmission can only obscure the divine message, and therefore we ought to try to weed them out, just as proofreaders ought to try and weed out all misprints, even if what is printed would be intelligible and generally reliable with the misprints there.'

J. I. Packer (1926–2020)[4]

FOR DISCUSSION

1. What is suggested concerning training of ministers of the word of God by these sections?
2. What principles for Bible translation are indicated by WCF 1:8? Evaluate the merit of several current translations.

3. "Of the Integrity and Purity of the Hebrew and Greek Text of the Scripture," in *The Works of John Owen*, ed. William H. Goold (Banner of Truth, 1968), 16:353,354,357 (italics in original).
4. *Honouring the Written Word of God:* The *Collected Shorter Writings of J.I. Packer* (Paternoster, 1999), 3:36.

3. "It is potentially damaging for a minister to pretend to his congregation that there are no differences or difficulties among the manuscripts. Sooner or later the pretence will be found out by those who use the minds God gave them, and the damage to faith may be far greater than if the existence of difficulties had been candidly admitted." (A. J. Brown in *The Quarterly Record of the Trinitarian Bible Society*, October/December 1984). Discuss.
4. Account for the differences which sometimes appear in quotations of the Old Testament in the New Testament.

CHARACTERISTICS OF SOME ENGLISH TRANSLATIONS

The *King James Version* (1611) is based on a consideration of those manuscripts and ancient versions available at the time. Its language has been updated several times, and the current text dates from 1769. The *New King James Version* (1983) uses the same underlying texts as the KJV, but footnotes variations from the form of text constructed using the much more abundant sources now available and used in most other modern translations, including the *Revised Standard Version* (1956) and its conservative updating, the *English Standard Version* (2002, 2011, 2016).

These above four translations tend to an approach to translation which is less interpretative than the 'dynamic equivalence' approach favoured by others such as the *Good New Bible* (1976) or the *New Living Translation* (1996). Still, all translations are to some degree interpretative. If we are interested in conveying meaning with clarity and accuracy a translation like the *New International Version* (1984, 2011) should be acceptable. The *Good News Bible* is excessively free, particularly in the Old Testament, and so is of less value, particularly for close study. It was intended for those for whom English is a second language.

The differences between the underlying texts should not be overemphasised, nor even the different approaches to translation. There will always be some difference of viewpoint but the ark of God in not in danger. Note that frequently the Septuagint Greek translation used by believers in New Testament times is quoted in the New Testament, although it can hardly be called a strictly literal translation and at points is quite free compared to the original Hebrew—as the reader can see from the common English translations.

1.9 The interpretation of Scripture

It is an infallible rule that Scripture is to be interpreted by Scripture. Scripture does not have several different meanings but one true and genuine meaning (which may embrace several different applications) arising from the words properly understood in context. Where there is any dispute, the meaning must be decided in the light of other passages that speak more clearly.[23#]

23. 2 Pet. 1:20,21; Acts 15:15,16.
For the sake of clarity this section 9 has been slightly expanded from the original 1646 text.

The Roman Church adhered to the idea of a 4-fold sense in Scripture (the *quadriga*). Along with the surface meaning of the words were three higher levels of spiritual interpretation. The *letter* taught merely the deed, the *allegory* of the passage what one was to believe, the *moral* meaning what one should do, and the *anagoge* what you should strive for. Consequently, without the expert guidance of the church and the pope one would be in doubt and lost in ambiguities. This remains Rome's teaching.[5]

But Scripture does not have a nose of wax to be shaped as we please. God is its primary author and Scripture is consistent with itself as a result. The Reformers rightly rejected the multiple meaning concept. The literal meaning to them was not necessarily the surface meaning of the words, but the intended meaning, and so the literal meaning might be figurative as in Genesis 3:15 or Matthew 5:29–30. There might be various aspects to the truth in a particular passage that were intended by the Holy Spirit, such as type and antitype, but there are not multiple levels of unrelated truths in a passage to be drawn out by applying the arbitrary concept of a 3-fold or 4-fold sense.

'The spiritual truth is contained in the proper sense of Scripture language' (John Macpherson). Scripture is to be understood organically

5. *Catechism of the Catholic Church* (1994), #115–119.

not atomistically. Proof-texting is often condemned, but there is nothing wrong with using texts of Scripture to prove a point so long as the text is being properly used. 'A text without a context is a pretext.'

FOR DISCUSSION

1. If asked, 'Do you take the Bible literally?' what would you say?
2. What advantages are there in a minister preaching through whole books or large parts of Scripture in an expository way?
3. Comment on the Devil's use of Scripture in Luke 4:9–11, and Jesus' use of Scripture in Luke 4:4,8,12.

1.10 Scripture and the Holy Spirit

The Holy Spirit speaking in the Scripture is the supreme judge by whom all religious controversies are to be decided, and all decrees of councils, opinions of ancient writers, human teachings, and claims to spiritual guidance are to be examined; with his decision we are to be content.[24]

24. Matt. 22:29,31; Eph. 2:20 with Acts 28:25.

The expression 'the Holy Spirit speaking in the Scripture' aims to express the conviction that when Scripture speaks it is really the Holy Spirit speaking. The Bible is no bare word but living and active in the Spirit's hands. He illumines our minds to understand the true meaning of Scripture. In effect the Confession asserts that over against the Papal tribunal is another tribunal from which the Spirit speaks and infallibly guides. The true sense of scripture is to be discovered from the Scripture itself as the Sprit brings conviction of the truth to our hearts.

The Scottish *Second Book of Discipline* (1578) Ch. 2.6, speaks of the extraordinary offices of apostle, evangelist and prophet 'which are not perpetual, and now have ceased in the Church of God, except when it pleased God, extraordinarily, for a time to stir some of them up again'. Westminster men like Rutherford and George Gillespie (*Miscellany Questions* [1649], Ch 5, 7) maintained that in *extraordinary* circumstances God might still raise up holy prophets (eg. some of the reformers), although 'prophecy' was defined as prediction of events bearing on the cause of Christ. This moderate 'cessationist' view contrasts with that the strict cessationist view of Dr. John Lightfoot, also a member of the Westminster Assembly, who held that supernatural manifestations ceased after 70 AD. Today there is a common claim that supernatural gifts, including but not limited to prophecy, are an *ordinary* part of healthy church life, and the sufficiency of Scripture tends to be devalued, especially in an age of expressive individualism.

I have rendered the words 'private spirits' in the 1646 text as 'claims to spiritual guidance'. The question has been raised as to whether 'spirits' in the original text has the sense of 'revelations' or 'opinions'. If, despite WCF 1.1, the former is correct, it would seem to imply the possibility of genuine private revelations but insist that all such be judged by the public revelation of Scripture. If the latter is right, false claims to revelation are included. I think my rendering covers the range intended.

THOUGHTS FROM OTHER MINDS

'But if the Holy Ghost speaking in the Scripture does not first of all inspire our minds and open the eyes of our understanding, for he alone can do it, assuredly it is lost labour to speak of any other argument or help; if we be not taught of God, and by his Holy Spirit, all other means shall profit us nothing at all.'

Robert Rollock (c.1555–1599)[6]

6. "A Treatise of Our Effectual Calling," *Select Works of Robert Rollock*, ed. William M. Gunn (Wodrow Society, 1849), 1:69.

> 'The Holy Scriptures which were the infallible dictates of the Spirit in the apostles, are more perfect than any of our apprehensions which come by the same Spirit. . . . Therefore we must not try the Scriptures by our most spiritual apprehensions but our apprehensions by the Scriptures. . . . This trying the Spirit by the Scriptures is not a setting of the Scriptures above the Spirit. . . . but is only a trying of the Spirit by the Spirit: that is, the Spirit's operations in ourselves. . . . by the Spirit's operations in the apostles, and by their revelations recorded for our use. For they and not we are called foundations of the church.'
>
> Richard Baxter (c.1555–1599)[7]

> 'Miracles and similar phenomena never happened on an ongoing basis. They occurred only at particular points in the history of redemption: in the exodus and the conquest, at or following the ministry of Moses; at the beginning of the prophetic period with Elijah and Elisha; and with the ministry of Jesus and the apostles.'
>
> Robert Letham[8]

FOR DISCUSSION

1. Is a prayerful attitude to Scripture, seeking God's help in understanding it, inconsistent with diligent study of the text of Scripture?

7. *A Christian Directory* (1673), Q. 163.
8. *Systematic Theology* (Crossway, 2019), 205.

CHAPTER 2
1–2: GOD'S BEING AND BLESSEDNESS

ANALYSIS *WCF 2:1–2*
1. What God is in himself
2. What God is in relation to other existences

Chapter 1 reminds us that God has spoken. In Chapter 2 the Confession has gathered together much of what God has told us of himself. The traditional order in dogmatics in followed in this chapter so the divine oneness is first considered in 2.1–2. The relation of the three persons follows on in 2.3.

2.1 What God is

There is but one, and only one,[1] living and true God,[2] who is infinite in being and perfection,[3] a completely pure spirit,[4] invisible,[5] without body, parts,[6] or other limitations of creatureliness.[7] He is unchangeable,[8] immensely great,[9] eternal,[10] incomprehensible,[11] almighty,[12] completely wise,[13] completely holy,[14] completely free,[15] and completely absolute.[16] He works all things according to the purpose of his own unchangeable and completely righteous will[17] for his own glory.[18] He is completely loving,[19] gracious, merciful, and long-suffering, abounding in goodness and truth, forgiving iniquity, transgression and sin.[20] He is the rewarder of those who diligently seek him.[21] Moreover, he is completely just and awesome in his judgments,[22] hating all sin,[23] and he will by no means leave the guilty unpunished.[24]

1. Deut. 6:4; 1 Cor. 8:4,6. 2. 1 Thess. 1:9; Jer 10:10. 3. Job 11:7–9; 26:14. 4. Jn 4:24. 5. 1 Tim. 1:17. 6. Deut. 4:15,16; John 4:24 with Luke 24:39. 7. Acts 14:11,15. [In lieu of 'other limitations of creatureliness'; the 1646 text reads 'passions'.] 8. James 1:17; Mal. 3:6. 9. 1 Kings 8:27; Jer 23:23,24. 10. Psalm 90:2; 1 Tim. 1:17. 11. Psalm 145:3. 12. Gen. 17:1; Rev. 4:8.

13. Rom. 16:27. 14. Isa. 6:3; Rev. 4:8. 15. Psalm 115:3. 16. Exod. 3:14. 17. Eph. 1:11. 18. Prov. 16:4; Rom. 11:36. 19. 1 Jn. 4:8,16. 20. Exod. 34:6–7. 21. Heb. 11:6. 22. Neh. 9:32–33. 23. Psalm 5:5–6. 24. Nah. 1:2–3; Exod. 34:7.

The existence of God is not treated speculatively in the Bible, and nor is it in the Confession. In thinking of God we are immediately reminded of God's claims upon us.

The description of God as 'living and true', 'infinite in being and perfection, a completely pure spirit' is elaborated in the words 'without body, parts or passions'—traditional church language also found, for example, in the Nicene Creed of 325 and in the Thirty-nine Articles of the Church of England, 1563. I can lose an arm or an eye and still be myself, but everything that belongs to God is essential to God—he cannot lose a 'part' of himself and still be God. God has no body such as would limit him in location, and he is 'without passions'. The word 'passions' historically refers to *human* passions, the fluctuations in our emotional life that belong to us as creatures, including our reactions arising from unforeseen circumstances, hence the rendering 'limitations of creatureliness' that I have provided and which is supported by the text cited (Acts 14:11–15). This does not make him God like an iceberg; rather it safeguards God's spiritual nature and the perfections of his being as the unchanging God. He is immensely or immeasurably great: even the heaven of heavens cannot contain him.

God as the Creator is infinite, eternal and unchangeable in all his perfections (WSC 4). That means that all his qualities are always in full 100% operation. As creatures we are limited and subject to growth and change. God being eternally perfect can neither improve nor be diminished. In regard to passages of Scripture which represent God as repenting, being angry, weeping and so on, we must, in the first place, recognise the passages that state God does *not* repent (eg. Num. 23:19) and that he does *not* change like shifting shadows do (James 1:17). We must take *all* the data and offer an explanation in which we reject human passions in God including actual change in God brought about by his creatures. Second, we must give the priority to statements referring to what God is in himself and avoid taking too literally the many and wide-ranging references to God's emotional attitudes to humans as if they were to be understood as having precise correspondence to our emotions. Third, God's affections (call them *divine* emotions if you like) arise from the fact that he is always perfectly passionate about all that belongs to his identity. When God represents himself to us as repenting, being angry, weeping &c., it may seem that God actually changes but in fact it is God's holy nature and character in its perfection relating to the change in us as in a manner consistent with himself, as Jeremiah 18:7–10 illustrates.

Much 20th century theology has thought of God as made in our image and so, contrary to Isaiah 55:8, his ways are regarded as too much like ours. That God cares about the world is one thing but to rush to the conclusion that he is changed in himself by our suffering is quite another. If outside influence can force God to change, where is our security, where the assurance that his love will not fail? Indeed, a God who changes in this way through interaction with his creatures cannot be eternal either.

When we read of God's eyes and ears, and so on, we understand such attributions of human characteristics to God are not to be taken literally but have real meaning all the same: God sees and knows all things. Although the infinite and perfect God does not experience the fluctuations characteristic of human emotions, yet God does have an emotional life of perfect love and joy in the fellowship of the Trinity. God's words of love and kindness to all (Psa 145:9), even his enemies (Matt 5:43–48), mean a great deal as do his words to those he chooses to save for he is 'distressed in their distress' (Isa. 63:9). We must also reckon with the wondrous reality of the incarnation of the divine person of the

Son of God. While his suffering for us was in his human nature it was nevertheless the suffering of the person of the Son of God. Thus we have a High Priest who is able to empathise with our weaknesses (Heb. 4:15), and through him and by the Holy Spirit we have access to our loving heavenly Father.

2.2 God in relation to others

God has all life,[25] glory,[26] goodness,[27] and blessedness,[28] in and of himself. He alone is all-sufficient in and to himself, nor does he need any of the creatures that he has made,[29] nor are they the source of any of his glory.[30] Rather, he reveals his own glory in, by, to and on them, for he is the only source of all being, of whom, through whom and to whom are all things.[31] He has completely sovereign dominion over them to do by, to or for them whatever he pleases.[32] In his sight all things are open and evident.[33] His knowledge is infinite and infallible, and does not depend upon any created thing,[34] so that to him nothing is conditional or uncertain.[35] He is completely holy in all his purposes, in all his works, and in all his commands.[36] To him is due whatever worship, service or obedience he is pleased to require from angels, human beings and all other creatures.[37]

25. Jn 5:26. 26. Acts 7:2. 27. Psalm 119:68 28. 1 Tim. 6:15; Rom. 9:5.
29. Acts 17:24–25. 30. Job 22:2–3. 31. Rom. 11:36.
32. Rev. 4:11; I Tim 6:15; Dan. 4:25,35. 33. Heb. 4:13.
34. Rom. 11:33–34; Psalm 147:5. 35. Acts 15:18; Ezek. 11:5.
36. Psalm 145:17; Rom. 7:12. 37. Rev. 5:12–14.

The first part of this section asserts the absolute self-existence of God. When it is said in the original text that God does not derive any glory from his creatures, it means that nothing that contributes to God's glory has its original source in man. Whatever in us contributes to God's glory, or the display of it, is ultimately from God himself.

Sovereignty must not be understood as tyranny or arbitrary rule but the holy rule of the holy God described in WCF 2, 1–3. The truths about God in this chapter provide the basis for the teaching on the divine decrees in WCF 3. God's knowledge extends to the springs of man's thought and action, yet it is not mere foresight but is independent of the creature and so free of all uncertainty. Consequently, God alone is worthy of all worship and all praise.

THOUGHTS FROM OTHER MINDS

'And let us not take it into our heads either to seek out God anywhere else than in his Sacred Word, or to think anything about him that is not prompted by his Word, or to speak anything which is not taken from that Word. But if some distinction does exist in the one divinity of Father, Son and Holy Spirit—something hard to grasp—and occasions to certain minds more difficulty and trouble than is expedient, let it be remembered that men's minds, when they indulge their curiosity, enter into a labyrinth. And so let them yield themselves to be ruled by the heavenly oracles, even though they may fail to capture the height of the mystery.'

John Calvin (1509–1564)[1]

'Impassibility, when attributed to God in the Christian tradition and, specifically, in medieval and Protestant scholastic thought, indicates, not a Stoic notion of apatheia, but an absence of mutation, distress, or any other sort of passions... Certainly the denial of passions to God...has primarily to do with the assumption that finite creatures do not alter the divine being or add new properties to it – and not at all with relationality to God.'

Richard Muller[2]

'God's freedom from passions is not impassivity, unconcern, and impersonal detachment in face of the creation; not insensitivity and indifference to the distresses of a fallen world; not inability or unwillingness to empathize with human pain and grief; but simply that God's experiences do not come upon him

1. *Institutes of the Christian Religion*, 1.13.21 (Battles' edition cited).
2. *Post Reformation Reformed Dogmatics* (Baker Academic, 2003), 3:310–311

as ours come upon us, for his are foreknown, willed and chosen by himself, and are not involuntary surprises forced on him from outside, apart from his own decision, in the way that ours regularly are.'

J. I. Packer (1926–2020)[3]

'...when the New Testament appeals to the moral force and constraint of Calvary, it is on the involvement of God the Father that it frequently focuses. The cross is the expression of his love and of his pity (John 3:16; Romans 8:32). He is the One whose conduct is the model of self-denial and cross-bearing. He is the One who bore the cost of redemption. Indeed, if he is so immobile and so passionless that Calvary cost him nothing, all talk of him must cease because our language about him is meaningless. If Calvary was painless for him, we are not made in his image and he does not love with our love. When Abraham offered Isaac, there was pain; when Jacob lost Joseph, there was pain; when David lost Absalom, there was pain. If things were different when God gave up his Son, then either he does not love his Son or his love is so radically different from ours as to be meaningless.... The Father did not suffer what the Son suffered (he was not crucified). But he suffered seeing the Son suffer and the even greater (and quite unfathomable) agony of being the One who had to bruise and forsake him.'

Donald Macleod[4]

FOR DISCUSSION

1. Take time to consider each of the texts supporting the statements in these sections.
2. Does the Confession adequately set out the love of God?
3. What is the value of the 'proofs' of God's existence?
4. How is it that the Scriptures speak of God as having human parts and characteristics? Can it speak in any other way?

3. "Theism for Our Time," in *God Who Is Rich in Mercy,* eds. Peter T. O'Brien and David G. Peterson (Baker, 1986), 16.
4. *Behold Your God* (Christian Focus, 1990), 19.

CHAPTER 2
3: GOD'S TRINITARIAN LIFE

ANALYSIS *WCF 2:3*

a. one God in three persons
b. the distinctions between the persons

2.3 One God in three persons

In the unity of the Godhead there are three persons, of one substance, power and eternity: God the Father, God the Son, and God the Holy Spirit.[38] The order seen in the external operations of the three persons reflects the eternal reality that each person possesses a property distinct from the others: the Father eternally possesses fatherhood in relation to the Son, the Son is eternally the son of the Father[39] and the Spirit is eternally from the Father and the Son.[40*]

38. [1 Jn. 5:7]; Mat 3:16–17; Matt 28:19; 2 Cor. 13:14.
39. John 1:14–18.
40. John 15:26; Gal. 4:6.
* In the 1646 text this sentence reads: The Father is of none, neither begotten, nor proceeding: the Son is eternally begotten of the Father: the Holy Ghost eternally proceeding from the Father and the Son. It has been rephrased in an attempt to express the fundamental teaching with greater clarity for ordinary readers (see below).

The doctrine of the trinity rests simply on the data of Scripture and is the result of Christian reflection upon the way God has shown himself to be present and active in the world in his mighty acts of salvation. The doctrine is not a simple one, but then God is Creator and we are but creatures. We must accept the information given in Scripture and resist the temptation to ignore or twist any part to make the conclusions easier to our minds.

Trinity as a word

The use of the term 'trinity' immediately reminds us we are not using a word found in Scripture. However, it is an uninformed, sectarian or latitudinarian spirit which mouths the cry, originally uttered by Anglican latitudinarian scholar William Chillingworth in 1638: 'The Bible, I say, the Bible only is the religion of Protestants.' In no case is this a true claim, for every group (Protestant or otherwise) claiming 'the Bible only' has its own interpretation. We do not wish to quibble over words but we do wish to adhere to the true meaning of Scripture. Hence the necessity and honesty of declaring our understanding of controverted teachings of Scripture in a public Confession of Faith.

Tertullian (AD c.160-c220), the Roman advocate who became a Christian about AD 197, contributed the term 'trinitas' to the doctrine of God as it was formulated in the 4th century. He used this term in his writings against Praxeas (AD c.215), who had taught that it was the Father who suffered on the cross. But neither Tertullian nor the Councils of the 4th century supposed that they were doing other than setting out and clearing up misrepresentations of the teaching about God found in the pages of Holy Scripture. That they used the language of their time was inescapable; that there were many unholy political skirmishes and worse in the conflict which raged on the subject is acknowledged; that they advanced speculations to account for the facts of Scripture is also true; but that they did correctly discern the leading points of Scripture is also our belief, and this has been succinctly incorporated in the Confession of Faith.

The essential doctrine

Well then, how do we state the doctrine? The Shorter Catechism reminds us: 'There are three persons in the Godhead, the Father, the Son and the

Holy Spirit; and these three are one God, the same in substance, equal in power and glory.' Such a statement is seeking to do full justice to the data of Scripture and may be otherwise expressed in three propositions:

i. there is only one God;

ii. the Father, the Son and the Holy Spirit is each God;

iii. the Father, the Son and the Holy Spirit is each a distinct person.

Now our language about God is of necessity accommodated to our capacity, and its inadequacy has always been recognised. We speak of three persons not because this language is adequate but because the Bible describes the relations of Father, Son and Holy Spirit in ways analogous to relations among human persons.

God is one in being or essence but within the singleness of his being there are three personal distinctions. Put plainly, we may say that God's life is not a solitary, lonely one, but has a richness and fulness reflecting the fact that God is a fellowship. Now to say God is a fellowship is not to say he is a committee, for a committee implies various individuals each with their distinctive origin, and might easily lead us to tritheism, belief in three Gods. To say God is a fellowship is to say that there is an intimacy of loving relationship and reciprocity in the nature of God in a manner consistent with the perfectly harmonious operation of the single divine will.

The last sentence in the 1646 text reflects discussions in the Christian church of the early centuries as believers reflected on the information in Scripture. In essence the church was saying that God is eternally what his revelation in history shows him to be. This does not imply an hierarchical ordering of the three persons as if the Son is eternally subordinate to the Father. The Bible shows the Father to be the one who plans, the Son the one who accomplishes and the Spirit the one who brings to fruition the works of Father and Son. This is seen in creation (Gen. 1:1–3) and in redemption. Full deity unqualifiedly belongs to the Son and the Spirit but the Son becomes God's servant as he takes our nature (sin excepted) to redeem and save. The traditional wording is important but less than unambiguously clear. It has been rephrased in an attempt to make it more meaningful.

Some Biblical illustrations

John beautifully expresses it: 'In the beginning was the Word and the Word was face to face with God and the Word was God' (Jn 1:1). Here is distinction and here is identity: distinction of person, identity of being. Or again, referring to the incarnation of the Son, we read: 'The only God who rests against the Father's heart, he has made him known' (Jn 1:18). Commenting on this passage, J. C. Ryle writes: 'As one who lies in the bosom of another is fairly supposed to be most intimate with him, to know all his secrets, and possess all his affections, so is it, we are to understand, in the union of the Father and the Son. It is more close than man's mind can conceive.'

Likewise the Spirit is referred to in terms of this intimacy and fellowship. Jesus says (Jn 14:15–17; 15:26; 16:13–15): 'If you love me you will obey what I command. And I will ask the Father, and he will give you another Counsellor to be with you forever—the Spirit of truth. . . . When the Counsellor comes, whom I will send to you from the Father, the Spirit of truth who goes out from the Father, he will testify about me. . . . He will not speak on his own; he will speak only what he hears. . . . He will bring glory to me by taking what is mine and making it known to you. All that belongs to the Father is mine. That is why I said the Spirit will take from what is mine and make it known to you.' So singular and essential is the Spirit's work in making known Christ that we have a virtual identity affirmed in the striking expression 'the Lord is the Spirit' in 2 Corinthians 4:17.

While it is proper to see anticipations of the doctrine of the trinity in the Old Testament, it is really only as we see the redemptive action of God disclosed in the New Testament that the distinctions in the very depths of deity itself are appreciated. By the same token, the truth of the Trinity would never have gained hold if it had not been intimately connected with the Christian understanding of salvation. Thus, the strictly monotheistic disciples have no embarrassment in affirming the deity of the Son and the Spirit in such a manner that we might well call the New Testament a distinctively trinitarian volume.

The Biblical presentation

The Biblical presentation of the Trinity is both specific and pervasive. There are brief statements of the doctrine (eg.: 1 Corinthians 12:4–6; 2 Corinthians 13:14; 1 Timothy 1:2–5; 1 Peter 1:2; Jude 20–21), extended passages which presuppose it and interweave it into practical instruction, as well as the passages which affirm deity of the Son (eg. John 5:18) or of the Spirit (eg. 1 Cor. 2:10–11).

1. *A specific passage: Matthew 28:19–20 (The Great Commission)*

Several points may be made in reference to the Great Commission passage:

1. In response to the argument that this must be a later addition, since elsewhere baptism is administered only in Jesus' name (Acts 2:38; 8:16; 10:48; 19:5; 1 Cor.1:13,15), it must be said that the textual witness in Matthew is not in any doubt.
2. In any event, I would argue that Matthew 28:19 in its original intention does not prescribe a formula so much as succinctly sum up

the fact that through the work of redemption the character of God has been declared definitively and he is to be recognised accordingly. Hence the initiatory rite of baptism as well as the teaching conveyed is to occur in just such a trinitarian context. This explanation fully corresponds with the situation in the early church as reflected in Acts and the Epistles. Where the gospel is rightly preached, people believe Jesus is the way to the Father, and rely upon him through the work of the Spirit (1 Cor.12:3).

3. The passage shows the importance of the truth of the Trinity. Herman Bavinck correctly affirms: 'the confession of the trinity is the sum of the Christian religion. Without it neither the creation nor the redemption nor the sanctification can be purely maintained. We can truly proclaim the mighty works of God only when we recognise and confess them as the one great work of Father, Son and Spirit. In the love of the Father, the grace of the Son, and the fellowship of the Holy Spirit is contained the whole salvation of men.'[1] In line with this approach we find very pervasive teaching throughout the New Testament.

2. *An extended passage: The Ephesian Letter*

Ephesians strikingly employs the truth of the Trinity. Chapter 1 verses 3–14 forms one sentence in the Greek and was written by a man who had not separated 'amazing' and 'grace'. Verse 3—'Praise be to the God and Father of our Lord Jesus Christ who has blessed us in the heavenly realms with every spiritual blessing [ie. blessings which come from the presence and power of the Spirit] in Christ'—is expanded in verses 4–6 in reference to the Father's election; in verses 7 to 12 in reference to the redemptive work of the Son, and in verses 13–14 in reference to the sealing work of the Spirit.

1. Herman Bavinck, *Our Reasonable Faith*, trans. Henry Zylstra (Baker Books, 1956), 161.

It is important to note the tone of doxology and devotion throughout the passage. There is nothing cold, hard and rationalistic about it. Similarly, although there is very strong emphasis on the sovereignty of God it is the sovereignty of the Triune God and not of some despot or arbitrary deity.

The action of the Triune God for our salvation is regarded as involving a new creation (1:3–2:10), the fruit of the incomparable riches of God's grace in Christ Jesus (2:8), a bringing from death to life. It results in a new community (2:11–3:21) which transcends barriers of race and background and, as the church, is the Heavenly Father's family on earth, characterised by new conduct (4:1–6:20). This new humanity in Christ, this new community, lives a life worthy of its calling (4:1), and imitates God in its life of love (5:2), with Christ as the great exemplar (5:2).

Characteristic, therefore, is unity in the truth (4:1–16 cf. John 17:20–23), a unity which allows for the diversity of gifts implicit in the metaphor of the body (4:16 cf. 1 Cor.12–14) and the pursuit of holiness (4:17ff): the old self put off and the new self put on (4:22–24). This is applied particularly to truth-telling, anger, stealing, purity of speech and behaviour.

In further application (5:15ff), the rejection of the drinking which results in uncontrolled, unwise and ungodly behaviour is contrasted with the constant infilling of the Spirit reflected in controlled, wise and godly conduct. The presence of the Spirit is seen from the four key imperatives which depend on the exhortation 'Go on being filled with the Spirit': speaking, singing (5:19), giving thanks (5:20), submitting (5:21), the last-named being expanded and applied in marriage, family and economic areas (5:22–6:9). In short, we have fellowship, worship, thankfulness and right relationships as a result of the work of the Triune God for and in his people.

Implications for Personhood

The truth of the Trinity helps us understand the nature of personhood. The modern world thinks in terms of self-contained individuality and thus of the separation of one person from another. However, the Biblical presentation would encourage us to understand personhood as individuality realised adequately only in community. God is supremely personal, and his own trinitarian life is characterised by fellowship and communion, an intimacy of loving relationship and reciprocity.

We are made in God's image and thus made for communion in relationship with God and with others who bear his image. It was not good for the man to be alone (Genesis 2:18) and the communion of marriage and family reflects a fundamental requirement of real human life. Ephesians 3:15 suggests that God is not merely like a human father but 'the pattern and archetype of all fatherhood' (John Macpherson, Ephesians (1892) 262). Over against the individualism which promotes the ego, alienates and separates, we must affirm and demonstrate the life that is self-giving, which reconciles and includes, while at the same time recognising the distinctiveness of each individual.

Already we are implying the Fall that progresses to utter isolation in hell, and the Redemption that leads to the embrace of God's people in the fellowship of God's trinitarian life here and now (cf. 1 John 1:3) with its climax in the world to come, a world of love. Peter affirms the believer's participation in the divine nature (2 Peter 1:4) not as if the Creator/creature distinction is lost, but to affirm that the un-begun and un-ending circle of the divine life is, as it were, opened to embrace his people.

Implications for the character of God

The correct understanding of the truth of the Trinity balances our belief in the sovereign power of God so that we see most clearly that it is not of a high-handed or arbitrary character. The God who predestines is the God who is love, the God and Father of our Lord Jesus Christ. The natural man does not receive the things of the Spirit of God and so he readily may represent God as a 'standover merchant'. However, believers should not contribute to harsh and unloving portraits of God, or even to a tendency to regard Biblical predestination as fatalism, let alone disregard the call to community and self-giving relationship in the body of Christ. We need a focus on God himself, on the God who wills that we are eternally embraced in his fellowship so that we might share in the glory the Son had with the Father before the world was. The Son has given us the pattern (Phil. 2:1–18). Lovelessness is the most contradictory aspect of the Christian life.

The belief in God as Triune, and thus in mutual self-giving and reciprocity, is also fundamental in anchoring a proper doctrine of atonement. Any suggestion of coercion on the part of the Father towards his Son is completely ruled out. There is never any conflict of will or purpose but a perfect harmony of love: it not only pleased the Father to put his Son to grief, but it was the delight of the Son to drink the cup the Father had given him (John 18:11), because it was the loving desire of both Father and Son, together with the Spirit, to bring many sons to glory. Sometimes we can give the impression that redemption is a mere legal arrangement of almost impersonal character, when it is the loving purpose of God who himself is the way back to himself.

Abraham was stopped from sacrificing his son, his only son, whom he loved, by the voice of God from heaven (Genesis 22), and the Genesis account is noteworthy in indicating no resistance on the part of Isaac.

But God the Father's love was so great and the Son's love so great that the Father did not stay the knife from his Son, his only Son, whom he loved, and the Son, because of the joy that was set before him—the joy of fellowship with redeemed sinners!—endured the cross, despising the shame. While the Son knew terrible fear as he anticipated his suffering, and his sweat was like drops of blood (Luke 22:44) he did not resist but willingly and lovingly went to the cross. Instead of a voice from heaven or a legion of angels, there was a loud cry from the earth which still resonates through the ages and expresses the impenetrable mystery of the immeasurable love of God: 'My God, My God, why have you forsaken me?'

It is that mysterious breach in communion, that utter isolation, that endurance of hell, if you will, in an intensity that cannot be fathomed, which constitutes the ground of our reconciliation, our inclusion, our assurance of eternal life with God. We are called to realise our life in communion, a communion of love through him who loved us. We love God and we love one another because God first loved us with a love so amazing, so divine that it 'demands my life, my soul, my all'.

THE GENDER OF GOD

Of recent years we have heard much about the gender of God, and of the efforts of the more extreme feminists to legitimise the addressing of God as our Father-Mother God or the like. While the terms 'Father' and 'Son' are metaphors yet it does not follow that they are without significance. In this connection the words of Herman Bavinck are relevant: 'The name of God in Scripture does not designate him as he is in himself, but in his manifold revelation and relation to the creature. Nevertheless, this name is not arbitrary, but God reveals himself as he is. . . . In Scripture 'to be' and 'to be called' indicate the same thing from different angles. God is that which he calls himself, and he calls himself that which he is.'[#]

The Son had glory with the Father before the world was (John 17:5), as the Father's equal and yet with a distinctive role. While some feminist theology involves reaction from inadequately expressed teaching about God, its fundamental approach can be characterised as one which does not take proper account of what is revealed in Scripture. The attempt by some to ascribe gender to God is quite misguided. The failure by many to appreciate that differentiation of *function* between male and female does not imply inferiority of *nature*, any more than it does among the persons of the Godhead, is lamentable.

Herman Bavinck, *The Doctrine of God* (Banner of Truth, 1951), 85

Simplifications to avoid

There are a number of simplifications which must be avoided since what God has revealed about himself is not subject to amendment by us unless we would be idolaters. First, is what is popularly called *unitarianism*. It affirms one God but denies the distinction of persons. Accordingly, the deity of Christ is denied and the personality of the Holy Spirit is rejected. This is the doctrine of Jehovah's Witnesses and Christadelphians today and of the Arians in the 4th century. Second, there is *modalism* which teaches the three persons are but several ways in which the one God has revealed himself, like an actor performing several roles in a play, but denies the distinction of persons. This was the error of Sabellius in the 3rd century (hence *Sabellianism*). Third, there is *tritheism*, which denies the one nature but affirms three persons thus teaching three gods. *Polytheism* (belief in many gods) is another simplification that divides the richness of God's character and attributes among many persons.

Explaining the doctrine

The doctrine of the Trinity, it must be emphasised, has no adequate human analogy. Further, the doctrine is the answer to the question, 'What is God like if he acts the way we know he does through Jesus Christ?' 'The proclamation is that God redeems us in Jesus Christ—the *doctrine* is that God therefore must be a trinity. It doesn't explain why God is like this, and neither does it pretend to—it simply states that God *must* be like this if he acts in the way that Christians know that he does'[2]. So the claim that the Trinity doctrine was unknown until the 4th century is misleading and irrelevant. As the church struggled to articulate its doctrine of God at that time there were those who oversimplified and made God to fit the human mind. It was the great Athanasius (c.298–373) who brought the church back to a true understanding by showing salvation depended on it.[3]

In discussing the Christian doctrine of God it will be helpful to remember the example of Athanasius, and relate the data of Scripture to the foundation of salvation. Certainly one could do well to first show that throughout Scripture we are exhorted never to put our trust in man but only in God himself; that Scripture exhorts us to honour the Son as we would honour the Father, and thus to worship the Son and trust him as 'Jehovah our righteousness' (Jer 23:6). The various Scriptures that ascribe deity to the Saviour may be quoted, together with passages that in the Old Testament are applied to Jehovah and in the New are applied to Christ.

It is usually claimed by anti-trinitarians that Jesus cannot possess true deity since he said that the Father is greater than himself (John 14:28). However, this is to confuse his subordination in *relation* to the Father with a subordination as to nature. It would seem that most objections to the doctrine of the trinity arise from inadequate views of human sinfulness and a consequent exalted sense of human wisdom. Begin then with the proclamation of Jesus Christ, the express image of the invisible God (cf. Hebrews 1:3). But those in cults such as the Watchtower Society really need to be challenged to examine their own religion critically: that is what they want you to do with yours so that you will see that it is wrong

2. Alister McGrath, *Understanding the Trinity* (1987), 115.
3. A good introduction is Peter Barnes' *Athanasius of Alexandria: His Life and Impact* (Christian Focus, 2019).

and they are right. They cannot think independently of the cult and are not permitted to read material other than their own. This needs to be taken into account when witnessing to such people, and the damning evidence from the cult's own history brought before them.

THE UNITY OF GOD AND THE THREE PERSONS	
Dynamic Monarchianism	God is one person with one nature who specially indwells Jesus. Originated 2nd century; Paul of Samosata, a notable advocate, was condemned in AD 268. Much liberal theology holds this view.
Modalistic Monarchianism	The Son and the Spirit are mere modes of manifestation of the one divine father, like roles in a play. The trinity of persons is denied. Sabellius c.AD 215 was a notable advocate; also called patripassianism (father-suffering). Common in some 20th century theology.
Arianism	Jesus a creature. Condemned at Nicaea AD 325. Champion of truth was Athanasius. Semi-arians said the Son was homoiousious, of like substance to the Father; orthodox said homoousious, of the same substance.

THOUGHTS FROM OTHER MINDS

'But God also designates himself by another special mark [in addition to his infinity and spiritual nature] to distinguish himself more precisely from idols. For he so proclaims himself the sole God as to offer himself to be contemplated clearly in three persons. Unless we grasp these, only the bare and empty name of God flits around in our brains, to the exclusion of the true God.'

John Calvin (1509–1564)[4]

'Between the Holy God and sinful man there is an infinite gulf; and only through one who is Deity, who takes man's nature upon himself and suffers and dies in his stead, can man's debt be paid. Nor could a Holy Spirit who falls short of Deity

4. *Institutes of the Christian Religion*, 1.13.2 (Battles' edition cited).

apply that redemption to human souls. Hence if salvation is to be had at all it must be of divine origin.... The fact of the matter is that God is the way back to himself, and that all the hopes of our fallen race are centred in the truth of the Trinity.'

Loraine Boettner (1901–1990)[5]

FOR DISCUSSION

1. Explain passages about the Angel of the Lord (Genesis 32:24 etc.).
2. Consider also Isaiah 6 in the light of John 12:39–41.
3. Can we speak of the Jehovahship of Jesus? [Compare Isa. 45:21ff with Phil. 2:9–11; Isa. 40:3 with Mark 1:3; Mark 3:3; Psalm 130:8 with Matt 1:21; Isa. 48:12 with Rev. 22:12,13.]
4. Reflect on the implications of the doctrine of God as Trinity for our understanding of ourselves.

5. *Studies in Theology* (P&R Publishing, 1947), 136.

CHAPTER 3
GOD'S ETERNAL PLAN

ANALYSIS *WCF 3:1–8*

1. The character and scope of God's plan
- a. flows from himself
- b. he is not the author of sin
- c. the freedom and responsibility of moral creatures is maintained
- d. he does not put aside ordinary relation of cause and effect

2. God's plan and God's knowledge
- a. God's plan not based on foresight
- b. conditions ordained as well as ends

3–4. God's plan and moral creatures
- a. embraces men and angels
- b. predestination to life
- c. foreordination to death
- d. absolutely unchangeable

5–6. God's plan and human salvation
- a. predestination in Christ
- b. reason for choice not in creature
- c. called in time through means of grace
- d. to the praise of God's grace

7. God's plan and human salvation
- a. sovereign preterition (passing by)
- b. judicial condemnation — 'for their sin'
- c. to the praise of God's justice

8. God's plan and human salvation
- a. how, to whom and why it is to be preached

The Confession of Faith aims to set out carefully and with precision the leading points on the subject of God's plan, especially as it affects moral creatures. Fifteen hundred years of history lie behind the formulation of this chapter, and it should not present a problem to the well-instructed believer, but rather the reverse (cf. WCF 3:8).

The 1646 chapter title is 'God's eternal decree' (singular) which emphasizes the comprehensive and unitary nature of God's plan for creation. The catechisms use the plural term 'decrees' so drawing attention to the individual aspects included in God's plan.

The amount of space allocated to this subject does not necessarily indicate its relative importance. Sufficient space is taken to fix all the important points. Critics often argue for omission or abbreviation, but history has shown that lack of clarity on God's decree means danger for the maintenance of the Gospel.

The content of this Chapter is not a peculiarity of Presbyterian bodies but is the common heritage of Protestant Christianity. It is true that the Lutheran Church did not follow Luther in this matter, but in essential points Luther agreed with Calvin (see Luther's great work against Erasmus, *The Bondage of the Will*). The Anglicans, Congregationalists and Particular Baptist groups had basic harmony in their understanding of God's decrees. Indeed, about 30% of the words in the Chapter come from earlier statements—chiefly the *Irish Articles* of 1615.

The Bible handles the subject in a variety of ways. In Romans, Paul brings in the doctrine in the course of explaining the unbelief of Israel, and after he has dealt with the doctrine of righteousness by faith and union with Christ. In Ephesians the same Paul includes predestination as an explicit part of his first chapter of praise to the God of salvation. But it would be wrong to draw the conclusion that Paul is dominated by predestination while in Romans he is more moderate.

The simple fact is that predestination has many implications and is particularly important in grounding assurance of salvation in Christ in the face of human inability. Much modern scholarship does not sufficiently consider this when (incorrectly) accusing 17th century Reformed theologians of deducing their theology from the single principle of predestination. Interestingly, those of a Barthian line of thought, who frequently advance the accusation of 'scholasticism' in the Westminster Confession, are opposed by Karl Barth himself, who says that careful reading is likely to 'give the impression that from the standpoint of its systematic range and importance they [the Westminster Confession and other Reformed theologians] gave the doctrine too little consideration rather than too much.'[1]

3.1 Character and scope of God's plan

From all eternity God, by the most wise and holy purpose of his own will, freely and unchangeably ordained whatever comes to pass. He does this in such a way that he is not the author of sin, nor does he force his moral creatures to act against their will, nor is the free working of secondary causes taken away but instead it is established.

1. Eph. 1:11; Rom. 11:33; Heb. 6:17; Rom. 9:15,18.
2. James 1:13,17; 1 Jn. 1:5.
3. Acts 2:23; Matt. 17:12; Acts 4:27,28; John 19:11; Prov. 16:33.

God's plan and purpose is like himself—wise and holy. God has decreed the existence of all things, including sin, but his relationship to sin is not the same as his relationship to good, although we cannot explain the mystery involved except to say God does not will sin but it does not come to pass apart from his will. Even Christ was delivered into the hands of lawless men to be crucified by the definite plan and foreknowledge of God (Acts 2:23). So we live in a creation that is not without purpose: everything has been predestined according to God's plan (Eph. 1:11) as he has freely decided and in that sense is unchangeable, fixed and certain '*yet so as thereby neither is God the author of sin, nor is violence offered to the will of the creatures, nor is the liberty or contingency of second causes taken away*' (1646 text). In other words, we do not live in a fatalistic world where human freedom and responsibility is minimised or is an illusion because

1. Karl Barth, *Church Dogmatics* II, 2 (T. & T. Clark, 1957), 78.

of the fact of God's sovereignty. God has ordained human freedom so we act as we see fit from the various options open to us and in this sense we live in a world where chance circumstances affect our lives. These secondary causes are seen also in nature. A sparrow cannot fall to the ground or a hair from the head apart from God's plan (Matt 10:29–30), yet the death of a bird due to age or being shot, or loss of hair due to dandruff or chemotherapy, is fully recognised. Similarly, when there is disaster in a city the Lord has done it (Amos 3:6) while yet it may be brought about by human invaders. The all-wise God ensures life is not a madhouse. Real relationship exists between means used and results obtained. God rules over all, not chance, so that even what seems to be random to us is also under his authority. More on human freedom in WCF 5.2 & WCF 9.

3.2 God's plan and God's knowledge

God knows everything that may or can occur under all conceivable conditions.[4] What he foresaw taking place in time is part of his decree, as is also the fulfilment of any condition.[5]

4. Acts 15:18; 1 Sam. 23:11,12; Matt. 11:21,23.
5. Rom. 9:11,13,16,18.

It has been claimed that some things are not decreed by God but are foreseen by God who acts upon them to bring about certain ends. This theory of conditional decrees is not infrequently advanced to support the notion that God's election of his people is conditioned on his foresight that they will have faith. However, Scripture makes plain that people have faith because God has ordained that they will repent and believe. If God had not fixed the entire future his knowledge to some extent would be imperfect. Moreover, God would be dependent upon a creature, and salvation would not be based on grace but human qualities; God would be reduced to 'a far-seeing statesman' (R. A. Finlayson). In short, God ordains the end, but also the fulfilment of all the conditions necessary to secure that end. He is not the prisoner of his creation, but its Lord.

Freedom can be a bit of a 'weasel' word, meaning different things to different people. The Biblical viewpoint is that freedom is not the ability to act *contrary to* our nature, but to act *in accordance with* our nature (see WCF 9). As we are spiritually dead towards God, spiritual life is the result of God's renewing work in our lives. God is in total control, yet we always have freedom within the bounds of our nature, and we are always fully responsible to God for our spiritual bondage, since our spiritual inability is our own fault. Some suppose that God's sovereignty and human freedom can be reconciled but at the expense of limitation on God's sovereignty (eg. Arminianism) or a limitation on human responsibility (eg. hyper-Calvinism), but the Confession rejects both.

Luis de Molina (1535–1600) acknowledged God knows everything about himself and all possibilities outside of him (*natural* knowledge) and he also knows factual reality—everything he in his freedom wills (*free* knowledge). But Molina argued for a *middle* knowledge between these. In order of logic, before God willed he foresees how humans will use their free will under all possible conditions and bases his predestination upon this foreknowledge and arranges the circumstances so that they freely do what he desires. Molina, a Spanish Jesuit, caused great controversy in the Roman Catholic church over these views, which did not square with official teaching, nor do they resolve the issue in question since God's use of middle knowledge rendered the outcome certain, while yet his sovereignty is qualified because something outside of God influences what he ordains. There has been a resurgence of this approach of recent years as in the work of the analytical philosophers Alvin Platinga (b.1932) and William Lane Craig (b. 1949). The last phrase of WCF 3.2 is directed against Molinism.

Molinism did not affect Protestantism directly at the time although Dutch Protestant **Jacob Arminius** (1560–1609) adopted Molina's idea of middle knowledge (without identifying his source) in his own restructuring of God's predestination. He denied God's foreknowledge of those who would be saved arose because God's had decreed their salvation. Rather he taught that God's foreknowledge left people in a position where their salvation depended on their use or otherwise of the grace God extended to all. Christ's death was for all and grace was extended to all, but belief and perseverance in faith were in the hands of the individual. Arminian teaching holds that God does what he can, but ultimately he must bow before the will of the creature. Arminian thought collided with Biblical and Reformed teaching at several points, including its understanding of the extent of man's depravity. It gave rise to the Synod of Dort in 1618–19 in which five criticisms were debated and rejected. Nevertheless, Arminian teaching made significant strides in the Church of England in the 17th century, was characteristic of the rise of Methodism under John Wesley (1703–91) and is very general today among evangelicals. The Confession rejects Arminian teaching.

Open Theism, or Arminian teaching 'with a twist', was advanced by people like Clark Pinnock (1937–2010) in the early 1990s. It describes the Reformed position as a 'determinist' position in which God treats us as puppets, doing what we are programmed to do. If we believe God is always responsive to his creatures, we can't accept this, says Pinnock, since it makes God like a stone pillar, frozen in time. Pinnock argues that God knows everything current, but not all the future. The future is partly settled and partly not settled, since it depends on the entirely free and undetermined acts of God's creatures. God cannot know these, otherwise they would not be free acts. Arminianism says that God has not planned the future but foresees what his creatures will do; Open Theism says creation is God's project, but only some parts are settled.

The appeal of openness teaching is found in stressing those passages of Scripture that speak of the future as uncertain, of God repenting, etc. (see under WCF 2.1). It holds that genuine interactions, truly free actions, cannot be exhaustively foreknown. Scientifically, novelty and chance are features of the world we know, it claims. Confidence in God should rest on the competence and resourcefulness of God who knows every possibility and is ready with a response. Thus far Open Theism.

The fatal weakness of openness theology is its failure to take all the Scripture data into account, as discussed previously, its philosophical (rather than biblical) notion of freedom, its failure to reckon with chance as a valid concept from our perspective yet still under the sovereignty of God (Proverbs 16:33), and its inability to meet the practical reality of suffering. Indeed, how can you be sure that the unsettled things won't unsettle the settled things? How can God speak about a happy ending if he has no control over the free decisions of human agents? When trouble or trial afflicts is it the case that God can do nothing? Far otherwise is the teaching of Scripture. Reformed theology does not profess to explain how God is fully sovereign while yet human decisions are free but we accept and hold these two truths as both taught in the word of God.

3.3 God's plan and moral creatures

By God's decree, to show his glory, some people and angels[6] are predestined to everlasting life; and others foreordained to everlasting death.[7]

6. 1 Tim. 5:21; Matt. 25:41.
7. Rom. 9:22,23; Eph. 1:5,6; Prov. 16:4.

In order to display his glorious perfections, and thus to communicate his blessedness to his moral creatures, God has predestined some to everlasting life—'a great multitude which no man can number.' Others have been foreordained to everlasting death. Notice that *predestination* is used in the Confession only of the saved while *foreordination* is reserved for the lost, and the term *reprobation* is not used. Predestination and foreordination as words are not dissimilar in their basic idea, but it is evident that the Confession follows its own teaching in 3:8, and thus makes an effort to highlight that God's dealings with the saved and the lost are based on different grounds. 'In the one instance we have an act of grace, determined by God's good will; in the other, an act of judgment, determined by the sin of the individual' (John Macpherson). 'Predestination reveals the goal of divine love and grace. . . . Since a goal is a perfect ideal, damnation is neither a goal nor an ideal. For even if sin and punishment are willed by God this is not an object of his delight as is the salvation of his elect'.[2] Thus we should avoid speaking of double predestination as if the salvation of the elect and the condemnation of others are based on precisely equivalent grounds. And we most certainly reject utterly the blasphemous claim that God has foreordained men to sin.

There was very careful debate on this section. Jeremiah Whitaker, an eminent Presbyterian pastor, wanted to modify this section, apparently by removing the closing words, but the Assembly refused to do so. It considered that important concerns were safeguarded by them.[3]

3.4 God's plan and moral creatures

These angels and people, thus predestined and foreordained, are individually and unchangeably designated, and their number so certain and definite that it cannot be either increased or reduced.[8]

8. 2 Tim. 2:19; John 13:18.

2. R. A. Finlayson, *Reformed Theological Writings* (Mentor, 1996), 262; Similarly, Herman Bavinck, *Reformed Dogmatics* (Baker Academic, 2004), 2:389
3. B. B. Warfield, *The Westminster Assembly and Its Work* (Oxford University Press, 1932), 131–133.

This straightforward section is designed to reaffirm that as the all-wise God is unchangeable and his plan perfect, so all within it is unchangeable. It is not fate or necessity but the Triune God's decree that renders events certain.

3.5 God's plan and human salvation

Those of the human race who are predestined to life, God has chosen in Christ to everlasting glory.[9] This choice was made according to God's eternal and unchangeable purpose and the secret wisdom and good pleasure of his will before the foundation of the world was laid. It arose solely from his free grace and love and was not influenced by or dependent on any cause or condition in the person, whether foresight of faith or good works, perseverance in faith or works, or anything else in the person.[10] God's purpose is that all praise might be to his glorious grace.[11]

9. Eph. 1:4,9,11; Rom. 8:30; 2 Tim. 1:9; 1 Thess. 5:9.
10. Rom. 9:11,13,16; Eph. 1:4,9.
11. Eph. 1:6,12.

Notice the time of God's choice, its nature as an act of grace, its reason as the good pleasure of God (cf. Matt 11:26), and the end in view—the praise of God's grace. Those predestined to salvation are chosen in Christ. Divine election is not apart from Christ, nor is the end of salvation divorced from the means. As also noted in 3:2 there is a rejection of the conditional decree theory. If foreseen faith is the *ground* of election then grace is denied. In fact, faith is a *fruit* of election, and the *gift* of God.

3.6 God's plan and human salvation

As God has appointed the elect to glory, he has also, by the eternal and completely free purpose of his will, foreordained all the means to this end.[12] Therefore, those who are elected, all being fallen in Adam, are redeemed by Christ;[13] they are effectively called to faith in Christ by his Spirit working at the appointed time, and are justified, adopted, sanctified,[14] and kept by his power, through faith, to salvation.[15] None but the elect are redeemed by Christ, effectively called, justified, adopted, sanctified, and saved.[16]

12. 1 Pet. 1:2; Eph. 1:4,5; Eph. 2:10; 2 Thess. 2:13.
13. 1 Thess. 5:9,10; Titus 2:14.
14. Rom. 8:30; Eph. 1:5; 2 Thess. 2:13.
15. 1 Pet. 1:5.
16. John 17:9; Rom. 8:28–39; John 6:64,65; John 10:26; Jn 8:47; 1 Jn. 2:19.

God has ordained the means of salvation, and this section states that he effectively applies those means or causes them to be effectively used. Those who are saved are reckoned as 'fallen in Adam'. A minority of the Reformed have been *supra*lapsarian ('*before* the fall'), viewing the matter from the final end God has in view. They thus think in terms of the logical order in God's decree being 'election-creation-fall' leading to eternal bliss or wrath, but run the risk of seeing creation and the fall as mere means to that end while at the point of election the elect are only hypothetical persons. Most Calvinists have been *infra*lapsarian ('*after* the fall'), that is, they consider the decree of election is reckoned in order of logic and history as contemplating people who are already fallen, thus 'creation-fall-election'. They are anxious to avoid any suggestion that the fall is ordained by God preferring to say that what is against God's will does not occur apart from God's will. Derek Thomas has shown that the language of 3.6 on this point is a studied ambiguity allowing either view.[4] While the majority view has always been infralapsarian, the two positions seem to divide the truth between them since they start from different perspectives—either the divine or the human, while both can easily overlook that the *ultimate* aim is not God's mercy and justice revealed in the salvation or damnation of sinners, but God's glory revealed in a renewed creation.

4. Derek W. H. Thomas, 'The Westminster Consensus on the Decree: The Infra/Supra Lapsarian Debate' in J. Ligon Duncan (ed.), *The Westminster Confession into the 21st Century* (Mentor, 2009), 3:267-290.

In the Confession the atonement is regarded as definite or particular that is, intended for and limited to the elect alone. In the endeavour to articulate clearly the nature of Christ's atonement in the early Reformation period it is understandable that there were debates among those who were agreed on the chief point but differed on how this related to an adequate ground for the free offer of the Gospel. The mainstream position was a truism dating from Peter Lombard (1100–1160), if not earlier, that Christ's atonement was 'sufficient for all but efficient for the elect'. The free offer of the Gospel is grounded in the command of Christ not on our knowledge of whom God has chosen.

Variations from the mainstream arose as justice was sought to be done to some of the Biblical passages that have a universal aspect, not least John 3:16.

There was a school of thought influenced by James Ussher (1581–1656), the Anglican Archbishop of Armagh who was delegated to the Westminster Assembly but did not attend because of his Royalist sympathies. A notable advocate of his approach was John Davenant (1572–1641), an English delegate to the Synod of Dort (1618–19) and later Bishop of Salisbury. His interpretation of 'sufficient for all but efficient only for the elect' was that the death of Christ secured a conditional remission of sin for all and so provided warrant for the indiscriminate preaching of the gospel. Nevertheless, Davenant separated the intercession of Christ from his death for sinners and held that God's intention was that the Son intercede for the elect alone securing to them alone remission of sin and all saving benefits. This so called 'hypothetical universalist' view has had some significant support among evangelicals in the English tradition down through the years, as for instance by Bishop J. C. Ryle of Liverpool. It requires some fine distinctions in an endeavour to avoid inconsistencies. It has never been judged heretical, and was advocated by several members of the Assembly, but it cannot be said with confidence that the final language of the Confession supports it.

The rather different 'hypothetical universalist' view of Moses Amyraut (1596–1664) of Saumur in France was current from the mid 1630s although it developed the thought of John Cameron (c.1579–1625). In the logical ordering of God's eternal decree Amyraut placed the decree of atonement for all before the decree of election, holding with the mainstream that those for whom he died are those for whom he intercedes. To avoid the notion that all will be saved it was explained that Christ died for the elect absolutely and for the reprobate only conditionally, in case they should believe. This form of particular redemption was controversial when advanced, received no positive endorsement in the Confession and seems clearly excluded by the opening words of WCF 8.8.

3.7 God's plan and human damnation

The rest of the human race God was pleased to pass by according to the unsearchable wisdom of his own will, by which he extends or withholds mercy, as he pleases. This he did to show the glory of his sovereign power over his creatures. Those he thus chooses to pass by he also ordains to dishonour and wrath for their sin, in order to bring praise to his glorious justice.[17]

17. Matt. 11:25,26; Rom. 9:17,18,21,22; 2 Tim. 2:19,20; Jude v.4; 1 Pet. 2:8.

Concerning the lost there are two points (1) passing by (what is technically called *preterition*) and (2) condemnation. The passing by is not because of their sin, otherwise all would be passed by and no one could be saved. The passing by is *sovereign*—for God's own reasons. God decides that they will go in their own way and in due time to punish them for their unbelief and sin. Grace prepares some for glory, sin fits others for destruction (Rom. 9:22–25). Only the deserving go to hell. And all the redeemed are underserving of God's gracious election in Christ.

One should keep in mind God's purpose with the entire creation. The Confession here and in WCF 33.2 could be more specific on the new creation in which final goal all God's perfections are reflected back to him by redeemed humanity, holy angels and the entire new creation.

3.8 The proper use of the doctrine of predestination

The doctrine of this profound mystery of predestination is to be handled with special prudence and care,18 so that people who hear the will of God revealed in his word and give obedience to it, may, from the certainty of their effective calling, be sure of their eternal election.19 Used in such a way this doctrine will give cause for praise, reverence and admiration of God;20 and will produce humility, diligence and abundant encouragement in all who sincerely obey the gospel.[21]

18. Rom. 9:20; Rom. 11:33; Deut. 29:29.
19. 2 Pet. 1:10.
20. Eph. 1:6; Rom. 11:33.
21. Rom. 11:5,6,20; 2 Pet. 1:10; Rom. 8:33; Luke 10:20.

Predestination may be a profound mystery but it is still to be preached. If there is lack of real fear of God, reverence and awe, if believers lack humility, are spiritually lazy and lack assurance—perhaps we may lay the blame at the door of those who do not preach and teach aright the doctrine of predestination.

ELECTION & REPROBATION: SOME IMPORTANT POINTS

1. The Confession does not teach or imply a double predestination. In an attempt to distinguish between election and reprobation it uses predestination for the elect and foreordination for the reprobate.
2. It shows that election and reprobation rest on different grounds: election on the redeeming love of God that undertakes the salvation of the lost; reprobation on the moral necessity to manifest to the universe the nature and consequences of sin in moral personality.
3. It teaches that means are used by God to fulfil the purpose of election, but that God uses no means to fulfil his purpose of reprobation. It is left to sin to run its course and receive its wages.

4. It shows that the fruits of election are attributable to divine grace, the fruits of reprobation to personal sin. This means that while there is grace to some, there is injustice to none.
5. It implies that, while God finds pleasure in the salvation of the elect, he has sworn by himself that he has no pleasure in the death of the wicked. God does not need sin or its retribution for his self-manifestation, but its reality in the universe can serve that end.
6. That the elect will constitute a recreation of the race under a new Head is evident, while the reprobate are but the branches cut off from the tree of humanity. Christ will be revealed as the Saviour of the world, though many are lost in the process.

R. A. Finlayson (1895–1989),
Professor of Systematic Theology,
Free Church of Scotland College (1946–65)[5]

THOUGHTS FROM OTHER MINDS

'Let this, therefore, be first before our eyes: to seek any other knowledge of predestination than what the Word of God discloses is not less insane than if one should purpose to walk in a pathless waste (cf Job 12:24), or to see in darkness. . . . Scripture is the school of the Holy Spirit, in which, as nothing is omitted that is both necessary and useful to know, so nothing is taught but what is expedient to know. Therefore we must be on guard against depriving believers of anything disclosed about predestination in Scripture, lest we seem either wickedly to defraud them of the blessing of their God or to accuse and scoff at the Holy Spirit for having published what it is in any way profitable to suppress.'

John Calvin (1509–1564)[6]

'*Article 3: The Infinite Value of Christ's Death*

This death of God's Son is the only and entirely complete sacrifice and satisfaction for sins; it is of infinite value and worth, more than sufficient to atone for the sins of the whole world.

5. Finlayson, *Reformed Theological Writings*, 262.
6. *Institutes of the Christian Religion*, 3.21.2–3 (Battles' edition cited).

Article 4: Reasons for This Infinite Value

This death is of such great value and worth for the reason that the person who suffered it is—as was necessary to be our Saviour—not only a true and perfectly holy human, but also the only begotten Son of God, of the same eternal and infinite essence with the Father and the Holy Spirit. Another reason is that this death was accompanied by the experience of God's wrath and curse, which we by our sins had fully deserved.

Article 5: The Mandate to Proclaim the Gospel to All

Moreover, it is the promise of the gospel that whoever believes in Christ crucified shall not perish but have eternal life. This promise, together with the command to repent and believe, ought to be announced and declared without differentiation or discrimination to all nations and people, to whom God in his good pleasure sends the gospel.

Article 6: Unbelief, a Human Responsibility

However, that many who have been called through the gospel do not repent or believe in Christ but perish in unbelief is not because the sacrifice of Christ offered on the cross is deficient or insufficient, but because they themselves are at fault.

Article 7: Faith God's Gift

But all who genuinely believe and are delivered and saved by Christ's death from their sins and from destruction receive this favour solely from God's grace—which God owes to no one—given to them in Christ from eternity.'

Synod of Dort[7]

'After the fall, after the race, adult and infant and all, has gone into the death grasp of violated and inexorable nature, the Calvinist, with joy and a shout of triumph, flies to the divine predestination, that counter decree which reverses destiny,

7. *The Synod of Dort 1619: Second Head of Doctrine.* Christian Reformed Churches of Australia Edition.

that only decree which can either lawfully or effectively countervail the doom of nature, and turn darkness into light, despair into hope, death into life, hell into heaven. . . . God must predestinate, or we are every one lost, whether we be an infant of eight days, or an old man of eighty years. He does predestinate: it is the sheerest madness in us to be bewailing the fact. We ought to bless the goodness that prompted him to predestinate: we ought to magnify the wisdom which devised a way by which he could predestinate in consistency with his justice: we ought to glorify the power which supports and makes effective his predestination. . . . It is predestination or it is damnation: the decree of God, or the decree of nature. Let us get the case very clearly: all were guilty, depraved, condemned, doomed; then God must predestinate if any are saved; if he predestinates, he must predestinate some or all; he determines to save some and to preterit [pass by] others and to leave them in the hands of nature. . . . Now "shall the thing formed say to him that formed it, why have thou made me thus?" "Who art thou that repliest against God?" I know not why God did not elect to save all: heaven proves he saved a multitude which no man can number: but I cannot see that any man can legitimately demand that God must save everybody, or nobody. What right, what ground in sound reason, has any sinner, in the grasp of violated nature, to force such an alternative upon his Maker?'

R. A. Webb (1856–1919)[8]

'Generally speaking, the formulation of the ultimate goal of all things as God's will to reveal his justice in the case of the reprobate and his mercy in the case of the redeemed, is overly simple and austere. The state of glory, Scripture tells us, will be rich and splendid beyond all description. We look for a new heaven, a new earth, a new humanity, a restored creation, an ever-progressing development never again stained by sin, To that end the creation and the fall, Adam and Christ, nature and grace, faith and unbelief, election and reprobation – all work together, each in its own way, not only consecutively but in concert.'

Herman Bavinck (1854–1921)[9]

8. *The Theology of Infant Salvation* (Presbyterian Committee of Publications, 1907), 273–275.

9. *Reformed Dogmatics* (Baker, 2004), 2:391.

FOR DISCUSSION

1. Why is the doctrine of predestination often ignored or rejected?
2. Is God 'arbitrary' in his actions?
3. What is the difference between predestination and fatalism?

CHAPTER 4
CREATION

ANALYSIS *WCF 4:1–2*
1. Creation in general
2. The creation of man

The doctrine of creation is absolutely foundational in Biblical thought. All Christians believe in creation: 'In the beginning God created the heavens and the earth' (Genesis 1:1). Indeed, the New Testament assures us that the Father created all things by Christ and for Christ (Colossians 1:16). Creation means that we are God's creatures. In fact we are made in his image (Genesis 1:26–27), so each individual has special value and each individual is accountable to the Creator. The cosmos has meaning and significance because God made it and continues to rule over it. His moral and ethical absolutes are as real as the law of gravity. He has given us authority and tasks in this world. We are stewards receiving talents and opportunities from God. We cannot ignore him and get away with it. Belief in God as Creator is absolutely fundamental.

By faith we Christians understand that the universe was framed by the word of God (Hebrews 11:3). Christians reject belief in the eternity of matter or belief in origination by chance of something when before there was nothing. These positions, the only alternatives to creation by God, cannot be demonstrated in a laboratory and in that sense are no more scientific than belief in Divine creation. In fact, they suggest credulity on the part of those holding such views, credulity that is often not acknowledged since the only alternative is creation by God. As that involves accountability to the Creator it is the unthinkable.

In our own time 'evolution' is often set against creation as an alternative, but this really involves confusion of thought. Strictly, evolution is a theory of development and presupposes something to evolve, so it is not an alternative to creation. In any event, everyone acknowledges a degree of variation among the creatures (micro evolution). However, in practice 'evolution' is often presented as if both the original stuff and all subsequent modifications are to be accounted for solely by inherent natural forces that have combined by chance. For example, Nobel prize-winner, Jacques Monod (1910-76), the eminent biochemist, shows himself to be a quite unreasoning fundamentalist scientist when he writes: 'Pure chance, absolutely free but blind, at the very root of the stupendous edifice of evolution: this central concept of modern biology is no longer one among other possible or even conceivable hypotheses. It is today the only conceivable hypothesis, the only one compatible with observed and tested fact. And nothing warrants the supposition (or the hope) that conceptions about this should, or ever could, be revised.'[1] Here we see an allegiance to the religion of humanism, with its closed system that cannot admit any criticism of its central commitment to naturalism. In the name of a supposedly objective science it would impose its religion upon us all if it could. This false religion must be rejected by all Christians.

Christians do not believe in the God of the gaps in our present scientific knowledge, but they believe in the God who rules over all, even over what appear to us random events. Biblically speaking, there is no such thing as a purely natural process, if by it we mean an event or process that operates independently of the divine decree. All processes are under the sovereign supervision of God as are all the events of providence. It is because of this that we can speak of God sending rain at the same time

1. Jacques Monod, *Chance and Necessity* (Knopf, 1971), 112.

as we offer a scientific explanation of the weather. Or as Jesus put it: A sparrow cannot fall to the ground without our Heavenly Father. Further, to offer a scientific explanation is not to provide a complete explanation, or even to say the most important thing about an event. As Australian Presbyterian, T. Jollie Smith put it: 'God is the cause, providence the process and the will of God the explanation.'[2] This can be illustrated in the death of Christ: you can see the second causes, the wicked hands of men, yet it was the outworking of the Divine purpose in every particular (Acts 4:24–28). See also WCF 3.1.

It has been suggested frequently that Genesis provides the *what* and *why*, but we are left to learn the *when* and *how* by scientific investigation. Things are not necessarily quite so neat, however, since the initial creation in the nature of the case must be instantaneous, profoundly mysterious and unrepeatable; similarly the movement from inanimate to animate. Further, it may be held that the Genesis narrative itself establishes matters of time and sequence, and a truly scientific investigation must reckon with this. But with these remarks, let us come to the text of the Confession.

4.1 Creation in general

In the beginning it pleased the Triune God—Father, Son, and Holy Spirit[1]—to make known the glory of his eternal power, wisdom, and goodness,[2] by creating, or making out of nothing, the world and all things in it, whether visible or invisible, in the space of six days, and all very good.[3]

1. Heb. 1:2; John 1:2,3; Gen. 1:2; Job 26:13; 33:4.
2. Rom. 1:20; Jer 10:12; Psalm 104:24; Psalm 33:5,6.
3. Gen. 1; Heb. 11:3; Col. 1:16; Acts 17:24.

a. *God*: If there is but one living and true God, Father, Son and Holy Spirit, the universe and anything in it can only have come into being

2. T. Jollie Smith, *Studies in Criticism and Revelation* (Epsworth Press, 1925), 153.

through his will. Genesis 1:2 mentions the Spirit of God moving on the face of the waters. Spirit in Hebrew is *ruah*, breath, but wind or Spirit are appropriate translations depending on the context. Here, with the word God, Spirit is the only adequate rendering. The idea is of God's Spirit watching (not brooding) over that which was formless and empty in order that it might be formed and filled.

We also note the emphasis (eight times in the six days) on God's word: 'And God said . . .' This is not a mere utterance but a potent command, an expression of God's will that carries creative energy. Compare the miracles of Christ. The repeated emphasis on God's word reinforces the teaching that all the various forms of life owe their existence to God: they do not arise haphazardly or by accident.

There is in the narrative, as Paul Beauchamp has said, 'the distant dawn of a trinitarian revelation.' The New Testament is explicit that the Father created the worlds by the Son: without the Word was nothing made that has been made (John 1:3).

b. *created:* The Genesis narrative expresses God's creative work in several ways: (1) God commands (eg. let there be light; let there be an expanse; let there be lights); (2) God orders existing elements (eg. let the earth bring forth vegetation; let the waters swarm . . .; let the earth bring forth; (3) he makes/creates in conjunction with (1) or (2) (eg. And God made the expanse; and God created great sea monsters; and God made the beasts of the field); (4) he makes after unique deliberation a creature in his own image from existing material and his own breath (Let us make man. . .).

The creation of light stands as a divine fiat. The Hebrew word *bara* (create) is a rare word in the Bible. It is used in Genesis 1:1 (the summary statement), 1:21 (of aquatic creatures and birds) and

1:27 (of humans). The word does not mean creation ex nihilo (out of nothing), yet it is always used of an act or activity of God without any reference to the means used. Thus it points to the power and accomplishment of God and can certainly imply *ex nihilo*. We can understand its presence in verse 1 and verse 27. In verse 21 it is immediately connected with the great sea monsters, perhaps because ancient cultures regarded these as rivals of the gods. The narrative (as well as other parts of Scripture which mention Leviathan and the Dragon, such as Isaiah 27:1; 51:9–10) firmly places them under the sovereignty of God along with the sun, moon and stars, which the heathen had likewise made gods.

The variety of ways in which the Genesis narrative speaks of creation shows that creation may be direct origination without process, or it may be origination involving the use of already existing materials over a period of time, however short.

c. *In the beginning:* The 'beginning' is not dated, nor is it dateable with precision from the genealogies later in Genesis, since they are not fully complete and do not appear to be intended to provide this information. In any event, it may be proper to distinguish the age of the worlds from the age of humanity. It is certainly true that written historical records of a reliable kind date back only to about 3,000 BC and the founding of Egypt.

It is important to recognise that time (and space) are necessary forms of existence for created beings, hence time and space began to exist in and with creation, as the great Augustine pointed out around AD 400. Genesis 1:1 is best taken as a statement of the initial creation of the universe with the work of the six days subsequent.

d. *in the space of six days:* Any objection to this phrase, first used by Calvin in 1554[3], tells equally against the Biblical text or, to put it positively, whatever the Biblical 'six days' means is the meaning of the expression in the Confession of Faith. The reason for saying this is that the words 'in the space of' do not define the length of the days. They really add nothing to the simple expression 'in six days'—unless an allegorical view of Genesis 1 is held that collapses the work of creation over six days into an instant of time. This 'instantaneous' position was very common in pre-Reformation times because of Augustine's influence. It was held by Cardinal Cajetan (1469–1534), and was often supported by a misconstruction of the words of the apocryphal book Ecclesiasticus at 18:1. The Divines did not support this instantaneous position, not because they were perfectly agreed on the length of the days, but because they were united in rejecting the interpretative method that made the instantaneous view possible (cf. WCF 1:9).

Creation was actually set out step-by-step from an initial stage to a finished state in six days, so as to provide an example for us. Creation in six days is dogma, since it is what Scripture teaches; creation in six 24 hour days is opinion, an opinion which was normal in the 16th and 17th century, when the physical sciences were in their infancy, but which assumes a particular interpretation of the Scripture text. Significantly, the Divines do not add words to teach a specific view of the six days as ordinary solar days. The question was not one that had been raised for serious debate in the 1640s; that would come later and would essentially be a matter of exegesis of Scripture. Indeed, it is notorious that the first few creation days were not regulated by the sun as are our days. Dr. John Lightfoot, a prominent member of

3. John Calvin, *Commentary on the First Book of Moses Called Genesis*, trans. John King (Eerdmans, 1948), 1:78

the Westminster Assembly, thought the first creation day was actually 36 hours long.[4] In Francis Turretin's time some writers even claimed that God had to occupy the whole day in creation work to provide an adequate example for us. Turretin himself thought in terms of eight distinct instantaneous creative acts spread out over six days.[5]

It is proper to describe the Bible as a book *for* science but it is hardly correct to call it a book *of* science. Without necessarily excluding scientific value in the narrative its chief focus must be found elsewhere. The simple yet subtle literary structure conveys a powerful message to every reader. The *origin* of creation in the sovereign will of God is affirmed. The *orderliness* of creation is seen in the way the formlessness and emptiness of verse 2 is matched by positive provision of form (days 1–3) and filling (days 4–6). The *purposefulness* of creation is seen in the increasing fullness of description from day 1 to day 6, and the attention-getting variations on day 6 in the normal pattern of description, which draw our attention to man's relation to God and creation. Its work is described as very good and the day, unlike the earlier ones, has the definite article in the Hebrew text. The *goal* of creation is emphasised in that the creation in six days is not to be viewed apart from the seventh day, while the *unity* of creation is very evident from the seven-day scheme.

The portrayal of the Divine Worker working as man is to work must not lead us to focus on chronology and duration. Our week is patterned on God's week, the definitive week for us. We are to imitate God's example. Exodus 20:11 and 31:17 state God created the heavens and the earth in six days, and rested the seventh, and we are to do likewise. While there is no identity there is a real similarity

4. John Lightfoot, *A Few, & New Observations upon the Book of Genesis* (T. Badger, 1642), 2.
5. Turretin, *Institutes of Elenctic Theology*, 1:444.

between God's week and ours that is sufficient to provide adequate foundation for our life.

It should be noted that the seventh day is not closed by the formula 'there was evening and morning'. The idea of God's unending sabbath was current among the Reformed.[6] Keeping in mind the very careful crafting of the creation narrative, this omission cannot be without meaning: *God's rest did not end.* Whereas we are to work six days and rest the seventh, *God* did not follow a pattern of recurring work and rest. He worked six days and then entered on an *enduring* rest into which he calls humanity, what is otherwise termed eternal life. This interpretation of God's seventh day is supported in John 5:17–19, where Jesus states that whatever the Father does the Son does, and so parallels his work of restoration on the *earthly* Sabbath with his Father's continual upholding and blessing of creation on his *heavenly* Sabbath. Note also Hebrews 3:7–4:11. In short, God does not work or rest as we do. He works by his word, and his rest is not like ours, even though Exodus 31:17 is bold to say 'he was *refreshed*' [ESV; not 'he rested' as in NIV], when we know God does not grow faint or weary. *God gives the creation account for our sakes!* God speaks to ordinary people like you and I, that all may grasp what we need to know of God, ourselves, and his purpose for us. In other words, God's week of creation is not a strict equivalent to our working week, but is a less precise but appropriate analogy which structures the life of creation. This view would not conflict with Exodus 20:11; 31:17—the only other passages (other than Hebrews) which connect the days with creation.

There is thus no occasion for office-bearers to plead the need for relief from full subscription to this phrase 'in the space of six days' as if it commits one to something unbiblical. In any case, denominations

6. eg. David Pareus (1548–1622) of Heidelberg's Latin Commentary on Genesis (1609).

have usually adopted the Confession with a well understood allowance of some breadth on this point, the more so as the doctrine of creation does not depend on precision in understanding the nature or length of the creation days. In the famous exposition of the Shorter Catechism by Thomas Watson (c.1620–1686), the nature of the days is not even mentioned.

e. *all very good:* The creation as it came from God's hands was very good. At a minimum this means that there was no moral evil in the universe, so the notions of dual principles of good and evil, and of the inherent evil of matter, are refuted. However, the expression does not mean that the original creation was the best of all possible worlds, for we know that the new creation will be better: there will be no possibility of losing that Paradise, while the natural will be transformed and elevated by the Spirit of God (cf. 1 Cor.15:44–46).

We live now in an interdependent, predatory world in which death is part and parcel of things, but we do not have the data to defend other than the position that death in the human family is the result of sin (Rom. 5). The curse on the ground, if not an objective change in the ground, certainly involves the providential working of creation against man rather than for him. But can we say that Adam's sin brought death upon the other creatures. I doubt it.

WAS THERE DEATH BEFORE SIN?
SOME POINTS TO CONSIDER

1. There was an intimacy of fellowship with God for Adam and Eve, and no sin or death in the human family.
2. The physical nature of our first parents did not correspond with the highest form of bodily existence possible – it was, like ours, of the earth, natural (1 Cor.15:44ff).
3. Our first parents did not have eternal life, that being in prospect only (Gen. 2:9; 3:22).

4. The environment was to be improved by godly dominion, so 'very good' does not mean 'beyond any improvement' but 'as God intended and free of moral evil'.
5. Eden in Scripture appears to be contrasted with the rest of the world, which lacked its paradise-like environment.
6. The reproductive capacities of the creatures involve their growth and thus ageing, and overpopulation if they do not die.
7. The taking of the life of other creatures is not expressly prohibited to man in Genesis 1, and Gen. 9:3 need not imply that meat was forbidden to man until after the Flood (so Calvin). What does 'rule over them' mean if it does not give man the right to use the fish, birds and the animals?
8. Scripture does not teach that eating meat is a moral evil: even our Saviour after his resurrection ate a fish in the presence of his disciples (Luke 24:42). The creation of all things 'good' is the reason why nothing is to be rejected in the way of food if it is received with thanksgiving (1 Tim. 4:4-5).
9. The threat of death and the promise of life involved in the tree of life seem to be cogent only if Adam knew at least something of death from it already existing in the lower orders of creation.
10. Organic death (plants/grasses) must be admitted pre-fall. Indeed, perhaps 1:29–30 aims to tell us how humans relate to the vegetation of day 3, just as on day 6 the other animals are placed under human authority. For if 1:29–30 is an exhaustive description of diet then it proves too much: milk and eggs would be forbidden as well as fish and meat.
11. The groaning of inanimate creation in Romans 8:18–27) appears to be not because of a curse that had radically changed the earth but because of the longing for the climax of God's purpose with humanity it is represented as sharing with redeemed believers and with the Holy Spirit.

THOUGHTS FROM OTHER MINDS

'Now although God was able to create all things in a moment, yet he willed to interpose some space in finishing his works: (1) to testify his own liberty; (2) to set forth his wisdom, power and goodness...; (3) to excite us to the distinct contemplation of his works; (4) to teach men by his own example that he must labour six days and rest the seventh...'

Francis Turretin (1623–1687)[7]

7. *Institutes of Elenctic Theology*, 1:445.

'The Bible does not state how old the earth is, and the question of the age of the earth is not the heart of the issue. What is the heart of the issue is whether God truly created or whether we, merely upon the basis of our observations of the universe, can place limits on the manner in which God worked.'

E. J. Young (1907–1968)[8]

FOR DISCUSSION

1. God didn't need to make the world, so why did he?
2. In what way does the teaching that God created all things provide a basis on which the scientific enterprise may proceed?
3. In the ancient world the sun, moon and stars were frequently worshipped, and the great sea creatures were thought of as rivals of the gods. What does Genesis 1 tell us about these ideas?
4. What would you say to a student who said: 'The Bible teaches (Gen. 1:11–12) that the plants were created before the sun. But we learn from science class that plants cannot live without the sun, so I can't be blamed for giving up reading the Bible, can I?' (Be careful answering this question!)
5. What are the weaknesses of the day-age theory of the creation days from a Scripture viewpoint? Is the harmony it aims at with science in principle good or bad?
6. What are the strengths and the weaknesses of the 'creation science' approach from both scientific and scriptural viewpoints? To what degree is it a polarised position in reaction to modernism in theology and naturalism in science?

---

8. E. J. Young, *Studies in Genesis One* (P&R Publishing, 1964), 102.

7. 'No one reads Genesis in the same way as a person 500 years ago or even 300 years ago. For example, no informed person today accepts that the sun rotates around the earth. So the issue is not whether or not our views of the physical world affect Scripture interpretation, but whether we are careful to avoid introducing ideas alien to the intent of scripture.' Discuss.
8. Matthew Poole (1624–1679), writing on Genesis 1:29, states: 'It is neither affirmed or denied that flesh also was granted to the first men for food, and therefore we may safely be ignorant of it.'[9] Discuss.

4.2 The creation of humanity

After God had made all other creatures, he created man, male and female.[4] He made them with reasoning and immortal souls,[5] and endowed with knowledge, righteousness, and true holiness, in his own image.[6] They had the law of God written in their hearts,[7] and power to keep it fully;[8] yet there was the possibility of transgression for he left their wills at liberty to disobey.[9] As well as this law written in their hearts, they received a command not to eat of the tree of the knowledge of good and evil.[10] As long as they kept God's law and this commandment, they were happy in their communion with God, and had authority over the other creatures.[11]

4. Gen. 1:27. 5. Gen. 2:7 with Eccl. 12:7 and Luke 23:43 and Matt. 10:28. 6. Gen. 1:26; Col. 3:10; Eph. 4:24. 7. Rom. 2:14,15. 8. Eccl. 7:29. 9. Gen. 3:6; Eccl. 7:29. 10. Gen. 2:17; 3:8–11,23. 11. Gen. 1:26–28.

The angels were created as individuals (Luke 20:35) and some failed their probation and some did not. But humanity was created a race to descend from one pair. The unity of humanity in Adam is a basic presupposition of Scripture (eg. Romans 5; 1 Corinthians 15). The description of God making the human as a potter would form clay on a wheel, has been variously interpreted. No less an orthodox confessional Calvinist than **B. B. Warfield** (1851–1921), the greatest of the Princeton theologians,

9. Matthew Poole, *Annotations upon the Holy Bible* (Robert Carter and Brothers, 1853), 1:5.

regarded it as at least possible that the human body could have a certain kind of evolutionary history with the soul specially created by God so as to constitute the human in the divine image from whose side ['rib' is the traditional but incorrect translation] the woman was specially made.[10] On the other hand, an equally orthodox confessional Calvinist such as **John Murray** (1898–1975) held that the human was constituted a living being upon God's inbreathing into a lifeless clay body.[11] **J. I. Packer** (1926–2020) sits somewhere in between insisting that we must counter evolutionism as a philosophy of life but recognise that Genesis does not address the intricacies of that debate. He insists we have history but written in a special way with some symbolic, parabolic features such as the creation of Eve from Adam's side and the representation of Satan as a snake, 'chosen in order to express the meaning and significance of things which we are not able to picture or conceive physically...'.[12]

In the ancient Near East the word 'image' can refer to a statue which represented the one imaged. It can also refer to the king as the adopted son of a god fulfilling the same role of representing the god in a portion of his kingdom. Genesis teaches that the human as human is God's vice-ruler. He represents God on earth and rules over it as God rules over his entire creation. The first human may therefore be called the son of God (Luke 3:38), made for fellowship with God, designed to show the family characteristics—righteousness, holiness and true knowledge (Eph. 4:24; Col. 3:10) – and assured of a son's inheritance. The image is not the spiritual part of man merely, but man himself in his totality. Note that Jesus is termed the express image of the invisible God (Heb. 1:3). It is best

10. See *Evolution, Science, and Scripture: Selected Writings*, ed. Mark A. Noll and David N. Livingstone (Baker, 2000).
11. John Murray, *Collected Writings of John Murray: Systematic Theology* (Banner of Trtuh, 1977) 6–13.
12. J. I. Packer, *Honouring the Written Word of God: The Collected Shorter Writings of J.I.Packer* (Paternoster, 1999), 3:182.

to say that the whole person is created after God's image—thus 'his soul, body, gifts, dignity and lordship', to use the words of William Bucan of Lausanne, an early Reformed theologian who died in 1603. The human is like God but on the creaturely level. Genesis 1 makes clear that both the man and the woman are equally the image of God.

An essential element in man's nature was God's law in the heart (to which our conscience still bears some witness) and power to fulfil it. But the possibility of contrary choice existed. Would man under test acknowledge God as his King or turn aside? The simple test through the giving of a specific command was with a view to establishing this. It is not for us to question this arrangement even if we cannot understand it.

THOUGHTS FROM OTHER MINDS

'Since Christ was totally without sin (Heb. 4:15), in Christ we see the image of God in its perfection...God the Father has given us in Jesus Christ a visual example of what the image of God is. There is no better way of seeing the image of God than to look to Jesus Christ. What we see and hear in Christ is what God intended for man'

A. A. Hoekema (1913–1988)[13]

FOR DISCUSSION

1. If you believe that God created man in his own image what difference will this make in your attitude to yourself, and in the way you treat others?

13. *Created in God's Image* (Eerdmans, 1986), 22.

CHAPTER 5
PROVIDENCE

ANALYSIS *WCF 5:1–7*

1. Nature of Providence

2–3. God's Providence and the use of means
- a. God has ordained everything including means
- b. Means are real
- c. God is not limited by means

4. Providence and sin in general

5. Providence and the sin of believers

6. Providence and the sin of the ungodly

7. Providence and the care of the church

5.1 The nature of providence

God, the great Creator of all things, upholds,[1] directs, arranges, and governs all creatures, actions and things,[2] from the greatest even to the least,[3] by his most wise and holy providence.[4] This he does according to his infallible foreknowledge[5] and the free and unchangeable purpose of his own will,[6] and all to the praise of the glory of his wisdom, power, justice, goodness, and mercy.[7]

1. Heb. 1:3.
2. Dan. 4:34,35; Psalm 135:6; Acts 17:25,26,28; Job, chapters 38,39,40,41.
3. Matt. 10:29–31. 4. Prov. 15:3; Psalm 104:24; 145:17.
5. Acts 15:18; Psalm 94:8–11. 6. Eph. 1:11; Psalm 33:10,11.
7. Isa. 63:14; Eph. 3:10; Rom. 9:17; Gen. 45:7; Psalm 145:7.

Providence is closely linked to creation. It is God's continued care for what he has created so that he both upholds it and governs it so that his purposes are accomplished. Cicero (106–43 BC), the Roman philosopher, said: 'Great things the gods care for, small things they neglect.' However, the Bible teaches that the very hairs of our head are all numbered (Luke 12:7). So all things are 'providential'.

5.2 God's providence and the use of means

In relation to the foreknowledge and decree of God, the absolute Creator, all things happen unchangeably and infallibly.[8] However, in his providence God directs events to occur through the agency of secondary causes. In relation to such secondary causes some events are inevitable, others depend on the voluntary choice of the creature, and others occur fortuitously.[9]

8. Acts 2:23. [In the 1646 text 'the First Cause' is used in lieu of 'the absolute Creator'.]
9. Gen. 8:22; Jer. 31:35; Exod. 21:13 with Deut. 19:5; 1 Kings 22:28,34; Isa. 10:6,7.

Our experience is that a certain end comes to pass as a result of a chain of contingent events. The Bible affirms that such an end is predetermined by God because he has ordained the means as well as the end. It is common for people to say that if God has decreed everything nothing we can do will make any difference. This is false. The truth is that since God has established means or second causes, such means are real. The Confession gives 'a simple statement of a mystery which cannot be explained: the consistency of a belief in the supreme all-determining first cause, and a belief in the reign of law in nature, and the freedom of action among intelligent creatures' (John Macpherson).

5.3 God's providence and the use of means

In the ordinary course of his providence God makes use of means,[10] yet, as he pleases, he is free to work without them,[11] to give them effect beyond what they normally possess,[12] and to work against their ordinary operation.[13]

10. Acts 27:31,44; Isa. 55:10,11; Hos. 2:21,22.
11. Hos. 1:7; Matt. 4:4; Job 34:20.
12. Rom. 4:19–21.
13. 2 Kings 6:6; Dan. 3:27.

It is God's wise and good will to use means that are suited to secure the desired end, but God is not bound by his ordinary way of working.

What we call a miracle—God working without, above or against ordinary means—is the outworking of God's freedom of action.

5.4 Providence and sin in general

God's almighty power, unsearchable wisdom, and infinite goodness are so far-reaching that his providence extends even to the first fall, and all other sins of angels and human beings.[14] It is not simply that he permits them,[15] for in a variety of ways he wisely and powerfully sets limits,[16] and appoints and governs them so that they fulfil his own holy ends.[17] Yet the sinfulness involved comes only from the creature, and not from God, who, being most holy and righteous, is not and cannot be the author or approver of sin.[18]

14. Rom. 11:32–34; 2 Sam. 24:1 with 1 Chron.21:1; 1 Kings 22:22,23; 1 Chron.10:4,13,14; 2 Sam. 16:10; Acts 2:23; 4:27,28.
15. Acts 14:16.
16. Psalm 76:10; 2 Kings 19:28.
17. Gen. 50:20, Isa. 10:6,7,12.
18. James 1:13,14,17; 1 Jn. 2:16; Psalm 50:21.

It is commonly represented by many Christians, and is the position of the Council of Trent of the Church of Rome, that God's relationship to sin is simply one of permission. However, mere permission or failing to prevent does not exhaust Scripture on this subject. Hence we can understand that the two statements concerning David's numbering of the people are both true: that God moved David to this act (2 Sam. 24:1) and that Satan did so (1 Chronicles 21:1). 'In regard to the action itself, which was sinful as produced or performed by Satan and David, God did more than merely permit it ... He did do something in the way of its being brought about'.[1] This is carefully expressed in the Confession, but of course is a matter of difficulty for our minds and is to be handled with great care.

1. William Cunningham, *Historical Theology* (Banner of Truth, 1960), 1:636.

5.5 Providence and the sin of believers

God, who is most wise, righteous and gracious, frequently leaves his own children to fall for a time into a variety of temptations, and to experience the corruption of their own hearts. This he does to chastise them for the sins they have committed, or to teach them humility by revealing to them the hidden strength of the corruption and deceitfulness remaining in their hearts.[19] He would also bring them to depend more fully and constantly on himself, put them on guard against all future opportunities for sin, and fulfil various other just and holy ends.[20]

19. 2 Chron.32:25,26,31; 2 Sam. 24:1.
20. 2 Cor. 12:7–9; Psalm 73 throughout; Psalm 77:1–12; Mark 14:66–72 with Jn 21:15–17.

In dealing with his own children God remains sovereign in respect of evil. They sin just as they do good, hence God disapproves the one and endorses the other. But through all, he works his holy purpose toward them.

5.6 Providence and the sin of the ungodly

God, as a righteous Judge, deals otherwise with wicked and ungodly people. For their former sins he blinds and hardens them.[21] He not only withholds from them the grace that might have enlightened their minds and changed their hearts,[22] but in some cases also withdraws the gifts he had given them,[23] and places them in situations on which their evil hearts seize as opportunities for sin.24 In this way he gives them over to their own lusts, the temptations of the world, and to the power of Satan,[25] with the consequence that they harden themselves, even under those means which God uses for the softening of others.[26]

21. Rom. 1:24,26,28; Rom. 11:7,8. 22. Deut. 29:4.
23. Matt. 13:12; 25:29. 24. Deut. 2:30; 2 Kings 8:12,13.
25. Psalm 81:11,12; 2 Thess. 2:10–12.
26. Exod. 7:3 with Exod. 8:15,32; 2 Cor. 2:15,16; Isa. 8:14; 1 Pet. 2:7,8; Isa. 6:9,10 with Acts 28:26,27.

God's providence also embraces the hardening of men in sin. This is a matter of justice because of their previous sins, and is largely a withholding of his gracious influences. The case of the Pharaoh of the exodus is significant. In the account of the first five plagues he is said to have hardened his heart, and only with the sixth plague do we read also that God hardened his heart. Still, before Moses returned to Egypt to lead his people God had said what he would do to display his power over Pharaoh (Exod. 4:21). 'By withdrawing any restraining influences on Pharaoh and by directly challenging his status, the LORD brought it about that the full extent of Pharaoh's stubbornness and opposition became evident. It would thus be manifest that what happened in the release of the Israelites was no voluntary act of Pharaoh, but a victory won over him by the superior power of Yahweh.'[2]

5.7 Providence and the care of the church

God's providence extends to all creatures, but in a very special way God directs it to the care of his church, and arranges all things for its good.[27]

27. 1 Tim. 4:10; Amos 9:8,9; Rom. 8:28; Isa. 43:3–5,14.

God's care extends to all things but has special reference to the church. It is not that God is a caretaker with little interest in the day to day affairs of the creation. Nor is he the God to whom we appeal simply in order to explain the gaps in our knowledge that we have not yet filled. But he is the God who holds the whole world in his hands and who directs all things to the destined end that all things might be brought under one head, even Christ (Ephesians 1:10 cf. vv 22–23).

THOUGHTS FROM OTHER MINDS

'The first turn that ever he [Satan] does he binds him. What binds he, his hands or his feet? No, he lets them loose, and lets him work on with them his own ruin, and run on to his own perdition. But he binds his eyes, or rather pulls them out, that the miserable body may not see the gracious face of Christ. Wherefore is he

2. John L. Mackay, *Exodus* (Mentor, 2001), 133.

sent to him? The cause is not only in the ordinance of God, but in the captive himself that maliciously resists the light, and will not receive the gospel; therefore the God of heaven sends the Devil to put out his eyes that he should not see.'

Robert Rollock (1555–1599)[3]

FOR DISCUSSION

1. 'If God controls everything, then things will turn out the same regardless of what we do.' Answer this objection.
2. Is taking out insurance a sign of distrusting God's care?
3. Suggest why the ungodly may do things in themselves praiseworthy.

3. *Select Works of Robert Rollock,* 1:394.

CHAPTER 6
SIN IN THE HUMAN RACE

ANALYSIS *WCF 6:1–6*

1. The entry of sin into the human family
2. The effects of sin for Adam and Eve
3. The effect of sin on their descendants
4. Sin and sins
5. Sin in believers
6. Sin's nature and consequences

6.1 The entry of sin into the human family

Adam and Eve, the parents of the human race, were deceived by the subtlety of Satan and sinned by eating the forbidden fruit. It pleased God, according to his wise and holy plan, to permit this sin of theirs, since he had purposed to direct it to his own glory.[2]

1. Gen. 3:13; 2 Cor. 11:3.
2. Rom. 11:32.

There is a biblical realism in this chapter and an absence of theorizing. The Confession does not deal with the origin of sin in God's creation but the origin of sin in the human race. This is all that is important for us. What is commonly called 'sin' is by some held to be the remnants of an animal nature that clings to us despite our evolutionary progress, and for which we are not responsible. The alternative position and the Biblical one is that sin is an intrusion into the original good order of creation and that we are morally responsible to our Creator for it. This intrusion has an historic origin at the beginning of the race: Adam and Eve were not mythical people, but real people who disobeyed God.

6.2 The effects of sin for Adam and Eve

By this sin our first parents fell from their original righteousness and communion with God,[3] and so became dead in sin,[4] and completely polluted in all the faculties and parts of soul and body.[5]

3. Gen. 3:6–8; Eccl. 7:29; Rom. 3:23.
4 Gen. 2:17; Eph. 2:1.
5 Titus 1:15; Gen. 6:5; Jer. 17:9; Rom. 3:10–18.

The result of the first sin so far as Adam and Eve are concerned is now stated. To become 'wholly defiled in all the faculties' (1646 text) does not mean totally defiled in degree but in extent, ie. every part of man's life was affected. The context is that of man's relation with God, whose communion was lost, hence the Larger Catechism Q25 states man is 'utterly disposed, disabled and made opposite to all that is spiritually good.' It is not meant to assert the obvious untruth that they are as evil as possible, or that there was nothing of relative good left (see WCF 16:7). As W. G. T. Shedd (1820-94) put it: 'Total depravity means the total absence of holiness not the highest intensity of sin.'[1]

6.3 The effects of sin on their descendants

Adam and Eve being the ancestors of the whole human race, the guilt of this sin was imputed,[6] and the same death in sin and corrupted nature was conveyed, to all those descending from them in the ordinary manner.[7]

6. Gen. 1:27,28 & Gen. 2:16,17 & Acts 17:26 with Rom. 5:12,15–19 & 1 Cor. 15:21,22,49.
7. Psalm 51:5; Gen. 5:3; Job 14:4; 15:14.

The imputation here stated is grounded on 'genetic solidarity'[2] not the covenant headship of Adam as in WCF 7.2 or even more explicitly stated in WLC 22 which was increasingly to the fore in discussions in the 1600s.

1. W. G. T. Shedd, *Dogmatic Theology* (Zondervan, 1969), 2:257.
2. Robert Letham, *Westminster Assembly* (P&R Publishing, 2009), 234.

How we inherit sin may be stated thus: Adam's sin brought guilt and corrupted his nature. We are represented by Adam therefore we are guilty; as an appropriate punishment we inherit Adam's corruption. As a result of our corrupt natures we commit actual sins. See also what was said in the notes for WCF 6:2 about good and evil, and WCF 9:3 & 16:7.

6.4 Sin and sins

This original corruption makes us completely disinclined, incapacitated, and opposed to all spiritual good,[8] and wholly inclined to all evil.[9] The actual sins that we commit are the fruit of this corrupt nature.[10]

8. Rom. 5:6; 8:7; 7:18; Col. 1:21. [The adjective 'spiritual' has been inserted before 'good' to clarify the meaning (see WCF 16:7, and note this word's inclusion in the text of WLC 25).]
9. Gen. 6:5; 8:21; Rom. 3:10–12.
10. James 1:14,15; Eph. 2:2,3; Matt. 15:19.

6.5 Sin in believers

During this earthly life this corruption of nature remains in those who are regenerated.[11] Although, through Christ, the corruption is pardoned and put to death, both it and everything flowing from it is truly and actually sin.[12]

11. 1 Jn. 1:8,10; Rom. 7:14,17,18,23; James 3:2; Prov. 20:9; Eccl. 7:20.
12. Rom. 7:5,7,8,25; Gal. 5:17.

Regeneration does not bring freedom from indwelling sin in this life. That believers are pardoned for Christ's sake does not relieve sin of its sinfulness, which remains as heinous as ever. The exhortation to believers to 'be perfect as your heavenly father is perfect' (Matt 5:48 cf. 1 Peter 1:15–16) is to be recognised, but in this life it cannot be realized. At various times there have been those who have preached the possibility of perfection in this life, but they must redefine sin to as to allow a lower attainable standard. A famous advocate, the great **John Wesley** (1703–91), never claimed the experience himself. The state of perfection or 'entire sanctification' claimed by some seems to arise from confusing experiences of God's love with sanctification. Sanctification is not an act, but a progressive work (cf. WCF 13).

6.6 Sin's nature and consequences

Every sin, both original and actual, transgresses the righteous law of God, and is contrary to it,[13] and so brings guilt on the sinner.[14] As a result he is brought under the wrath of God[15] and the curse of the law,[16] and thus is subject to death,[17] with all spiritual,[18] temporal[19] and eternal miseries.[20]

13. 1 Jn. 3:4. 14 Rom. 2:15; 3:9,19. 15. Eph. 2:3. 16. Gal. 3:10
17. Rom. 6:23. 18. Eph. 4:18. 19. Rom. 8:20; Lam. 3:39.
20. Matt. 25:41; 2 Thess. 1:9.

Guilt lies on us for all transgressions—the sin of our natures and the sin of our lives, and justly incurs the consequences noted.

THOUGHTS FROM OTHER MINDS

'Man brought forth children of the same nature as himself after the fall. That is to say, being corrupt he brought forth corrupt children. The corruption spread, by God's just judgment, from Adam to all his descendants, except for Christ alone —not by way of imitation (as in former times the Pelagians would have it) but by way of the propagation of his perverted nature.'

Synod of Dort[3]

FOR DISCUSSION

1. What is meant by 'total depravity'?
2. How are we involved in Adam's first sin?
3. Jesus said a good tree cannot bring forth bad fruit (Matt 12:33–35). What does this imply concerning our nature?
4. What is perfectionism? Is holiness attained by crisis or process? (Be careful in your answer!)

3. *Canons of the Synod of Dort* (1618–19), 3-4:2

CHAPTER 7
GOD'S COVENANT WITH MAN

ANALYSIS *WCF 7:1–6*
1. The general necessity of God's dealing by covenant
2. Its first expression
3. Its second expression
4. Its testamentary/inheritance aspect
5–6. Its administration in the OT and the NT

One of the most basic of biblical terms is covenant (in Hebrew: *berith*; in Greek: *diatheke* as distinct from *suntheke*, compact). Whereas covenants made between men may be worked out by mutual agreement, the covenants made by God with men are sworn promises in terms set by God in his sovereignty and grace. The word contract or compact is not a suitable synonym. Accordingly, in the Greek New Testament *diatheke* not *suntheke* is used. The actual derivation of the term *berith* is as uncertain to us as to the writers of the Confession, although we are more aware of covenant relationships between rulers and their vassals in ancient times than they were.

God administers his kingdom by way of his covenant. Arising from the creation covenant with Adam, which he broke, we have a series of related redemptive covenants—with Noah, Abraham, Moses and David, and also in the promise of 'a new covenant' fulfilled in a measure in the return from exile, and in fullness in Jesus Christ. The covenant with Noah (Gen. 9:8ff) is a promise that the earth will remain a suitable theatre for the development and fulfilment of God's purpose in creation (cf. Gen.

1:28). The covenants with Abraham, Moses and David, and the remnant that returned from exile embody the promise: 'I will be your God.' (Gen. 17:7; Exod. 25:8; 2 Sam. 7:14; Jer 31:33). In other words, God commits himself to those with whom he makes covenant. The full depth of this commitment is seen in the new covenant in Christ's blood (Luke 22:20), for there we see God himself making the way back to himself, the Father not sparing his belovèd Son. What had been promised and portrayed in type and figure is now realised in deed and truth. God's covenant involves the giving of law to be kept in response to the grace that has justified the believer (Noah: Gen. 9:1; Abraham: 17:1; Israel: Exod. 19:6; 20:1; believers: Matt. 5:47).

WCF 7 stresses that there are not different ways of salvation for sinners in the Old and New Testaments but one way—that of grace, which is administered in different ways at different times. Thus, while the Old Testament *as understood* by *Judaizers in New Testament times* can be stigmatised as law, this does not mean its substance, correctly understood, was salvation by law (see Gal. 3:15f). Further, the successive redemptive covenants in history are related to the purpose of God in creation. Redemption does not involve abandonment of creation but the realization of God's purposes for it. Humanity will ultimately rule effectively as a kingdom of priests through the Last Adam who succeeds where the First failed.

An explicit theology of covenants of works (before the fall) and grace (after the fall) belongs to the late 16th century with writers like Amandus Polanus (1561–1610) of Basel, and Robert Rollock (1555–99) of Edinburgh in 1589 and 1597 respectively. It soon becomes the norm and appears in brief in the *Irish Articles* of 1615, which were a primary source for the Westminster Confession.

In the comments that follow it will become evident that the Confession sketches the main lines of what we call 'covenant theology' in a consensus approach appropriate to the 1640s. There were in the 1640s, and remain now, variations in understanding aspects of the subject.

7.1 The general necessity of God's dealing by covenant

The distance between God and the creature is so great that although creatures endowed with reason owe obedience to him as their Creator, yet they could never have any enjoyment of him as their blessedness and reward, except by some voluntary condescension on God's part. This he has been pleased to express by way of covenant.[1]

1. Isa. 40:13–17; Job 9:32–33; 1 Sam. 2:25; Psalm 113:5–6; Psalm 100:2–3; Job 22:2–3; Job 35:7–8; Luke 17:10; Acts 17:24–25.

This section teaches that the necessity for covenant relationship between man and God predates sin and belongs to man as man. In other words, man cannot fulfil the purpose of his existence—to glorify God and enjoy him forever—apart from a gracious condescension on God's part.

Many writers seem to have regarded the covenant relationship as established after man's creation. Therefore one could contrast an initial state of relative servitude in which God owed man nothing (cf. Luke 17:10) with a subsequent covenant relationship in which God made generous promises on the condition of continued obedience, and so obliged himself to give to obedience what it could not otherwise have obtained. This is what WCF 7:1 sounds like at first glance. However, there were not wanting voices which emphasised that the covenant with Adam was made between friends already in covenant in some sense from the moment of creation, and that God's goodness and favour was richly evidenced from the beginning. The Larger Catechism 93 seems to suggest a promise of life is attached to the keeping of the moral law written on the heart, which would make it an implicit covenant, while WCF 19:1

appears to conflate the law written on the heart and the arrangement of Genesis 2 under the term covenant.

The notable Dutch covenant theologian, Herman Witsius (1636–1708), writes: 'I lay this down as an acknowledged truth, that God owes nothing to his creature. By no claim, no law is he bound to reward it. For all that the creature is, it owes entirely to God; both because he created it, and also, because he is infinitely exalted above it.... Whatever then is promised to the creature by God, ought all to be ascribed to the immense goodness of the Deity.... Nor can God on account of this his goodness refuse to communicate himself to, or give the enjoyment of himself to, an innocent, an holy creature.... He does not love in reality, who desires not to communicate himself to the object of his affection.... The sum of the divine commands is ...love me above all things.... But how is it conceivable that God should thus speak to the soul, and the soul should religiously attend to, and diligently perform this, and yet never enjoy God...[for God to say] "long after me, but on condition, never of obtaining thy desire..."'[1]

God's voluntary condescension is thus better placed at the point of his free decision to create a creature in his image than at a point subsequent to man's creation. The arrangement of Genesis 2 should be seen as 'a particularisation of the Covenant, which was designed to bring man to self-conscious choice and realisation of his covenant relation with God' (Morton H. Smith - 1923–2017)[2]. Adam was never in a merely legal relationship with his Creator, a position where God owed him something, for on the basis of his deeds man never can earn God's favour. The relationship was covenantal—personal as well as legal—in order that man might be blessed (compare this aspect with marriage as a covenant).

1. Herman Witsius, *The Economy of the Covenants,* trans. William Crookshank (R. Baynes et al., 1822), 1:76–79.
2. Morton H. Smith, *Systematic Theology* (Greenville Seminary Press, 1994), 1:280

7.2 The first expression of God's covenant with humanity

The first covenant made with the human race was a covenant of works.[2] In it life was promised to Adam and, in him, to his descendants,[3] on condition of perfect and personal obedience.[4]

2. Gal. 3:12. [In the Shorter Catechism Q.12 the term used is 'covenant of life'.]
3. Rom. 10:5; Rom. 5:12–20.
4. Gen. 2:17; Gal. 3:10.

In writing of the first covenant with man, the position of those who held to a covenant of redemption within the trinity as the foundation of the covenant of grace is safeguarded. In accordance with the terms of this covenant of redemption, Christ fully met all the obligations of the covenant of works as the Last Adam and secured the Holy Spirit for his people. Many in the 1640s in effect viewed the covenant of redemption (the pactum salutis) and the covenant of grace as one, and this was later popularised by Thomas Boston. But the other view, held by men like Samuel Rutherford, one of the Scottish Commissioners to the Assembly, also became widespread, and enables the stating of the issues with clarity.

The existence of the covenant: We do not read the word *covenant* of the relationship between God and our first parents unless Hosea 6:7 is an exception, as I believe it is.[3] However, the elements of a covenant are present in Genesis 2 (parties, promise, condition, penalty); the probationary character of the Adamic administration implies it; and the analogy with the covenant of grace and the headship position of Adam and Christ 'the last Adam' (1 Cor.15:45 cf. Rom. 5:12ff) demands it.

Further, while the word 'covenant' first appears in the history of Noah (Genesis 6:18), it is obvious that God's covenant of blessing with Noah (Genesis 9) has in essence the same content as the blessing and

3. Covenant theologians did not rest their case on the interpretation of this verse. However, a parallel between Adam and Israel is being drawn: Adam broke the covenant God made with him and was driven from Eden; Israel has broken the covenant God made with her and will be driven out of the land God gave her, cf. Hosea 1:9.

commission to Adam ('be fruitful and multiply, fill the earth and subdue it'). In short, when the original blessing of our first parents is repeated to Noah it is called a covenant. Therefore the original relationship to Adam was covenantal. Genesis 6:18 refers to *continuing* an existing relationship not commencing a new one. Those blessings in Genesis 1 are covenantal blessings. To the same effect is Jeremiah's reference to God's 'covenant for day and night' (33:20ff). This passage refers back beyond Genesis 9:8 to Genesis 1 and God's blessing of his good creation, as Jeremiah 31:35 makes clear. Thus we see God's covenant commitment at the very beginning of creation in the making of a creature in his image, dependent and responsive.

Naming the covenant: One can look at the relationship from different angles. As the original relationship it may be called the covenant of *creation*. As it was to be fulfilled by man in the strength with which he is endowed it may be called the covenant of *nature*. Being made with Adam before sin it may be called the covenant of *innocence*. As made between parties who were friends it may be called the covenant of *friendship* (but not a covenant of reconciliation since the parties were not estranged). The blessing in view may lead us to call it a covenant of *life*, as does the Shorter Catechism Q12, while the requirement of obedience to God suggests the term *legal* covenant, covenant of *obedience* or covenant of *works*. Consideration of the tender love and generosity God showed may suggest the term covenant of *favour*. A more neutral term could be *Adamic* covenant. All these terms appear in the classic literature of the 17th century.

The condition of the covenant: The terminology is not the real issue. The distinctive significance of the Adamic covenant is the issue, and it must be seen as one requiring obedience to the covenant terms as the principle required in order to the blessing. In Protestant theology covenant of *works* has been the common expression and is contrasted with the covenant of *grace* instituted after the entry of sin. The covenant of grace is not a separate covenant so much as that disclosure of God's following disobedience which shows God does not abandon his covenanted commitment to his creation but relates to it redemptively, Christ fulfilling the covenant of works as the basis for the covenant of grace. The covenant of works does not imply the relationship is purely legal. Adam was God's son (Luke 3:31) in his image: the filial and the legal are not contrary to each other. The blessing would be found in the way of obedience, but the notion of meriting reward is uniformly rejected by the 17th century writers, except in the sense that God, by his covenant with Adam, obligates himself to reward obedience.

The blessing promised: The Confession affirms life was promised to Adam. The nature of this life was a matter of some difference of opinion in the 1640s. As the New England preacher Peter Bulkeley (1583–1659) put it: '[The covenant of works and the covenant of grace] agree in this, that in both there is a promise of life and blessedness; the Covenant of works saith, *Do this and live*; the covenant of grace saith, *Believe and live.* Life is promised in both. Now whether the same life is promised in both, or whether a terrene [earthly] felicity and life here on earth, be promised in the one, and a heavenly in the other, as some think, or whether a heavenly life and glory in both, as some others think, I will not determine, it not being much material. It's enough to know that life and blessedness was and is promised in both'[4].

Scripture does not expressly state that life was promised to Adam, but, as God's son, he had an inheritance, and the threat of death is effectively the loss of the inheritance. The supposition that he should always have continued in life, but with the possibility of falling, was generally rejected. His sin brought eternal death and his obedience would have brought eternal life. At some point he would have been confirmed. Hence it

4. Peter Bulkeley, *The Gospel Covenant* (Matthew Simmons, 1651), 55.

was usual to speak of a probation climaxed by a gracious reward, while recognising that in the event what would have happened is somewhat hypothetical.

The representative or federal principle: Adam was the fountainhead of the race and in him God dealt with all who should descend from him in the ordinary course. We may not understand this procedure, although it is illustrated in our ordinary life in a variety of ways. For example, the acts of a President or Prime Minister may bind the nation. More to the point, the principle is illustrated in the method of redemption. Jesus is representative of his people to pay their debt and meet their obligations. The covenant headship of Adam does not mean we actually committed his sin, but that his disobedience in some just way is reckoned to us so that we are charged with its guilt and share its consequences.

7.3 The second expression of God's covenant with humanity

By the fall the human race made itself incapable of life by that covenant, and so the Lord was pleased to make a second,[5] commonly called the covenant of grace. In this covenant he freely offers to sinners life and salvation by Jesus Christ, requiring of them faith in Jesus Christ that they may be saved,[6] and he promises to give his Holy Spirit to all those who are ordained to life to make them willing and able to believe.[7]

5. Gal. 3:21; Rom. 8:3; Rom. 3:20–21; Gen. 3:15; Isa. 42:6.
6. Acts 16:30,31 [as substitute for Mark 16:15–16 in original]; John 3:16; Rom. 10:6–9; Gal. 3:11.
7. Ezek. 36:26–27; Jn 6:44–45.

As discussed earlier, the covenant of (redemptive) grace has historic manifestations in the promise of redemption (Gen. 3:15), and in the various biblical covenants which God made with his people and which culminated in the new covenant ratified by Christ's death. The parties to this second covenant with humanity are not stated in the Confession, nor are they in Shorter Catechism 20. In Larger Catechism 31 the parties are said to be God, and Christ as representing the elect. This view of the covenant of grace, which does not distinguish the covenant of redemption from the covenant of grace, is followed by Thomas Boston in his justly influential book, *Human Nature in its Fourfold State* (1720). However, the alternative and, in my view, clearer and more correct position, is to regard the parties to the covenant of grace as God and the believer. Abraham is called the father of the faithful and is a pivotal example for those justified by faith in every age (eg. Rom. 4:1). The requirement of faith on our side is not a work or condition in order to meet the requirements of salvation, but it is the means by which we enter into relationship with Christ in history. Like the totality of salvation, faith is itself a blessing of the covenant given to the elect on the basis of the work of Christ (Eph. 2:8).

The obedience and sacrifice of Christ, rendered as the covenant head of his people in terms of the covenant of redemption, is the ground of the covenant of grace. All who are 'in Christ' by faith share in the salvation he has merited. Note that the parallel between Adam and Christ is not precisely equivalent (cf. Romans 5:12ff). Adam could not have merited life but it was necessary for the Redeemer to do so, since the fall had introduced demerit.

7.4 The testamentary aspect

This covenant of grace is frequently described in Scripture as inaugurated by the death of Jesus Christ, and as securing an everlasting inheritance for all believers.[8]

8. Heb. 9:15–17; Heb. 7:22; Luke 22:20; 1 Cor. 11:25. The 1646 text reads: *This covenant of grace is frequently set forth in Scripture by the name of a Testament, in reference to the death of Christ the Testator, and to the everlasting inheritance, with all things belonging to it, therein bequeathed.*

Only in Hebrews 9:16,17 is the Greek word *diatheke* (covenant) likely to have the meaning 'testament' and even here there is doubt. The rewording expresses what is clearly supported by the original texts of Scripture cited. Either way, the doctrinal point remains valid: Christ's work is testamentary since our salvation is through his death, and what we receive from him is the inheritance of the children of God that was forfeited by Adam.

7.5 The administration of the covenant of grace

The covenant was administered in different ways in the time of the law and in the time of the gospel.[9]

Under the law it was administered by promises, prophecies, sacrifices, circumcision, the Passover lamb, and other types and ordinances given to the Jewish people, all of which foreshadowed Christ to come.[10] These were sufficient and effective for that age, through the operation of the Spirit, to instruct and build up the elect in faith in the promised Messiah,[11] by whom they had full remission of sins and eternal salvation. This covenant administration is called the Old Testament.[12]

9. 2 Cor. 3:6–9.
10. Hebrews chs. 8–10; Rom. 4:11; Col. 2:11–12; 1 Cor. 5:7.
11. 1 Cor. 10:1–4; Heb. 11:13; Jn 8:56.
12. Gal. 3:7–9,14.

7.6

Under the gospel, Christ, the reality,[13] has been revealed.

The ordinances in which the covenant of grace is now dispensed are the preaching of the word of God and the administration of the sacraments of Baptism and the Lord's Supper.[14] These ordinances are fewer in number and administered with more simplicity and less outward glory than was the case under the Old Testament. However, in them the covenant of grace is held forth in more fulness, clarity, and spiritual power[15] to all nations,[16] both Jews and Gentiles. This administration is called the New Testament.[17]

Therefore there are not two covenants of grace, differing in substance, but only one covenant of grace, administered under different dispensations.[18]

13. Col. 2:17. 14. Matt. 28:19–20; 1 Cor.11:23–25.
15. Heb. 12:22–28; Jer 31:33–34. 16. Matt. 28:19; Eph. 2:15–19.
17. Luke 22:20.
18. Gal. 3:14,16; Acts 15:11; Rom. 3:21–23,30; Psalm 32:1 with Rom. 4:3,6,16–17,23,24; Heb. 13:8; Acts 15:11.

The gracious character of the Old Testament must not be denied by appeal to the Mosaic administration which came later (cf. Galatians 3). Indeed, the character of the Mosaic economy was one in which grateful and obedient response to the covenant Lord was the ethic, and not legalism or self-righteousness. The Exodus deliverance came before the law at Sinai (cf. Exod. 19:4; 20:2).

When the apostle John reminds us that 'the law was given through Moses; grace and truth were realised through Jesus Christ' (John 1:17), the contrast is not between two ways of salvation. Rather, the contrast is between the prefiguring of Christ and his work through the Mosaic administration, and the reality that has come in Jesus Christ. The clear and full revelation now given means the ceremonies and sacrifices in which the Messiah was veiled and prefigured are no longer to be observed.

There is a system of thought known as dispensationalism which arose in the 19th century. It is associated with the *Scofield Reference Bible* (1909), writers such as J. N. Darby, C. I. Scofield and L. S. Chafer, and institutions such as Dallas Theological Seminary. It seeks to reckon with the historic unfolding of God's purposes but tends to create periods which are not properly linked by the unifying factor of God's grace.

The dispensational scheme employs a radical literalism which leads to the view that God has separate and distinct purposes for Israel and the Church, the one earthly and the other heavenly. Israel in Scripture always means earthly Israel, it is claimed. Israel rejected the earthly Davidic kingdom offered her and crucified her king. Consequently, the Lord, through the Apostles, introduced the Church age with a heavenly message for the Gentiles. This parenthesis will continue until God again renews the kingdom to ethnic Israel during an earthly millennium. Before that happens the Gospel must be preached to all the nations as a testimony, but a pessimism about both its reception and the faithfulness of the organised church is characteristic. A great tribulation will precede the millennium, but the church will be raptured away to heaven *before* it occurs although some say a*fter*.

On the other hand, covenant theology sees the choice of Israel as part of God's preparation for the coming of Christ when salvation would be proclaimed among the nations. The kingdom of Israel was intended to provide an illustration of the kingdom of God inaugurated by Christ, just as surely as the sacrificial system provided types of Christ's saving work. Old Testament promises about the future employed the images of the institutions of Israel without at all meaning to limit the fulfilment to a mere earthly reproduction of them. The notion that the Old Testament promises are fulfilled other than in and through the church as the expanded Israel of God is anathema. The unity of the church in every age is basic (Rom. 11). Literal interpretation means the intended meaning, not necessarily the surface meaning. The shallow views of many evangelical Christians about the nature of the Old Testament dispensation need correction.

THOUGHTS FROM OTHER MINDS

Herman Bavinck (1854–1921), the finest of modern Dutch covenant theologians, insists that without covenant no religion in the sense of fellowship with God, is possible. True fellowship with God can exist only because God is both infinitely great and condescendingly good. In his goodness God gives rights to his creatures. The covenant of works and the covenant of grace do not differ in their final goal but only in the way that leads to it. True religion must take the form of covenant in which love is not coerced but humans serve God willingly, moved by love to love in return. His the gift, ours the gratitude. Adam lived in the state of one who was changeably good. He had a positive obligation to God's law written on his heart from the beginning. The negative probationary command provided a test of his attitude to God to the moral law – either God's word or man's insight. The image of God is ultimately only adequately realized in a humanity counting billions of members summed up in one head, spread over the earth. Humanity as prophet proclaiming the truth of God, as priest dedicating itself to God, as ruler controlling the earth and the whole of creation – that is the fully finished image of God, in New Testament terms the body of Christ and the temple of the Holy Spirit

Summarised from Herman Bavinck (1854–1921)[5]

'Man brought forth children of the same nature as himself after the fall. That is to say, being corrupt he brought forth corrupt children. The corruption spread, by God's just judgment, from Adam to all his descendants, except for Christ alone —not by way of imitation (as in former times the Pelagians would have it) but by way of the propagation of his perverted nature.'

John Murray (1898–1975)[6]

FOR DISCUSSION

1. Distinguish between a covenant and a contract. To what extent does the former include aspects of the latter?
2. God initiates the covenants he makes with humans, setting the terms of them; in that sense they are one-sided. But his covenants always call for obedient response to him; in that sense they are two-sided. Discuss.
3. One important implication of covenant theology is that the church is one in all ages. Discuss, citing relevant Scriptures.
4. What is the error of dispensationalism? How would you refute it?

---

5. *In the Beginning: Foundations of Creation Theology* (Revell, 1999), 204ff. [section of his *Reformed Dogmatics*, 2:534ff].
6. *Collected Writings of John Murray: Studies in Theology* (Banner of Trtuh, 1977), 4:233.

CHAPTER 8
CHRIST THE MEDIATOR

ANALYSIS *WCF 8:1–8*
1. **The appointed Mediator**
2. **The God-Man**
3. **The anointed Mediator**
4. **His work as Mediator**
5. **The atonement and its fruit**
6. **The atonement and those who lived before it**
7. **The relations of the natures in the Mediator**
8. **The application of redemption**

The salvation of those God has chosen to be saved from the fallen race of mankind (cf. WCF 3:3–6) is through a covenant of redemption. In it the Son of God undertakes to meet everything necessary on their behalf (cf. WCF 7) so that the covenant of grace may operate in their favour. In this chapter—one of the longest in the Confession—the central theme of Christ as Mediator is set out.

8.1 The appointed Mediator

In his eternal purpose it pleased God to choose and appoint the Lord Jesus, his one and only Son, to be the mediator between God and man,[1] the Prophet,[2] Priest,[3] and King,[4] the Head and Saviour of his Church,[5] the Heir of all things,[6] and Judge of the world.[7] From all eternity God gave him a people to be his seed,[8] and to be in time by him redeemed, called, justified, sanctified, and glorified.[9]

1. Isa. 42:1; 1 Pet. 1:19,20; Jn 3:16; 1 Tim. 2:5. 2. Acts 3:22
3. Heb. 5:5,6. 4. Psalm 2:6; Luke 1:33. 5. Eph. 5:23. 6. Heb. 1:2.
7. Acts 17:31. 8. Jn 17:6; Psalm 22:30; Isa. 53:10.
9. 1 Tim. 2:6; Isa. 55:4,5; 1 Cor.1:30.

The head of the elect church is not the Son as Son, but the Son in his capacity as Mediator, thus the incarnate Son, the Lord Jesus Christ. The office of Mediator embraces the functions of prophet (since we are ignorant), priest (since we are guilty) and king (since we are in bondage). To this office the Son was appointed by the Father. He was to make peace between God and man and was given power to ensure that peace was accomplished. His kingly office rests on his priestly office (cf. Phil. 2:6–11) and includes all authority in heaven and on earth in order that he might bring to glory all those for whom he died.

8.2 The God-Man

The Son of God, the second person of the Trinity, is truly and eternally God, of one substance and equal with the Father. In the fulness of time he took to his divine person a human nature,[10] with all its essential characteristics and ordinary frailties, with the exception of sin.[11] He was conceived by the power of the Holy Spirit, in the womb of the virgin Mary, of her substance.[12] Thus two complete, perfect and distinct natures, the divine and the human, were inseparably joined together in the person of the Lord Jesus, without being changed, mixed or confused.[13] So the Son of God is now both true God and true man, yet one Christ, the only Mediator between God and man.[14]

10. John 1:1,14; 1 Jn. 5:20; Phil. 2:6; Gal. 4:4.
11. Heb. 2:14,16,17; Heb. 4:15.
12. Luke 1:27,31,35; Gal. 4:4.
13. Luke 1:35; Col. 2:9; Rom. 9:5; 1 Pet. 3:18; 1 Tim. 3:16.
14. Rom. 1:3,4; 1 Tim. 2:5.

In this section we consider more particularly the constitution of the person who is Mediator. The Mediator could not be God simply, but nor could he be man simply. Man has sinned and cannot meet his obligations. God is the one sinned against and he cannot ignore man's guilt. Hence, God himself is the way back to himself. The Son takes to his divine person a true human nature, a body and a soul like ours, but sin excepted. The human nature of Christ never had a separate personal existence. His humanity began to exist in the Virgin's womb through the power of the Spirit, but his person existed from eternity. This union of natures in the one person is called the *hypostatic* union.

The mystery of the two natures in the one person remains a mystery, but it fits the Biblical evidence. He was not two persons, nor were the two natures mixed so as to form one new nature. His humanity did not become divine (then it would not be human and he could not act for us), nor did his deity take the limitations of humanity (then God would destroy himself). He did not cease to be what he was from eternity, God's Son, when he became what he was not, the Son of Man. Compare the succinct statement of the Shorter Catechism Q21: *The only Redeemer of God's elect is the Lord Jesus Christ who, being the eternal Son of God, became man and so was and continues to be both God and man in two distinct natures and one person for ever.*

THE NATURES IN THE PERSON OF CHRIST

False views which deny that Jesus Christ is both God and man, but affirm he is only man, only God or neither God nor man, may be summarized as follows:

Docetism	Jesus only seemed to be man but was in fact a kind of angel. Many Gnostics held this. The NT seems to know of its presence (eg. 1 John 4:2; 5:6).
Ebionitism	Denied reality of divine nature along the line of those Jews who opposed the gospel in NT.
Arianism	Jesus halfway between God and man. Condemned Nicaea AD 325.
Apollinarianism	Denied integrity of human nature saying that it had been taken up into the divine nature, so that the two natures were mingled. Condemned AD 377–381.
Nestorianism	Endangered the unity of the person and in effect held two persons, a divine and human, existing in the incarnate Christ. Condemned AD 431.
Eutychianism	Called monophysitism (single nature). It was a reaction to Nestorianism. Condemned AD 449–451. Still held by Coptic, Ethiopian and Syrian Jacobite Churches at least in theory.

Monothelitism	Monophysites were divided over whether or not the will belonged to the person or the nature; the Monothelites held the former hence denied Christ had a human will.

8.3 The Anointed Mediator

His human nature thus united to the divine, the Lord Jesus was set apart and anointed with the Holy Spirit to an unlimited extent.[15] He had in him all the treasures of wisdom and knowledge,[16] and in him it pleased the Father that all fulness should dwell.[17] The Father's purpose was that Jesus, being holy, harmless, undefiled, and full of grace and truth,[18] might be completely equipped to exercise the office of a mediator and guarantor.[19] Jesus did not take this office on his own initiative, but was called to it by his Father,[20] who put all power and judgment into his hand, and commanded him to exercise it.[21]

15. Psalm 45:7; Jn 3:34. 16. Col. 2:3. 17. Col. 1:19.
18. Heb. 7:26; Jn 1:14. 19. Acts 10:38; Heb. 12:24; Heb. 7:22.
20. Heb. 5:4,5. 21. John 5:22,27; Matt. 28:18; Acts 2:36.

The effect of the hypostatic union was to give the human nature of Jesus dignity and honour. The anointing by the Spirit and the commissioning of God the Father, rendered him completely fit to be Mediator. This receiving of authority and power from the Father accounts for passages in Scripture which place Jesus in a subordinate relationship to the Father (eg. 1 Cor.11:3; John 14:28). 'In essential being, the Son is the equal of the Father; in relation to his official work, the Son takes on him the form of a servant ... It is as Mediator, as manifested to us in the incarnation, that he subordinates himself to his Father's will, in order that the Father, by the execution of that will, may secure our salvation.' (John Macpherson)

8.4 The work of the Mediator

The Lord Jesus undertook this office of Mediator most willingly.[22] In order that he might discharge it, he became subject to God's law[23] and perfectly fulfilled it;[24] he endured extremely severe torments in his soul[25] and most painful sufferings in his body;[26] was crucified, and died,[27] was decay.[28] On the third day he rose from the dead[29] with the same body in which he suffered,[30] and with which he also ascended into heaven. There he sits at the right hand of his Father[31] making intercession,[32] and shall return to judge all people and angels, at the end of the world.[33]

22. Psalm 40:7,8 with Heb. 10:5–10; Jn 10:18; Phil. 2:8. 23. Gal. 4:4.
24. Matt. 3:15; 5:17. 25. Matt. 26:37,38; Luke 22:44; Matt. 27:46.
26. Matt. chapters 26 & 27. 27. Phil. 2:8.
28. Acts 2:23,24,27; Acts 13:37; Rom. 6:9. 29. 1 Cor.15:3,4.
30. John 20:25,27. 31. Acts 2:33–36 [as substitute for Mark 16:19 in original].
32. Rom. 8:34; Heb. 9:24; Heb. 7:25.
33. Rom. 14:9,10; Acts 1:11; Acts 10:42; Matt. 13:40–42; Jude 6; 2 Pet. 2:4.

Christ's work was entirely voluntary. See the quotation at the end of this chapter. Further, his work was **active** and *passive*—that is, it was a course of **obedience** which involved *suffering*. Note that the suffering of Christ in his death was not something merely done to him in which he was inactive – that is not what passive means in this context—but it was something he did in loving obedience: he was active in his death, as a priest offering himself to God. Finally, the Mediator did his work in a state of humiliation and in a state of exaltation, in both states his glory as Mediator being evident. His resurrection with 'the same body' does not mean there were not different qualities, cf. WCF 32:2–3.

8.5 The atonement and its fruit

By his perfect obedience to God's law, and the unrepeatable sacrifice of himself, which he offered up to God through the eternal Spirit, the Lord Jesus has fully satisfied the justice of his Father.[34] He has purchased both reconciliation and an everlasting inheritance in the kingdom of heaven for everyone whom the Father has given to him.[35]

34. Rom. 5:19; Heb. 9:14,16; Heb. 10:14; Eph. 5:2; Rom. 3:25,26.
35. Dan. 9:24,26; Col. 1:19,20; Eph. 1:11,14; Jn 17:2; Heb. 9:12,15.

It is popular to deride explanations of the atonement as mere theories. While we will do well to recognise the aspects of truth in some other views, the heart of Christ's work is that of satisfaction in the sinner's place, that is, penal substitution. This is held by Roman, Greek and orthodox Protestant Christianity. The effect of Christ's mediatorial work is to make a perfect satisfaction to God's justice, and to secure an everlasting inheritance for believers. The atonement is to be understood in the context of Christ as mediator of the covenant and thus is made for those who are represented by Christ and bound up with him. This is not a mechanical or commercial transaction.

A very general view is that the atonement of Christ does not secure salvation but rather access to salvation if we choose it by our 'free will'. In other words, it is held that Christ died for all people but only those who believe will be saved. Human free will operates to limit the effects of the atonement. Now while there is a sense in which it may be said that Christ died for 'all men' or for 'the world', the context of Scripture passages to this effect sometimes shows that the universalism meant is set in contrast to the single nation of the Jews or to a particular class of humans. In such cases the meaning is that Christ died for people of every class from all the nations, and that a great multitude will be saved. On the other hand, one must not miss those passages that speak of the love of God for all, such as the desire of the One who is his exact image to gather them that they be saved (Matthew 23:37), and Christ's reminding us that as God loves his enemies so we are to do the same and indeed desire the salvation of all, beseeching them to be reconciled to God, a lesson Jonah had to learn. We cannot use mere human logic to harmonise these facts with the equally valid facts of God's special redemptive love for the elect alone, Christ's atonement being for those whom the Father had given him, and the spiritual inability of those dead in trespasses and sin.

8.6 The atonement and those who lived before it

Although the work of redemption was not actually accomplished by Christ until after his incarnation, yet its inherent value, operative power and benefits were given to the elect in all ages from the beginning of the world. Through promises, types and sacrifices, Christ was revealed and shown to be the seed of the woman who should bruise the serpent's head, and the Lamb slain from the beginning of the world. He is the same yesterday, today and for ever.[36]

36. Gal. 4:4,5; Gen. 3:15; Rev. 13:8; Heb. 13:8.

The question of the redemption of those who lived before the incarnation of Christ is answered in this section (see also WCF 7:5). Jesus tells us that Abraham rejoiced to see Christ's day and he saw it and was glad (John 8:56). The phrase 'the foundation of the world' linked with 'the Lamb slain' in Rev. 13:8 indicates that the death of Christ was a redemptive sacrifice decreed in the counsels of eternity. An alternative rendering which dates the writing of believers' names in the book of life to the foundation of the world would not provide the water-tight argument required by the context for believer's security given Rev. 3:5, and it is not the most natural construction of the Greek syntax either.

8.7 The relations of the natures in the Mediator

In his work of mediation, Christ acts according to both his natures, by each nature doing what is appropriate to it.[37] However, because of the unity of the person, what is appropriate to one nature is in Scripture sometimes attributed to his person named according to the other nature.[38]

37. Heb. 9:14; 1 Pet. 3:18.
38. Acts 20:28; Jn 3:13; 1 Jn. 3:16.

Christ's divine person renders his obedience and sufferings in our nature of infinite worth and value. All the acts of Christ are acts of the divine person. Each nature contributes what is proper to the mediatorial work

Christ undertakes without becoming mixed or confounded with the other nature (see 8.2). Because of the unity of both natures in the one person what is proper to either nature belongs to the person, and Scripture sometimes applies names appropriate to the natures to the person. For example, it is said that the Son of Man came from heaven (John 3:13) or that God purchased the church 'with his own blood' (Acts 20:28; perhaps more correctly, 'the blood of his own one'), or that God laid down his life for us (1 John 3:16 KJV), or that the Lord of Glory was crucified (1 Cor.2:8).

Martin Luther held the position that the two natures in one person demand the participation of the exalted humanity of Christ in the omnipresence of God, hence the Lutheran doctrine of *consubstantiation* in the Supper; i.e. that Christ is really present *by, with and under* the elements of bread and wine. This confusion of the natures undermines the perfection of Christ as Mediator (see Section 2) and is evidently an inadequate attempt to move away from the Roman theory of *transubstantiation*, an actual change of the elements.

8.8 The application of redemption

Christ makes absolutely certain that redemption reaches to and is effectively received by all those for whom he purchased it.[39] He makes intercession for them,[40] reveals the mysteries of salvation to them in and by the word,[41] effectively persuades them by his Spirit to believe and obey, and governs their hearts by his word and Spirit.[42] He overcomes all their enemies by his almighty power and wisdom, using the ways and means that are most in agreement with his wonderful and unsearchable administration of all things.[43]

39. Jn 6:37,39; John 10:15,16.
40. 1 Jn. 2:1,2; Rom. 8:34.
41. John 15:13,15; Eph. 1:7–9; Jn 17:6.
42. John 14:26; Heb. 12:2; 2 Cor. 4:13; Rom. 8:9,14; Rom. 15:18,19; Jn 17:17.
43. Psalm 110:1; 1 Cor.15:25,26; Mal. 4:2,3; Col. 2:15.

In 8:5 the satisfaction rendered by Christ was set forth. Here the actual application of that satisfaction is described. The harmony in the work of redemption is thus brought out (see also WCF 3:6). Christ made satisfaction for those the Father gave to him, and Christ, through the Spirit, effectively applies this redemption to those for whom he died. Some aspects touched on in this section will be taken up in WCF 10—God's Effective Call.

THOUGHTS FROM OTHER MINDS

'The voluntariness of Christ's service is everywhere throughout Scripture made most clear. He willingly undertook the office of Mediator, assuming a nature which was subject to weakness and pain, and a position that necessarily involved suffering unto death. This voluntariness of the Redeemer does not mean that he allowed himself to show occasional signs of weakness and fatigue, and permitted temptation to approach him. It applies rather to his willing entrance into and continuance upon that path in which all these real trials had of necessity to be encountered.'

John Macpherson (1847–1902)[1]

FOR DISCUSSION

1. Is it proper to make pictures in say a child's story Bible to represent Christ? What about in a devotional context or in a church building?
2. Why was it necessary for Christ to be equipped by the Holy Spirit?
3. Locate several Scriptures which teach that Christ acted voluntarily as Mediator.
4. Explain 1 Timothy 4:10; Titus 2:11.

1. *The Confession of Faith* (T. & T. Clark, 1882), 73

5. Were the OT animal sacrifices able to take away sin?
6. If Christ died for all men but only some are saved, what was achieved by Christ's death?

CHAPTER 9
HUMAN FREEDOM

ANALYSIS *WCF 9:1–5*

1. Human freedom basics

2. Freedom in the state of innocence

3. Freedom in the state of sin

4. Freedom in the state of grace

5. Freedom in the state of glory

9.1 Human freedom basics

God has given the human will a natural liberty so that it is neither forced nor, by any necessity arising from within itself, compelled to good or evil.[1]

1. Matt. 17:12; Jas 1:14; Deut. 30:19.

The Confession states that man has a natural liberty of will which prevents it being determined to good or evil by such causes or influences as would exclude deliberate choice and spontaneous agency. The freedom or bondage of the four possible states of man described in the following sections must be taken in the light of this foundational teaching. In short, the human will is a reality; it is not a delusion as if our will was compelled to choose a certain way by an inbuilt necessity over-riding desire and deliberate choice. Choice is made, it is made freely, and the agent is responsible.

We must not set the sovereignty of God over against the freedom of man as if the former eliminates the latter so that man has no will of his own but is driven by God's will or, on the other hand, as if belief in man's freedom of necessity limits the sovereignty of God. The Bible does not envisage human freedom as freedom from all restrictions or a freedom to act autonomously, nor does it regard God's sovereignty as a threat to man's freedom, or vice versa. When, as is often the case, man wants to assert his freedom over against God, he is acting as a rebel enslaved by sin, not as a son who submits to his Father. For the Bible does not regard freedom in an abstract or philosophical way, nor as the opposite of submission, but it regards freedom as realised in submission to God (compare 2 Peter 2:18–19).

We would do well in keeping very carefully to the Biblical emphasis on the nature of human freedom. A great deal of fruitless speculation and harmful teaching and division has arisen through failure to do so. Much popular thought in Christian circles builds on the idea of freedom as an ability to act autonomously as if man dictates to God who will be saved. This is common in those sections of the Roman church uninfluenced by Augustine (AD 354–430), but it is far more widespread than this. It arose in the 17th century in the form of Arminianism (named after Jacob Arminius) which asserts the freedom of man *over against* God's sovereignty.

Those who followed Arminius, perhaps going further than he did, were called Remonstrants. They raised five objections to the Biblical scheme of salvation which gave rise to five answers by the Synod of Dort (1618–19). These are commonly called the five points of Calvinism but the mnemonic TULIP to recall them dates only from the early 20th century. Of course Calvinism is much more than these five points. Arminianism was widely influential in English Methodism and undergirds much popular evangelicalism today. The general idea of the Arminian view is that the will is neutral so that free will is a power of choice that is not controlled by the moral nature of the chooser. However, Christ teaches that the nature of the fruit *is* determined by the nature of the tree on which it grows (Matthew 12:33–35). In a more refined form Arminianism admits that man needs God's grace to repent and believe, but it is still held that this grace is granted to all with the ultimate decision for or against being in the hands of man because of his 'free' will. See further WCF 3.2.

9.2 Freedom in the state of innocence

In the state of innocence man had freedom and power to will and to do what was good and well pleasing to God,[2] but with the possibility of change so that he might fall from this state.[3]

2. Eccl. 7:29; Gen. 1:26.
3. Gen. 2:16,17; Gen. 3:6.

In the state of innocence before Adam's disobedience, man had freedom for he was created in fellowship with God and 'very good'. His position had to be personally and freely accepted; his freedom had to be vindicated by personal choice of righteousness or sin—hence the test in Eden. But if there was the necessity for choice, there was no necessity for the actual choice made. There can be no explanation but the wilful abuse of his freedom.

9.3 Freedom in the state of sin

As a consequence of his fall into a state of sin, man has lost all ability to will any spiritual good related to salvation.[4] In his unregenerate state he is completely opposed to that spiritual good,[5] and dead in sin.[6] Hence he is not able, by any strength of his own, to convert himself or even to co-operate with God that he might be converted.[7]

4. Rom. 5:6; Rom. 8:7; Jn 15:5.
5. Rom. 3:10,12.
6. Eph. 2:1,5; Col. 2:13.
7. John 6:44,65; Eph. 2:2–5; 1 Cor. 2:14; Titus 3:3–5.

The fall meant that man enslaved himself by his free choice, consequently the term 'free will' is a misnomer in much popular usage. For man does not now live in submission to God but is enslaved by sin. Certainly he still makes free and conscious choices (cf. 9:1), but his prior free act of will has brought him into subjection to evil. He chooses what he desires, but he does not desire God any more. He may do many decent and worthy things in the eyes of men, but he does not choose what is spiritually good. 'Those who are in the flesh cannot please God', Paul reminds us (Romans 8:8). Indeed, man claims 'freedom' to act independently of God, and this cherishing of autonomy is the expression of self-will and proud rebellion against his Creator. So this is not a freedom to boast about, but a freedom that is slavery. Hence Martin Luther (1483–1545) regarded his book, *The Bondage of the Will,* written in 1525 against Erasmus, as his most important, along with his *Small Catechism*, for in it the fundamental issue was addressed—the hollowness of man's claim to freedom.

The last part in the 1646 text reads: *or prepare himself thereunto*. This does not mean *God* does not prepare a person for conversion, nor does it mean that the use of the means of grace is beyond man's power. Rather, it relates to the common idea of man co-operating with God to bring about conversion—something utterly impossible for the one dead in sin, but something man in his pride likes to suppose he contributes to his salvation.

It should be clearly noted that the sinful enslavement of mankind through the fall is one for which we are fully responsible. The inability to do what God demands of us does not excuse us since our inability is self-inflicted. In other words, responsibility to obey God's word does not now imply ability to obey. Second, if our inability is really recognised it produces urgency to find relief, not indifference, as would be the case if we believed we had ability. Third, no appeal to the secret will of God is legitimate if it is used to deny or undermine the reality and sincerity of God's revealed proposals of mercy made to sinners in the Gospel.

9.4 Freedom in the state of grace

When God converts a sinner and brings him into the state of grace, he frees him from his natural bondage under sin,[8] and by his grace alone enables him freely to will and to do that which is spiritually good.[9] Nevertheless, corruption remains, so that he does not perfectly and constantly will good but also wills what is evil.[10]

8. Col. 1:13; John 8:34,36.
9. Phil. 2:13; Rom. 6:18,22.
10. Gal. 5:17; Rom. 7:15,18,19,21,23.

It follows from man's bondage in sin that the application of salvation must be accomplished by God's grace—by the mighty working of God's power through the Holy Spirit (compare John 6:44,65). This is the context in which our understanding of the following chapters must be understood. Accordingly, effective calling of the elect will not be seen as an arbitrary procedure but as a gracious activity by which the salvation purchased by Christ becomes the possession of those sinners to whom it has pleased the Lord to grant salvation. Being thus brought into submission by the Holy Spirit in the day of *his* power, man's freedom is more than restored, since he has freedom in Christ, that is, freedom through the covenant of grace. He continues to make free and conscious choices but the miracle of regeneration has given him a new nature which enables the choice of what is good once more. Not left to himself but enabled to do and to will what is good by God's grace, he is on the way to glory, the perfection of grace. Although he remains imperfectly sanctified in this life, and so also chooses evil, a decisive break has been made at the entry to the Christian life, the life of freedom in Christ.

9.5 Freedom in the state of glory

Only in glory is the human will made perfectly and unchangeably free to will good and good alone.[11]

11. Eph. 4:13; Heb. 12:23; 1 Jn. 3:2; Jude 24.

In this life the believer has freedom from the power of sin but not from its presence. Perfect freedom is only realised in glory when we are perfectly conformed to the image of Christ. Through grace sin has been freely excluded and it has no more place in our lives.

THOUGHTS FROM OTHER MINDS

'Surely, if no Christian will dare say this, "It is not of God that shows mercy but of man who wills", lest he should openly contradict the Apostle, it follows that the true interpretation of the saying, 'It is not of him who wills, nor of him who runs, but of God who shows mercy' [Romans 9:16], is that the whole work belongs to God who both makes the will of man righteous, and thus prepares it for assistance, and assists it when it is prepared.'

Augustine (354–430)[1]

If we are tempted to infer that there is no point in trying to persuade spiritually-dead men and women that it is their duty to repent and believe, we may ask:

'Why then did the great Calvinist evangelists venture forth to the scattered hamlets and great cities of Britain and America, and to the mission fields of India, Africa and China, to plead with all who heard them to turn to the living God? Did they not believe in the bondage of the will? Of course they did! How then could they motivate themselves to such a futile action? The short answer is, Because they took their cue not from human logic, but from the example of

1. *Enchiridion* 32.

the Lord and his apostles, and accordingly saw it as their mission not only to proclaim the Gospel but to persuade people to believe it.'

Donald Macleod[2]

FOR DISCUSSION

1. In what sense is man free and in what sense bound? Is there a parallel in God's will?
2. If the will of man is not the decisive factor in coming to salvation what is the decisive factor and how is man's will involved?
3. Name the five points the Remonstrants' asserted against Biblical doctrine. How significant is the understanding of human freedom and divine grace which Arminianism reflects?

2. *Compel Them to Come In* (Christian Focus, 2020), 16–17.

CHAPTER 10
GOD'S EFFECTIVE CALL

ANALYSIS *WCF 10:1–4*

1. **Persons with reason who heed the call**
2. **Passivity in regeneration underscored**
3. **Infants and incapables who cannot answer the call**
4. **Persons with reason who do not heed or who do not hear**

10.1 Persons with reason who heed the call

All those whom God has predestined to life, and those only, he is pleased to call effectively[1] by his word and Spirit at the right time as he decides.[2] He calls them out of the state of sin and death in which they are by nature, to grace and salvation by Jesus Christ.[3] Their minds are enlightened spiritually and savingly so as to understand the things of God;[4] their hearts of stone are taken away and hearts of flesh given them;[5] their wills are renewed, and by his almighty power they are set to seek and to follow that which is good,[6] and are effectively drawn to Jesus Christ:[7] yet in this they come most freely, being made willing by God's grace.[8]

1. Rom. 8:30; Rom. 11:7; Eph. 1:10,11. 2. 2 Thess. 2:13,14; 2 Cor. 3:3,6.
3. Rom. 8:2; Eph. 2:1–5; 2 Tim. 1:9–10.
4. Acts 26:18; 1 Cor. 2:10,12; Eph. 1:17–18.
5. Ezek. 36:26. 6. Ezek. 11:19; Phil. 2:13; Deut. 30:6; Ezek. 36:27
7. Eph. 1:19; John 6:44,45. 8. Song 1:4; Psalm 110:3; Jn 6:37; Rom. 6:16–18.

Man being enslaved to his sinful nature, salvation must be a work of divine power and grace, but God has not chosen to save all but only those who are his called or the elect—a multitude which no man can number. Those of God's elect who can be called through the outward means of the word are also called effectively through the inward ministry of the Spirit. The logical distinctions are that the *mind* is illuminated so that the truth can be truly seen, the *heart* is awakened to hate evil and love what is good, and the *will* is renewed so that a genuine and willing response is given to the call of Christ in the gospel. We make these distinctions in logic although we cannot separate them in experience.

10.2 Passivity in regeneration underscored

This effective call is entirely the outcome of God's free and special grace. It does not depend on anything at all God foresaw in the person called.[9] The person so called is entirely passive until, by being made alive and renewed by the Holy Spirit,[10] he is enabled to answer this call and to embrace the grace offered and conveyed in it.[11]

9. 2 Tim. 1:9; Titus 3:4,5; Eph. 2:4,5,8,9; Rom. 9:11.
10. 1 Cor. 2:14; Rom. 8:7; Eph. 2:5.
11. John 6:37; Ezek. 36:27; Jn 5:25.

We distinguish between regeneration proper, which is a new birth or a new creation, and conversion. Regeneration is monergistic, that is, God is the only worker of it, and the one *dead* in sin is (naturally) utterly *passive*. But, illumined in the mind, awakened in the heart and conscience and renewed in the will, the subject of the effective call closes with Christ as he is freely offered in the gospel. Strictly speaking this is called conversion, and the person is *active* in this. To put it another way, repentance and faith are evidence of a prior renewal; they are evidences that the Spirit of God has quickened one who was formerly dead in trespasses and sins. There may be resistance on our part but that resistance is overcome to bring us 'clothed and in our right mind' to the feet of Christ. Grace is not just offered for man to choose but is actually bestowed so producing the will to believe and the belief itself.

10.3 Infants and incapables who cannot answer the call

Those elect persons, including elect infants dying in infancy,[12*] who are incapable of being outwardly called by the ministry of the word, are regenerated and saved by Christ through the Spirit,[14] who works when, where, and how he pleases.[13]

12. Luke 18:15,16; Acts 2:38,39; Jn 3:3,5; 1 Jn. 5:12; Rom. 8:9 all compared.
13. John 3:8
14. 1 Jn. 5:12; Acts 4:12.

The natural question to raise at this point is, 'What about elect persons who cannot be outwardly called by the ministry of the word because they are infants or mentally incapable?' Section 3 answers this by affirming that such persons are saved by Christ through the Spirit, just as are any other elect persons. In short, such persons, being members of a fallen race, need salvation, but they have it on the same basis as others. Ordinarily, persons show the fruit of regeneration in repentance, faith and evangelical obedience, whereas this fruit is not evident to us in the case of elect infants dying such or those mentally incompetent. However, regeneration may still occur, and issue in its fruit in glory.

Since the confession is dealing with *the way* by which infants may be saved and *not the number* of such persons, the appropriateness of the term '*elect* infants' is clear. This term implies the need of redemption for infants and thus safeguards against the notion that original sin is not of itself damning. Failure to recognise this orientation of this section of the Confession has led many to infer that there are some in the category of infants who are not elect. This is not a necessary inference and in fact the larger number of Calvinists have always held that the children of believers who die in infancy or in the womb are saved, and many have held that *all* infants dying such are saved.

It is of interest that *some* editions of the Baptist Confession of 1689, which was modelled on Westminster, remove the word *elect* qualifying infants in this section and so assert the regeneration of all children dying in infancy. The PCUSA did the same in 1903. Still the lack of a positive assertion to this effect is desirable. A plausible inference should not be bound on the conscience in a creed even though it be the common belief, nor should any suggestion that children do not need redemption be allowed a place. All who are saved are saved because they are elect out of a fallen humanity.

This section is important. It is certainly true that Calvinists have the only satisfactory basis for affirming the salvation of any infants or of any grown persons who have never had the power of reason. For those predicating salvation on participation in the sacraments cannot point the finger at the Confession, nor can those who predicate salvation on the possession of conscious faith. But salvation predicated on the electing love of the Father, the atonement of Christ and the regeneration of the Spirit finds no obstacle to the salvation of those who cannot be called by the outward ministry of the word. Hence, it is open to a subscriber to the Confession to believe *all* infants dying such are saved in this way, although he cannot assert it as the authoritative teaching of the church.

10.4 Persons with reason who do not heed or do not hear

Others not elected may be called by the ministry of the word[15] and may have some common operations of the Spirit.[16] However, they never truly come to Christ, and therefore cannot be saved.[17] It is even more obvious that persons not professing the Christian religion cannot be saved in any other way whatsoever, no matter how diligent they are in living their lives according to their conscience and the teaching of the religion they profess.[18] To assert and maintain that they can be saved in such other way is very harmful and should be detested.[19]

15. Matt. 22:14. 16. Matt. 7:22; Matt. 13:20,21; Heb. 6:4,5.
17 John 6:64–66; Jn 8:24. 18. Acts 4:12; Jn 14:6; Eph. 2:12; John 4:22; 17:3.
19. 2 Jn. 9–11; 1 Cor. 16:22; Gal. 1:6–8.

The Confession now turns to the position of those who are finally lost. The theoretical possibility may be granted that the phrase *others not elected* includes non-elect infants dying such and non-elect persons who have never had the faculty of reason, but this is not asserted as such. At any rate, the focus in this final section is on non-elect persons who are rationally capable but either do not heed or do not hear the Christian gospel, and so do not come to Christ and do not profess the Christian religion.

Take the case of those who do not heed the gospel though it is presented to them, and who die in that condition. It follows that their dislike of, and opposition to, God has not been overcome by God's effective call, for they have not come to Christ, but have chosen to remain rebels.

As to those who have never heard the gospel, the Confession does not actually affirm that they are lost, but it does affirm that they cannot be saved except by coming to Christ. This amounts to the same thing in practice. It may be that we should not underestimate the value of remnants of special revelation which have become embedded in the traditions of people who have not been regularly exposed to the gospel, and which God may use in bringing them to feel their sin and to trust in Christ, if they knew of him. But *if* there are cases of this kind, as American theologian W. G. T. Shedd (1820-94) thought, they only prove the rule: If people call on the Lord, they will be saved; in order to call on him, they must believe; in order to believe, they must hear; in order to hear, the gospel must be brought to them (Romans 10:13–17). Hence we must be diligent in bringing the gospel to every creature. God has revealed no other means of salvation for men than through a knowledge of Christ and a closing with him as he is freely offered in the gospel.

It is often claimed that, if those who have never heard the gospel are lost, it is through no fault of their own. This claim ignores the fact that God has given a clear revelation of himself through what he has made to which none conform, and so all are justly without excuse (Romans 1:18ff cf. WCF 1:1). Leaving to one side the guilt of Adam's sin imputed to his posterity, every human person knows enough to merit damnation. It is also characteristic of mankind to seek salvation on the ground of personal worth and 'good works.' But we are enslaved by sin. The only way of salvation is through Christ and his atonement. To reject this is to make shipwreck, hence such teaching is to be detested.

THOUGHTS FROM OTHER MINDS

'If a man is dead in a natural or physical sense it is apparent to all and will readily be granted by all, that there is no possibility of his performing any physical action. A corpse cannot act in any way whatever, and that man would be deemed to have taken leave of his senses who ventured to assert that it should be assumed to have power to act. In what other way, then, are we to understand the declaration that man is dead in sins and trespasses except that he is utterly unable to do anything of a true spiritual character, that he cannot raise himself up into life and that he is just as much dependent upon an act of sovereign power to raise him to spiritual life as the naturally dead man would be dependent upon an act of omnipotence for his physical resurrection to life? Nothing less than omnipotence could raise a dead Lazarus. Nothing less than omnipotence, working in grace, can raise a dead soul.'

K. J. Gardner[1]

'However, just as by the fall man did not cease to be man, endowed with intellect and will, and just as sin, which has spread through the whole human race, did not abolish the nature of the human race but distorted and spiritually killed it, so also this divine grace of regeneration does not act in people as if they were blocks and stones; nor does it abolish the will and its properties or coerce a reluctant will by force, but spiritually revives, heals, reforms, and—in a manner at once pleasing and powerful—bends it back. As a result, a ready and sincere obedience of the Spirit now begins to prevail where before the rebellion and resistance of the flesh were completely dominant.'

Synod of Dort[2]

1. *The God of All Grace* (Presbyterian Church of Australia, 1980), 13.
2. *Canons of the Synod of Dort* (1618–19), 3-4.16

FOR DISCUSSION

1. Show from Scripture that regeneration must precede conversion.
2. Explain and justify the phrase 'elect infants' in Section 3.
3. Why cannot the earnest practice of a religion other than Christianity save?

CHAPTER 11
JUSTIFICATION

ANALYSIS *WCF 11:1–6*

1. Justification defined
 a. gracious act of God
 b. involving complete pardon and full acceptance
 c. grounded on the righteousness of Christ
 d. imputed and received through faith alone

2. Justification in its relations
 a. Christ the ground
 b. faith the instrument
 c. works the evidence

3. Justification and God's character

4. Justification in relation to God's purposes

5. The sins of the justified

6. Justification before Christ's resurrection

Roman Catholicism was and is a religion emphasising salvation by grace through faith. But closer examination shows that human merit is not excluded. Traditions God never gave us to keep, and practices inconsistent with a truly gracious salvation, are required. They are regarded as instrumental causes of salvation along with faith in Christ. That is even written into the theory since the Council of Trent (1545–63), and it is certainly intertwined in popular grass-roots Roman Catholicism to the present.

Judaism in New Testament times was somewhat similar. It was fully recognized that Israel was in covenant with the Lord through his goodness. That was obvious from the Biblical history. It was recognized that the covenant brought the demand of obedience to God's law. In the understanding of the religious leaders one should therefore set oneself to careful obedience to the law. Those who did so were termed "righteous" and those who did not were regarded as "sinners". The righteous did not suppose they were absolutely perfect; after-all, there were sacrifices in Israel to atone for failures. But they were convinced that their careful observance of the law of Moses in its whole range of requirements, including circumcision, Sabbath, and dietary laws (which very obviously marked them off from non-Jews), to which they added their own carefully worked out traditions, would be pleasing to the Lord and ensure a place in the kingdom of heaven. They were already in by covenant membership and they would stay in by covenant obedience.

Jesus' teaching was regarded as shocking. He associated with 'sinners' and even ate with them (Luke 15:2). He said he had not come to call the righteous but sinners to repentance (Matt 9:13). He assured his disciples that their righteousness must exceed that of the scribes and Pharisees, otherwise they would not enter the kingdom (Matt 5:20). The Law had been given to regulate life but could not transform it. Jesus said he did not come to destroy the Law and the Prophets but to fulfil them (Matt 5:17), which he did by his death on the cross when he brought them to the goal intended.

Sometimes someone claims that they could not be bad enough for Christ to die in their place. Doubtless this was part of Paul's thinking, until he came to see that Jesus' death demonstrated with the utmost clarity the powerlessness of the law to save. Christ's death redeems from the curse due for transgression of the law. Consequently, Paul came to see that working and believing in Christ were polar opposites. 'To him who does not work but trusts God who justifies the wicked, his faith is credited as righteousness' (Rom. 4:5), a faith that is itself God's gift. Hence, we are justified by faith alone – the empty hand that receives the gift of God. Christians are not suspicious of good works, but they put them in their proper place as fruits of the new relationship. We broke God's law and came under its condemnation; Christ fulfilled God's law for us and bore our condemnation. Set free, now the righteousness of the law is fulfilled in us through the Spirit (Rom. 8:3–4).

We cannot think of our acceptance with God in terms of our faithfulness to the covenant, but only in terms of Christ's obedience as our representative head. Paul discards everything he could have through law-keeping so as to have the righteousness which is through faith in Christ (Phil. 3:9).

The remarks in the preceding paragraphs have been written in the light of the so-called 'New Perspective' on Paul which has had increasing advocacy since about 1980. It claims that justification in Paul is not about how we are right before God, but about who is to be included in God's new community, the church. The Jews wanted to insist on the 'boundary markers' of ethnic privilege—circumcision, the Sabbath, the dietary code—but Paul insists these are not to be laid on Gentiles. They have been made members of the covenant by God when they acknowledged Jesus as Lord, and they are to stay in the covenant by non-meritorious works done through the enabling of the Spirit. This 'New Perspective' downplays, if it does not deny, the imputation of Christ's righteousness to the ungodly, and speaks of righteousness primarily in terms of God's covenant faithfulness. It relates faith and works in a way somewhat similar to Roman Catholic doctrine. While articulate advocates like N. T. Wright have some excellent things to say, one cannot avoid the conviction that at the key point a serious shift has been made that has repercussions all down the line. Paul was not Luther, but the emphasis on justification by faith alone by the Protestant Reformers is fully in line with Paul's teaching, and the teaching of the Scriptures as a whole.

11.1 Justification defined

Those whom God effectively calls he also freely justifies.[1] He does this, not by infusing righteousness into them, but by pardoning their sins, and by accounting and accepting them as righteous. This he does for Christ's sake alone and not for anything done in them or by them. He does not consider their faith itself, the act of believing, as their righteousness, nor any other obedient response to the gospel by them, but he credits the obedience and satisfaction of Christ to them.[2] For their part, they receive and rest by faith on Christ and his righteousness, and this faith does not originate with themselves but is the gift of God.[3]

1. Rom. 8:30; Rom. 3:24.
2. Rom. 4:5–8; 2 Cor. 5:19,21; Rom. 3:22,24,25,27,28; Titus 3:5,7; Eph. 1:7; Jer 23:6; 1 Cor. 1:30,31; Rom. 5:17–19.
3. Acts 10:43; Gal. 2:16; Phil. 3:9; Acts 13:38,39; Eph. 2:7,8.

The question of how a person may be just before God is absolutely fundamental. The Bible teaches that people are righteous in God's sight because he declares them to be so for Christ's sake. In other words, justification is a legal term whose opposite is condemnation. Thus, Romans 8:33–34: 'Who will lay anything to the charge of God's elect? It is God who justifies. Who is he who will condemn?' The Gospel is primarily about the righteousness of God which comes through faith in Jesus Christ to all who believe (Rom. 3:22). William Cunningham, the 19th century Scottish theologian, aptly says somewhere, 'The righteousness of God is the righteousness which the righteousness of God requires him to require.'

Before God's tribunal we may be condemned or justified, declared guilty or declared righteous. Now God does not make the guilty guilty by, for instance, pouring sin into them. He simply declares what they are. Similarly, God does not accept us as righteous by pouring righteousness into us, but by declaring us to be righteous and putting us in that category. Hence justification is *an act*. He is able to do this because he views us in Christ the covenant head of the redeemed. So it is *an act of grace*. Our sins were placed to Christ's account and he has paid the penalty for them. Christ has also procured complete righteousness on our behalf, which is placed to our account. Our sins are laid on Christ and his righteousness reckoned to us. We call this a double imputation. Justification is *an act of grace grounded on the merit of Christ*.

God does not look at our faith or some other response to the gospel when making his verdict, but he looks at the righteousness of God in the gospel, the righteousness Christ has procured. But faith is the instrumental cause of salvation since it is the means by which Christ is appropriated. Hence, Paul (Romans 4) can speak of the experience of Abraham whose faith was counted as righteousness, because faith holds on to Christ. But as he is expounding the meaning of Romans 3:21–26, none should mistake faith as other than the *instrumental* means; it's not a work.

The subject of justification is a very important one and remains a major issue between the Church of Rome and orthodox Protestantism. Rome certainly teaches the necessity of grace, and that salvation apart from Jesus Christ and his merit is impossible. But Rome confuses justification and sanctification in her teaching set out as dogma in 1547 at the Council of Trent. She holds that justification means the forgiveness of sins and moral renovation, and she regards faith and the new ethical disposition as a ground of acceptance with God. Rather than the emphasis on the righteousness of God in the gospel, the emphasis falls on the subjective experience of the individual, hence the impossibility of real assurance. Bound up with this is the understanding of faith as assent to the teachings of the church rather than trust in the person of Christ. Rome also sees divine grace as tied to the sacraments and to a mediating priesthood, so creating more confusion. It is not surprising that Martin Luther regarded justification as the key test of a standing or falling church. Mind you, the remarkable Scottish Presbyterian Dr. John

Duncan (1796–1870) well said: 'The Person of Christ is fundamental.' He adds: 'Justification by faith is the meeting-point of many doctrines, a rallying centre of theology; but it is not the foundation doctrine'[1].

11.2 Justification in its relations

The faith that receives and rests on Christ and his righteousness, is the sole means of justification.[4] Yet it is never alone in the person justified, but is always accompanied by all other saving graces; it is not a dead faith, but works by love.[5]

4. John 1:12; Rom. 3:28; Rom. 5:1.
5. James 2:17,22,26; Gal. 5:6.

Rome professed concern for morality in her objection to justification by faith alone, but she does not see the marvel of God's saving purposes as she ought. This section affirms that faith is the only means, that it rests on Christ, and that it shows its reality by what accompanies or flows from it. Good works are fruits of a new relationship, not means of establishing it. Faith alone justifies because it looks away from itself and is centred in the person of Jesus Christ. In some sections of Protestantism there is a nominalism which, while rejecting the additions of Rome, nevertheless rests content with a faith which is traditional or historical. This 'cheap grace' concept (as it has been called) might properly be termed a dead faith. A faith not evidenced by deeds is a spurious faith, as James reminds us in his epistle.

In summary: We are justified by Christ *meritoriously*, by faith *instrumentally*, and by works *evidentially*.

11.3 Justification and God's character

By his obedience and death Christ paid in full the debt of all those who are justified, and made a proper, real, and full satisfaction of every claim

1. J. M. Brentnall (ed.), *'Just a Talker': Sayings of John ('Rabbi') Duncan* (Banner of Truth, 1997), 102

of his Father's justice on their behalf.[6] Since it was not for anything in them that Christ was freely given by the Father for them,[7] and his obedience and satisfaction freely accepted in their place,[8] their justification is only of free grace.[9] Hence, both God's exact justice and his rich grace are glorified in the justification of sinners.[10]

6. Rom. 5:8–10,19; 1 Tim. 2:5,6; Heb. 10:10,14; Dan. 9:24,26; Isa. 53:4–6,10–12.
7. Rom. 8:32. 8. 2 Cor. 5:21; Matt. 3:17; Eph. 5:2. 9. Rom. 3:24; Eph. 1:7.
10. Rom. 3:26; Eph. 2:7.

The price of justification has been fully met by Christ but the justification of the elect remains an act of free grace since all that was required God himself provided at his cost. Notice again that the atonement is described as a sacrifice by which satisfaction has been made to the Father's justice (cf. WCF 8:5). The atonement did not procure the Father's love but flowed from it. Free justification does not mean the ruin of God's character, but its vindication. He remains just and the one who justifies whoever believes in Jesus (Rom. 3:25–26).

11.4 Justification in relation to God's purposes

From all eternity God decreed to justify all the elect,[11] and when the time was right Christ died for their sins and rose again for their justification.[12] Nevertheless, the elect are not justified until in due time the Holy Spirit actually applies Christ to them.[13]

11. Gal. 3:8; 1 Pet. 1:2,19,20; Rom. 8:30.
12. Gal. 4:4; 1 Tim. 2:6; Rom. 4:25.
13. Col. 1:21,22; Gal. 2:16; Titus 3:3–7.

None can be saved apart from the eternal decree and the work of Christ but none are actually justified until the redemption purchased by Christ is applied to them in regeneration and they, as a consequence, believe. The eternal decree includes the time of application to the individual. Until then they are children of wrath like others (Eph. 2:3) although, viewed in union with Christ, they shared in Christ's resurrection, ascension and session at God's right hand (Eph. 2:4–6).

11.5 The sins of the justified

God continues to forgive the sins of those who are justified.[14] Although they can never fall from their justified state,[15] they may fall under God's fatherly displeasure because of their sins, and they may not have the light of his countenance restored to them until they humble themselves, confess their sins, ask for forgiveness, and renew their faith and repentance.[16]

14. Matt. 6:12; 1 Jn. 1:7,9; 2:1,2.
15. Luke 22:32; John 10:28; Heb. 10:14.
16. Psalm 89:31–33; 51:7–12; 32:5; Matt. 26:75; 1 Cor. 11:30,32; Luke 1:20.

Believers still sin, feel it, and pray for forgiveness each day. Justification, being God's act apart from anything in them, cannot be destroyed, but their sins are deservedly, and perhaps severely, punished by fatherly chastisement. 'The justified may fall under the Father's displeasure but they never fall out of his purpose of grace.'[2]

11.6 Justification before Christ's resurrection

The justification of believers under the Old Testament was in all these respects identical with the justification of believers under the New Testament.[17]

17. Gal. 3:9,13,14; Rom. 4:22–24; Heb. 13:8.

The texts cited provide ample proof of this section, and further expansion may be found in WCF 7:3–6. The case of Abraham is decisive. Indeed, it is to God's covenant with Abraham that every spiritual blessing Christians enjoy may be traced.

2. James B. Green, *A Harmony of the Westminster Presbyterian Standards* (The John Knox Press, 1951), 86.

THOUGHTS FROM OTHER MINDS

'That faith is properly called justifying by which we rely upon Christ for the remission of sins and for salvation. For Christ is a sufficient object for justifying faith. Faith justifies only by apprehending the righteousness by which we are justified. That righteousness does not lie in the truth of some proposition to which we give assent, but in Christ alone who has been made sin for us that we might be righteousness in him, 2 Cor. 5:21.'

William Ames (1576–1633)[3]

'Now this faith which unites to Christ and justifies a man who has hitherto been ungodly is itself a fruit of the new birth. It does not by any means precede that birth, nor is it in any degree the cause of it. It is not its cause but its outcome. Yet it is so the fruit of the new birth as that no interval of time elapses between that birth and the breathing of the new life of faith. In the order of time there is not a space that would allow for a razor's edge to come in between them. Yet in the order of nature or of cause and effect the one is the cause of the other. The new birth in this sense is the working or the production of faith in the heart and the heart acts that faith as soon as it is wrought.'

John Macleod (1872–1948)[4]

FOR DISCUSSION

1. Justification may be said to be a forensic act. Explain what this means and why it is important. Why do non-christians think it unimportant?
2. How is God's justification of the ungodly just?
3. Explain imputation in reference to our sins and Christ's righteousness.

3. *The God of All Grace*, 13.
4. *Scottish Theology in Relation to Church History Since the Reformation* (1946; repr., Banner of Truth Trust, 1974), 125.

4. Paul asserts Abraham to be an example of justification by faith (Romans 4:1ff), while James 2:23–24 says Abraham is an example of justification by works. Explain this apparent contradiction.
5. Can a person be regenerate without being a believer?

CHAPTER 12
ADOPTION

ANALYSIS *WCF 12:1*

Adoption an act of grace based on the obedience of the Son of God by which the status of God's child is restored and the spirit of adoption is conferred—a status received through faith and which will be publicly revealed at the resurrection.

12.1

Participation in the grace of adoption is conferred by God on all the justified for the sake of his only Son, Jesus Christ.[1] By this act they are numbered with and enjoy the liberties and privileges of the children of God.[2] They have his name put upon them,[3] receive the spirit of adoption,[4] have access to the throne of grace with boldness,[5] and are enabled to cry, 'Abba, Father'.[6] They are pitied,[7] protected,[8] provided for,[9] and chastened by God, as by a father.[10] Yet they are never cast off,[11] for they have been sealed for the day of redemption,[12] and so inherit the promises[13] as heirs of everlasting salvation.[14]

1. Eph. 1:5. 2. Gal. 4:4,5; Rom. 8:17; Jn 1:12. 3. Jer. 14:9; 2 Cor. 6:18; Rev. 3:12. 4. Rom. 8:15. 5. Eph. 3:12; Rom. 5:2. 6. Gal. 4:6. 7. Psalm 103:13. 8. Prov. 14:26. 9. Matt. 6:30,32; 1 Pet. 5:7. 10. Heb. 12:6. 11. Lam. 3:31. 12. Eph. 4:30. 13. Heb. 6:12. 14. 1 Pet. 1:3,4; Heb. 1:14.

Early Reformation writers and many in the European tradition give little attention to adoption, and some treat it as a mere element of justification. The WCF is the first creed to treat adoption as a distinct subject.

Originally, man was not only a loyal subject of God's rule but also a son in God's house, for Adam is called the son of God (Luke 3:37) and was an heir of the future held out to him in Eden. We are thus talking about an intimacy of spiritual relationship and privilege which far surpasses that of a mere citizen or servant, and which reflects something of the relation between God the Father and God the Son. As a result of his sin man loses his rights as a citizen and also as a son, and has the nature of a rebel. He needs a new nature, restoration of his citizenship and restoration of his sonship, hence regeneration, justification and adoption.

The fact that there is a sense in which all of the human family are sons of God by reason of creation must not be overlooked (Acts 17:25–29; Heb. 12:9; James 1:18). Still, it must not be overplayed, as it is in that form of theology which supposes that our creaturehood is the guarantee of our adoption into God's family. 'To substitute the message of God's universal fatherhood for that which is constituted by redemption and adoption is to annul the gospel; it means the degradation of this highest and richest of relationships to the level of that relationship which all men sustain to God by creation. In a word, it is to deprive the gospel of its redemptive meaning.'[1]

The term 'adoption' is applied to the present position of the believers in Romans 8:15, Gal. 4:5 and Eph. 1:5. It implies that since the fall we are not sons of God in a proper sense and that we become so by an act with some analogy to what is involved in human adoption, that is, an act of transfer. So adoption is a legal act or declaration by God as is justification, and cannot be separated from it. It is the justified who are adopted. But if justification and adoption are closely related, they ought also to be clearly distinguished if we would have the fullest appreciation of God's grace toward us.

Regeneration (the new birth) implants a new heart and disposition appropriate for the child of God but it does not restore rights. Since justification deals with sin and righteousness, and adoption deals with slavery and sonship, 'justification recovers his lost citizenship; adoption

1. John Murray, *Redemption Accomplished and Applied* (Banner of Truth, 1961), 135–136.

recovers his lost sonship' (R.A.Webb). Scripture teaches that this right of adoption is received by those who believe (John 1:12) hence it is distinct from the new birth. It is the reinstatement of a lost sonship, so that we can call God our Father again, and it is based on the ground of Christ's obedience as the incarnate Son. Of course, the eternal Sonship of Jesus Christ is unique and we can never share it. However, as the incarnate Son of God, Jesus learned obedience through the things he suffered (Heb. 5:8). Adoption is based on this obedience, and secures a church of sons not merely of servants (Heb. 2:10).

Romans 8:23 speaks of our adoption as sons taking place at the resurrection of the body. This is best understood as a future public acknowledgment of the present reality and may have a parallel in Roman adoption practice in which the legal adoption in private was later declared in a public ceremony.

The logical order in the chain of salvation is: regeneration, faith, justification, adoption, sanctification, glorification. In the gospel we do not call upon men to regenerate themselves, but we assure them of the blessings promised to all who believe, blessings which include adoption.

'How great is the love the Father has bestowed upon us, that we should be called children of God! And that is what we are!' (I John 3:1). God regenerates by his Spirit, declares us justified through faith, and declares us his children. Accordingly, he fulfils the duties of a father (gives us his name, pities, protects, provides and chastens) and enables us to fulfil the duties of children by conferring the spirit of adoption so that we draw near with boldness and have grace to use the promises.

THOUGHTS FROM OTHER MINDS

'It is an exhibition of unspeakable love for God to bring back man to himself a disobedient and run-away slave, but grace is magnified upon grace, and love is laid over upon love with more than a threefold thickness, when man as the child of sin and banishment is translated from the kingdom of Satan into the family of God's dear Son and made an heir to a glory incorruptible, undefiled and that fades not away. The grace of Adoption deserves to be richly magnified by all those who glory in the achievements of divine grace.'

R. A. Webb (1856–1919)[2]

FOR DISCUSSION

1. 'I believe in the Fatherhood of God and the brotherhood of man.' What truth and what error may be involved in this statement?
2. Discuss the meaning of Romans 8:16–17.

---

2. *Christian Salvation: Its Doctrine and Experience* (Presbyterian Committee of Publication, 1921), 405.

CHAPTER 13
SANCTIFICATION

ANALYSIS *WCF 13:1–3*

1. Sanctification described

a. its subjects
b. its nature
  - definitive — in regeneration
  - progressive — in the course of the Christian life
c. its basis
d. its means
e. its necessity

2. The constant conflict in this life

3. The aim and goal of sanctification

13.1 Sanctification described

Those who are effectively called and regenerated thereby have a new heart and a new spirit created in them. They are further sanctified, actually and personally, through the virtue of Christ's death and resurrection[1] and by his word and Spirit dwelling in them.[2] Sin's mastery over them is completely broken,[3] the evil desires to which it gives rise are more and more weakened and put to death,[4] and they are more and more stimulated and strengthened in all saving graces[5] for the practice of true holiness, without which no one shall see the Lord.[6]

1. 1 Cor. 6:11; Acts 20:32; Phil. 3:10; Rom. 6:5,6.
2. John 17:17; Eph. 5:26; 2 Thess. 2:13. 3. Rom. 6:6,14.
4. Gal. 5:24; Rom. 8:13. 5. Col. 1:11; Eph. 3:16–19. 6. 2 Cor. 7:1; Heb. 12:14.

While sanctification is an inevitable accompaniment of justification, and logically follows it, sanctification begins in regeneration hence the subjects of sanctification are described as 'the effectively called and regenerated'. This reminds us that sanctification begins in a new creation, and initiates the change of which progressive sanctification is the development. Hence

Paul's insistence that those united to Christ cannot go on in sin: 'How shall we who died to sin still live in it?' (Rom. 6:2).

13.2 Constant conflict in this life

This sanctification extends to every part of the person,[7] yet remains incomplete in this life. Some remnants of corruption still remain in every part[8] causing within the person a continual and irreconcilable war, the flesh opposing the Spirit, and the Spirit opposing the flesh.[9]

7. 1 Thess. 5:23.
8. 1 Jn. 1:10; Rom. 7:18,23; Phil. 3:12.
9. Gal. 5:17; 1 Pet. 2:11.

Sanctification touches every part of our life—mind, heart and will—but finds every part of our life has some remnants of corruption. As a result there is a constant struggle. However, there is a difference between the remnant of sin and the reign of sin. Sin does not reign nor are we to allow it to do so. Sanctification is not a matter of 'letting go and letting God' but it is a matter of engaging in the good fight of faith.

13.3 The aim and goal of sanctification

Although in this war the remaining corruption may strongly prevail for a time,[10] the new nature overcomes through the continual supply of strength from the sanctifying Spirit of Christ.[11] And so the saints grow in grace,[12] advancing constantly in holiness in the fear of God.[13]

10. Rom. 7:23.
11. Rom. 6:14; 1 Jn. 5:4; Eph. 4:15,16.
12. 2 Pet. 3:18; 2 Cor. 3:18.
13. 2 Cor. 7:1.

The believer is able to engage in this struggle with confidence as a result of his position in Christ as dead to sin but alive to God. He is constantly to appreciate this and prosecute the war by mortification of sin and growth in holiness. The role of the Scriptures, prayer and worship are important (Romans 12:1–2; Heb. 10:25) and so is disciplined living so that bad habits are replaced by good ones, faith working by obedience to the directions of God's word. A very large part of the New Testament consists of exhortations and directives to believers with a view to furthering their sanctification. The outcome is beyond doubt. [The 1646 text reads: 'the regenerate *part* doth overcome' for 'the new nature overcomes,' a slightly ambiguous and less than happy expression for the Christian's growth in holiness given that a new heart has been given to him (WCF 13:1).]

Perfectionism, in the sense that a person can in this life attain to what God requires, confuses several things. Believers are saved from sin but not yet saved from sinning. Perfectionism requires the redefinition of sin so as to exclude the motivation for actions and the evil desires of our hearts. In this sense it breeds complacency and hypocrisy, but it also furthers legalism (the wrong use of the law) since the concentration is on outward things. Entire sanctification is not a crisis experience by which inbred sin is cleansed away but it is the consummation of a process rooted in a radical break with sin at conversion. Perhaps the failure to emphasise the radical break with sin involved in any real conversion contributed by way of reaction to the erroneous perfectionist views of holiness churches in the older Methodist tradition. But perfectionism remains unbiblical and harmful in its consequences. Strikingly, its great advocate, **John Wesley** (1702–91), never claimed the experience. It is alarming that so many lesser lights do.

THOUGHTS FROM OTHER MINDS

'It is a fact too frequently overlooked that in the New Testament the most characteristic terms that refer to sanctification are used, not of a process, but of a once-for-all definitive act. . . . When a person dies he is no longer active in the sphere or realm or relation in reference to which he has died. . . . In accord with this analogy, the person who lives in sin, or to sin, lives and acts in the realm of sin—it is the sphere of his life and activity. And the person who died to sin no longer lives in that sphere. His tie with it has been broken, and he has been translated into another realm.'

John Murray (1898–1975)[1]

'If the old man is considered an inescapable part of me, I then have a handy, built-in excuse for sinning. Whenever I do something wrong, I can always say, "Oh, I can't help doing that; you see, that's the old man in me." But this kind of reasoning is precisely what the Bible warns us against. The old man is the old self that I repudiated when I became a Christian. I am now a new person in Christ, who has voluntarily adopted a new life-style. When I therefore slip back into an old-man way of living, I have no excuse. All I can do is confess that I did wrong, and to try again in the strength of the Spirit to live in accordance with my real self. Holding on to the positive self-image the Bible prescribes, therefore, should be a deterrent to slipping back into wrong ways of living.'

A. A. Hoekema (1913–1988)[2]

FOR DISCUSSION

1. Note 1 John 3:6,9 and compare with 1 John 1:8 & 3:3. How are these two aspects to be reconciled? Similarly Romans 6 and Romans 8:13.
2. Is effort on the part of the believer needed for progress in sanctification?
3. What is the consequence of an exaggerated emphasis on justification compared to sanctification, and vice versa?

1. *Collected Writings of John Murray: Systematic Theology*, 277, 279.
2. *The Christian Looks at Himself* (Eerdmans, 1975), 96.

CHAPTER 14
SAVING FAITH

ANALYSIS *WCF 14:1–3*

1. The origin of faith

a. God's gift to the elect
b. the work of the Holy Spirit
c. the role of the means of grace

2. The working of faith

a. a. it accepts everything that is revealed in Scripture
b. b. it responds appropriately to everything revealed in Scripture
c. c. its principal work is trust in Christ alone for salvation

3. The varying degrees of faith

Faith and repentance could have been taken after WCF 10, which dealt with God's effective call, since they result from it, and faith is the instrumental cause of justification, the topic of WCF 11. But the Confession treats first of the gracious work of God before turning to the human response to grace.

Saving faith (WCF 14) and true repentance (WCF 15) are two sides of the one coin—whoever truly repents believes, and whoever truly believes repents—but are treated in separate chapters for convenience. 'Repentance denotes that aspect of change whereby the soul turns from sin and experiences true abhorrence of it. Faith denotes that aspect of change whereby the soul turns to Christ and experiences true attachment to him.'[1]

1. G. I. Williamson, *The Westminster Confession for Study Classes* (P&R Publishing, 1964), 97.

14.1 The origin of faith

The grace of faith by which the elect are enabled to believe to the saving of their souls[1] is the work of the Spirit of Christ in their hearts.[2] Normally it is accomplished by the ministry of the word of God.[3] It is also increased and strengthened by the word, by the administration of the sacraments and by prayer.[4]

1. Heb. 10:39.
2. 2 Cor. 4:13; Eph. 1:17–19; Eph. 2:8.
3. Rom. 10:14,17.
4. 1 Pet. 2:2; Acts 20:32; Rom. 4:11; Luke 17:5; Rom. 1:16,17.

Faith is a grace, that is, a divine gift to the elect, by which they lay hold of salvation. Faith does not secure election but is a fruit of it. In the case of those who have the faculties to hear the external call the Spirit of God uses the word of God in working this faith. It continues to be strengthened by the means of grace blessed by the Spirit of God.

There are varieties of faith other than saving faith. Traditional faith or historical faith are all very well but as they do not appropriate Christ as Saviour so they cannot save. Faith is not mere assent but it is belief and commitment wrought by a supernatural agency (cf. WCF 1:1).

14.2 The working of faith

By this faith a Christian believes everything to be true that is revealed in the word because of the authority of God who speaks in it.[5] He responds appropriately to each particular passage: he gives obedience to the commands,[6] trembles at the threatenings,[7] and embraces the promises of God concerning this life and that which is to come.[8] But the principal acts of saving faith are accepting, receiving and resting upon Christ alone for justification, sanctification and eternal life by virtue of the covenant of grace.[9]

5. John 4:42; 1 Thess. 2:13; 1 Jn. 5:10; Acts 24:14.
6. Rom. 16:26.
7. Isa. 66:2.
8. Heb. 11:13; 1 Tim. 4:8.
9. John 1:12; Acts 16:31; Gal. 2:20; Acts 15:11.

Saving faith brings a person to accept, on the ground of the testimony of the Spirit of God, all that God has revealed in the Bible. This testimony is not apart from the objective witness of Scripture, for the testimony of the Spirit is not the communication of new revelation, but the bringing of the individual to accept and embrace already given revelation. So there is the appropriate response to each particular part according to its meaning.

It is important to emphasise that the rational demonstration of the excellencies of Scripture will not itself bring saving conviction that it is God's word (cf. WCF 1:1). The work of the Spirit is indispensable. Scripture is a proper instrument for the Holy Spirit to employ because it is his own production, but it does not have magical or automatic powers. 'The true knowledge of God is gained with a teacher and a grammar, the Holy Spirit and the Sacred Writings.'[2] Similarly, as the testimony of the Spirit is not the communication of facts but the persuasion of truthfulness, it does not mean that questions of language, background, fact and interpretation are communicated by the Spirit.

Saving faith is not simply a matter of understanding certain doctrines. It involves the understanding, the emotions and the will, and brings the sinner to close with Jesus Christ as he is set forth in the Scriptures.

14.3 The varying degrees of faith

Saving faith has different degrees of strength and weakness.[10] Often and in different ways it may be attacked and weakened but it gains the victory.[11] In many believers it develops to attainment of a full assurance through Christ,[12] who is both the author and perfecter of our faith.[13]

10. Heb. 5:13,14; Rom. 4:19,20; Matt. 6:30; Matt. 8:10.
11. Luke 22:31,32; Eph. 6:16; 1 Jn. 5:4-5.
12. Heb. 6:11,12; Heb. 10:22; Col. 2:2.
13. Heb. 12:2.

2. Bernard Ramm, *The Witness of the Spirit* (Eerdmans, 1960), 64.

Faith varies in degree, but it is not the strength of faith but its nature as having Christ as its object that is important. A true saving faith will ultimately progress to victory and full assurance, because he who has begun a good work in us will perfect it.

THOUGHTS FROM OTHER MINDS

'God did not bring forth his word among men for the sake of a momentary display, intending at the coming of his Spirit to abolish it. Rather, he sent down the same Spirit by whose power he had dispensed the word, to complete his work by the efficacious confirmation of the word . . . the children of God . . . know no other Spirit than him who dwelt and spoke in the apostles, and by whose oracles they are continually called to the hearing of the word.'

John Calvin (1509–1564)[3]

'In the phraseology of Scripture faith is not simply an assent of the understanding, but implies an act of volition, accepting the Saviour and relying upon him for salvation. This does not proceed upon any previous knowledge which the sinner has of his election; nor upon any persuasion that Christ died intentionally for him more than for others, for it is impossible to come to a knowledge of these things prior to believing; nor does it proceed upon the persuasion that Christ died equally for all men, and therefore for him in particular; nor upon the perception of any good qualities in himself to distinguish him from others; but it proceeds solely upon the free, unlimited offer and promise of the gospel to the chief of sinners.'

Robert Shaw (1795–1863)[4]

---

3. *Institutes of the Christian Religion*, 1.9.3 (Battles' edition cited).
4. *The Reformed Faith: An Exposition of the Confession of Faith* (1845) on WCF 14:2

FOR DISCUSSION

1. Why cannot saving faith and true repentance exist separately?
2. Consider the parable of the Sower (Matthew 13) as illustrating different responses to the Gospel.

CHAPTER 15
REPENTANCE LEADING TO LIFE

ANALYSIS *WCF 15:1–3*

1. Repentance in relation to faith
- a. an evangelical grace
- b. a sister grace to faith

2. The nature of repentance
- a. a true sense of sin leading to penitence
- b. a grasping of God's mercy in Christ

3–4. The necessity of repentance
- a. is not meritorious means of salvation
- b. is that without which there is no justifying faith
- c. to reject it is to destroy oneself

5–6. The practice of repentance
- a. requires thoroughness: general and particular
- b. requires confession
  - privately to God
  - privately or publicly to other believers
- c. restitution evidences reality
- d. the penitent to be received in love

15.1 Repentance in relation to faith

Repentance leading to life is an evangelical grace.[1] The doctrine of repentance leading to life is to be preached by every minister of the gospel along with the doctrine of faith in Christ.[2]

1. Zech. 12:10; Acts 11:18.
2. Luke 24:47; Mark 1:15; Acts 20:21.

True repentance is not produced merely by the terrors of God's law working on the conscience (as has been held by some) but it is a grace wrought by the gospel and thus involves both the terrors of the law and the persuasions of grace. It should be noted that repentance is not merely a change of mind but it is a change of heart. While repentance is not the instrumental grace of salvation, it is inseparably linked with faith, which is. Hence, repentance is absolutely necessary. A preacher is not to rest content with preaching the necessity of faith without emphasis on the necessity of repentance. Note how Scripture sometimes speaks of the one thing needful to salvation being repentance (eg. Acts 2:38) and at other times faith (eg. Acts 16:31). The weakness of much Christianity is due to weakness in preaching the doctrine of repentance.

15.2 The nature of repentance

By this grace of repentance a sinner sees and feels the danger of his sins and also their filthiness and odiousness as being contrary to the holy nature and righteous law of God. On grasping God's mercy in Christ to the penitent, he so grieves for and hates his sins, that he turns from them all to God,[3] resolving and endeavouring to walk with him in all the ways of his commandments.[4]

3. Ezek. 18:30,31; Ezek. 36:31; Isa. 30:22; Psalm 51:4; Jer 31:18,19; Joel 2:12,13; Amos 5:15; Psalm 119:128; 2 Cor. 7:11.
4. Psalm 119:6,59,106; Luke 1:6; 2 Kings 23:25.

This section shows the two factors involved in true repentance. The actual experience of repentance will vary depending on the temperament of the individual, his course of life—whether marked by many flagrant sins or otherwise—and the clarity of his sense of the sinfulness of sin. The claim that all must experience a crisis conversion is contrary to Scripture and the facts of experience.

15.3 The necessity of repentance

Repentance is not to be regarded as satisfaction for sin in any way or as being a basis for forgiveness.[5] The only basis of forgiveness is God's free grace in Christ.[6] Nevertheless, repentance is so necessary that no sinner may expect forgiveness without it.[7]

5. Ezek. 36:31,32; Ezek. 16:61–63.
6. Hos. 14:2,4; Rom. 3:24; Eph. 1:7.

7. Luke 13:3,5; Acts 17:30,31.

15.4 The necessity of repentance

Even the smallest of sins deserves damnation[8] but there is no sin so great that it will bring damnation on those who truly repent.[9]

8. Rom. 6:23; Rom. 5:12; Matt. 12:36.
9. Isa. 55:7; Rom. 8:1; Isa. 1:16,18.

Repentance does not atone for sin or propitiate God. Rather, it is the path along which God brings his elect to trust in him. None should presume and none should despair on account of his sins. While all manner of sin may be forgiven, persistence in unbelief is a sin not only against the command of God in the Gospel but a sin for which there is no remedy.

15.5 The practice of repentance

No one should be satisfied with a general repentance only, but it is everyone's duty to endeavour to take particular care to repent of his particular sins.[10]

10. Psalm 19:13; Luke 19:8; 1 Tim. 1:13,15.

15.6

It is everyone's duty to make private confession of his sins to God, praying that they may be forgiven.[11] Those who thus confess and pray for forgiveness, forsaking their sins, will find mercy.[12] Similarly, anyone who has wronged his fellow believer or the church of Christ, ought to be willing by a private or public confession and sorrow for his sin, to declare his repentance to those whom he has offended.[13] Following such repentance, those he has wronged are to be reconciled to him and to receive him in love.[14]

11. Psalm 51:4,5,7,9,14; Psalm 32:5,6.
12. Prov. 28:13; 1 Jn. 1:9.
13. Jas 5:16; Luke 17:3,4; Josh. 7:19; Psalm 51.
14. 2 Cor. 2:8.

Too many are content with a general acknowledgment: 'I don't claim to be perfect; I've done some wrong things in my time.' This is inadequate for it has the implication that I am not so bad after all, and that I think God will accept me on that ground. True repentance leads us to recognise the basic corruption of our nature and the necessity of re-creative grace (Psalm 51:5,10). 'True repentance is no mere external thing. It does not essentially consist in lopping off, but in rooting out; not in reforming the sinful life, but in removing the sinful heart. Thoroughness in repentance, however, can only follow that hatred of the sinful principle which renders one jealous of every single manifestation thereof.' (John Macpherson) The recognition of particular sins and repentance of them will teach us humility and lead to dependence on God's grace.

All sins need appropriate confession. 'Forgive us our trespasses as we forgive those who trespass against us' is a prayer applicable to the whole course of a Christian's life. The Church of Rome teaches the necessity of regular confession to one of her priests. The Bible teaches confession to God through Jesus Christ our great High Priest, and confession to others in a public or private way depending on the circumstances. Those believers who have been wronged by our sins are bound to receive us in love when the wrong is repented of and that loving reception is itself a factor in furthering our sanctification. Genuine repentance is shown by appropriate restitution.

THOUGHTS FROM OTHER MINDS

'But the true conversion and repentance does not consist of such a sorrow which regrets the consequences of sins but consists rather of an inner breaking of the heart (Psalm 51:19 and Acts 3:37), or a grief because of sin itself, because it is in conflict with God's will and provokes his wrath, and of a sincere remorse and a hating and fleeing of sin. Such repentance does not come up out of the old but out of the new man. It assumes a saving faith and is the fruit of such faith. It is a grief which God wills and which God works and its bearings are towards God, and it brings about a repentance not to be repented of (2 Cor. 7:10). When the lost son has come to his senses, and concludes to return home, he says: I will arise and go to my Father, and I will say to him, Father, I have sinned against heaven and before thee (Luke 15:18). He takes the name of Father upon his lips even though he is still far from him. He dares to go to the Father and confess his sins before his face because in the depths of his heart he believes that the Father is his Father. We should not dare to turn around towards God if we did not trust inwardly in our souls through the Holy Spirit that as a Father he will accept our confession of sins and forgive us.'

Herman Bavinck (1854–1921)[1]

FOR DISCUSSION

1. What is the difference between true repentance and 'doing penance'?
2. Consider Zacchaeus as an example of repentance (Luke 19:1–10).
3. What estimate would you form of Saul's repentance (1 Sam. 15)?
4. Psalm 51 is the record of a backslidden believer's repentance. What did he learn through the experience?

---

1. *Our Reasonable Faith*, trans. Henry Zylstra (Baker, 1956), 437.

CHAPTER 16
GOOD WORKS

ANALYSIS ***WCF 16:1–3***

1. Good works defined

2. The place and value of good works

3–5. Praise for good works

6. God's acceptance of good works

7. The works of unbelievers

16.1 Good works defined

Good works are only those which God has commanded in his holy word.[1] They do not include works without the warrant of the word of God which are of human invention, whether arising from blind zeal or from a claim of good intentions.[2]

1. Mic. 6:8; Rom. 12:2; Heb. 13:21.
2. Matt. 15:9; Isa. 29:13; 1 Pet. 1:18; Rom. 10:2; Jn 16:2; 1 Sam. 15:21–23.

Saul of Tarsus thought he was serving God when he persecuted the early Christians, and multitudes have grievously sinned by mistaking a prejudiced understanding of the Scriptures for the truth. One sees it in the traditions the Pharisees laid upon the people, and the same feature has infected Christendom to a marked degree. Others suppose that what they consider to be a good intention is sufficient to render an act good in God's sight. But only what is required by God is truly good before him.

16.2 The place and value of good works

Good works done in obedience to God's commandments are the fruits and evidences of a true and living faith.[3] By means of them believers show their thankfulness,[4] strengthen their assurance of salvation,[5] edify their fellow believers,[6] adorn the profession of the gospel,[7] deprive their opponents of arguments against it,8 and glorify God.[9] It is God who has made believers what they are, creating them in Christ Jesus with a view to good works,[10] so that, bringing forth fruit that evidences holiness, they may have its outcome, eternal life.[11]

3. James 2:18,22. 4. Psalm 116:12,13; 1 Pet. 2:9. 5. 1 Jn. 2:3,5; 2 Pet. 1:5–10. 6. 2 Cor. 9:2; Matt. 5:16. 7. Titus 2:5,9–12; 1 Tim. 6:1. 8. 1 Pet. 2:15. 9. 1 Pet. 2:12; Phil. 1:11; John 15:8. 10. Eph. 2:10. 11. Rom. 6:22.

All who take the name Christian (except antinomians) believe in the necessity of good works but not all put them in the right place. Good works are fruits of a right relationship not means of establishing it. Their uses are here helpfully stated.

16.3 Praise for good works

The ability of believers to do good works is not at all from themselves, but entirely from the Spirit of Christ.[12] In addition to the graces they have already received from him, they need the Holy Spirit's actual influence to work in them the will and ability to do the works that please God.[13] Yet they are not on this account to grow careless as if they were not bound to perform any duty without a special leading of the Spirit, but they ought to be diligent in stirring up the grace of God in them.[14]

12. Jn 15:4-5; Ezek. 36:26,27.
13. Phil. 2:13; Phil. 4:13; 2 Cor.3:5.
14. Phil. 2:12; Heb. 6:11,12; 2 Pet. 1:3,5,10,11; Isa. 64:7; 2 Tim. 1:6; Acts 26:6,7; Jude 20,21.

16.4

Those believers who attain to the greatest heights of obedience possible in this life are not able to go beyond what is necessary and do more than God requires; in fact, they fall short of much that they are duty bound to do.[15]

15. Luke 17:10; Neh. 13:22; Job 9:2,3; Gal. 5:17.

16.5

We cannot by our best works merit forgiveness of sin or eternal life at the hand of God. This is so because of the great disproportion between our best works and the glory to come. In addition, because of the infinite distance between us and God, our best works can neither profit God nor pay the debt of our former sins,[16] for when we have done all we can we have only done our duty and are unprofitable servants.[17] Moreover, the goodness in our best works comes from God's Spirit, not from us,[18] while the good works done by us are defiled and mixed with so much weakness and imperfection that they cannot meet the searching standard of God's judgment.[19]

16. Rom. 3:20; Rom. 4:2,4,6; Eph. 2:8,9; Titus 3:5–7; Rom. 8:18; Psalm 16:2; Job 22:2,3; Job 35:7,8.
17. Luke 17:10. 18. Gal. 5:22,23.
19. Isa. 64:6; Gal. 5:17; Rom. 7:15,18; Psalm 143:2; 130:3.

These sections show that whatever good believers are enabled to do all praise belongs to God. It is the Spirit who empowers believers (section 3) yet remaining sin means their works are imperfect in this life (section 4). These two points are repeated in Section 5. Section 4 has in view the treasury of merit teaching of the Church of Rome, which led to the dispensing of indulgences. But no believer can do more than is required and there is no scriptural authority for the notion of a store of surplus merit on which weaker believers may draw to make up their deficiencies. Further, the idea that the duties of everyday life are less worthy than the duty of fulfilling a monastic vow voluntarily taken is also unscriptural. It already presupposes the erroneous idea that it is possible to do more than is required.

16.6 God's acceptance of good works

Nevertheless, since the persons of believers are accepted through Christ, their good works also are accepted in him.[20] It is not that they are in this life completely without blame and beyond reproof in God's sight,[21] but that God, looking on them in his Son, is pleased to accept and reward that which is sincerely done, although accompanied by many weaknesses and imperfections.[22]

20. Eph. 1:6; 1 Pet. 2:5; Exod. 28:38; Gen. 4:4 with Heb. 11:4.
21. Job 9:20; Psalm 143:2.
22. Heb. 13:20,21; 2 Cor. 8:12; Heb. 6:10; Matt. 25:21,23.

The good works of believers are accepted because they themselves have been accepted in and through Christ.

16.7 The works of unbelievers

Unregenerate persons may do things that God commands and that are useful to themselves and others.[23] However, these things are sinful because they do not come from a heart purified by faith,[24] are not done in a right manner as prescribed in the word,[25] nor are directed to the right end of glorifying God.[26] Such works can neither please God nor make a person fit to receive grace from God.[27] Yet neglecting to do what God commands is even more sinful and displeasing to God.[28]

23. 2 Kings 10:30,31; 1 Kings 21:27,29; Phil. 1:15,16,18.
24. Gen. 4:5 with Heb. 11:4; Heb. 11:6. 25. 1 Cor. 13:3; Isa. 1:12.
26. Matt. 6:2,5,16.
27. Hag. 2:14; Titus 1:15; Amos 5:21,22; Hos. 1:4; Rom. 9:16; Titus 3:5.
28. Psalm 14:4; Psalm 36:3; Job 21:14,15; Matt. 25:41–43,45; Matt. 23:23.

All unregenerate persons are sinful before God: 'those who are in the flesh *cannot* please God' (Rom. 8:8) and 'without faith it is impossible to please God' (Heb. 11:6). They may do things that are good as far as the matter goes but lack those things which make their deeds good and acceptable in God's sight. But as some sins are more serious than others, so neglecting duties on the plea that one cannot do them in a manner acceptable to God is more sinful.

THOUGHTS FROM OTHER MINDS

'Just as God the Creator continues in providence to uphold and govern his creation, so does God the Spirit continue to strengthen and direct His new creation in its spiritual course. He who will daily accomplish good works before God, must have his inward man renewed day by day. Dependence on the Spirit, however, must not be made an excuse for sloth.... He who is faithful in little, will have ampler opportunities given, and will be fitted for showing his faithfulness in much. Those who honestly address themselves to the discharge of any duty, not sparing themselves any more than if all had to be done by them, and yet humbly and heartily acknowledging before God that only his Spirit's power can secure success, will have the spiritual influence bestowed if the work is for God's glory and should be done by them.'

John Macpherson (1847–1902)[1]

FOR DISCUSSION

1. Discuss why Abel's offering was acceptable but Cain's was not (Genesis 4:2ff cf. Heb. 11:4).
2. Is a Christian to wait for a special impression on his heart before performing a duty?

1. *The Confession of Faith*, 106

CHAPTER 17
THE PERSEVERANCE OF THE SAINTS

ANALYSIS *WCF 17:1–3*

1. The fact of endurance

2. The grounds of endurance

3. The difficulties along the way

17.1 The fact of endurance

Those whom God has accepted in his Beloved Son and effectively called and sanctified by his Spirit can never totally or finally fall out of the state of grace, but shall certainly persevere in that state to the end and be eternally saved.[1]

1. Phil. 1:6; 2 Pet. 1:10; John 10:28,29; 1 Jn. 3:9; 1 Pet. 1:5,9.

Since salvation is of the Lord and since believers have been brought into a state of grace, their endurance in it to the end is certain (compare also WCF 11:5 and 13:3). This does not mean they cannot stumble or backslide (compare Section 3) but only that they cannot finally fall away. 'The saint may fall down, but he does not fall out.' (J. B. Green) Notice that it is not all who profess to be Christians, but those who are truly so, who are said to persevere.

17.2 The grounds of endurance

This perseverance of the saints does not depend on their own free will, but on the unchangeable decree of election flowing from the free and unchangeable love of God the Father;[2] on the powerful operation of the merit and intercession of Jesus Christ;[3] on the indwelling of the Spirit and of the life of God within them;[4] and on the nature of the covenant of grace.[5] These grounds provide the certainty and infallibility of the perseverance of the saints.[6]

2. 2 Tim 2:18,19; Jer. 31:3.
3. Heb. 10:10,14; 13:20,21; Heb. 9:12–15; Rom. 8:33–39; John 17:11,24; Luke 22:32; Heb. 7:25.
4. John 14:16,17; 1 Jn. 2:27; 1 Jn. 3:9.
5. Jer. 32:40.
6. John 10:28; 2 Thess. 3:3; 1 Jn. 2:19.

If salvation resulted from an act of 'free will' it could be undone the same way, but since salvation is of the Lord what he purposes he accomplishes. Five reasons for the perseverance of God's people are given: the Father's unchanging and unconditional love for his chosen, Christ's work for them, the Spirit's indwelling, the work of regeneration, and the nature of the covenant of grace in securing these benefits.

17.3 The difficulties along the way

God's people may fall into serious sins,[7] and continue in them for a time.[8] The causes are the temptations of Satan and of the world, the corruption remaining in them, and the neglect of the means provided for their preservation. In this way God's people incur his displeasure[9] and grieve his Holy Spirit.[10] They lose some measure of their graces and comforts,[11] have their hearts hardened[12] and their consciences wounded,[13] hurt and offend others,[14] and bring temporal judgments on themselves.[15]

7. Matt. 26:70,72,74.
8. Psalm 51 title and verse 14.
9. Isa. 64:5,7,9; 2 Sam. 11:27.
10. Eph. 4:30.
11. Psalm 51:8,10,12; Rev. 2:4; Song 5:2–4,6.
12. Isa. 63:17; Mark 6:52; Psalm 95:8 [as substitute for Mark 16:14 in original].
13. Psalm 32:3,4; Psalm 51:8.
14. 2 Sam. 12:14.
15. Psalm 89:31,32; 1 Cor. 11:32.

The world, the flesh and the devil provide sources of temptation. If the means of preservation—such as prayer, Scripture study, public worship, fellowship with other believers, diligence in making one's calling and election sure—are neglected, serious backsliding and bitter fruits will follow. Those professing Christians who live a careless, slothful Christian life, neglecting known duties, are in a serious state. They cannot rightly entertain the hope of salvation while living in such a way, for the grace of perseverance includes the duty of perseverance. If their profession is real they will heed the admonitions of the word of God and so persevere. When Satan whispers: 'If you sin, you can repent,' one may respond in Samuel Waldron's words: 'Yes, and you will, but to truly repent is to vomit up the sin. All the enjoyment of eating the dainty morsel of sin is more than made up for by the miserable nausea and vomiting. There will always be more misery than pleasure in sin for a true Christian.'[1]

THOUGHTS FROM OTHER MINDS

'We must appreciate the lengths and heights to which a temporary faith may carry those who have it. This is brought to our attention to a certain extent in the parable of the sower. Those compared to seed sown on rocky soil received the word with joy and continued in this joyful experience for a season. In terms of the similitude there was the blade and sometimes there may be the ear. There is not only germination; there is also growth. The only defect is that there is never the full corn in the ear. To a greater extent it is brought to our attention in the language of the epistle to the Hebrews when it speaks of those 'who were once enlightened and tasted of the heavenly gift and were made partakers of the Holy Spirit and tasted the good word of God and the powers of the age to come' (Hebrews 6:5–6). It staggers us to think of the terms of this description as applicable to those who may fall away. They advise us however, of forces that

1. Samuel Waldron, *A Modern Exposition of the 1689 Baptist Confession of Faith* (Evangelical Press, 1989), 222.

are operative in the kingdom of God and of the influence of these forces upon those who finally demonstrate that they have not been radically and savingly affected by them. . . . We do not attain to the prize of our high calling of God in Christ Jesus automatically. Perseverance means the engagement of our persons in the most intense and concentrated devotion to those means which Christ has ordained for the achievement of his saving purpose.'

John Murray (1898–1975)[2]

FOR DISCUSSION

1. Can one believe in the perseverance of the saints while rejecting total depravity, unconditional election, definite atonement and unconquerable grace?
2. Contrast the experiences of Judas and Peter (Matt 26:69–27:10) as illustrating the effects of apostasy from a false profession and backsliding from a true profession.

2. *Redemption Accomplished and Applied*, 152–153,155.

CHAPTER 18
ASSURANCE OF GRACE AND SALVATION

ANALYSIS *WCF 18:1–4*
1. The privilege of assurance
2. The nature and basis of assurance
3. The experience of assurance
4. Fluctuation in assurance

18.1 The privilege of assurance

Hypocrites and other unregenerate persons may vainly deceive themselves with false hopes and worldly presumptions that they are in God's favour and in a state of salvation.[1] This hope of theirs will perish.[2] However, those who truly believe in the Lord Jesus, and love him in sincerity, endeavouring to conduct themselves in all good conscience before him, may in this life be certainly assured that they are in a state of grace,[3] and may rejoice in the hope of the glory of God, a hope that will never disappoint them.[4]

1. Job 8:13,14; Mic. 3:11; Deut. 29:19; Jn 8:41.
2. Matt. 7:22,23.
3. 1 Jn. 2:3; 1 Jn. 3:14,18,19,21,24; 1 Jn. 5:13.
4. Rom. 5:2,5.

The possibility of assurance is here affirmed alongside a warning of the possibility of false assurance. True assurance comes in the way of faith in Christ, sincere love to him and attention to the everyday duties of the Christian life, whereas false assurance presumes because it bypasses these essentials. True assurance arises out of faith, and results in assurance that we are saved. The Church of Rome holds that assurance is not generally given to believers but only to select specially holy persons by special revelation. Others neglect the importance of godly living and assert assurance that they belong to Christ as if it is known other than in the way of a faithful walk—by subjective feelings or by head knowledge.

18.2 The nature and basis of assurance

This certainty is not mere conjecture and probability based on a fallible hope,[5] but is an infallible assurance arising from saving faith and based on the divine truth of the promises of salvation,[6] the evidence in our hearts of those graces to which these promises are made,[7] and the testimony of the Spirit of adoption witnessing with our spirits that we are the children of God.[8] The Spirit is the pledge guaranteeing our inheritance, and by him we are sealed for the day of redemption.[9]

5. Heb. 6:11,19. 6. Heb. 6:17,18.
7. 2 Pet. 1:4,5,10,11; 1 Jn. 2:3; 1 Jn. 3:14; 2 Cor. 1:12.
8. Rom. 8:15,16. 9. Eph. 1:13,14; Eph. 4:30; 2 Cor. 1:21,22.

'Assurance of faith' (1646 text) means assurance arising from faith. It is based on the gracious promises of the gospel centred in the person and work of Jesus Christ, the internal evidence that one has believed the gospel (faith, repentance, other graces of the Spirit) and the testimony of the Spirit bearing witness with our spirits.

18.3 The experience of assurance

The relationship of this infallible assurance to the essence of faith is such that a true believer may wait long and contend with many difficulties before he experiences it.[10] However, being enabled by the Spirit to know the things freely given him from God, he may attain to this assurance in the right use of ordinary means without extraordinary revelation.[11] Therefore it is the duty of everyone to be as diligent as possible in making his calling and election sure,[12] so that his heart may be enlarged in peace and joy in the Holy Spirit, in love and thankfulness to God, and in strength and cheerfulness in the duties of obedience.[13] These, and not carelessness, are the natural consequences flowing from assurance of salvation.[14]

10. 1 Jn. 5:13; Isa. 50:10; Mark 9:24; Psalm 88; Psalm 77:1–12.

11. 1 Cor. 2:12; 1 Jn. 4:13; Heb. 6:11–12; Eph. 3:17–19. 12. 2 Pet. 1:10.
13. Rom. 5:1–2,5; Rom. 14:17; Rom. 15:13; Eph. 1:3–4; Psalm 4:6–7; Psalm 119:32.
14. 1 Jn. 2:1–2; Rom. 6:1–2; Titus 2:11–12,14; 2 Cor. 7:1; Rom. 8:1,12; 1 Jn. 3:2–3; Psalm 130:4; 1 Jn. 1:6–7.

The original wording which begins this section reads: *This infallible assurance doth not* so *belong to the essence of faith ...*, and thus seems to leave the much debated question of whether or not assurance is of the essence of faith undecided (but note WLC 81 which states assurance is not of the essence of faith). Assurance can be considered a reflex act of faith, but it is possible to believe without being sure that one believes. This is why Scripture urges us to press on to full assurance. It is to be noted that Calvin and other leading Reformers tended to identify assurance with faith in reaction to the prevalent teaching of the Roman church which denied the possibility of assurance for ordinary Christians. The New Testament picture is generally one where assurance is normal but the pastoral experience of most of the Divines showed them the frequency of lack of assurance in the tempestuous time in which they lived and they framed their comments accordingly.

18.4 Fluctuation in assurance

True believers may have the assurance of their salvation in different ways shaken, diminished or temporarily absent. This may result from carelessness in preserving it, or from falling into some special sin which wounds the conscience and grieves the Spirit, or from some sudden or very strong temptation, or by God's withdrawal of the light of his countenance and allowing even those who fear him to walk in darkness and have no light.[15] Yet true believers are never utterly deprived of the nature which is born of God, the life of faith, the love of Christ and of other believers, or of sincerity of heart and conviction of duty. As a result of the presence of these graces their assurance may in due time be revived through the working of the Spirit,[16] while in the meantime they are kept from utter despair.[17]

15. Song 5:2,3,6; Psalm 51:8,12,14; Eph. 4:30,31; Psalm 77:1–10; Matt. 26:69–72; Psalm 31:22; Psalm 88; Isa. 50:10.
16. 1 Jn. 3:9; Luke 22:32; Job 13:15; Psalm 73:15; Psalm 51:8,12; Isa. 50:10.
17. Mic. 7:7–9; Jer. 32:40; Isa. 54:7–10; Psalm 22:1; Psalm 88.

The presence of sin is the chief factor which takes away the believer's assurance, but there can be the discouragement which follows a testing experience or spiritual and physical exhaustion (cf. Elijah) as well as an unexplained withdrawal of God's comfortable presence.

THOUGHTS FROM OTHER MINDS

'1. It is a mistake to think that every one who is in Christ knows that he is in him; for many are truly gracious, and have a good title to eternal life, who do not know so much, until it is made out afterwards: "These things are written to them that believe, that they may know they have a title to eternal life" (1 John 5:13); that is, that they may know they are believers, and so it is supposed they knew it not before.

2. It is a mistake to think that all who come to the knowledge of their interest in Christ attain an equal certainty about it. One may say, "He is persuaded nothing present or to come can separate him from the love of God" (Rom. 8:38); another comes only this far, "Lord, I believe, help my unbelief." (Mark 9:24)

3. It is a mistake to think that every one who attains a strong persuasion of his interest always holds there; for he who today may say of the Lord, "He is his refuge" (Psalm 91:2) and "his portion" (Psalm 119:57), will at another time say, "He is cut off" (Psalm 31:22), and will ask, "if the truth of God's promise fails for evermore?" (Psalm 77:7–9)

4. It is also a mistake to think that every one who attains a good knowledge of his gracious state can formally answer all objections to the contrary; but yet they may hold fast the conclusion and say, "I know whom I have believed." (2 Tim. 1:12) There are few grounds of the Christian religion of which many people are

so persuaded that they are able to maintain them formally against all arguments brought to the contrary; and yet they may and will hold the conclusion steadfastly and justly; so it is in the case in hand.'

William Guthrie (1620–1665)[1]

FOR DISCUSSION

1. Is assurance normal immediately on one's conversion?
2. What are the proper results flowing from true assurance?
3. Consider the account of Christian losing and finding his Roll in Bunyan's *The Pilgrim's Progress*.

1. *The Christian's Great Interest* (Banner of Truth, 1969), 35–36.

CHAPTER 19
1–4: THE DIVINE LAWS

ANALYSIS *WCF 19:1–4*

1–2. The moral law
- a. its creation origin
- b. its Mosaic repetition

3. Israel's ceremonial law
- a. its purpose and fulfilment

4. The final authority of Scripture
- a. has perished with the theocracy
- b. elements of general equity remain valid

19.1 The moral law

God gave to Adam a law in the form of a covenant of works, by which he bound him and all his posterity to personal, complete, exact and perpetual obedience. God promised life if Adam kept the law and threatened death if he broke it, and gave him power and ability to keep it.[1]

1. Gen. 1:26,27 with Gen. 2:17; Rom. 2:14,15; Rom. 10:5; Rom. 5:12,19; Gal. 3:10,12; Ecc 7:29; Job 28:28.

In WCF 4:2 we saw that our first parents 'had the law of God written in their hearts' and that 'in addition to this law written in their hearts they received a command not to eat of the tree of the knowledge of good and evil.' The relation of the moral law written on the heart at creation to the explicit command about the fruit is this: the former is the precondition for the latter. Our first parents' attitude to the express command concentrates, or brings into focus, their attitude to the former. So the explicit command, which is the point of testing in the covenant, really involves the entire moral law written on Adam's heart from the beginning, hence the statement here, cf. WCF 7.2. Note also the essential identity of this moral law and the Ten Commandments given (see WCF 19:2).

19.2 The moral law

After Adam fell, this law continued to be a perfect rule of righteousness. As such it was given by God on Mount Sinai in ten commandments written on two stone tablets.[2] The first four commandments contain our duty towards God, and the last six contain our duty towards man.[3]

2. James 1:25; James 2:8,10–12; Rom. 13:8–9; Deut. 5:32; Deut. 10:4; Exod. 34:1.
3 Matt. 22:37–40.

The moral law was a rule of judgment by which disobedience was condemned, but it was also a rule of righteousness reflecting the divine requirement. It continues as such for God's people under the covenant of grace (see also WCF 19:6 below). The Mosaic dispensation was a particular administration of the covenant of grace. Its requirements were to be fulfilled in the context of grateful response to the God of salvation who had redeemed them from bondage in Egypt. If we speak of the giving of the Ten Commandments as a republication of the law written on the heart in a form of words appropriate for its recipients—and it is correct to do so—we need to remember the context of redemptive grace in which the giving occurred.

Roman Catholics and Lutherans arrange the commandments by combining the first two and dividing the last one into two (coveting wife and coveting possessions), but the arrangement of the Hebrew Bible is followed by the Confession as also by the Greek Orthodox and by Protestants. (Traditional Jewish interpretation takes the preface as the first commandment as requiring strict monotheism, and combines two and three.) One should not assume from popular representations that four commandments were written on one tablet and six on another. Almost certainly all were written on each tablet, so that two copies existed in line with ancient treaty practice. Further, a neat division between the first four and the last six cannot be made because of the unity of the law—if we offend in one point we are guilty of all. After all, the underlying principle is love to God and our neighbour, the latter flowing from the former (James 2:8–11).

The unique position of the moral law is seen in the fact that: (1) only the Ten Commandments were spoken by God's voice; (2) they alone were accompanied by the shaking of Mount Sinai; (3) they alone were written by his finger; (4) they alone were written on enduring stone tablets rather than merely being written in a book (Deut. 4:10–14; Exod. 24:4) and (5) they alone of the various laws were placed in the ark of the covenant (Deut. 10:5). (6) They formed the introduction to the Mosaic covenant which, in fact, expounds them in a manner appropriate for the people at that time (Deut. 6–26). (7) Of course they were also fully complete, the tablets being written on the front and the back, so that there was no room for other commandments of the same unique kind for there were none (Exod. 32:15), and (8) they were regarded as superior to the ceremonial law (eg. Psalm 51:16–19; Jer 7; Amos 5). (9) It should also be remembered that the greatest commandment, on which depends everything else, is total love for the Lord (Matt 22:37 quoting the exposition of the first commandment in Deut. 6) and also love for one's neighbour—a command which, while explicit in a context of laws of different character, is a necessary corollary to the other given that humans bear the divine likeness (Lev. 19:18 cf. Matt 7:12). Hence, (10) these considerations lead to the common view that the Decalogue is a reflection, in a form suited to the historical situation of Israel, of the moral law, the law of love, written on Adam's heart at his creation.

Although the ten commandments can be distinguished, Christians do not obey them because commanded by Moses, but as they receive them from Christ in the Gospel. For we are not under the covenant given through Moses, but under the new covenant given through Christ. Thus one can readily admit that the law of Moses as a unit is superseded yet highlight the ten commandments as of abiding relevance. This is so, not because they are part of the law of Moses, but because in essence they date from creation, the Lord merely republishing them in a particular context and form through Moses.

19.3 Israel's ceremonial law

As well as this law, commonly called the moral law, God was pleased to give to the people of Israel—as the church in a preparatory stage of development—various ceremonial laws which contained types of things to come. Some of these laws were rites of worship prefiguring Christ, his graces, actions, sufferings and benefits,[4] and others instructed in moral duties.[5] All these ceremonial laws are now discontinued by virtue of the new covenant.[6]

4. Heb. 9; Heb. 10:1; Gal. 4:1–3; Col. 2:17.
5. 1 Cor. 5:7; 2 Cor. 6:17; Jude 23.
6. Col. 2:14,16,17; Dan. 9:27; Eph. 2:15,16.

The ceremonial laws are agreed by all to have been abrogated by the ratification of the new covenant by Christ since the reality of grace shadowed by them has come, as also the fulfilment of truth (John 1:17). Yet there are exceptions to this agreement: classical dispensationalists speak of a restored temple and a revival of the ancient worship of Israel in an earthly millennium to begin at the return of Christ. This is contrary to all right understanding of the covenant of grace and the purpose of God in the choice of Israel. Others accept that Christ fulfilled the ceremonial law yet reintroduce symbolic worship into Christian worship—candles, incense, bowing to the east, sacred buildings, fancy dress, and so on. This seems to reflect a failure in practice to understand the newness that has come in Christ, or else an indifference to the sufficiency of Scripture so that human additions that are unauthorised by God, but considered useful by men, are introduced.

19.4 Israel's judicial laws

God also gave to the people of Israel laws to govern them as a nation and these came to an end with the theocracy. These judicial laws are not obligatory on any other people now except to the extent that general principles of justice and right incorporated in them may require.[7]

7. Exod. 21; Exod. 22:1–29; Gen. 49:10 with 1 Pet. 2:13,14; Matt. 5:17 with Matt. 5:38,39; 1 Cor. 9:8–10.

The civil or judicial laws were given to Israel in her special position as the theocratic nation and reflected the requirement that Israel be a holy people. One might also speak of these laws in their nature and penalties as prefiguring righteousness in Christ, and also the destruction of sin through Christ. At any rate, the civil law of Israel does not bind any other people now, since no earthly nation today is in the same theocratic position as ancient Israel.

The New Testament church is the proper continuation of Israel—not a replacement of Israel, but an expansion of Israel which supersedes the theocracy to establish the 'holy nation' (1 Peter 2:9 cf. Exod. 19:6) among all the nations. From this viewpoint church authorities must take seriously the Old Testament laws, particularly those that were marked by the death penalty or exclusion ('cutting off') from the nation. It would seem that professing believers who commit similar offences today are subject to the equivalent penalty—spiritual death, that is, excommunication if they do not repent (compare the position of the incestuous man at Corinth, I Cor 5:1ff and Lev. 18:8,29).

Civil authorities today, especially those living in the light of special revelation, can learn from the Old Testament judicial laws too. However, the civil ruler today will not apply Mosaic civil laws or penalties because they are prescribed by the Mosaic law, but because he discerns that the law or the penalty reflects a basic principle of justice and right that ought always to be applied in a manner appropriate to a particular society. An obvious example is the law of incest; another is the law of negligence. Some laws will have no civil application today because they were set with the special holiness of theocratic Israel in mind. As to penalties, the emphasis in the law of Moses on restitution rather than incarceration is noteworthy, as is the principle of equality before the law. It is also worthy of note that penalties were not always applied—eg: David's adultery or the sabbath breakers in Nehemiah's day (Exod. 31:14–15; Neh. 13:15–22).

The verses cited by the Confession from Matthew 5 are interesting. Verse 17 reminds us Jesus did not come to destroy the law but to fulfil it, while verses 38–39 refer to turning the other cheek rather than applying the eye for an eye principle of the Mosaic law. In other words the citing of these texts appears to suggest that the 'fulfilment' of the law in this case was by its abrogation and the realisation of its ultimate purpose by the application of the law of forgiveness.[1] One does not need to agree exactly with this interpretation of verses 38–39 to accept the principle behind it.

Paul sees the equity principle in an Old Testament passage forbidding muzzling working oxen, and uses it to exhort the adequate financial support of ministers (1 Cor.9:9–12; 1 Tim. 5:18). Similarly, the use by the Assembly of particular texts in the civil law, particularly in the section on the commandments in the Larger Catechism, shows they distinguished the civil law in the Mosaic code from the principle of equity, fairness or

1. S. B. Ferguson, "An Assembly of Theonomists? The Teaching of the Westminster Divines on the Law of God," in *Theonomy: A Reformed Critique*, eds. W.S. Barker & W.R. Godfrey (Zondervan, 1990), 336.

justice behind it. Note their use (WCF 22.7) of Numbers 30 as proof that vows not according to the word of God are forbidden, when that passage is dealing with the right of a father to cancel the vows of his wife or daughters. They do not follow the law, but they recognize a principle of justice behind it.

The civil ruler will not necessarily find all the answers in the Mosaic legislation. For example, there is no penalty provided for a man having intercourse with a prostitute but the death penalty is prescribed for adultery. Does this mean that a Christian country today should not have laws against prostitution and that it should attach civil penalties to adultery? Among those united in opposing such behaviour opinions vary as to how best to combat these evils. Such differences are found in discussions both before and after the Westminster Confession was adopted, and no doubt will continue.

It should be noted that the Noahic provisions of Genesis 9:6, which include the death penalty for murder, belong to the race as a whole and predate the existence of Israel. It is here and not in the Mosaic legislation that the foundation for capital punishment should be sought. Certainly the tendency to extend such a punishment to a multitude of lesser crimes should be resisted.

THOUGHTS FROM OTHER MINDS

'The Westminster Divines were arguing that the law was judicially outdated. Just as a person would appeal to a court of equity if he believed the common law was not designed for his particular situation, so also the Westminster Divines appealed to general equity because they did not believe that the "common law" of Moses was designed for seventeenth-century England. They presumed that one should not appeal to the civil law of Moses to establish a certain practice for today, unless one could demonstrate that the equity in, under or behind that particular law is an abiding principle for all societies and cultures based upon God's moral law. To put it another way, the judges of Britain, who would be expected to adhere to the Confession of the Churches of England, Ireland and Scotland, were not expected to view the Mosaic law as the common law of the land. Rather, they were to use the Mosaic law as a guideline to train their consciences in principles of justice and equity, where such principles were clearly taught or demonstrated.'

A. Craig Troxel and Peter J. Wallace[2]

FOR DISCUSSION

1. Give grounds for distinguishing the Ten Commandments from the ceremonial and judicial laws of the Old Testament.
2. In what sense do the judicial laws have authority over modern states? What principles of 'general equity', if any, can be found in (a) the distribution of the land among the twelve tribes; (b) the principle of an eye for an eye; and (c) the principle of the tithe.

2. "Men in Combat over the Civil Law: 'General Equity' in WCF 19.4" in *Westminster Theological Journal* 64 (Fall 2002): 313.

CHAPTER 19
5–7: GOD'S MORAL LAW

ANALYSIS *WCF 19:5–7*

5. The moral law's permanence and universality

6. The uses of the moral law

a. a. for all persons
b. b. for believers

7. The harmony of the moral law with grace

19.5 The moral law's permanence and universality

All people at all times, both those who are justified and those who are not, are under binding obligation to obey the moral law.[8] This obligation arises out of its content and also because of the authority of God the Creator, who gave it.[9] In the gospel, Christ in no way lessens this obligation but greatly strengthens it.[10]

8. Rom. 13:8–10; Eph. 6:2; 1 Jn. 2:3,4,7,8.
9. James 2:10,11.
10. Matt. 5:17–19; James 2:8; Rom. 3:31.

The moral law is that which was originally written by the Creator on the human heart, hence the basis of our obligation to obey it is twofold: because God is its author and because of its content. Man as a creature is necessarily subject to his Creator's law, and finds true liberty in conformity to it. Jesus did not come to destroy the law but to fulfil it. The previous section employed Matthew 5:17 in conjunction with other verses to show that some things in the Mosaic law do change. In this section the same text is used to indicate that the moral law does not change but is reinforced by the other changes that Christ brought. Christ does not change the basis of our obligation but he adds the additional reasons which arise from his redeeming love. Thus for example, his *new* commandment: to love one another *as I have loved you* (John 13:34).

19.6 The uses of the moral law

Although true believers are not under the law as a covenant of works by which they are justified or condemned,[11] the law is of great use to them as well as to others.

As a rule of life it informs them of God's will and their duty, and directs and binds them to live accordingly.[12]

It also reveals to them the sinful pollution of their nature, hearts and lives,[13] so that as they examine themselves by the light of the law they may be further convicted of sin, humbled because of it and brought to hate it more,[14] as well as to see more clearly their need of Christ, and the perfection of his obedience.[15]

The law is also useful to the regenerate because, by forbidding sin, it restrains their corruptions,[16] while its threatenings serve to show what even their sins deserve, and what afflictions they may expect for them in this life, even though freed from the curse due for them threatened in the law.[17] Similarly, the promises attached to the law show them God's approval of obedience and the blessings they may expect to follow such obedience[18] These blessings do not accrue to them as their due from the law considered as a covenant of works.[19]

So it follows that a person cannot be said to be under the law rather than under grace merely because he is motivated to obedience by the law's promises, or refrains from evil out of regard to its threatenings.[20]

11. Rom. 6:14; Gal. 2:16; Gal. 3:13; Gal. 4:4,5; Acts 13:39; Rom. 8:1.
12. Rom. 7:12,22,25; Psalm 119:4–6; 1 Cor. 7:19; Gal. 5:14,16,18–23.
13. Rom. 7:7; Rom. 3:20. 14. James 1:23–25; Rom. 7:9,14,24.
15. Gal. 3:24; Rom. 7:24,25; Rom. 8:3,4. 16. James 2:11; Psalm 119:101,104,128.
17. Ezra 9:13,14; Psalm 89:30–34.
18 Lev. 26:1–14 with 2 Cor. 6:16; Eph. 6:2,3; Psalm 37:11 with Matt. 5:5; Psalm 19:11.
19 Gal. 2:16; Luke 17:10.
20 Rom. 6:12,14; 1 Pet. 3:8–12 with Psalm 34:12–16; Heb. 12:28,29.

The Reformed faith holds to the 3-fold use of the moral law: (1) restraining sin in society; (2) to humble, leading to self-knowledge and faith in Christ for justification; (3) to aid believers in inward and outward obedience flowing from free justification in Christ. Luther, with his central concern of a free justification, could be less positive about the third use as he placed more emphasis on the spontaneity of the believer's obedience out of concern to avoid legalism or moralism. Some evangelicals have distinguished between Christ as Saviour and Christ as Lord to the extent of rejecting the law as a rule of life for believers, and the general understanding of this subject is exceedingly poor in most Christian circles.

Unbelievers are under the law as a covenant of works but they, as well as believers, find the law to be a rule of life, a measure of what God requires. The law can be a tutor to teach the things of Christ. In addition, believers find the law of further value in their progress in the Christian life. They find the promises of reward for obedience an encouragement to earnest endeavours through the grace of God through whom they can do all things. The threatenings and attendant chastisements for disobedience enhance their sense of the sinfulness of sin and what it deserves and spur them on in the good fight of faith. The use of threat and reward to encourage a proper response to God's law is not legalism nor is such a motivation inherently sub-Christian for the believer does not seek to be accepted in God's sight on the basis of his own works of faith.

19.7 The harmony of the moral law and grace

The previously mentioned uses of the law are not contrary to the grace of the gospel but are in complete harmony with it,[21] for the Spirit of Christ subdues and enables the will of man to do freely and cheerfully those things, which the will of God, revealed in the law, requires.[22]

21. Gal. 3:21.
22. Ezek. 36:27; Heb. 8:10 with Jer 31:33.

The purpose of Christ's redeeming work is to deliver us from sin and disobedience so that the righteousness of the law might be fulfilled in us through the Spirit (Romans 8:4). Our obedience to the law is imperfect in this life but the believer sees the law as the expression of God's will to which, by God's grace, he now aspires and to which he will be brought to full conformity at the last by that same grace.

THOUGHTS FROM OTHER MINDS

'When men are considered as unregenerate or regenerate, then law and gospel must be understood as opposites; when men are considered as regenerate, then the law must be subordinated to the gospel.

Such is the opposition indicated by the apostle: 'You are not under the law but under grace' (Rom. 6:14). Here he indicates the state of man before and after regeneration. Unfaithful man is said to be 'under law' because (1) he is subject to the curse of the law; (2) he is subject to the severity of the law, by which it demands perfect righteousness and obedience; and (3) because he looks for occasion of sinning on account of law, according to the proverb: 'We always seek what is forbidden, and we desire that which we have been denied' (see Rom. 7:8).

Faithful man is said to be under grace because (1) he has been freed from the curse of the law; (2) he has been freed from the severity of the law and the demand for perfect righteousness, since Christ has discharged it; and (3) because he has been freed from sin ruling in him, so that he no longer desires sin on account of the law, but rather begins to do what the law requires, through the Holy Spirit and because of his gratitude.

The law is presented as subordinate to the gospel when Christ is called the end of the law: (Rom. 10:4); and the law a 'tutor unto Christ' (Gal. 3:24), and when the law is said not to be opposed to him who does the works of the Spirit (Gal. 5:22–23). Indeed, the gospel gives to faithful man, in Christ, all the righteousness that the law requires. And although we are not able to satisfy the law in this life, yet the reborn, through the gift of sanctification, begin to do so.'

Johannes Wollebius (1586–1629)[1]

FOR DISCUSSION

1. Expound the meaning of the text, 'Sin shall not have dominion over you for you are not under law but under grace.' (Romans 6:14)
2. Is a Christian under less obligation to keep God's law or is the obligation greater? Give reasons for your answer.

1. *Compendium Theologiae Christianae* (1626). This quotation is from the translation in J. W. Beardslee, trans. and ed. *Reformed Dogmatics* (Baker, 1965), 86.

CHAPTER 20
CHRISTIAN LIBERTY AND LIBERTY OF CONSCIENCE

ANALYSIS *WCF 20:1–4*

1. Christian liberty defined
- a. under the gospel (New Testament)
    - freedom from guilt, condemnation & curse
    - free access to God and child-like obedience
- b. under the law (Old Testament)
    - identity with gospel freedom
    - yet a relative restriction

2. Liberty of conscience defined
- a. to whom obliged
    - God alone — the Lord of the conscience
- b. to what beliefs/practices not obliged by conscience
    - anything contrary to Scripture
    - anything additional to Scripture in matters of faith/worship
- c. responsibilities
    - to ensure Scripture informs the conscience
    - to reject coercion of the conscience

3–4. The perversion of Christian liberty
- a. in private life: liberty is not licentiousness
- b. in public life: liberty is not individualism

20.1 Christian liberty defined

The liberty which Christ has purchased for believers under the gospel comprises freedom from the guilt of sin, the condemning wrath of God and the curse of the moral law.[1] It includes deliverance from this present evil world, from bondage to Satan and from sin's domination,[2] as well as from the evil of afflictions, the sting of death, the victory of the grave, and everlasting damnation.[3] It also includes free access to God,[4] and the giving of obedience to him out of childlike love and readiness rather than out of slavish fear.[5] All of these blessings were also enjoyed by believers during Old Testament times,[6] but in the New Testament dispensation the liberty of Christians is extended since they are freed from the yoke of the ceremonial law to which the Jewish Church was subjected,[7] they have greater boldness of access to the throne of grace,[8] and through the Spirit of God who brings freedom they have fuller gifts than believers normally enjoyed previously.[9]

1. Titus 2:14; 1 Thess. 1:10; Gal. 3:13.
2. Gal. 1:4; Col. 1:13; Acts 26:18; Rom. 6:14.
3. Rom. 8:28; Psalm 119:71; 1 Cor. 15:54-57; Rom. 8:1. 4. Rom. 5:1,2.
5. Rom. 8:14,15; 1 Jn. 4:18. 6. Gal. 3:9,14
7. Gal. 4:1–3,6–7; 5:1; Acts 15:10–11.
8. Heb. 4:14–16; 10:19–22. 9. Jn 7:38–39; 2 Cor. 3:13,17–18.

This section explains what Christian liberty is, shows that it is common to all believers, but that the consciousness of it was not in general so clear in the Old Testament as it is under the new covenant.

20.2 Liberty of conscience defined

God alone is Lord of the conscience.[10] He has left it free from all doctrines or human commandments which are contrary to his word, or which, if matters of faith or worship, are additional to that word.[11] One who believes such doctrines or obeys such commands for the sake of conscience betrays true liberty of conscience.[12] Moreover, to require an unquestioning faith in something not established out of the word of God, or to require total and blind obedience, is destructive of liberty of conscience and the proper use of reason as well.[13]

10. James 4:12; Rom. 14:4.
11. Acts 4:19; Acts 5:29; 1 Cor. 7:23; Matt. 23:8–10; 2 Cor. 1:24; Matt. 15:9.
12. Col. 2:20,22,23; Gal. 1:10; Gal. 2:4,5; Gal. 5:1.
13. Rom. 10:17; Rom. 14:23; Isa. 8:20; Acts 17:11; Jn 4:22; Hos. 5:11; Rev. 13:12,16,17; Jer 8:9.

God speaking in his word is the only rule for the human conscience. God's truth is to be acknowledged and tyranny has no place, whether the absolutism of the Stuart dynasty or the tyranny of 51%. The individual conscience cannot be surrendered to the church, or to any man or organisation. Here is the charter of true freedom.

Many editions of the Confession perpetuate a typographical error in that the word *in* replaces *if* in the statement of the original: '. . . and has left it free from the doctrines and commandments of men which are in any thing contrary to his word; or beside it, *if* matters of faith or worship.' The error obscures the fact that the conscience is *never* bound to anything *contrary* to God's word, and in matters of faith or worship is not bound to anything *additional* to what is revealed in Scripture (as explained in WCF 1:6). The result of the application of this 'regulative principle' to matters of faith and worship is simply to exclude all the additions of the ages and bring us back to apostolic standards. It also places limits on the rights of civil government. A civil government may require us to use seat belts in our cars, contribute to a Pension Fund or pay a particular tax. These are not matters of faith or worship, nor are they contrary to Scripture. Such laws should therefore be obeyed. Similarly, restrictions on public gatherings including worship services because of the need to limit the spread of infectious disease are in principle acceptable (cf. Lev. 13).

20.3 The perversion of Christian liberty — private life

Those who practise any sin or cherish any lust in the name of Christian liberty destroy the purpose of Christian liberty, namely, that being delivered out of the hands of our enemies, we might serve the Lord without fear, in holiness and righteousness before him, all the days of our life.[14]

14. Gal. 5:13; 1 Pet. 2:16; 2 Pet. 2:19; Jn 8:34; Luke 1:74,75

Freedom is not licence; spiritual freedom is not a throwing off of all constraint. History is littered with examples of those who have made this mistake. Nor does spiritual freedom mean that I must stop doing whatever someone, somewhere, particularly a fellow Christian, believes to be wrong. I must not use my liberty as a cover for evil doings, but if all other things are permissible not all are beneficial and not all are constructive (1 Cor.10:23). Again, 'one man's faith allows him to eat everything, but another man, whose faith is weak, eats only vegetables.

The man who eats everything must not look down on him who does not, and the man who does not eat everything must not condemn the man who does' (Rom. 14:2–3). 'God alone is Lord of the conscience ...'

20.4 The perversion of Christian liberty — public life

The authorities ordained by God and the liberty Christ has purchased are not intended by God to destroy but mutually to uphold and preserve one another. Those who in the name of Christian liberty oppose any lawful civil or ecclesiastical power or the lawful exercise of it, resist the ordinance of God.[15] Anyone who publishes opinions or maintains practices that are contrary to the common conscience of humanity or to the known principles of Christianity concerning faith, worship or conduct, or contrary to genuine godliness, may lawfully be called to account,[16] and subjected to church discipline, and to the power of the civil authorities. The same applies also to erroneous opinions or practices that, either of themselves or in the manner of publishing or maintaining them, are destructive to the external peace and order which Christ has established in the church.[17*]

15. Matt. 12:25; 1 Pet. 2:13,14,16; Rom. 13:1–8; Heb. 13:17.
16. Rom. 1:32 with 1 Cor. 5:1,5,11,13; 2 Jn. 10,11 & 2 Thess. 3:14 & 1 Tim. 6:3–5 & Titus 1:10,11,13 & Titus 3:10 with Matt. 18:15–17. 1 Tim. 1:19,20; Rev. 2:2,14,15,20; Rev. 3:9.
17. Deut. 13:6–12; Rom. 13:3,4 with 2 Jn. 10,11; Ezra 7:23,25–28; Rev. 17:12,16,17; Neh. 13:15,17,21,22,25,30; 2 Kings 23:5,6,9,20,21; 2 Chron.34:33; 2 Chron.15:12,13,16; Dan. 3:29; 1 Tim. 2:2; Isa. 49:23; Zech. 13:2,3.

* In affirming its continued adherence to the teaching of the Confession, the 1846 *General Assembly of the Free Church of Scotland* declared that a fair interpretation of the Confession did not favour intolerance or persecution. [See below also the note on WCF 23.3]

True liberty is the liberty to do what is right. As a citizen of the state and as a church member, the Christian has responsibilities. If he misuses his liberty he is subject to appropriate action from one or both of these institutions. The American editions of the Confession usually exclude the right of the civil authorities to censure religious opinions and practices resulting from them, an amendment dating from qualifications made by the Synod of Philadelphia in September 1729. However, it should be noted that the Confession does not regard the mere holding of an heretical opinion as censurable, although under the English *Court of High Commission* such was the case up to 1640.

It is the public propagation of deviations from fundamental matters of the faith, as well as divisive and disorderly behaviour arising from the advocacy of such errors, which a state living under the light of revelation is obliged to deal with in a way appropriate in the circumstances if it would be, as it should be, a Christian nation. Of course, erroneous opinions may often be ignored, and left to be combated by the spiritual means the church possesses, but there may be situations where the free expression of views must be restricted—particularly when gross ignorance prevails, crimes are committed, or actions subversive of good order occur. WCF 23:3 envisages that heresy is dealt with by the church. The civil power is merely to encourage the church to do its duty.

It is important to note that liberty as a citizen is not founded upon an abstract ground, such as is commonly advocated by modern liberal democratic states. This kind of liberty is based in the will of man rather than the word of God and leads to all manner of evils being propagated under the guise of 'freedom of religious expression' or as a result of the tyranny of 51%. The previous chapter of the Confession has reminded us that all owe allegiance to the moral law, and that responsibility is not diminished when a person exercises civil office. Of course the church and the state are not to be subjected to each other, but they ought to co-operate in a manner which recognises the autonomy of each, because they aim at the same end, the glory of God and the good of man, although using different means. What God's word says is the proper basis for a free society. It will be found to secure true liberty where applied by leaders of wisdom and integrity.

The declaration noted above by the Free Church of Scotland is to be taken as a rejection of the interpretation of this section of the Confession that alleges that the involvement of the state in matters concerning religion is *ipso facto* contrary to liberty of conscience and the right of private judgment, and necessarily of a persecuting, coercive character. This was the interpretation argued by the extreme 'Voluntaries' in Scotland in the 19th century who were among the forerunners of the secular/atheistic state ideal which has afflicted much modern life. But it is one thing to separate church and state; it is another to say that the state has nothing to do with religion, or that freedom of religion means that the national recognition of the Christian faith is improper in predominantly Christian states. A Christian state will not coerce the conscience, nor persecute minority religions within its borders. It will in fact protect them and even take in the refugee and the dispossessed of other cultures, but not at the price of abandoning its Christian foundations or adopting neutrality in religion.

No serious thinker accepts that the state has no concern with morality, and no state can long endure without fundamental moral and spiritual values that direct and inform its life. All states restrict certain forms of product advertising, engage in media campaigns to influence opinion on many subjects, conduct psychological counselling programmes that reflect particular theories of human nature, and mandate educational programmes based on presuppositions which may or may not be Christian. The claim of a state to be strictly secular is a religious claim in itself, and the fruits of this religion, particularly in the communist states of the 20th century, show its tyrannical character. That there are difficulties in a Christian state dealing with various evils in a multicultural society is undoubted. Modern liberal democracies also have difficulty giving satisfaction in non-homogeneous communities.

A Christian state will not try to take over the church's role but it will seek to provide a framework of law, education and welfare expressive of the principles of the word of God, and in other ways give positive encouragement and support to the church (see further on this subject WCF 23:3 and 31:2).

THOUGHTS FROM OTHER MINDS

'I admit at once that the language there (in Chapter 20:4) is capable of a harsh construction, and probably was so construed by stricter English and Scottish Covenanters. Yet the words do not necessarily require such a construction, and were not so construed by all who assented to them. If an unlimited toleration of all teaching however blasphemous, and of all practices however revolting, is not to be openly proclaimed (and no Christian state has yet ventured to proclaim it, nor any Christian church to recommend it), and if all power is not to be taken from the magistrate of guarding the sanctity of the Lord's day and the marriage bond, and of preserving peace between contending sects, both Christian and non-Christian, I do not see how less can well be affirmed, to bring out the truth that men are not to turn liberty into licentiousness, but are responsible to God and society when they abuse it.'

A. F. Mitchell (1822–1899)[1]

FOR DISCUSSION

1. Examine each of the texts adduced for Section 1 and discuss the elements of Christian liberty set out there.
2. Is obedience to the church authorities an essential part of our obedience to God? What limits are there?
3. Is obedience to the civil authority an essential part of our obedience to God? What limits are there?

1. *Minutes of the Sessions of the Westminster Assembly of Divines* (William Blackwood and Sons, 1874), lxx.

CHAPTER 21
1–6: RELIGIOUS WORSHIP

ANALYSIS *WCF 21:1–6*

1. The duty of worship
- a. the light of general revelation
- b. the light of special revelation

2. The nature of worship
- a. its object is God
- b. its medium is Christ

3–4. Prayer as a part of worship
- a. what is required
- b. how it is to be offered
- c. its scope and content

5. Other parts of worship

6. The places of worship

21.1 The duty of worship

God's revelation in his works shows the existence of a God who has dominion and sovereignty over all, who is good and does good to all, and who is therefore to be feared, loved, praised, called on, trusted and served with all one's heart, with all one's soul and with all one's might.[1] But the only acceptable way of worshipping the true God is appointed by himself in accordance with what he has revealed in his word. Therefore he is not to be worshipped according to human ideas or inventions, nor according to the suggestions of Satan, nor by means of visible representations, nor in any other way not prescribed in the Holy Scripture.[2]

1. Rom. 1:20; Acts 17:24; Psalm 119:68; Jer 10:7; Psalm 31:23; Psalm 18:3; Rom. 10:12; Psalm 62:8; Josh. 24:14; Mark 12:33.
2. Deut. 12:32; Matt. 15:9; Acts 17:25; Matt. 4:9,10; Deut. 4:15–20; Exod. 20:4–6; Col. 2:23.

The light of nature teaches the duty of worship, but a sinner cannot obtain knowledge of mercy and redemption from this source. Special revelation is needed and accordingly the word of God directs us how to worship God. Taking up the point made in WCF 20:2, the requirement of divine institution is affirmed. It is God's prerogative to lay down how he is to be worshipped.

21.2 The nature of worship

Religious worship is to be given to the Triune God, the Father, Son, and Holy Spirit and to him alone.[3] It is not to be given to angels, saints, or any other created thing.[4] Since the fall of mankind into sin, worship cannot be given except through a mediator, nor is it to be given in the mediation of any other except Christ alone.[5]

3. Matt. 4:10 with John 5:23 & 2 Cor. 13:14.
4. Col. 2:18; Rev. 19:10; Rom. 1:25.
5. Jn 14:6; 1 Tim. 2:5; Eph. 2:18; Col. 3:17.

Only the true God is to be worshipped. Veneration of 'saints' was approved by the Nicene Council in AD 787. This Council distinguished between *latreia*, the worship due to God alone; *hyperdulia*, the inferior worship due to the Virgin Mary; and *dulia*, the lower worship due to the saints and martyrs. These distinctions lack authority in the word of God, and are not in practice distinctions the simple understand. Worship of the saints involves belief that they are not just holy examples for our faith but actual agents, with a religious role of interceding powerfully for us and aiding us through their merits, and so is not merely a weakness of the simple but is highly offensive to the character of Christ as the only mediator.

21.3 Prayer as a part of worship

Prayer with thanksgiving is one special part of religious worship[6] which God requires of all people.[7] In order that it might be acceptable, prayer is to be made in the name of the Son,[8] by the help of his Spirit,[9] according to God's will.[10] Prayer is to be offered with understanding, reverence, humility, fervour, faith, love and perseverance.[11] United prayer must be offered in a language understood by those present.[12]

6. Phil. 4:6. 7. Psalm 65:2 8. John 14:13,14; 1 Pet. 2:5.
9. Rom. 8:26. 10. 1 Jn. 5:14
11. Psalm 47:7; Eccl. 5:1,2; Heb. 12:28; Gen. 18:27; James 5:16; James 1:6,7; Mark 11:24; Matt. 6:12,14,15; Col. 4:2; Eph. 6:18.
12. 1 Cor. 14:14.

Prayer is more than a privilege; it is a duty. Inability to pray does not release from the moral obligation and thus the unbeliever should begin with the sinner's prayer (Luke 18:13), and the believer may well pray with the disciples, 'Lord, teach us to pray.' To go through the mere form of prayer does not comply with the conditions for the acceptance of prayer. Prayer must be in the confidence of the merit and intercession of Christ because we are sinners and he is the only way to the Father, and it is offered through the help of the Spirit whom God will give to those who ask him. *'To pray in the name of Christ is, in obedience to his command and in confidence in his promises, to ask mercy for his sake not by a bare mentioning of his name but by drawing our encouragement to pray and our boldness, strength and hope of acceptance in prayer, from Christ and his mediation.'*[1] Although God knows all things, he has appointed prayer as a means by which he will bestow his blessings. 'Ask and you will receive' (Matt 7:7).

21.4 Prayer as a part of worship

Prayer is to be made for things that are in agreement with God's law[13] and for all kinds of people living now or who may live in the future.[14] But prayer is not to be offered for the dead[15] nor for those who are known to be guilty of 'the sin that leads to death'.[16]

13. 1 Jn. 5:14.

1. WLC Q. 180.

14. 1 Tim. 2:1,2; Jn 17:20; 2 Sam. 7:29; Ruth 4:12.
15. 2 Sam. 12:21–23 with Luke 16:25–26; Rev. 14:13.
16. 1 Jn. 5:16.

Given the duty and privilege of prayer, we are warranted to pray concerning everyday needs as well as spiritual needs (Matt 6:32–33). Our prayers should embrace a wide range, including future generations, and specific individuals. However, the dead cannot be helped by our prayers, nor help us, and so it is wrong to pray for them or to them.

But what is the sin that leads to death? John is explicit in his advice not to pray for the person who has committed this sin. The sin that leads to death appears to be apostasy from the faith once professed so that there is wilful rejection of Jesus Christ. It occurs in a context of a loving Christian community characterised by truly Christian concern for one another and evidences of the powerful operation of the grace of God. So it is a deliberate spurning of the grace of God by one who knows what he is doing. We may feel we cannot be certain that a person has committed the sin that leads to death, but our reluctance may be an index of our relaxed attitude to sin compared to the New Testament standard (cf. Luke 12:10; Heb. 6:4–6; 10:26–31).

In our day there are some wrong approaches to prayer. Some of these are associated with 'prosperity' teaching, or with belief in territorial spirits and/or with the notion that the more time we spend in prayer the more we are likely to receive an answer. But also there is a general tendency to have a wish list approach to prayer, in which our needs are to the forefront. We need to remember the pattern of the prayer Jesus taught us and have God and his glory first in our thinking—'not my will but yours be done'.

21.5 Other parts of worship

The reading of the Scriptures with godly fear,[17] the sound preaching[18] and conscientious and obedient hearing of the word of God with understanding, faith, and reverence,[19] the singing of psalms with grace in the heart,[20] the due administration and worthy receiving of the sacraments instituted by Christ—these are all parts of the ordinary religious worship of God.[21] In addition, religious oaths,[22] vows,[23] solemn fasting,[24] and thanksgiving on special occasions,[25] are to be used in a holy and reverent manner at appropriate times.[26]

17. Acts 15:21; Rev. 1:3. 18. 2 Tim. 4:2.
19. James 1:22; Acts 10:33; Matt. 13:19; Heb. 4:2; Isa. 66:2.
20. Col. 3:16; Eph. 5:19; Jas 5:13. 21. Matt. 28:19; 1 Cor. 11:23–29; Acts 2:42.
22. Deut. 6:13 with Neh. 10:29. 23. Isa. 9:21 with Eccl. 5:4,5
24. Joel 2:12; Esth. 4:16; Matt. 9:15; 1 Cor. 7:5. 25. Psalm 107; Esth. 9:22.
26. Heb. 12:28.

Trends in the late 20th century suggest the teaching of this section needs to be emphasised. Notice the balance in the statement of the elements of worship. Not only the form but the manner is set forth. Purity of worship is not limited to the outward but embraces the inward also.

In regard to the sung element in public worship, the term 'psalms' is not intended to settle the limits of sung praise although all agreed to replace the English Psalter of 1562 and the Scottish Psalter of 1564. There were completing claims. Francis Rous had produced a Psalter in 1640 and this was used as a basis to produce the Westminster Version published in April 1646. While the Commons approved it, the House of Lords did not but favoured William Barton's version (1644) as did the London ministers. The political situation soon changed so the English church continued with the 1562 Psalter. The Scots took the Westminster Version, thoroughly revised it over a period of 28 months, and approved it in November 1649. This is the famous Scottish Metrical Version still used in some churches today.

The singing of inspired songs in public worship, thus primarily the Psalter, was the position in practice of all Reformed Churches in the 17th century, and particularly of the Church of Scotland. This is not to say that the Confession is adopting an 'exclusive psalmody' position. The 1562 English Psalter had some pieces additional to the 150 Psalms, while the day after the Church of Scotland approved the Confession in August 1647 it sought to have the 'other Scripture Songs' rendered into metre with a view to use, a decision not then implemented although revived after the Revolution of 1688. The stance in both England and Scotland reflects an inspired songs practice but even so the exegetical tradition on the relevant texts was diverse and use of other doctrinal accurate compositions had advocates and would gain ground later, particular in the last half of the 19th century.

The WCF certainly requires recognition of the principle that worship is not to be offered according to our desires but God's appointment. This principle will exclude much in modern self-centred worship that can be more a theatrical performance than worship, and bring the Psalter to the fore again. There are currently a number of accurate Psalters available in English in a variety of metres including *The Book of Psalms for Singing* (Reformed Presbyterian Church of North America 1974, revised 2009), *The Complete Book of Psalms for Singing with Study Notes* (Presbyterian Church of Eastern Australia, Melbourne 1991), and *Sing Psalms* (Free Church of Scotland 2003) as well as English versions of the Genevan Psalter to the original French tunes.

The Reformed replaced choral singing (usually in Latin) by choirs with organs. They introduced congregational singing of the psalms in the language of the people, so organs became redundant in Scotland and almost all other Reformed Churches. In May 1644 Parliament ordered the removal of organs from all churches in England which had them, so the Confession had no need to refer to that subject. In Scotland there was a long-standing practice of unaccompanied singing. In any event, the absence of reference to musical accompaniment indicates such is not an essential part of Christian worship. It's certainly absent from the church in New Testament times. If it has any place, it is a subsidiary one of helping the singing stay in tune. It is of interest to note that the great Baptist preacher C. H. Spurgeon (1834–92) had no musical instruments in the large church he pastored.

21.6 The places of worship

In the New Testament dispensation, prayer and other parts of religious worship are not tied to or made more acceptable by any place in which they are performed or towards which they are directed.[27] Rather, God is to be worshipped everywhere[28] in spirit and truth.[29] He is to be worshipped in families[30] daily,[31] in private by individuals,[32] and, with greater solemnity, in public worship services. Attendance at public services is not to be carelessly or deliberately neglected or given up when God, by his word or providence, gives opportunity for such attendance.[33]

27. John 4:21. 28. Mal. 1:11; 1 Tim. 2:8. 29. Jn 4:23,24.
30. Jer 10:25; Deut. 6:6,7; Job 1:5; 2 Sam. 6:18,20; 1 Pet. 3:7; Acts 10:2.
31. Matt. 6:11. 32. Matt. 6:6; Eph. 6:18.
33. Isa. 56:6,7; Heb. 10:25; Prov. 1:20,21,24; Prov. 8:34; Acts 13:42; Luke 4:16; Acts 2:42.

There were holy places on earth in the Old Testament period, but this has passed with the inauguration of the new covenant: the locality of our worship is now heaven itself (Heb. 10:19) and worship is through the one who is Truth by the enabling Spirit (John 4:24). If we appreciate as we ought the excellency of the priesthood of Christ, such things as ritualistic worship, sacred buildings, bowing to the east, will be seen as a regression which obscures if it does not deny the reality of the believer's entry by faith into the celestial splendour of the eternal courts through the perfect accomplishment of his faithful High Priest.

Worship each day in the family and in private is appropriate. However, public worship is not to be neglected either. Worship is response to God in the context of his covenant. The original title to WCF 21, *Of Religious Worship and the Sabbath Day,* suggests indeed the great importance of public worship on the Lord's Day. The Lord has promised to meet with his people as they gather as his covenant community, and the elders are warranted to require such a use of the Lord's Day.

THOUGHTS FROM OTHER MINDS

'The ecclesiastical rites and ceremonies of the Old Testament were used by God for communicating the spiritual truth in part, and were continued until the truth was fully revealed in Jesus Christ, and the old order is now inconsistent with the spiritual nature of worship. 'In that he saith, a new covenant, he hath made the first old. Now that which decayeth and waxeth old is ready to vanish away' (Heb. 8:13). Ritualism distracts rather than aids spiritual worship. Its object is to create an atmosphere which appeals to the emotions through the senses and to give a halo of sacredness to an earthly sanctuary, the work of men's hands, while the Scriptures clearly state that the sanctuary is now in the heavens, 'For Christ is not entered into the holy places made with hands, which are the figures of the true; but into heaven itself, now to appear in the presence of God for us' (Heb. 9:24). And we are called upon to enter by faith into the celestial splendour of the eternal courts, 'Having therefore, brethren, boldness to enter into the holiest by the blood of Jesus, by a new and living way, which he hath consecrated for us through the veil, that is to say, his flesh' (Heb. 10:19). We are also reminded that our altar is heavenly, 'We have an altar whereof they have no right to eat which serve the tabernacle' (Heb. 13:10). Our altar is connected exclusively with spiritual worship.'

Arthur Allen (1902–1958)[2]

2. *Writings and Addresses* (Presbyterian Church of Eastern Australia, Sydney 1964), 43

'In our church practice we need to take the Old Testament more seriously. It astounds me, given the overwhelming use of psalms as central to gathered worship in the first four centuries, the absolute importance given to psalmody for the first two centuries of the post-Reformation Reformed churches, and the fact that the Book of Psalms is the only hymn book which can claim to be universal in its acceptance by the whole of Christendom and utterly inspired in all its statements—it astounds me, I say, that so few psalms are sung in our worship services today. Moreover, nothing seems to earn the scorn and derision of others than the suggestion that more psalms should be sung in worship. Indeed, the last few years have seen a number of writers strike out against exclusive psalmody. Given that life is too short to engage in pointless polemics, I am left wondering which parallel universe these guys come from, where the most pressing and dangerous worship issue is clearly that people sing too much of the Bible in their services. How terrifying a prospect that would be! Imagine: people actually singing songs that express the full range of human emotion in their worship using words of which God has explicitly said, 'These are mine!"

Carl R. Trueman[3]

FOR DISCUSSION

1. Discuss the value of spiritual preparation beforehand in order to blessing in worship.
2. Is the fault the minister's or the hearer's if the message from the word does not profit? What solutions are there?
3. How should one assess orchestral effects, dimmed lighting and theatrical features in much modern worship?
4. 'Whenever the Psalter is abandoned, an incomparable treasure vanishes from the Christian church. With its recovery will come unexpected power' (Dietrich Bonhoeffer). Discuss.

3. 'The Marcions Have Landed' in *The Presbyterian Banner* (March 2003).

CHAPTER 21
7–8: THE SABBATH OR REST DAY

ANALYSIS *WCF 21:7–8*

7–8. The special day of worship

a. the creation sabbath
b. the sabbath in the Decalogue
c. the day changed but the sabbath preserved
d. how to observe the sabbath

21.7 The special day of worship

All people, as God's creatures, know that a proper proportion of time should be set apart for the worship of God. Accordingly, in his word, God has specially appointed one day in seven as a sabbath to be kept holy to him. The commandment to this effect is a positive, moral and perpetual one which binds all persons in all ages.[34] From the beginning of the world to the resurrection of Christ the Sabbath was the last day of the week, but when Christ's resurrection took place it was changed to the first day of the week.[35] In Scripture this day is called the Lord's Day.[36] It is to be continued to the end of the world as the Christian Sabbath.[37]

34. Exod. 20:8,10,11; Isa. 56:2,4,6,7.
35. Gen. 2:2,3; 1 Cor. 16:1,2; Acts 20:7.
36. Rev. 1:10.
37. Exod. 20:8,10 with Matt. 5:17,18.

The emphasis in the fourth commandment is not so much on the sequence of the days, as if the moral content includes the last day of the week, but on the meaning of the sabbath itself. Nowhere does the Old Testament tell us: Keep the seventh day *of the week*, but it tells us to keep the weekly sabbath. Whether the sabbath follows or precedes the other six days of the week, it is still a seventh day in relation to the other six days.

Further, the different reasons stated in Exodus 20:11 (creation) and in Deuteronomy 5:15 (redemption) to enforce sabbath observance certainly help understand the significance of the sabbath, but in the nature of the case cannot be part of the strictly moral content. Rather, they are a form of words appropriate to the situation of the recipients. The unchangeable or strictly moral content of the fourth commandment must be found in the principle of a due proportion of time with the actual time to be set by other factors such as creation or redemption.

a. *The sabbath at creation*

God instituted the sabbath or rest day at creation (Genesis 2:2–3), so it was part of the order established for man from the first. As Jesus said, 'The sabbath was made for man' (Mark 2:27). It follows that (1) the sabbath is of universal relevance quite apart from the later entrance of sin into the human race; (2) subsequent significance which might become attached to the sabbath day because of the provision of redemption cannot alter its basic character; and (3) it is no argument against the origin of the sabbath in creation to point to the lack of references prior to Moses since (a) an argument from silence is risky, eg.: there is no mention of the sabbath between Moses c.1400 BC and the time of Elijah c.840BC (2 Kings 4:23); and (b) corruption and or neglect of sabbath observance are amply explained by human sinfulness.

Even if one does not understand the creation days to be of the same length as our solar days, it is agreed by all that the narrative of God's creation week aims to provide a pattern for man's activity. The sabbath is *not* a mere weekly memorial day for a past work nor is it a kind of afterthought tacked on to something more important, but it points forward to creation's purpose and goal—an entering into the higher destiny of God's 'rest,' which is attested to by the tree of life in the midst of the garden. Man is made for more than work—he is made for God, and that purpose and destiny gives his work its true meaning.

b. *The sabbath in Israel*

Whatever happened in other nations it is admitted by all that the sabbath became a special feature in the life of Israel. The redemptive reason attached to the fourth commandment in Deuteronomy 5:12–15 is not an additional but secondary emphasis to creation, but is closely allied to the basic meaning of the sabbath. How can fallen man reach the goal of eternal fellowship with God apart from redemption? But God redeemed Israel, their destiny is with him, therefore they are to keep the sabbath. Hence the eschatological principle of the sabbath was elaborated in various applications beyond the weekly day.

When the people of God settled in the Promised Land following the Exodus from Egypt and the wilderness wanderings, they entered into the place God had prepared for rest, but they had not thereby reached their ultimate rest (see Hebrews 4:8–9). To those of Abraham-like faith there lay ahead 'a heavenly country', 'a city which is to come', of which blessing the sabbath was both an emblem and a pledge. A greater than Joshua would bring them into this true rest. Canaan was only a type or picture of the heavenly country.

c. *Jesus and the sabbath*

During Jesus' ministry we find that Jesus is regular in his attendance at the synagogue on the sabbath day (Luke 4:16), and that he also healed many people on this day. The healing of a man at the pool of Bethesda called forth the criticism of the Pharisees, whereupon Jesus responded: 'My Father is always at his work to this very day, and I, too, am working.' The Jewish leaders then sought the more to kill him since, in their eyes, he not only was breaking the sabbath but committing blasphemy 'calling God his own Father, making himself equal with God' (John 5:18). But Jesus answers that whatever the Father does the Son also does. In other words, Jesus justifies his healing of a man on the (earthly) sabbath by the parallel case of his Father in continuing to sustain the creation each moment during his (heavenly) sabbath.

For our present purpose two points may be noted: (1) God's rest following creation (Genesis 2) is unclosed since it embraces history, yet during it the Father is not idle but continues to uphold his creation and act for its benefit; and (2) Jesus' healing of the man is entirely in character with the observance of the earthly sabbath just as are the Father's activities during his heavenly sabbath. Thus, not to do good on the sabbath is to profane it (cf. Matthew 12:12).

One of the most remarkable sayings of Jesus is found in Mark 2:27–28: 'The sabbath was made for man, not man for the sabbath. So the Son of Man is Lord even of the sabbath.' In context the saying does not mean merely that Jesus has the right to free the sabbath from Pharisaic abuses. Who doubts that he has such right? But it means that his relationship to it is such that he has full authority to determine all things related to it. After all, the sabbath was made for man to ensure his well-being, not to make him a slave to legalistic regulations. The term 'Son of Man' has its background in Daniel 7. It indicates universal authority as Messiah, while the emphasis '*even* of the sabbath', stresses the greatness of that authority. It is a Messianic claim.

As the sabbath points to the eternal fellowship with God which comes alone through him who is the way (John 14:6), the saying includes the thought that Jesus is Lord of the sabbath to bring to realisation what the day represents. In Matthew's account (12:1–8) Jesus points out that the work of the priests in the temple on the sabbath defiled it yet they were innocent. He adds, 'something greater than the temple is here.' The priests were carrying out God's work in offering the sacrifices, but Jesus, the true Servant of the Lord, had now come, and inaugurated the time of the new wine that old wineskins could not hold without splitting (Mark 2:21–22). As Christ inaugurates a new creation, the renewal of the pre-Mosaic, pre-fall Edenic sabbath is not at all inappropriate but the reverse. In principle we have rest in Christ but we look forward to the consummation when we enter into the heavenly country.

d. *The day changed*

The New Testament shows that the resurrection of Christ, which secures the eternal destiny of Christ's people, occurred on the first day of the week, very early, and not on the sabbath day as then observed. Christ is 'the firstfruits' of those who have fallen asleep (1 Corinthians 15:20), and this reminds us of the first sheaf of the harvest which was to be presented *the day after* the (Saturday) sabbath at the close of Passover (Leviticus 23:9–14). On the day of his resurrection Christ appeared to his disciples, and likewise a week later (John 20:19, 26). After his final parting from them, marked by the Ascension, he poured out the Spirit. This event occurred on the Day of Pentecost, 50 days after Passover, and also fell on the first day of the week. Pentecost is otherwise known as the feast of firstfruits (Exodus 34:22; Leviticus 23:15ff), and the outpouring of the Spirit marks the beginning of the harvest of which Christ, the firstfruits, is the guarantee.

Christ is not only the one through whom all things were created; he is also 'the beginning and the firstborn from among the dead' (Colossians 1:18). He has inaugurated a new order of existence, a new creation. Still, the redemption he brings does not annul the first creation but restores and perfects it. In Christ, believers have all things, but they have not yet entered into the heavenly country which is their inheritance. They still have the recurring sign of the believer's hope in the gift of the sabbath, but a sabbath enriched by Christ's accomplishment of redemption. *The change of day reflects the reality of what has come*, that creation's goal is through the Risen Lord, *while the continuation of the day of rest points to what is yet to be* in the consummation.

It is in the light of such principles that the true significance of the New Testament emphasis on the first day of the week is seen. The significance of Christ's honouring of the first day of the week is as great as the divine example provided in Genesis 2.

e. *The goal of our pilgrimage*

A very important statement on the significance of the present time in the light of the achieved salvation is provided in Hebrews 3:7–4:11. The writer presupposes that Israel in the wilderness and the church on earth today are in parallel situations. Both receive a promise of rest (3:11; 4:1), and both are subject to dangers and temptations which can lead to failure to enter the rest (3:19; 3;12), and so both receive exhortation to obedience in faith. The rest is defined as the rest of God's seventh day (4:4), is represented as future and as a place of rest to be entered by believers as was Canaan, although Canaan was not the true rest (4:8). *This language does not fit a subjective experience of rest the believer gains now.* The true rest into which believers will enter is a heavenly country (11:16), the city with foundations (11:10), the city which is to come (13:14). God's purpose in the creation is thus realised through the consummation of redemption: the redeemed enter into God's creation rest.

This being the perspective of Scripture, the gift of the earthly sabbath has as much relevance today as in the beginning. As Hebrews 4:9 states: 'There remains, then, a sabbath-rest (Greek: *sabbatismos*) for the people of God.' The weekly sign of this eternal hope continues. Believers find rest in the Lord. They therefore rejoice in his works and go forth to labour for his glory. They have the assurance, that through the Last Adam, they have a blessed destiny even though it is not yet their experience.

Other holy days?

In regard to Festival days, commonly called Holy-days, these arose over time as a Christianising of Old Testament festivals, the first being Passover-Easter (2nd century) with the addition of commemoration of the birth of Christ in the 4th century. Rome and also many in the English Church insisted that the festival days of Christ's birth, death, resurrection, ascension and Pentecost were specially holy to be consecrated as special sabbaths. They contained a mystical element and were made holier than other days by the extraordinary works and great benefits of God which happened on them which was even appropriated to the annual commemoration of them.[1] The Scottish Church had taken a firm stand against Festival days of this kind (and obviously holy days associated with 'saints') from 1560.

Some Reformed churches also kept the days just referred to. Usually there was some pressure from the civil authorities but Francis Turretin (1623–87) in Geneva explains the practice of Reformed Churches clearly in his *Institutes*.[2] Commemoration of certain events in Christ's ministry in some Reformed churches was not based on divine prescription but human appointment, were not obligatory having no special sanctity or requiring a sabbath rest and they were capable of being abolished or changed 'if utility and the necessity of the church should demand it'.

Some Protestant assessments of the date of Christ's birth and of Easter as originating in paganism need correction as these originated before pagan impact in the church. (i) The term Easter for the Resurrection festival is now generally regarded as derived from High German *eostarum* (=dawn) and not *Eostrae,* the Anglo-Saxon goddess of fertility. (ii) The date for the birth of Jesus was calculated by the Christian historian Sextus Julius Africanus (180–250) about 221 in his chronology of the world. The

1. George Gillespie, *A Dispute against the English Popish Ceremonies, Part II* (Naphtali Press, 2013) 145,146.
2. Turretin, *Institutes*, 2:100–104.

Christian martyr Hippolytus of Rome (170–235) is to the same effect. In these chronologies the conception of Jesus occurred on what the authors believed was the anniversary of the world's creation (25 March) and his birth 9 months later (25 December). This date did not correspond to the time of pagan celebrations of Saturnalia (which finished 17 December) or the cult of Sol Invictus (which features much later in the 3rd century) but became general in the 4th century after Christianity became a tolerated religion (313) and especially after it became the official religion of the Roman Empire in 380. The birth of Jesus was first observed as a festival in Rome in 336.

At any rate, every Lord's Day commemorates the resurrection of Christ and the new creation, and is the only holy day under the New Covenant.

21.8 The special day of worship

In order to keep the Christian Sabbath holy to the Lord, it is necessary for people to prepare their hearts and attend to their ordinary affairs beforehand. They are then to observe a holy rest all the day from their own works, words and thoughts concerning their everyday employment and recreations,[38] and to devote the whole time to the public and private exercises of God's worship and to the duties of necessity and mercy.[39]

38. Exod. 20:8; Exod. 16:23,25,26,29,30; Exod. 31:15–17; Isa. 58:13; Neh. 13:15–19,21,22.
39. Isa. 58:13; Matt. 12:1–13.

The Old Testament has very little on the subject of sabbath observance. The essential emphasis is the cessation of ordinary employment and the use of the day for spiritual celebration. Psalm 92—a psalm for the sabbath according to its title—indicates that praising the Lord, making music to him, singing for joy at the work of God's hands, trusting in his righteousness, and praising his constant love and power, are sabbath activities. The sabbath was not to be a day of doing nothing nor a day of mere external religious duties, but a day of heart-felt spiritual activity and of doing good.

As for specific prohibitions, work during the ploughing and harvest times was prohibited on the sabbath (Exodus 34:21), presumably because people claimed that the limited period available to complete these tasks justified ignoring the sabbath. Jeremiah (17:21–27) and Nehemiah (13:15–22) prohibited the bearing of burdens on the sabbath, but the context indicates commercial activity was involved. There are two other prohibitions. Fire in dwellings is banned in Exodus 35:3, but occurs in the context of instructions about the building of the tabernacle, no doubt to offset any tendency to justify working on the materials for the tabernacle on the sabbath. In other words, building a place of worship was not a proper activity for God's day. The other reference in Numbers 15:32–36 sets the death penalty for gathering wood, but the context is that of defiant transgressors. The case in question is that of a fuel merchant who plies his trade on God's day. One other passage (Exodus 16:23) has been taken as excluding any preparation of food gathered the previous day, but this is to draw too much from the passage.

These few general statements stand in marked contrast with the more than 1,000 rules built up by the Pharisees in the time of Jesus, and even their rules were not always as rigid and detailed as those of other Jewish sects. But detailed rules tend to side-track from the right recognition that the day belongs to the Lord. It is his gift for our good. Let us beware the encroachments that can so easily be made upon it by less important things. Let us grasp its great principle and apply it gladly and whole-heartedly for our spiritual profit. We can use it for worship, fellowship, spiritual enrichment—and how we need these! Also, as we put aside the ordinary activities of the week, we may enjoy spiritual, physical and emotional refreshment in activities which further the aim of the day. Avoiding business, shopping and the like, we are to be active in doing good.

In some occupations there will be everyday work on this day, and rightly so (the cows must be milked, the hospitals must be open, police will be needed) for the sabbath is made for man and not the reverse. There will be particular difficulties in some occupations in our industrialised society, but obviously a Christian will not be anxious to cut into the opportunities for Christian worship by working overtime on Sunday without good reason.

The present impoverishment of the church and our national direction owes much to neglect of God's provision of the Lord's Day. We are great on physical muscle-building and find great amounts of time and money for it. But what about our spiritual muscles? Consider the human restlessness characteristic of our time because God's rest is ignored. How important it is to raise our eyes heavenward! And will not the church find sufficient funds for the spread of the gospel if on the first day of the week—the day that reminds us of the destiny we have in Christ because of his love for us—we set aside as the Lord has prospered us (1 Corinthians 16:2)!

THOUGHTS FROM OTHER MINDS

'The statement of the Confession as to the way the Sabbath should be sanctified is moderate and wise. The devotional and the practical are not sundered. The obligation of the second great commandment is recognised as well as that of the first, the worship of God and the duty owing to our fellow-men. The religious and secular theories of the day are apt to overlook one or other. The secularist professes to worship by the simple discharge of relative duties. The extreme religionist sometimes gives us the impression that he is inclined to minimise the claims of necessity and mercy.'

John Macpherson[3]

3. *The Confession of Faith*, 131.

'To speak of the 'abolishment' of the Sabbath under the new covenant does not involve merely the denial of the continuing significance of the Mosaic decalogue. It involves a breach of the very orders of creation, history, and consummation as revealed in Scripture. Instead of resisting the role of the Sabbath in redemption, the participant in the new covenant should rejoice in the privileges associated with God's consummating Sabbath-ordinance.'

O. Palmer Robertson[4]

FOR DISCUSSION

1. The answer to human restlessness is to rest in the Lord. Discuss.
2. How is Paul's indifference to religious days in Romans 14:5–6 to be reconciled with his condemnation of them in Galatians 4:9–11? Is he thinking of the Mosaic administration and the varying motivations for still observing it? Could he have the fourth commandment in view too? If not, why not?
3. Discuss Dr. Robertson's comment quoted above.

4. *The Christ of the Covenants* (P&R Publishing, 1980), 72.

CHAPTER 22
LAWFUL OATHS & VOWS

ANALYSIS *WCF 22:1–7*

1. Definition of an oath

2. Basis

3. Limits

4. Obligations

5. Definition of a vow

6. To whom made and in what manner

7. Limits

22.1 Oath defined

A lawful oath is a part of religious worship.[1] On proper occasions the person swearing solemnly calls on God to witness what he declares or promises, and to judge him according to the truth or falsehood of what he swears.[2]

1. Deut. 10:20.
2. Exod. 20:7; Lev. 19:12; 2 Cor.1:23; 2 Chron.6:22,23.

22.2 The basis of a lawful oath

The name of God is the only name by which people ought to swear, and when they do so his name is to be used with all holy fear and reverence.[3] Therefore to swear vainly or rashly by that glorious and dreadful name or to swear at all by any other thing is sinful and to be abhorred.[4] Yet in matters of weight and importance an oath is warranted by the word of God, under the New Testament as well as under the Old,[5] and so in such matters a lawful oath required by lawful authority ought to be taken.[6]

3. Deut. 6:13.
4. Exod. 20:7; Jer. 5:7; Matt. 5:34,37; James 5:12.
5. Heb. 6:16; 2 Cor. 1:23; Isa. 65:16.
6. 1 Kings 8:31; Neh. 13:25; Ezra 10:5.

An oath is a solemn act in which God is invoked as witness and as judge of what is asserted or what is promised. WCF 21:5 has already stated that oaths are a part of religious worship. This is here reaffirmed. But if those who believe in the one true and living God cannot swear by any other, nor can those who do not believe in him properly swear by him. It would be mockery to invoke the name of God if one does not acknowledge him and his absolute righteousness. So the provision for an affirmation in our civil courts, although reflecting decline in religion, is not inappropriate.

On the other hand, the view that Jesus' words, 'Swear not at all' (Matthew 5:33–37) forbid Christians to take an oath in any circumstances is rightly rejected in the Confession. No doubt Christians should so speak that their simple 'yes' means yes and their 'no' means no. No doubt all vain and rash oath-taking should be avoided as well as the use of euphemisms for God which avoid the formal use of his name. No doubt in the world to come there will be no occasions for oath taking either. But we are not in the world to come yet, and there is nothing in the New Testament dispensation which even suggests a break in continuity in the use of oaths in appropriate circumstances as recognised in the Old Testament. God himself made a self-maledictory oath to confirm his word (Gen. 15:9ff cf. Hebrews 6:13–16), Christ allowed himself to be put on oath (Matthew 26:63), and Paul's life provides examples (Romans 1:9; 2 Corinthians 1:23). The lawfulness of oath taking *per se* was denied by some of the Anabaptists and by the Society of Friends (Quakers), and that denial is echoed today in some evangelical circles. Jesus' words in their context deal with hypocritical oaths which seek to gain acceptance for our words while avoiding strict honesty.

22.3 Limits in oath-taking

Whoever takes an oath ought to give due consideration to the great seriousness of such a solemn act, and in the oath swear to nothing but what he is fully persuaded is the truth.[7] No one may bind himself by oath to anything except to what is good and just, what he himself believes to be so, and what he is able and determined to perform.[8] Yet it is a sin to refuse an oath required by lawful authority concerning any good and just thing.[9]*

7. Exod. 20:7; Jer 4:2.
8. Gen. 24:2,3,5,6,8,9.
9. Num. 5:19,21; Neh. 5:12; Exod. 22:7–11. [* This sentence was deleted by the American Presbyterian Assembly in 1789.]

22.4 Obligations in oath-taking

An oath is to be taken in the plain and ordinary sense of the words, without equivocation or mental reservation.[10] It cannot require a person to sin, but in respect of any thing not sinful it binds him to perform it even if it causes loss to him.[11] A lawful oath is not to be violated, even though made to heretics or unbelievers.[12]

10. Jer. 4:2; Psalm 24:4.
11. 1 Sam. 25:22,32–34; Psalm 15:4.
12. Ezek. 17:16,18,19; Josh. 9:18,19 with 2 Sam. 21:1.

An oath to commit sin cannot be lawful and to keep such an oath is to compound the sin of making it in the first place (cf. Mark 6:23,26). Oaths which are not in themselves sinful but which result in loss are to be kept for truth's sake and for God's sake. Roman Catholic moral theology allows mental reservation and equivocation in a just cause. If the other party does not know that the words are used with a private or unusual meaning that is his fault, is the argument. As Rome identifies the voice of the church with the voice of God, and claims to be the moral arbiter of the individual conscience, the just cause becomes the advancement of the church's interests and the dictates of the church will justify setting aside an oath. Rome's all too frequent practice of not keeping faith with heretics has ample illustration in history. So has the practice of Protestant ministers and elders subscribing statements of faith but teaching contrary to them.

Sometimes the propriety of lying in time of war is raised and the example of Rahab, a person of faith, adduced (Joshua 2; Heb. 11:31; James 2:25). It is a common maxim that 'truth is the first casualty in war'. It must be admitted that one is not obliged to tell others things that are not their business, while subterfuge (eg. the use of ambush) is certainly a necessary element in war in every age. Rahab's dominant motive was belief in the righteous cause of Israel's God but, as she and we are imperfect people in an imperfect world, our actions done in faith are often tainted with sin. It is one thing for her to be commended for her faith, but it is not apparent that Scripture justifies her lie even though good resulted.

22.5 A vow defined

A vow is similar to an oath promising something and ought to be made with the same religious care and be performed with the same faithfulness.[13]

13. Isa19:21; Eccl. 5:4–6; Psalm 61:8; Psalm 66:13–14.

An *oath* is a promise between parties which God is called upon to witness. A *vow* is a promise made to God as the other party (and the witness) and is to be kept for the same reasons as an oath—for truth's sake and for God's sake.

22.6 Parties to a vow and how made

A vow is not to be made to any creature but only to God.[14] An acceptable vow is one made voluntarily, arising from faith and conviction of duty, expressing thankfulness for mercy received or the desire for what we want. By taking a vow we more strictly bind ourselves to necessary duties; or, in so far and for as long as may be appropriate to the obtaining of what we desire, we bind ourselves to other things.[15]

14. Psalm 76:11; Jer. 44:25,26.
15. Deut. 23:21–23; Psalm 50:14; Gen. 28:20–22; 1 Sam. 1:11; Psalm 66:13,14; Psalm 132:2–5.

22.7 Parties to a vow and how made

No one may vow to do anything forbidden in the word of God, anything which would hinder any duty it commands, or anything not in his power to do and for the performance of which he has no promise of ability from God.[16] In this connection, vows of perpetual celibacy, poverty and obedience within Roman Catholic monastic orders are not degrees of higher perfection but are actually superstitious and sinful snares in which no Christian may entangle himself.[17]

16. Acts 23:12,14; Mark 6:26; Num. 30:5,8,12,13.
17. Matt. 19:11,12; 1 Cor. 7:2,9; Eph. 4:28; 1 Pet. 4:2; 1 Cor. 7:23.

Vows by which we freely accept and promise to observe, by God's grace, the duties set out in the word of God (to which we are already bound) are very proper. The most common vow is the vow of church membership, the renewal of such vows in the sacrament of the Lord's Supper, and vows on other occasions to follow more fully the ways of the Lord. The covenants subscribed in 17th century Scotland and subsequently come under this head.

However, vows to perform special tasks with the aim of securing something from the Lord or expressing thanks for mercies received are much more likely to lead to difficulty, given that special revelation has ceased. It is possible to entangle oneself very easily by falling into will-worship, and also into erroneous conceptions of the Christian life. The monastic orders cited are examples of this. Paul made a vow (Acts 18:18) although its nature is not clear.

A vow cannot continue to bind in cases where its continued observance is found clearly to be inconsistent with our spiritual vow.

THOUGHTS FROM OTHER MINDS

'The phrase *not at all* has deceived many, making them think that it was a general condemnation of every sort of swearing. Some men in former days were driven to this excessive rigour—not bad men, I may say—because of the unbridled freedom of swearing which they saw prevailing on all sides in their world. The Anabaptists too, used this pretext for a great uproar, saying that Christ allowed no reason for taking oaths, in telling men to swear not at all. . . . Briefly, it comes back to this, that there are other ways than perjury for God's name to be taken in vain. So we must abstain from all unnecessary freedom in swearing, for when a right reason compels it, the Law not only allows the oath but explicitly enjoins it. . . . Christ requires that our words possess candour and constancy, that we may not need to swear any more. . . . Christ, as I see it, says that it is a human failure that leads men to swearing. If good faith flourished among them, if they were not inconsistent and changeable in their speech, they would still preserve the simplicity which nature dictates. Yet it does not follow that we may not legitimately take an oath as often as necessity demand it, for the use of many things is innocent, though their source be vitiated.'

John Calvin (1509–1564)[1]

'A vow cannot 'continue to bind in cases where its continued observance is found clearly to be inconsistent with our spiritual interests; for then it is certain God does not wish it, and a promise can never bind when the party to whom it is made does not desire it to be kept.'

A. A. Hodge (1823–1886)[2]

FOR DISCUSSION

1. Explain how Matthew 5:33–37 is in harmony with the provisions for swearing an oath given in the Old Testament.
2. Discuss Psalm 15:4b.
3. Discuss the practice of promising to serve God in some special way if he will do something for you such as healing a sick loved one?

1. *A Harmony of the Gospels* (St Andrew Press, 1972), 1:191-193.
2. *The Confession of Faith* (Banner of Truth, 1958), 291.

CHAPTER 23
CIVIL GOVERNMENT

ANALYSIS *WCF 23:1–4*

1. Civil Government
- a. divine institution
- b. divine purpose
- c. coercive power

2. Public Duties and the Christian
- a. a lawful vocation
- b. may engage in war

3. Duty of State to Church and Religion
- a. what the state may not do
- b. what the state may do

4. Civil Allegiance

23.1 Civil government

With a view to his glory and the public good, God, the world's supreme Lord and King, has ordained civil authorities answerable to himself to be over the people. To accomplish his aims, God has armed them with the power of the sword to defend and encourage those who are good and to punish evil doers.[1]

1. Rom. 13:1–4; 1 Pet. 2:13,14.

The Bible does not specify any particular form of civil government such as monarchy, republic or democracy but it does affirm that the ultimate foundation of human government is in God's appointment. The 'powers that be' are not independent of God or equal with God, but under God. In this sense all civil authority might be called constitutional, for the purposes of the institution are linked to the institution itself, and all exercising the office are accountable. No countenance is given to tyranny or despotism, nor to the tyranny of the 51% found in much modern democracy which erroneously bases the source of what is right in the will of the majority. It is far more important to have the rule of right law—the law of God—than 'one man one vote'. On the other hand, in the multitude of counsellors is safety (Proverbs 11:14), hence the Reformed faith has tended to favour republicanism over monarchy, and an electoral base broadened beyond the few nobility.

It is worth noting that the institution of civil government is not founded in grace but in nature before sin. The Fall and God's redemptive purpose introduce new factors which must be taken into account in fulfilling its basic and unchanged purpose of God's glory and the public good. The expression 'public good' should not be defined as 'secular interests' rather than spiritual, nor moral interests as contrasted with spiritual. The division of life into 'sacred' and 'secular' sounds neat but is untenable.

23.2 The Christian and public duties

It is lawful for Christians to accept and carry out the duties of public office when called to do so.[2] In carrying out such tasks they ought to take care to uphold piety, justice and peace in accordance with the sound laws of each commonwealth they serve,[3] and in so doing the New Testament permits them to engage in war if there is just and necessary cause.[4]

2. Prov. 8:15,16; Rom. 13:1,2,4.
3. Psalm 2:10–12; 1 Tim. 2:2; Psalm 82:3,4; 2 Sam. 23:3; 1 Pet. 2:13.
4. Luke 3:14; Rom. 13:4; Matt. 8:9,10; Acts 10:1,2; Rev. 17:14,16.

It is not unlawful for Christians to be involved in political and civil affairs. It *is* improper for Christians to make their religion so private that the interests of piety, justice and peace are not furthered. Not everyone is called to work as a public official, for God gives gifts which fit people for various vocations. The Christian fitted for such tasks should not shirk from the important work of guiding the affairs of national life, and the institutions of welfare and justice. Contrary to the Anabaptists, who held that the holding of civil office was sinful for Christians, in theory none should be better fitted for such work.

The use of the force of law or arms is a legitimate function of civil government. War is really an aspect of the power of the sword. The concept of a just war is of long standing in Christian theology dating particularly from Augustine (354–430). Just war principles are usually stated as: having just cause, being declared by a proper authority, possessing right intention, having a reasonable chance of success, and the end being proportional to the means used. The Confession gives no countenance to individuals engaging in war on their own initiative but places the responsibility in the hands of the civil powers. The Reformed have held that inferior civil rulers may act against a tyrannical superior if necessity demands. War always has evil consequences. The concept of a just war is not meant to justify war but to bring it under the control of justice. In this way it limits and restricts war into definite bounds.

From a Biblical perspective it is hard to conclude that a Christian or anyone else must be a pacifist, although all ought to be peacemakers. A Christian may scruple a particular war in the light of the knowledge he has, and such a person should be accommodated, rather than forced to act against his conscience. In reality it often seems otherwise: the pacifist is given exemption, but the objector to a particular war is not.

23.3 Duty of the state to the Church and religion

The civil authorities may not take to themselves the administration of the word and sacraments, or interfere in the spiritual government of the church,[5] yet they have authority, and it is their duty, to see to it that unity and peace is preserved in the Church, the truth of God is kept pure and complete, all blasphemies and heresies are suppressed, all corruptions and abuses in worship and discipline prevented or reformed, and all the ordinances of God duly established, administered and observed.[6] To carry out these ends more effectively in circumstances where the church is disorganised or corrupt, the civil authorities have power to call synods, to be present at them, and to insist that whatsoever is transacted in them be according to the mind of God.[7*]

5. 2 Chron.26:18 with Matt. 18:17 & Matt. 16:19; 1 Cor. 12:28,29; Eph. 4:11,12; 1 Cor. 4:1,2; Rom. 10:15; Heb. 5:4.
6. Isa. 49:23; Psalm 122:9; Ezra 7:23,25–28; Lev. 24:16; Deut. 13:5,6,12; 2 Kings 18:4; 1 Chron. 13:1–9; 2 Kings 23:1–26; 2 Chron. 34:33; 2 Chron. 15:12,13.
7. 2 Chron. 19:8–11; 2 Chron. chapters 29 & 30; Matt. 2:4,5.
* This sentence has been reworded from the 1646 original to reflect the qualifications in the Adopting Act of the General Assembly of the Church of Scotland, 27 August 1647. The American wording of 23.3 dating from 1788 is as follows (see discussion in commentary): 'Civil magistrates may not assume to themselves the administration of the word and sacraments; or the power of the keys of the kingdom of heaven; or in the least interfere in matters of faith. Yet, as nursing fathers, it is the duty of civil magistrates to protect the church of our common Lord, without giving the preference to any denomination of Christians above the rest, in such a manner that all ecclesiastical persons whatever shall enjoy the full, free, and unquestioned liberty of discharging every part of their sacred functions, without violence or danger. And as Jesus Christ hath appointed a regular government and discipline in his church, no law of any commonwealth should interfere with, let, or hinder, the due exercise thereof, among the voluntary members of any denomination of Christians according to their own profession and belief. It is the duty of civil magistrates to protect the person and good name of all their people, in such an effectual manner as that no person be suffered, either upon pretense of religion or infidelity, to offer any indignity, violence, abuse, or injury to any other person whatsoever: and to take order, that all religious and ecclesiastical assemblies be held without molestation or disturbance.'

The civil authorities may not treat the church as a department of state or take on the role of the spiritual officers Christ has appointed in his church. The church has a distinct government and this is not to be usurped or interfered with by the civil authority. The original text allowed the civil power to call synods, but this right the Church of Scotland, when adopting the Confession in 1647, expressly limited to 'kirks not settled or constituted in point of government.' The last sentence in the above text has been modified accordingly.

But if the state may not usurp the government of the church, it does not follow that it has nothing to do with it. Both church and state seek the glory of God and the good of man, although by different means. The state should see to it that unity in the church is preserved and the truth of God maintained. In ordinary circumstances the civil power cannot convene synods and it can never usurp church government, but it can still do a great deal to encourage and exhort the church to base its proceedings on the word of God. In a somewhat similar way, the state encourages and regulates the arts and sciences, but does not presume to determine authoritatively matters discussed by these disciplines. [See further on WCF 20:4.]

The Confession envisaged a situation of a national church endowed by the state (the divines had subscribed the *Solemn League and Covenant* in 1643). Today we usually find that a country has a multiplicity of denominations, none of which is established as the official church, and none of which receives direct government financial support for its church buildings and pastors' housing and stipends. Voluntary support by adherents may well be a preferable course in present circumstances in many countries. Indeed, endowment and recognition are really distinct and separable. Thus the Church of Scotland was established by law in 1560, but was not endowed until 1567. The large section of the Established Church of Scotland which withdrew in 1843 to form the Free Church, continued to hold the principle of the duty of the state set out in the Confession, but supported itself by voluntary givings. This was because the conditions on which the state gave endowment had become intolerable in the light of God's word.

American wording

The American Presbyterian church reworded WCF 3.3 (also 20:4 & 31:1–2) in 1788 to affirm a three-fold duty of the state in reference to religion: (1) to protect the church; (2) to protect citizens; (3) to ensure freedom of assembly [text above]. However, the duty of the state to encourage the unity of the church and the maintenance of the truth is not asserted, and all denominations of Christians are placed on an equal basis. This is a pragmatic position which might well be judged appropriate in religiously divided societies but it hardly seems the ideal to be aimed at. The underlying principle is at best that the state's duty does not encompass anything but the encouragement of a lowest common denominator Christianity, and at worst that the state has nothing to do with religion except to protect people in the free exercise of it—the actual current practice in the United States of America. In any event, the vision of a thoroughly Christian state has been a little dimmed by the denominational ideal.

23.2 The Christian and public duties

It is the duty of people to pray for those in authority in the state,[8] to honour their persons,[9] to pay them taxes or other dues,[10] to obey their lawful commands, and to be subject to their authority, for the sake of conscience.[11] The civil power's just and legal authority is not made void by reason of him being an unbeliever or of different religious beliefs, nor are the people freed from their due obedience to such.[12] Church office-bearers are not exempt from the obedience due to the civil authorities.[13] Still less has the pope any power and jurisdiction over civil rulers in their dominions or over any of their people, and, least of all, has he any power to deprive them of their dominions or their lives, if he considers them to be heretics or chargeable with any other fault at all.[14]

8. 1 Tim. 2:1,2. 9. 1 Pet. 2:17. 10. Rom. 13:6,7. 11. Rom. 13:5; Titus 3:1.
12. 1 Pet. 2:13,14,16.
13. Rom. 13:1; 1 Kings 2:35; Acts 25:9–11; 2 Pet. 2:1,10,11; Jude 8–11.
14. 2 Thess. 2:4; Rev. 13:15–17.

The authority of the state is here affirmed and the role of the church limited to its scriptural bounds. The position of a king like Charles II must be seen in the light of his breach of the *Solemn League and Covenant* to maintain and further the reformed religion according to the word of God which was sworn by him in 1650 and 1651. What was 'just and legal' was determined by that covenant not by the mere will of the king. For all that the Scottish ideal might be termed 'theocratic', it included very advanced ideas of the rights of the people.[1]

THOUGHTS FROM OTHER MINDS

'Politics is simply the art or science of government. . . . Now we believe it is through the ordinances of God that the state exists, in order that man's sin may not wholly corrupt his life and the life of others despite the depravity of human nature. In these ordinances is to be seen part of God's providential directing of history.. . . . politicians are particularly subject to temptation, and also certain undesirable types are particularly attracted by politics. But surely this is all the more reason for Christians to enter public life, and for those who do, to pay all the greater attention to the means of grace.'

F. M. Bradshaw (1910–1992)[2]

FOR DISCUSSION

1. In what circumstances in a modern liberal democracy would it be appropriate for a church office-bearer to take his church to the civil court and on what basis would it be proper for the civil court to be involved? Is 1 Corinthians 6:1–8 a relevant prohibition or is it more a case of the rich Christians exploiting the poor Christians, through the latter's inability to prosecute legal remedies.
2. Suppose 10% of your taxes are spent on some immoral purpose. Should you hold back a corresponding share of your tax bill?
3. Discuss the kind of framework of law, education and welfare which Christians might aim to see implemented?

1. See Samuel Rutherford's book *Lex, Rex: The Law and the Prince* (John Field, 1644).
2. R. S. Ward, ed. *A Witness for Christ* (Presbyterian Church of Eastern Australia, 1996), 411ff.

CHAPTER 24
MARRIAGE AND DIVORCE

ANALYSIS *WCF 24:1–6*

1. The nature of marriage
- a. between a man and a woman
- b. monogamous

2. The four-fold purpose of marriage
- a. mutual help
- b. procreation
- c. godly children
- d. preservation of purity

3. The general rule and the Christian rule
- a. in general all entitled to marry
- b. informed consent necessary
- c. Christians should marry only 'in the Lord'

4. Forbidden degrees

5–6. The ending of a marriage
- a. by death
- b. by adultery (porneia)
- c. by irremediable desertion

24.1 The nature of marriage

Marriage is to be between one man and one woman. It is not lawful for any man to have more than one wife, nor for any woman to have more than one husband, at the same time.[1]

1. Gen. 2:24; Matt. 19:5-6; Prov. 2:17.

Marriage is constituted by the public commitment of a man and a woman to a many-faceted life-long union so that a man leaves his father and mother and cleaves to his wife and the two become one flesh. So called homosexual marriages are an abomination to God. The rule for marriage is monogamy.

The polygamy which existed among the patriarchs, such as Abraham, Jacob and David, is generally not expressly condemned in Scripture, but it is contrary to the foundational character of marriage as given in Genesis 2:24. Scripture is normally content to show us that polygamy violates God's norm by indicating the bitter consequences in the families of those who practised it.

24.2 The four-fold purpose of marriage

God ordained marriage for the mutual help of husband and wife,[2] for the legitimate increase of mankind, to provide the church with holy children,[3] and for the prevention of moral impurity.[4]

2. Gen. 2:18.
3. Mal. 2:15.
4. 1 Cor. 7:2,9.

The Church of Rome tends to stress that procreation is the fundamental purpose of marriage, whereas the Protestant position is that it is only one of the purposes, and then not the primary one. However, one should not be too ready to wish to prevent the birth of children, since children are to be regarded as a blessing from the Lord. God does not bypass the family, a relationship he established, in his gracious dealings with us. His promise is to be the God of his people and their children.

Contraception is not in principle wrong in itself but like anything else, may involve sin because of the motive of selfishness. Contraception may be wrong in itself if the particular method causes the destruction of human life. Methods which operate to destroy the fertilised ovum (eg. IUDs and the 'morning after' pill) are illegitimate. Some other methods (the ordinary contraceptive pill) may have side effects with long-term use but in principle are not illicit. The use of a condom and the 'natural' ('Billings') method are also acceptable in principle. A responsible approach is needed with good communication between the parties. It goes without saying that sexual intercourse between persons not committed to each other in marriage falls far short of God's purpose and is sin. True love involves commitment.

The fundamental nature of marriage is intended to be such that children are raised in the knowledge of their Creator. Properly speaking, however, marriage cannot have been ordained at creation for the increase of the church unless we take 'church' here more loosely as 'the people of God', since the church in order of history comes after creation and the fall. But given human sin and the provision of redemption, the ideal of marriage is properly realised only where there is community of faith between the parties.

24.3 The general rule and the Christian rule

It is lawful for all sorts of people to marry, provided that they can give informed consent.[5] Yet is it the duty of Christians to marry only in the Lord.[6] Therefore, those who profess the true reformed religion should not marry with unbelievers, Roman Catholics* or other idolaters; nor should those who are godly be unequally yoked by marrying those who are notoriously wicked in their life or who maintain soul-destroying heresies.[7]

5. Heb. 13:4; 1 Tim. 4:3; 1 Cor. 7:36–38; Gen. 24:57,58.
6. 1 Cor.7:39.
7. Gen. 34:14; Exod. 34:16; Deut. 7:3,4; 1 Kings 11:4; Neh. 13:25–27; Mal. 2:11,12; 2 Cor. 6:14.

* The 1646 text has 'papists'.

The Bible does not prohibit marriage other than as mentioned in 24:3–4. Inter-racial marriage, the marriage of persons who have disabilities or the marriage of older persons, are all lawful, although the advisability in any case may be another question.

In reference to religiously mixed marriages, one would say these are not advisable. Of course, sometimes a mixed marriage results from one person being converted after marriage. In such a case the marriage holds, unless the unbeliever refuses to remain. But Scripture goes further than advising against to actually forbid Christians to enter a marriage contract with an unbeliever, although such a marriage is valid if made. To keep this command one needs to avoid situations which will create difficulty in obedience—such as dating a person who is not eligible religiously.

24.4 Forbidden relationships

Marriage ought not to be within the degrees of blood relationship or kinship forbidden by the word of God.[8] When such incestuous marriages occur they can never be made legitimate by any human law or by agreement between the parties involved so that such persons can rightly live together as man and wife.[9] The man may not marry any of his wife's kin who are nearer in blood than he may of his own, nor the woman of her husband's kin who are nearer in blood than of her own.[10]

8. Leviticus chapter 18; 1 Cor. 5:1; Amos 2:7.
9. Mark 6:18; Lev. 18:24–28.
10. Lev. 20:19–21.

There are also natural restrictions arising from blood or family relationships. The idea of laws against incest is to provide safeguards against genetic problems which have emerged since the early history of the human race and to guard the freedom and purity of family life by ensuring the integrity and intimacy of family life is realised.[1] Sometimes the restrictions on marriage partners among the nations are far narrower than the Bible. For example, prior to 2005 South Korea still maintained the Confucian practice inherited from China.

The Scripture prohibits marriage to anyone closer than a first cousin whether by blood or marriage. Although the law on this subject forms part of the Mosaic code, these restrictions appear to rest on a more general basis since the Gentiles were judged for their violation before the law was

1. Cf. V. Poythress, *The Shadow of Christ in the Law of Moses* (P&R Publishing, 1991), 216–218

given to Israel through Moses (Lev. 18:24–30). They cannot be explained simply as restrictions created by the Jewish law.

The last sentence in the text was scrupled in the 19th century (particularly in the 1870s), and in most cases Presbyterian denominations deleted or no longer enforced it so that marriage to a deceased wife's sister is not rejected. Some have supposed the relevant Scripture (Lev. 20:21) is addressing the case of bigamy (cf. Lev. 18:18), although the apparently lighter penalty ('they will be childless') compared to other illicit relations ('they must be cut off') does not seem to fit this supposition. The Levirate law (Deut. 25:5–10) allowed, and even required, an unmarried brother or close relative to marry a deceased brother's wife if she was childless, so one assumes the deceased wife's sister in view in Lev. 20:21 already had children. A marriage in these circumstances was forbidden, clearly to discourage such marriages, but could continue with the penalty of being stripped of (legitimate) children, which is as much as to say, of honour and respect in Israel.

24.5 Ending a marriage – death or porneia

Adultery or fornication committed after a commitment to marry has been made but discovered before the marriage, gives the innocent party just cause to withdraw from the agreement.[11] In the case of adultery after marriage, it is lawful for the innocent party to sue for divorce[12] and, after the divorce, to marry someone else as if the offending party were dead.[13]

11. Matt. 1:18–20.
12. Matt. 5:31,32.
13. Matt. 19:9; Rom. 7:2,3.

Dissolution of a marriage is a serious matter. The main Old Testament reference is Deuteronomy 24:1–4. Strictly, it does not authorise divorce but recognises it in the course of regulating an aspect of it, namely, prohibiting the remarriage of a divorced wife to her former husband after she had married another man who had divorced her or died. Such a remarriage is said to be an abomination to the Lord. A permitted divorce was one where the man 'found some unclean thing' in his wife, and a properly attested divorce procedure had to be followed. Jesus affirms that 'Moses permitted you to divorce your wives because your hearts were hard. But it was not this way from the beginning' (Matt 19:8; Mark 10:5). What Jesus says reinforces the sanctity of marriage as given by God, and that must remain central in our thinking. The regulation in Deuteronomy 24 does not give positive approval to divorce, but provides for legal evidence and safeguards against hasty divorce which may be regretted later in that one could not return to his original wife.

The question is whether or not Jesus repeals the Mosaic permission. However, nothing in the reason he gives suggests he repeals it since human hearts are still hard. And when Jesus goes on to say that divorce and remarriage, except for *porneia*, is adultery (Matthew 19:9), perhaps he reaffirms Moses in a way which more clearly defines 'an unclean thing' than was common in his time.

The argument among many Jews could and did go like this: The Hebrew word *'erwat* (unclean) can apply to illicit sexual intercourse, but that cannot be the meaning in Deuteronomy 24, since illicit intercourse was punishable by death (pre-marital with a third party, Deut. 22:13–21; adultery, Deut. 22:22–27; bestiality, Lev. 20:15–16; homosexuality, Lev. 20:13). Therefore 'an unclean thing' must be something else, such as lack of beauty, childlessness etc. So it would be argued that divorce is permissible for many reasons, virtually anything, so long as the prescribed legal procedure was followed. This was the view of Rabbi Hillel (d.AD 10) while Rabbi Shammai (d. AD 30) confined the grounds for divorce to illicit sexual intercourse—a position with some credibility given that capital punishment does not seem to have been applied to all sexual offenders under the Old Testament (cf. David; also Joseph's approach in Matthew 1:19), and was formally abandoned about AD 30.

When Jesus stigmatises divorce and remarriage which occurs 'except for marital unfaithfulness' [Greek *porneia*] he rejects the liberal position of Hillel. The term *porneia* seems to interpret *'erwat* in Deut. 24. Porneia is not the Greek word for adultery (that would be *moicheia*), but best describes illicit sexual intercourse of all kinds (compare our word *pornography*). It follows that remarriage by the innocent party following a divorce on grounds of *porneia* is lawful in God's eyes.

Remarriage after divorce

The Church of Rome, which holds a sacramental view of marriage, teaches that remarriage of a person so divorced can only occur when the guilty party is dead. On this theory the divorce is really a permanent separation. But the Bible knows nothing of marriage obligations when a marriage is lawfully ended. One is either married or one is not. Against this view it is argued that Matthew 5:31–32, which also affirms the legitimacy of divorce on the grounds of *porneia*, goes on to say that whoever is divorced, other than on grounds of *porneia*, is made to commit adultery, and whoever marries a divorced woman commits adultery; hence, even the unjustly divorced have no remedy. But the passage must not be understood apart from its context.

The passage says that the innocent party is *made to commit adultery* by the divorce, and this can only be because such a person will normally remarry and thus, judged by the position established at creation, she commits adultery and so does whoever marries her. Remarriage by the innocent party is not literally adulterous. However, as remarriage would not have occurred apart from the sin of the man who divorced his wife improperly, Jesus draws out the consequences of his wrong attitude to

God and to his wife in a striking way: far from keeping God's requirement by attention to forms, the wrong attitude compounds the departure from God's norm for marriage, and in this sense the normally to be expected remarriage of the rejected wife can be described as adulterous. Jesus does not say that she cannot remarry, in fact he implies that she will, but this situation comes about because of the first husband's sin. A necessary implication of the passage is that a husband who divorces his wife for marital unfaithfulness is free from the sin of adultery should he remarry. Are we to suppose that a faithful woman cast out of her marriage by an unjust husband is in a less favourable position? Certainly not.

In Mark 10:1–12, which parallels Matthew 19, the exception clause and the statement implying remarriage of the unjustly divorced as the normal consequence, do not appear as they do in Matthew 5. Rather, the basic principle of the sanctity of marriage is affirmed: divorce is not to be contemplated. It was not relevant to Mark's purpose to include the exception. We also have the initiative of a woman in obtaining a divorce (v12). In other words, in marriage the two become one flesh but illicit sex violates the one flesh, hence either party may initiate divorce. Luke 16:18 gives a further condemnation of divorce and remarriage without stating the exception. The context (Luke 16:1–17) is that of the Pharisees' manipulation of the law to allow man's desires, and the statement of the essential principle was appropriate.

In short, whereas the scribes and Pharisees stressed the correct documentation Jesus stressed the fundamental principle, confined the grounds for divorce to sexual immorality, and showed how a loose approach to divorce inevitably furthered the evil.

Remarriage by a guilty party

The question of remarriage by a guilty party who repents is one requiring very careful consideration. Obviously reconciliation is impossible if the divorced spouse has remarried. The prospect of a fresh marriage is suggested by the need to direct the sexual impulse into proper channels, and by the claims of Christian compassion and forgiveness.

24.6 Ending a marriage – desertion

The sinful character of man is such as tends to look for excuses to justify the divorce of those whom God has joined together in marriage. However, only adultery# or deliberate desertion which cannot be remedied by the church or the civil authority is a sufficient ground for dissolving the marriage bond.[14] Divorce proceedings are to be conducted in a public and orderly manner so that the parties concerned in it are not left to decide the matter as they see fit.[15]

Strictly, illicit sexual intercourse of all kinds as defined in the exception clause of Matt 19:9.
14. Matt. 19:8,9; 1 Cor.7:15; Matt. 19:6.
15. Deut. 24:1–4.

This section cautions against finding excuses for divorce, requires divorce proceedings to be properly regulated, and affirms that divorce on the grounds of irremediable desertion (the so-called 'Pauline privilege') is also legitimate. Jesus had addressed the position of marriage among the covenant nation, but the spread of the Gospel among all nations presented new situations.

In 1 Corinthians 7 Paul deals with various matters concerning marriage. Verses 17–24 state the general principle of remaining in the social situation one has when one becomes a Christian. In verses 1–7 Paul insists that deprivation of sexual relations by wives who think this a spiritual course is wrong. It leads the men into immorality. Paul insists that there is to be no abuse of sexual relations, no manipulation, no depriving, no abstinence except on the basis of mutual agreement for a limited time for purposes of prayer. In verses 8–9 he says that it is perfectly proper for widowers[2] and widows to remain as they are. Marriage is an appropriate course for any who are already sinning. In verses 10–11 Christian married couples are not to divorce. Separation may sometimes be appropriate but reconciliation is always to be the aim. In verses 12–16, concerning mixed marriages, divorce is not to be sought simply on the ground of religious difference. The believer's life (not so much the words) should be eloquent so that the unbeliever may be won for Christ. But if the unbeliever will not remain the believer is *not bound* in such cases. Paul's emphasis is that everything possible should be done to maintain the marriage but if the unbeliever does leave let him do so—the marriage is at an end. A parallel passage in Romans 7:2 shows Paul's usage where he says a wife is *bound* to her husband as long as he lives. Thus we conclude that wilful desertion by an unbeliever, after the spouse has become a believer, with the intent the desertion be final allows the formal termination of the marriage. This being so remarriage is possible for the one deserted.

The principle of 1 Corinthians 7:15 would seem capable of extension to cases of wilful and permanent desertion in situations not precisely of the kind noted by Paul, for example by a professing Christian who deserts a spouse (and repudiates thereby his or her Christian profession), or cases of such cruelty that there is a virtual repudiation of the marriage vows. But one should always approach marriage on the basis that there is no easy way out, that vows are to be kept, and that work and effort is needed to build and strengthen any relationship. The Bible does not approve divorce; in fact, God says he hates it (Mal. 2:16), but he does allow it as a means of controlling one of the evils sin has brought. Interestingly, God kept his marriage covenant with Israel but Israel did not, so God gave her a certificate of divorce (Jer 3:8) and she went into exile. Judah too was unfaithful and was sent away but without a certificate of divorce (Isa.

2. The Greek word *agamois* has traditionally been rendered 'the unmarried' but good reasons for the translation 'widowers' are given in G. Fee, *The First Epistle to the Corinthians* (Eerdmans, 1987) 287–288.

50:1) so the exile in Babylon was not the end for Judah but a separation (Isa. 54:6–7) followed by restoration.

THOUGHTS FROM OTHER MINDS

'We may not discount or underestimate the fact that marriage is the divine provision for the sex impulses with which God has endowed us. These impulses are not ignoble; they are implanted by God, ingenerated in our nature. Since God had created man with these sex instincts, there would have been an imperfection in God's creation if he had not made provision for the satisfaction of these impulses. It is not in line with biblical thought to underestimate the motivation and urge to marriage arising from the sex impulse in the more restricted sense of desire for the sexual act. There is a wholesome candour about the way in which Paul develops and applies that truth. His treatment is a protest against the false asceticism which has too frequently been entertained, practised, and propagated in connection with the sexual urge. Ironically enough this asceticism lies close to the grossest kinds of sexual indulgence.'

John Murray (1898–1975)[3]

FOR DISCUSSION

1. Has a small local church any responsibility to assist young Christians to have contact with a circle from whom a marriage partner might be found?
2. Is the problem of divorce due to easy divorce laws, or to deeper spiritual problems?
3. How does Rome use annulment to get around her view of divorce?

---

3. *Principles of Conduct: Aspects of Biblical Ethics* (Eerdmans, 1957), 77.

4. What can we learn from our Lord's strict teaching on marriage and yet his pastoral care in the case of the Samaritan woman (John 4:16ff), or the woman taken in adultery (John 8:3ff)?

CHAPTER 25
THE CHURCH

ANALYSIS *WCF 25:1–6*
1–2. The church's identity
3. The church's marks and task
4-5. The church's purity
6. The church's head

The Roman Church makes the claim to be the one true church. This was pointedly expressed in the bull *Unam sanctam* of Pope Boniface VIII in 1302, which asserted that it was necessary for all human beings for their salvation to be subject to the bishop of Rome. Pope Leo X reaffirmed this at the Fifth Lateran Council in 1516, just prior to the Reformation. This sweeping claim is still made today although some qualifications are made to relate separated brethren and even those of other faiths to the Roman Catholic Church so that the possibility of their salvation can be admitted. The decree of Vatican Council II in 1964 entitled *Dogmatic Constitution of the Church* reminds us that although the bishops have a role '…the Roman Pontiff, by virtue of his office as Vicar of Christ, namely, and as pastor of the entire Church, has full, supreme and universal power over the whole church, a power which he can always exercise unhindered.'

At the time of the Reformation the Reformers did not devalue the church as the visible society of God's people. Rather, they insisted that the true church was characterised by a striving for conformity to God's word, and they contrasted this with the false church which 'assigns more authority to itself and its ordinances than to the Word of God. It does not want to submit itself to the yoke of Christ. It does not administer the sacraments as Christ commanded in his word, but adds to them and subtracts from them as it pleases. It bases itself more on men than on Jesus Christ. It persecutes those who live holy lives according to the word of God and who rebuke the false church for its sins, greed and idolatries'.[1]

A church is either striving for conformity to God's word or it is not, and so in this sense there are no degrees of trueness. A church is a true church or it is not. But to speak of striving for conformity to God's word is to imply that such conformity is not attained: there is impurity and sin in every true church. Thus, although the Lutherans did not generally recognise the Reformed in the 16th and 17th centuries, the Reformed, with few exceptions, did recognise the Lutheran Church as a true church and accepted Lutheran members at the Lord's Table in Reformed churches, and likewise with the members of the Anglican Church. The errors the Reformed held existed in the Lutheran Church, particularly on the nature of the presence of Christ in the Supper, were not regarded as in the fundamentals of the blood, suffering, death and obedience of Jesus Christ in whom believers have forgiveness of sins, nor did these errors arise from a despising of Scripture, but from a misunderstanding of it.

Rome placed such stress on the church as a visible organisation that she lost sight of the essence of the church as a congregation of believers. Coupled with the stress on the infallibility of the church, the church was placed beyond substantial criticism, hence Rome's fierce rejection of the Reformation.

The New Testament teaches that there is one flock and one shepherd (John 10:16), one body, one Spirit, one hope, one Lord, one faith, one baptism, one God and Father of all (Eph. 4:4). Scripture recognises that the essential unity of the church given by the Spirit may be inadequately

1. *Belgic Confession* (1561), 29.

expressed (Eph. 4:3), and our Lord prayed about this (John 17:21), but Scripture does not accommodate the definition of the church to the anomalies produced as a result of sin, such as the presence of hypocrites. Thus Paul can write to churches as those called to be saints and sanctified in Christ, yet speak of the need for putting out a grossly erring member (1 Cor. 1:1,2; 5:1ff). We conclude then that the church is not to be defined as including chaff and wheat, but that it is addressed according to its calling and profession.

The Reformers employed the idea of the church as invisible to emphasise that the church's life depends on divine election, and the operation of the Spirit which are not infallibly discerned by men. The distinction has often been misunderstood. It does not mean there are two churches, but that the one church may be viewed in two ways, and that the church as we see it ought not to be thought of apart from its nature as a holy congregation of true Christian believers. In short, hypocrites and evil persons may be admitted into the church, administered as it is by fallible men, but they are not thereby assured of salvation. The distinction between the visible and invisible aspects has also been misapplied as a means of escape from facing the obligation of unity, and as an excuse for failure to address doctrinal and moral error in a particular denomination. But this is just as wrong as is losing sight of the invisible aspect belonging to the church by an over-emphasis on the visible aspect.

25.1 The church's identity as the totality of the redeemed

The catholic or universal church is not visible to us for it consists of the whole number of the elect, who have been, are, or shall be gathered into one, under Christ, its Head. This church is the bride,* the body, the fulness of him who fills all in all.[1]

* The 1646 text has 'spouse'.
1. Eph. 1:10,22,23; Eph. 5:23,27,32; Col. 1:18.

Christians confess belief in 'one holy catholic church.' This one church embraces all of God's elect in every age and place, but until the consummation it will not be gathered into one place under its Head. Neither the elect gathered to date, nor their totality at the consummation, is seen by us, and so the holy catholic (=universal) church is believed in as an article of our faith. 'Let all our views, impressions, and conduct in regard to the visible church, and its different branches, be regulated by *some* reference to this great invisible spiritual reality,—that thus we may be led to estimate the purity and efficiency of visible churches mainly by a respect to the spiritual character and attainments of their individual members.'[2]

25.2 The church's identity as militant on earth

The catholic or universal church, as visibly existing on earth under the gospel, is not confined to one nation as it was under the law of Moses. This church consists of all those throughout the world who profess the true religion,[2] together with their children.[3] It is the kingdom of the Lord Jesus Christ,[4] the house and family of God,[5] outside of which there is no ordinary possibility of salvation.[6]

2. 1 Cor. 1:2; 1 Cor. 12:12,13; Psalm 2:8; Rev. 7:9; Rom. 15:9–12.
3. 1 Cor. 7:14; Acts 2:39; Ezek. 16:20,21; Rom. 11:16; Gen. 3:15; Gen. 17:7.
4. Matt. 13:47; Isa. 9:7. 5. Eph. 2:19; Eph. 3:15. 6. Acts 2:47.

If the catholic church from one viewpoint is invisible, from another it is visible in the association of believers here on earth. The contrast with section 25.1 is not between two churches, one invisible and one visible, but between the holy catholic church (section 1) and the church militant on earth (section 2). There is only one church but it must be viewed under these two aspects if justice is to be done to the teaching in Scripture. 'We can avoid the inconsistency of admitting on the one

2. Cunningham, *Historical Theology*, 1:26.

hand, that hypocrites and evil men may be in the purest churches on earth, and yet, on the other hand, claiming for the Church militant all the attributes of faultlessness and perfect holiness, only when we make the former statement with reference to the visible Church and the latter with reference to the Church as invisible.'[3] The relevance of this position for the refutation of the Roman Catholic view is evident. It refutes the Separatists and Independents too, for they recognised only the visible church and made it consist of the regenerate only.

The wording of this section implies the essential unity of the covenant of grace and of the church in both Old and New Testaments. The church on earth is the covenant people of God, and embraces those who profess the true religion and their children in accordance with the covenant promise.

The church is catholic because it does not consist of individual competing parts but parts of one whole, a world-wide empire. 'The Churches of the different nationalities constitute the provinces of this empire; and though they are so far independent of each other, yet they are so one, that membership in one is membership in all, and separation from one is separation from all. . . . This conception of the Church, of which, at least in some aspects, we have *practically* so much lost sight of, had a firm hold of the Scottish theologians of the seventeenth century.'[4]

The reference to those who profess the true religion must not be taken as a mere declaration, but as a serious, apparently sincere profession evidenced in apparent subjection to Christ. Such a person is admitted a member of the church not because the church judges him or her to be regenerate (that would require men to judge the genuineness of spiritual graces), but because the profession is appropriate for one who is regenerate, called of God and not of man.

3. John Macpherson, *The Doctrine of the Church in Scottish Theology* (Macniven & Wallace, 1903), 70.
4. James Walker, *The Theology and Theologians of Scotland* (T. & T. Clark, 1872), 95–6.

The children of the faithful are also members of the church. The *Westminster Directory for Public Worship* (January 1645) states: 'The promise is made to believers and their seed, and the seed and posterity of the faithful, born within the church, have by their birth, interest in the covenant, and right to the seal of it.' The following implications may be drawn: (1) Those baptised in infancy who do not profess faith in their maturity, do not have a right to baptism for their children. Their unbelief disqualifies them from that privilege.[5] (2) Presbyterians, possibly because of a certain application of the visible/invisible church distinction, have usually only reckoned church membership by communicants. However, the baptised but not yet professing members of the church should also be recorded on a church membership roll, as is the practice of Reformed churches in Europe.

This section also affirms the importance of the church. 'When we say that out of the visible church there is no ordinary possibility of salvation, we guard against the error of supposing that connection with the church as an institution necessarily secures salvation, and equally against the notion that God regards the use of his own appointed means of grace as of slight importance. By sovereign power he can work savingly apart from those means, but ordinarily he does not.'[6] The church is not so bound to the marks of the church (see below) that all outside it—such as unbaptised believers, unbaptised infants of believers, and the wrongfully excommunicated, are lost, but church membership is still a matter of the utmost seriousness.

25.3 The marks of the church and its task

In order to gather and perfect the saints in this life to the end of the world, Christ has given to this universal visible church the ministry, the

5. There has not been full consistency of practice on this point. Some situations (as in the Scottish Highlands) reflect an historical or cultural development which requires sensitive pastoral handling.
6. Macpherson, *The Confession of Faith*, 143.

message to be proclaimed, and the ordinances of God to be observed. By his own presence and Spirit, according to his promise, he makes these means effective for this gathering and perfecting of the saints.[7]

7. 1 Cor. 12:28; Eph. 4:11–13; Matt. 28:19,20; Isa. 59:21.

The preaching of the word and the administration of the sacraments are indicated as two means by which believers are gathered and built up in their faith. Thus they are also marks of the church. Church discipline, the third mark commonly affirmed by the Reformed church, is treated in WCF 30 cf. 20:4; 15:6. The statement, that to the church 'Christ has given ... *the ministry*', reminds us that in a real sense the church exists in the effective call of God before the ministry. The question of the validity of a ministry, so much regarded by those who define the church in terms of a claimed succession of valid orders from apostolic times, is secondary to the existence of a body of believers promoting and maintaining the fundamental principles of Christian truth according to the apostolic writings. It is granted that ordination by existing spiritual rulers is the regular means of setting apart new ministers, but this is not essential to validity if, in God's providence, a body of Christians have no opportunity to secure a ministry in the regular way and instead acknowledge as a minister one suitably gifted in their congregation.[7]

25.4 The church's purity

This universal church has been sometimes more, sometimes less visible.[8] The particular churches belonging to it are more or less pure, depending on how the doctrine of the gospel is taught and embraced, the ordinances administered and public worship performed.[9]

8. Rom. 11:3,4; Rev. 12:6,14.
9. Revelation chapters 2 & 3; 1 Cor. 5:6,7.

7. Cunningham, *Historical Theology*, 1:31.

The spread of the church and the number and faithfulness of local and national churches has varied enormously in different ages and places. Sometimes the church has seemed almost non-existent. The purity of a particular church is to be judged by the fidelity or otherwise to the doctrine of salvation, the use of the sacraments and the observance of worship. The proof texts from Revelation 2 & 3 and 1 Corinthians 5 indicate there is no suggestion that the relative purity of any local church is a matter of no consequence, for Christ in his word in general, and these passages in particular, calls his church to faithfulness. But failure to acknowledge the relative purity of any particular church in her pilgrim life on earth leads to schism by those seeking a purity which cannot be attained, or else it leads to sectarianism.

25.5 The church's purity

The purest churches under heaven are subject both to impurity and error.[10] Some churches have so degenerated that they have ceased to be churches of Christ and have become synagogues of Satan.[11] Nevertheless, there will always be a church on earth to worship God according to his will.[12]

10. 1 Cor. 13:12; Revelation chapters 2 & 3; Matt. 13:24–30,47.
11. Rev. 18:2; Rev. 11:18–22.
12. Matt. 16:18; Psalm 72:17; Psalm 102:28; Matt. 28:19,20.

The assertion that the purest churches are subject to impurity does not mean that there is an absolutely pure church which, however, is liable to fall. It means that the purest church is still only relatively pure because evil is ever mixed with good, and the striving to do all things according to Christ's word always falls short. Errors of greater or lesser significance will be present. Errors can multiply, and the lampstand can be taken away. Compare the case of English Presbyterian churches which descended into Unitarianism in the 18th century, or once Bible-loving churches dominated by liberal theology in the 20th century.

The marks of the church (pure preaching of the word, sacraments rightly administered, scriptural discipline maintained) are important tests for judging whether or not a church is true. We cannot deny the name of church to a body which strives to maintain the truth of God and holds fast to the fundamental truths of the word of God. True unity exists when all such churches recognise each other and strive more and more to fight against Satan and come to a fuller understanding of Christ's will in Scripture: in this sense *a Reformed church is always reforming.*

The mere presence of some errors or abuses will not be sufficient to cause us to withdraw from a church. The nature of the errors, the insistence with which they are advocated, and the freedom or otherwise we have from compliance, will be relevant in deciding whether or not we can remain in the body. Certainly, withdrawal is not to be contemplated lightly. The multiplicity of denominations today makes it easier for one to find a spiritual home, but we must not think that denominational differences are unimportant, or that different churches are equally acceptable if they hold basic fundamentals. The church is called to contend earnestly for the faith, to teach *all* Christ commanded, and there must be readiness to submit to Scripture in everything.

A church may fall to a level which makes it unlawful for a believer to hold communion with it, even though it be admitted that it contains true believers. John Calvin writes:

'However, when we categorically deny to the papists the title of *the* church, we do not for this reason impugn the existence of churches among them. Rather, we are only contending about the true and lawful constitution of the church, required in the communion not only of the sacraments (which are the signs of profession) but also especially of doctrine. Daniel [Dan. 9:27] and Paul [2 Thess. 2:4] foretold that Antichrist would sit in the Temple of God. With us, it is the Roman pontiff we make the leader and standard bearer of that wicked and abominable kingdom. The fact that his seat is placed in the Temple of God signifies that his reign was not to be such as to wipe out either the name of Christ or of the church. From this it is evident that we by no means deny that the churches under his tyranny remain churches. But these he has profaned by his sacrilegious impiety, afflicted by his inhuman domination, corrupted and well-nigh killed by his evil and deadly doctrines, which are like poisoned drinks. In them Christ lies hidden, half buried, the gospel overthrown, piety scattered, the worship of God nearly wiped out. In them, briefly, everything is so confused that there we see the face of Babylon rather than that of the Holy City of God. To sum up, I call them churches to the extent that the Lord wonderfully preserves in them a remnant of his people, however woefully dispersed and scattered, and to the extent that some marks of the church remain—especially those marks whose effectiveness neither the devil's wiles nor human depravity can destroy. But on the other hand, because in them those marks have been erased to which we should pay particular regard in this discourse, I say that every one of their congregations and their whole body lack the lawful form of the church.'[8]

Similarly, the 17th century Scottish Presbyterian writers, men of no narrow focus, abhorred schism, regarded the Lord's Table as the table of the universal church not of one part of the church, recognised baptism by Roman Catholic priests, and the discipline of even corrupted churches, if it was not in the matter of the corruption itself. This admirable ecumenical ideal, combined as it was with the utmost jealousy for purity of doctrine, worship and discipline, is worthy of imitation.

The continuance of the church of Christ is guaranteed by the election of God, the redemption of Christ and the activity of the Holy Spirit.

8. Calvin, *Institutes*, 4.2.12.

Particular churches may disappear, but the church persists, even if sometimes reduced so as to be a small remnant.

25.6 The church's head

There is no other head of the church but the Lord Jesus Christ.[13] The Pope of Rome can in no sense be the church's head. The general spirit and distinctive features of the Papal system are opposed to Christ, and represent a serious departure from Christian truth and practice, a departure which was predicted in Scripture itself.[14*]

13. Col. 1:18; Eph. 1:22.
14. Matt. 23:8–10; 2 Thess. 2:3,4,8,9; Rev. 13:6.
* The 1646 text of the last part reads '*but is that antichrist, that man of sin, and son of perdition, that exalteth himself in the church against Christ, and all that is called God.*'

The first two sentences of this section are agreed by all Presbyterians. The last sentence in the original form as footnoted, which derives from the *Irish Articles* (1615) art. 80, has been scrupled over the past century, although without real basis in my view. Some also think (and rightly) that the Confession's statement conflicts with the ideals of tolerance and inclusive ecumenicity presently popular. Some churches have deleted these words and others have reworded them (see below).

Identification of the papacy with antichrist goes back many centuries before the Reformation, with not only dissidents and heretics but notable churchmen using the term when they wished to castigate abuse of power by the Bishop of Rome. While no real objection can be raised against the original expressions if the scope and context is kept in mind, the wording given in the modernised text indicates the essence of the original text in a straightforward way not likely to be misconstrued. For the doctrinal positions of the Confession in 25:6 are (1) that the Pope is not the head of the church; (2) that he exalts himself as if he were, which (3) proves him to be activated by the anti-Christian spirit which seeks religious veneration (Matt 23:8–9) and persecutes the godly (Rev. 13:6), and so illustrates the truth of the prediction of apostasy in the church (2 Thess. 2:3–4,8–9). Sadly, all of this is still true today.

The man of sin passage was regarded by virtually all 17th century Protestants as referring to a movement of error in history, under the guise of friendship to Christ, that had come to dominate in the organised church. Its seed-bed is in the heart of any who do not sincerely embrace the authority of Christ in his word, yet profess to be his friends, and its outgrowth is evident not only in the Papacy but in apostate Protestantism and the like. The lurid pictures of popular imagination must be put to one side.

The reformers did not teach that the Church of Rome is no church at all, and this section of the Confession distinguishes the church and the papacy as the quotation from Calvin given earlier also illustrates. Nor is the possibility of change for the better in Rome excluded by the antichrist identification, since 'the breath of Christ's mouth' (2 Thess. 2:8 cf. Isaiah 11:4), that is, the truth of the Gospel, overcomes the apostasy, although the complete elimination of error in the church under the guise of truth awaits Christ's return.

That the language of 2 Thess. 2 is fittingly applied to the papacy is evident, but that one is thereby committed to a detailed scheme of prophetic interpretation is not implied. This follows from the fact that the context is 'The Headship of the Church' not 'The Interpretation of Prophecy', from our knowledge that the framers of the Confession did not intend to insert such debatable elements in it, and from the distinction between the interpretation of a text as referring to apostasy and its application to a particular manifestation. Thus, those who agree that the Papal system is anti-Christian but regard the Biblical passages as having their further fulfilment in a future individual are not prevented from subscribing the Confession. The present writer does not favour this futurist position on exegetical grounds,[9] and it was not at all usual among 17th century Protestants either, but he admits that it may be held consistently with the Confession, if errors such as dispensationalism are not held with it.

The Presbyterian Church in the United States (the Southern Church) rewrote the section in 1939 so as to read: *The Lord Jesus Christ is the only head of the church, and the claim of any man to be the vicar of Christ and the head of the church, is without warrant in fact or in Scripture, even anti-Christian, an usurpation dishonouring to the Lord Jesus Christ.* With the exception of the words 'even anti-Christian' this was virtually identical to an earlier modification by the Northern Church.

THOUGHTS FROM OTHER MINDS

'But while spurious unity is to be condemned, the lack of unity among churches of Christ which profess the faith in its purity is a patent violation of the unity of the body of Christ, and of that unity which the prayer of our Lord requires us to promote. . . . The unity prayed for was one that would bear witness to the world, and therefore belonged to the realm of the observable. The implications for visible confession and witness are unavoidable.'

John Murray (1898–1975)[10]

FOR DISCUSSION

1. What is right and what is wrong about the modern ecumenical movement?

---

9. See my article, 'The Man of Sin', *Banner of Truth Magazine* (December 1977), 26-32. For a sample of some positive views on the future of the Gospel see I. H. Murray, *The Puritan Hope* (Banner of Truth, 1971).
10. *Collected Writings of John Murray: Systematic Theology*, 335.

2. Biblical descriptions of the church include that of a building, a body and a bride. Discuss each of these.
3. What are the principles to determine which particular church we should join?
4. What do you think of 'birds of passage', those spiritual tramps who move constantly from one church to another? How can this problem be reduced?

CHAPTER 26

THE COMMUNION OF THE SAINTS

ANALYSIS *WCF 26:1–3*

1. Its foundation

2. Its practical expression

3. Its qualifications

26.1 The foundation of communion among believers

All saints are united to Jesus Christ, their head, by his Spirit and by faith, and have fellowship with him in his grace, sufferings, death, resurrection, and glory.[1] United to one another in love, the saints have communion in each other's gifts and graces,[2] and are under obligation to perform such duties, public and private, as promote their mutual good, in both spiritual and temporal concerns.[3]

1. 1 Jn. 1:3; Eph. 3:16–19; Jn 1:16; Eph. 2:5,6; Phil. 3:10; Rom. 6:5,6; 2 Tim. 2:12.
2. Eph. 4:15,16; 1 Cor. 12:7; 1 Cor. 3:21–23; Col. 2:19.
3. 1 Thess. 5:11,14; Rom. 1:11,12,14; 1 Jn. 3:16–18; Gal. 6:10.

The communion of saints is not a matter only of the life to come when we will enjoy the fellowship of other believers. The reality of fellowship here and now with other believers by virtue of union with Christ is the subject of this chapter. It follows on naturally from the teaching about the church in WCF 25. The fellowship or communion of which this chapter speaks is not simply on a spiritual level but is worked out in very practical ways too. We are able to have, and desire to have, this fellowship with other believers, because of the new relationship which we have to Christ, and the workings of his grace in our lives.

26.2 The practical expression of this communion

By their profession of Christ, saints are committed to maintain a holy fellowship and communion in the worship of God, and in performing such other services as help them build each other up in spiritual things;[4] and they are also bound to assist each other in temporal things according to their different abilities and needs. This communion is to be extended, as God gives opportunity, to all those in every place who call upon the name of the Lord Jesus.[5]

4. Heb. 10:24,25; Acts 2:42,46; Isa. 2:3; 1 Cor. 11:20.
5. Acts 2:44,45; 1 Jn. 3:17; 2 Cor. 8 & 9; Acts 11:29,30.

The two areas in which this fellowship is shown are the spiritual and the temporal. It is to be noted that no restriction is placed on the obligation of extending fellowship to believers. We are to do good to all men, but especially to those of the household of faith. There is no sectarianism here, but all who are members of the family of God are to be recipients of our care. This includes fellow believers of different racial or social background as well as believers in other denominations than our own. Note the specific comment about worship, an important emphasis given the tendency to neglect the public means of grace.

26.2 Some qualifications

The communion which the saints have with Christ, does not make them in any way sharers of the substance of his Godhead nor does it make them to be equal with Christ in any respect, and to affirm either is impious and blasphemous.[6] Nor does sharing with one another as saints take away or infringe the right of ownership and use each person has of his own goods and possessions.[7]

6. Col. 1:18,19; 1 Cor. 8:6; Isa. 42:8; 1 Tim. 6:15,16; Psalm 45:7 with Heb. 1:8,9.
7. Exod. 20:15; Eph. 4:28; Acts 5:4.

Union with Christ is a fundamental Christian teaching. It is a union by covenant and representation and does not involve any confusion of persons as some mystical strains of teaching have held. Compare James Denny's comment: 'I would rather be found in Christ than lost in God.' But as the covenant of marriage results in a personal relationship, so the covenant of grace means that 'our life is bound up in the bundle of the life of our Lord and Saviour Jesus Christ' (Thomas Goodwin), and the cardinal experiences of our Lord have a parallel in our experience. Christ dwells in us by his Spirit, but there is something ultimately mysterious about the mystical union of Christ and the believer.

Similarly, our fellowship with other believers does not mean that the individual is lost in the crowd. There was a voluntary sharing of property in the needy Jerusalem church (Acts 2:44–45; 4:32–35), but it was not a compulsory measure (Acts 5:4). The general principle of the New Testament is acceptance of the social position we have when we become believers (1 Cor.7:20), and recognition of the needs of others so that the whole body is built up, we being members one of another.

THOUGHTS FROM OTHER MINDS

'If we are all one, why then is it the case that our property is not common? We must remind ourselves of the foundation. We are one in and through Christ. We are not one directly. Therefore our property first belongs to Christ and only through him to each other. Thus, for example, we have no right to demand of our brother his car. Rather, our attitude must be one of humility and thankfulness for all that we receive. We must respect the fact that our brother's property belongs to him as a divine stewardship. We have no direct claim upon his goods. With that stewardship we have no right to interfere.'

Sam Waldron[1]

1. *A Modern Exposition of the 1689 Baptist Confession of Faith*, 336.

FOR DISCUSSION

1. Does union with Christ begin or climax the Christian life? What different conception of Christianity is involved in the two possible answers?
2. What is wrong with the notion that one can live the Christian life without church attendance? How would you deal pastorally with a person holding this position?
3. What is the purpose for which Christ gives particular gifts to particular members of his church?

CHAPTER 27
THE SACRAMENTS IN GENERAL

ANALYSIS *WCF 27:1–5*

1. Definition
- a. their origin
- b. their nature
- c. their purpose

2. Relationship between sign and thing signified

3. Effectiveness
- a. not inherent or dependent on intention
- b. depends on Spirit and the word

4. Number

5. Relationship of New to Old Testament sacraments

27.1 The foundation of communion among believers

Sacraments are holy signs and seals of the covenant of grace.[1] They were directly instituted by God[2] to represent Christ and his benefits, and to confirm our participation in him.[3] They also mark a visible difference between those who belong to the church and the rest of the world,[4] and solemnly pledge them to the service of God in Christ, according to his word.[5]

1. Rom. 4:11; Gen. 17:7,10. 2. Matt. 28:19; 1 Cor. 11:23.
3. 1 Cor.10:16; 1 Cor. 11:25,26; Gal. 3:27.
4. Rom. 15:8; Exod. 12:48; Gen. 34:14.
5. Rom. 6:3,4; 1 Cor. 10:16,21.

The word sacrament (something sacred) is a useful one to express biblical teaching, although it has had a varied meaning in church history. The first sentence succinctly states what is elaborated in the second sentence. The sacraments are not simply sacred things but sacred things instituted by Christ. As signs and seals of the covenant of grace they point to and confirm the vital truths of the Gospel. The sacraments also serve to mark off those who profess faith in Christ, and they involve a vow of commitment to loyal service.

27.2 The sign and the thing signified

In every sacrament there is a spiritual relationship or sacramental union between the sign and the thing signified. This is why the names and effects of the one are sometimes attributed to the other.[6]

1. Gen. 17:10; Matt. 26:27,28; Titus 3:5.

The sign and the thing signified must not be identified as by those who teach baptismal regeneration. Still, there is a relationship between the outward sign and the spiritual blessing it represents so that the sacrament can be spoken of as if it were the grace represented, and vice versa. In short, the sacrament cannot be separated from the sign but nor may it be identified with them.

27.3 The sign and the thing signified

The grace which is set forth in or by the correct use of the sacraments, is not conferred by any power in them, nor does the effectiveness of a sacrament depend on the character or intention of the one who administers it.[7] Rather, the effectiveness of a sacrament depends on the work of the Spirit[8] and the word of institution, for God's word not only authorises their use but also promises benefits to those who receive them rightly.[9]

7. Rom. 2:28,29; 1 Pet. 3:21.
8. Matt. 3:11; 1 Cor. 12:13.
9. Matt. 26:27,28; Matt. 28:19,20.

Two false views of Rome are here rejected. (1) The sacraments do not have an inherent power so that they more or less work automatically (*ex opere operato*) as, in effect, is the Roman teaching which says that, so long as the receiver puts no obstacle in the way, grace is actually conferred. (2) Rome taught that the priest must intend to do what the church teaches for the sacrament to be valid (*Council of Trent*, VII,11). This doctrine of intention leads to uncertainty in any particular case as to whether the sacrament has been validly administered, since no one can see the real intention of another.

The section teaches that the grace received by the sacraments is received in the way of faith in the objective promise of God and dependence on the work of the Spirit, rather than depending on the shifting states of human consciousness or on some inherent power. Faith is not to be equated with the right disposition or proper motive of the Roman teaching since 'the disposition that puts no obstacle in the way' is really a co-operation with grace and a contribution to salvation, whereas the Biblical way of faith is an assertion of dependence on the one in whom we believe. It is to be noted that the section also points out that the character of the administrator does not affect the validity of the sacrament. A Christian minister may be a hypocrite or later reject the faith, but the validity does not depend on his character but on the sure promise of God and the work of the Spirit.

27.4 Number

There are only two sacraments ordained by Christ our Lord in the gospel, namely, Baptism, and the Lord's Supper; neither of these may be dispensed by any person other than a lawfully ordained minister of the word.[10]

10. Matt. 28:19; 1 Cor. 11:20,23; 1 Cor. 4:1; Heb. 5:4.

The Church of Rome has taught for about 1,000 years that there are seven sacraments (baptism, confirmation, the eucharist, penance, holy orders, marriage, holy unction). She makes much of the symbolism of seven and links each sacrament to the stages of life reflecting the thought that 'the totality of man's life from birth to death is flooded with sacramental, supernatural light. . . . Roman Catholic theology fixes the number of sacraments on the basis of its view that they constitute a series of supernatural acts that infuse supernatural grace into all of life from beginning to end, rather than upon an indubitable foundation of biblical exegesis'.[1] The controversy over the number of sacraments is at root a controversy over the nature of grace.

Rome, because of the way she ties grace to the sacraments, gives lay persons the right to administer baptism to those who are ill and at risk of death. The principle of the Confession that only a minister should administer the sacraments follows from the fact that sacraments are seals of the word and are not to be administered without the word, and that the ministry is a gift of Christ and a stewardship in which a man must be faithful. Others not called to it should not intrude into it. The intent of this statement is not to suggest that the effectiveness of the sacrament depends on the character of the administrator, a view specifically rejected in WCF 27:3, but to ensure proper order and to check superstitious views as to the absolute necessity of the sacraments as taught by Rome. Probably most Presbyterian denominations have given to persons not ordained in the full sense a limited right to preach and to administer the sacraments in the capacity of Home Missionaries, lest persons in remote areas, with only rare visits from ordained ministers, be utterly deprived of the sacraments.

27.5 Relationship of sacraments in the OT & NT

The sacraments of the Old Testament signified and set forth essentially the same spiritual things as those of the New Testament.[11]

11. 1 Cor. 10:1–4.

1. G. C. Berkouwer, *The Sacraments* (Eerdmans, 1969), 30,36.

In 27:2 we saw that the relationship between the sign and the thing signified is such that the sacrament can be spoken of as the grace it signifies and vice versa. The text cited (1 Cor.10:2) speaks of the baptism of the Israelites whereas they were in fact circumcised, while in Colossians 2:11–12, Paul speaks of the Christians being baptised by the circumcision of Christ, ie. Christ's death is the basis of true circumcision and equivalent to union with Christ of which baptism is the seal. In 1 Corinthians 5:7 Paul refers to the Passover when in fact it was the Lord's Supper which the Corinthians observed (1 Cor.11). From such passages we can see that circumcision and the passover were essentially the same in spiritual significance to baptism and the Lord's Supper. We could infer the same from the broad principles of biblical teaching.

THOUGHTS FROM OTHER MINDS

'But in addition, to crown His infinite goodness, He has willed to add to the preaching of His Word certain actions which are designed to compel the most uneducated and stubborn in the world to believe more and more that God is not mocking them in offering them eternal life by this most wondrous means—the death of His own Son. Thus, by such signs and actions, all their senses are driven to consent to the doctrine of the Gospel, as if they were already fully enjoying the salvation which is promised to them . . . While we are here below, we possess the Heavenly Kingdom only by hope (Rom. 8:24; 1 Cor.13:9); it is needful that we be supported to grow in this and persevere to the end (Eph. 5:15).'

Theodore Beza (1519–1605)[2]

'It is certainly true that we get no new thing in the Sacrament; we get no other thing in the Sacrament than we get in the Word. For what more could you ask than really to receive the Son of God himself? . . . The Sacrament is appointed that we may get a better hold of Christ than we got in the simple Word, that we

2. *The Christian Faith* (1558, tr. J. Clark 1992) 50,51

may possess Christ in our hearts and minds more fully than we did before, by the simple Word.... The Sacraments also serve to seal up and confirm the truth that is in the Word.... Although you believed the evidence before, yet by the seals you believe it better.... Therefore the whole concern of Christians should be, when they see the sacraments and hear the Word, to find and feel in their hearts and minds, that which they hear and see.'

Robert Bruce (1554–1631)[3]

FOR DISCUSSION

1. Discuss the following comparative table derived from that given by G.I. Williamson is his commentary on the Confession:

Circumcision-Baptism	*Passover-Lord's Supper*
1. Administered once only	1. Administered repeatedly.
2. Administered to believers and to their children.	2. Administered to believers only.
3. Pictures inception of union with God (cleansing, justification etc.)	3. Pictures maintenance of union with God (nourishment, growth, sanctification, etc.)
4. Recipient wholly passive (he receives what another performs)	4. Recipient active (he partakes by his own act)

2. What is a sign and what is a seal? How do these apply to the sacraments? Look up the Biblical references.

3. *The Mystery of the Lord's Supper*, trans. T.F.Torrance (James Clarke, 1958), 63f.

CHAPTER 28
BAPTISM

ANALYSIS *WCF 28:1–5*

1. Nature and meaning
2–3. Mode
4. Subjects
5. Necessity
6. Effectiveness
7. Frequency

28.1 Nature and meaning of baptism

Baptism is a sacrament of the New Testament, ordained by Jesus Christ[1] for the solemn admission of the person baptised into the visible church,[2] and to be to him a sign and seal of the covenant of grace,[3] of his being grafted into Christ,[4] of regeneration,[5] of remission of sins,[6] and of his surrender to God, through Jesus Christ, to live a new life.[7] By Christ's own appointment this sacrament of baptism is to be continued in his church until the end of the world.[8]

1. Matt. 28:19. 2. 1 Cor. 12:13. 3. Rom. 4:11 with Col. 2:11,12. 4. Gal. 3:27; Rom. 6:5. 5. Titus 3:5. 6. Mark 1:4. 7. Rom. 6:3,4. 8. Matt. 28:19,20.

The nature of a sacrament has been discussed in the previous chapter. Baptism is the initiatory rite of the Christian church. In accordance with the root meaning of the word (a washing that involves a transformation), baptism speaks of a new relationship being cemented with the one in whose name you are baptised (1 Cor. 10:1–2). If you are baptised in Paul's name you belong to him (1 Cor. 1:13), so being baptised in the name of the Triune God means you belong to him. Hence, it is not surprising that the New Testament does not envisage a person as a Christian who has not been baptised. This new relationship with God is through incorporation into Christ by grace through faith. God's covenant speaks of the manifold riches of God's goodness to us and our baptism is a pledge and commitment also. The arguments over baptism must not lead us to the easy option of giving up its use altogether as in the Salvation Army and the Society of Friends (Quakers). Christ has instituted it; we must not despise it.

28.2 Mode of baptism

The outward element to be used in this sacrament is water, with which the person is to be baptised in the name of the Father, and of the Son, and of the Holy Spirit, by a lawfully-called minister of the gospel.[9]

9. Matt. 3:11; John 1:33; Matt. 28:19,20.

Water is a natural cleansing agent but the new relationship of which baptism speaks has been made effective through the Holy Spirit. He makes us part of Christ's body (1 Cor. 12:13). Scripture very directly connects the water of baptism and the pouring out of the Spirit at Pentecost (Matt. 3:1) as if the one is emblematic of the other.

A valid baptism requires the use of water and the name of the Triune God, for the one baptised now belongs to God. No contradiction should be supposed between references in Scripture to being baptised in the name of Christ or the Lord Jesus (eg Acts 19:5) and the words of the Great Commission in Matthew 28:19. There is no relevant textual uncertainty in Matt 28:19, and the tenor of New Testament teaching is pure trinitarianism, far more than the citing of a few explicit texts might suggest (see WCF 2:3). An obvious way of harmonising the Scripture references is to suppose that the candidate was baptised in the name of the Father and the Son and the Holy Spirit following his confession of Jesus as Saviour and Lord, just as is common today. In any event, Matthew 28:19 does not prescribe a formula so much as succinctly sum up the fact that through redemption by Christ the character of God has been declared definitively and he is to be recognised accordingly. Hence the initiatory rite occurs in just such a trinitarian context as Acts and the Epistles reflect.

28.3 Mode of baptism

Dipping of the person into the water is not necessary. Baptism is rightly administered by pouring or sprinkling water on the person.[10]

10. Heb. 9:10,19–22; Acts 2:41; Acts 16:33; Mark 7:4.

Two years earlier the Westminster Assembly had specified in their *Directory for Public Worship* (1644) that the minister 'is to baptize the child with water, which for the manner of doing is not only lawful but expedient to be by pouring or sprinkling water on the face of the child, without any other ceremony.' In debate the previous day (7 August 1644) the proposal to include dipping as well as pouring and sprinkling was excluded 25 votes to 24. It should be noted that the debate was not between dipping and the other modes, as is sometimes stated, but on the propriety of putting dipping on the same level as the other modes. The next day the question was dealt with afresh and the statement above agreed to. 'But as for the dispute itself about dipping, it was thought fit and most safe to let it alone'.[1] The statement of the Westminster Confession in this section reflects a similar line. Pouring or sprinkling are lawful and expedient. Immersion is not necessary although of itself it does not make the sacrament invalid.

The water is a symbol of a change beyond the power of the water, and so the quantity is not of much importance. Still, the positive teaching

1. John Lightfoot, *Journal of the Proceedings of the Assembly of Divines* (J. F. Dove, 1824), 13:301.

of Scripture is that baptism involves putting water on the person not putting the person into water, and the parallel with Holy Spirit baptism (Matt 3:11 cf. Acts 2) confirms this. A simple mode suitable to all kinds of people and situations is implied by the New Testament descriptions. Total immersion lacks Old Testament precedent or clear New Testament justification.

The root idea of the Greek word *baptizo* is not total immersion, but an intensive dipping which involves a transformation (cf. dyeing). Metaphorical uses became common in Greek literature in which mode has no place: being overwhelmed with cares; drunk with wine etc. However, because of the richness of the covenant of grace of which baptism is a sign and seal, baptismal language can be used for many aspects of Christian experience, and some misapply Romans 6:1ff in this connection. In that passage Paul is speaking of the implications of union with Christ (which is implied in Christian baptism) without at all reflecting on the *mode* of baptism. It is the *meaning* of baptism which Paul has in mind. Further, the idea that the mode of baptism is essentially a portrayal of our death to self and rising with Christ (as immersionists argue) is impossible. Paul would have to say '*out of* which you were also raised with him' if he was thinking of baptismal water. *Our* baptism is not the grave in which we die spiritually. Who dies in a grave? Baptism speaks of union with Christ in whose name we are baptised, and thus of union with him in *his* death (by crucifixion), *his* burial (in a cave in the side of a hill), which certified the reality of his death (and shows that subsequent life must be of a new order), and *his* resurrection.

28.4 The subjects of baptism

Not only those who actually profess faith in and obedience to Christ are to be baptised[11] but also the infants of one or both believing parents.[12]

11. Acts 16:31–34 [in lieu of Mark 16:15,16 in original]; Acts 8:37,38.
12. Gen. 17:7,9 with Gal. 3:9,14 & Col. 2:11,12 & Acts 2:38,39 & Rom. 4:11,12; 1 Cor. 7:14; Matt. 28:19; Mark 10:13–16; Luke 18:15.

The missionary situation of the early church means that most explicit cases of baptism in the New Testament focus on adult converts. Nevertheless, there is not lacking evidence of household baptisms, while the statement of Jesus that the infants of those who believe in him belong to the kingdom (Luke 18:15–17) is ultimately only comprehensible on the basis of the continuation of the administration of God's covenant on the 'family descent' principle. God's commitment is 'to you and to your children.' His gracious activity works against sin, not against the family. Baptism as thus understood puts the emphasis on God's action and God's initiative.

Still, covenant children have obligations along with their parents. Although children may be cut off from God's family because of unbelief, the expectation of the parent who seeks to honour the Lord in bringing up the children God gives, should be that they will accept the obligations of the covenant as they are trained in the ways of the Lord. Children of believers who die in infancy are doubtless saved through the mercy of Christ who renews them in his grace (WCF 10:3).

Those who reject the baptism of the believer's infants, frequently do so because of an individualistic approach which is not a product of the Biblical idea of community. Infant dedication services lack Biblical warrant but do reflect the Christian consciousness of parents. Yet one wonders how *real* consolation can be gained from such services without recognition of the covenant grace of God. Doubtless all well-exercised believers recognise implicitly what they do not all recognise explicitly.

28.5 The necessity of baptism

Although it is a great sin to despise or neglect this ordinance,[13] yet grace and salvation are not so inseparably connected with it that no person can be regenerated or saved without it,[14] nor are all those who are baptised undoubtedly regenerated.[15]

13. Luke 7:30 with Exod. 4:24–26.
14. Rom. 4:11; Acts 10:2,4,22,31,45,47.
15. Acts 8:13,23.

Rome teaches the necessity of baptism as a means of regenerating grace. The Reformed teach the necessity of baptism as God's direction to us: it is God's command, but does not accomplish salvation of itself. Christ appointed it; disobedience is sin.

28.6 The effectiveness of baptism

The effectiveness of baptism is not tied to that moment of time in which it is administered.[16] Nevertheless, by the right use of this ordinance, the grace promised is not only offered, but truly set forth and conferred by the Holy Spirit in God's appointed time to all, including infants, to whom in the purpose of God that grace belongs.[17]

16. John 3:5,8.
17. Gal. 3:27; Titus 3:5; Eph. 5:25,26; Acts 2:38,41.

Baptism as the token of God's covenant may not have its spiritual reality fulfilled at the time of administration, but sooner or later as God wills, it will accomplish its object in those God intends for salvation. It will testify and confirm that union that the believer has with Christ. Those who scruple the circumstances of their baptism if it was associated with a mere nominal church connection, should be encouraged by this.

28.7 The frequency of baptism

The sacrament of baptism is to be administered once only to any person.[8]

18. Tit. 3:5.

The statement of the Confession follows from the nature of the sacrament as an initiatory rite (see WCF 28:1). It is not without significance that the Reformers and the Westminster men held to the validity of Roman Catholic baptism, but not to the lawfulness of receiving baptism from a Roman priest (illustrated by the quote below).

THOUGHTS FROM OTHER MINDS

'In this belief we declare that, properly speaking, there can be no church where the word of God is not received, nor profession made of subjection to it, nor use of the sacraments. Therefore we condemn the papal assemblies. . . . Nevertheless, as some trace of the church is left in the papacy, and the virtue and substance of baptism remain, and as the efficacy of baptism does not depend upon the person who administers it, we confess that those baptised in it do not need a second baptism. But on account of its corruptions, we cannot present children to be baptised in it without incurring pollution.'

French Confession[2]

FOR DISCUSSION

1. How is God's grace shown in baptism?

2. Discuss 'improving' one's baptism—using it to good effect. Consider Larger Catechism 167 in this connection (my modernised English version follows):

2. *French Confession* (1559), 28.

167. How is our Baptism to be used by us to good effect?

The necessary but much neglected duty of using our Baptism to good effect is an obligation throughout our lives, especially in times of temptation and when we are present at the administration of Baptism to others.[1] Baptism is used to good effect by serious and thankful consideration of its nature, the purposes for which Christ instituted it, the privileges and benefits conferred and sealed by it, and our solemn vow made in it;[2] by being humbled for our sinful defilement, for our falling short of and living contrary to the grace of Baptism and our pledges;[3] by growing up to assurance of pardon of sin, and of all the other blessings sealed to us in Baptism;[4] by drawing strength from the death and resurrection of Christ, into whom we are baptised, for the putting to death of sin and making alive in grace;[5] and by making every effort to live by faith,[6] to conduct ourselves in holiness and righteousness[7] as those who in Baptism have enlisted in Christ's service,[8] and to walk in brotherly love as being baptised by the same Spirit into one body.[9]

---

[1] Col. 2:11–12, Rom. 6:4,6,11. [2] Rom. 6:3–5. [3] 1 Cor. 1:11–13, Rom. 6:2–3. [4] Rom. 4:11–12, 1 Pet. 3:21. [5] Rom. 6:3–5. [6] Gal. 3:26–27. [7] Rom. 6:22. [8] Acts 2:38. [9] 1 Cor. 12:13,25–27.

CHAPTER 29
THE LORD'S SUPPER

ANALYSIS *WCF 29:1–8*

1. **Institution**
2. **Nature**
3. **Right administration**
4. **Certain abuses rejected**
5. **Relation of signs to things signified**
6. **Transubstantiation rejected**
7. **Christ's real presence explained**
8. **Unworthy recipients**

29.1 The institution of the Supper

Our Lord Jesus, on the night in which he was betrayed, instituted the sacrament of his body and blood, called the Lord's Supper, to be observed in his church to the end of the world, for the perpetual remembrance of his sacrificial death. It was also instituted as the seal of all the benefits of that sacrifice to true believers, and to promote their spiritual nourishment and growth in him, their increased commitment in and to all the duties which they owe to him, and to be a bond and pledge of their communion with him and with each other, as members of his mystical body.[1]

1. 1 Cor. 11:23–26; 1 Cor. 10:16,17,21; 1 Cor. 12:13.

The institution of the Supper is inseparably linked with the direction of the Saviour shortly before his death. It belongs to the church and so is to be observed congregationally, not privately (compare 29.4), and is to be supervised by the church (section 8). Note the six purposes.

29.2 The nature of the Supper

In this sacrament, Christ is not offered up to his Father, nor is any real sacrifice for remission of sins of the living or the dead made at all.[2] Rather, the sacrament is a commemoration of Christ's once-for-all offering up of himself, by himself, on the cross, and involves a spiritual offering of all possible praise to God for this once-for-all sacrifice.[3] Hence the Roman Catholic sacrifice of the mass, as they call it, is a detestable insult to Christ's one and only sacrifice, the sole propitiation for all the sins of his elect.[4]

2. Heb. 9:22,25,26,28.
3. 1 Cor. 11:24,25,26; Matt. 26:26,27.
4. Heb. 7:23,24,27; Heb. 10:11,12,14,18.

This sacrament is not a true, though bloodless, sacrifice as has been held by many and still is. Rather, it is a commemoration which proclaims the death of the Lord, (that which is of supreme praise), until he comes again. In Roman Catholic teaching the mass is regarded as a bloodless re-enactment of Christ's sacrifice, and thus 'it obscures the finished and completed character of Christ's work and robs him of his glory by daring to see it as repeated'[1]. It might be added here that the tendency even in Protestant circles to speak of the Lord's Table as an 'altar' is improper. An altar is a place of sacrifice; a table is a place of fellowship with the one who has reconciled us to God by his death and now lives and is present with us.

29.3 The administration of the Supper

In this ordinance, the Lord Jesus has appointed his ministers to declare his word of institution to the people, to pray, and to bless the elements of bread and wine, and in this way to set them apart from a common to a holy use. They are to take and break the bread, then to take the cup, and to give both to the communicants, and they are to partake with the congregation;[5] but the elements are not to be given to any person is not then present in the congregation.[6]

1. Waldron, *A Modern Exposition of the 1689 Baptist Confession of Faith*, 365.

5. Matt. 26:26–28 & Mark 14:22–24 & Luke 22:19,20 with 1 Cor. 11:23–26.
6. Acts 20:7; 1 Cor. 11:20.

The administration of the sacrament is always to be accompanied by the words of institution which give it its meaning, as well as prayer for the presence in blessing of the Lord as the sacrament is dispensed. The breaking of the bread is regarded as a significant action in the Confession. A very general view in the Reformed church has associated this action with the manner of Christ's death but it was a custom at every meal. The Supper must not become a passion play but must point us to the result of Christ's self-offering in the spiritual banquet which nourishes our souls for eternal life. The table at which the disciples reclined with our Lord is an outward aspect of communion which ought not to be disregarded when considering its spiritual nature. It was in fact the common practice of Reformed and Presbyterian churches to provide a table around which the communicants were seated.

29.4 Some abuses to avoid

Private masses, receiving this sacrament alone from a priest or anyone else,[7] denial of the cup to the people,[8] worshipping the bread and wine, lifting them up or carrying them about for adoration, and reserving them for any supposed religious use, are all contrary to the nature of this sacrament, and to the institution of Christ.[9]

7. 1 Cor. 10:16.
8. Mark 14:23; 1 Cor. 11:25–29.
9. Matt. 15:9.

Several Roman abuses are here expressly rejected. They arose from erroneous views of the sacraments. In the *first* case, the sacrament was held to have inherent virtue and was received privately; in the *second* case, the doctrine of transubstantiation (see 29.6) was held to make giving the cup to the laity unsuitable lest the blood of Christ be spilt. Hence, the

Council of Constance in AD 1414 forbade giving the cup to the laity; in the *third* case, the doctrine of transubstantiation (which developed gradually and was formally promulgated in AD 1215) was associated with worship of the elements since, after consecration, they were held to be the actual body and blood of Christ under the appearance of bread and wine.

During the pandemic in 2020 the question of the Lord's Supper by electronic means came to the fore. It is also a consideration for those living where there are no regular Christian gatherings who have become believers through hearing or reading on the internet. But it is in the context of the of the church as the assembly of God's new covenant community that the sacramental meal is observed. In extraordinary situations we still have the word of God to which the sacraments are subordinate. That we cannot observe the Supper in all its physicality 'in the church' (1 Cor.11:18,22) as the gathered people of God we should miss as we do the regular services. It is good to avoid insisting on or justifying our individualism by doing our own thing which does not pay enough regard to Christ's institutions or the community of the redeemed. On the other hand, Reformed churches have sometimes arranged for representatives of the congregation to have worship with a church member who is bedridden or hospitalised.

29.5 The sign and the thing signified

When the outward elements in this sacrament are duly set apart to the uses appointed by Christ they are related to him as crucified in a true yet sacramental way. Therefore they are sometimes called by the name of the things they represent, that is, the body and blood of Christ.[10] However, in substance and in nature they still remain truly and only bread and wine, as they were before their sacramental use.[11]

10. Matt. 26:26–28.
11. 1 Cor. 11:26–28; Matt. 26:29.

There is a relationship between the sign and the thing signified. When Jesus said, 'This is my body' he is not to be taken in a crassly literal sense, any more than when he says, 'I am the door.' He means that the elements of bread and wine represent his body and blood surrendered for our salvation. Bread and wine nourish physically; Christ's death for us nourishes us spiritually.

29.6 Transubstantiation rejected

The doctrine of transubstantiation, which teaches that the substance of the bread and wine is changed into the substance of Christ's body and blood through consecration by a priest or in any other way, is repugnant not only to Scripture but even to common sense and reason. It overthrows the nature of the sacrament, and has been and is the cause of all kinds of superstitions as well as flagrant idolatries.[12]

12. Acts 3:21 with 1 Cor. 11:24–26; Luke 24:6,39.

This section repudiates the doctrine of transubstantiation held by the Church of Rome. It is indicative of the central role of this teaching in Roman Catholic theology that the Confession specifically rejects it. It is contrary to the nature of a sacrament because it identifies the sign and the thing signified. It is thoroughly unscriptural, not merely beyond reason but contrary to it, and it is productive of many errors. Once consecrated, the elements are held by Rome to be truly Christ's body and blood offered again on the altar. As a crumb of bread could fall to the ground or wine be spilt, wafers were introduced in place of ordinary bread and the cup was held back from the people.

29.7 Christ's real presence explained

When worthy recipients outwardly partake of the visible elements in this sacrament,[13] they also at the same time receive and feed on Christ crucified and all the benefits of his death. This they do in a real and true, but inward and spiritual, manner by faith, and not by the mouth in a physical manner. The body and blood of Christ are not physically present in, with or under the bread and wine, but are present in the sacrament to the faith of believers in a spiritual way just as the bread and wine are present to their physical senses.[14]

13. 1 Cor. 11:28.
14. 1 Cor. 10:16.

Those who partake of the Supper in the way of faith do have the real but spiritual presence of Christ. The Lutheran teaching, which asserts that the bread and wine remain bread and wine but that Christ is physically present in, with and by the elements (what is called consubstantiation), is rejected. It confounds the sign and the thing signified and asserts a physical presence. This requires the teaching of ubiquity, ie. that Christ has become everywhere present in his human nature because his glorified humanity partakes of the attributes of deity, a teaching contrary to the perfection of Christ's humanity. It also implies that all who receive the elements receive Christ irrespective of faith (see next section). The Reformed believe in the real presence of Christ in grace and forgiveness, but it is a spiritual presence. 'Just as the bread and wine are present to the outward senses, so the body and blood of Christ, as spiritual nourishment, are present to the spiritual apprehension of those who receive the outward elements in faith.'[2]

29.8 Unworthy recipients

Although ignorant and wicked persons receive the outward elements in this sacrament, they do not receive what is signified by it. Their unworthy participation makes them guilty of the body and blood of the Lord to their own condemnation. It follows that all ignorant and ungodly persons, being unfit to enjoy communion with Christ, are also unworthy to come to the Lord's table. While they remain like this they cannot, without great sin against Christ, partake of these holymysteries[15]

2. Macpherson, *The Confession of Faith*, 157.

or be admitted to them.[16]

15. 1 Cor. 11:27–29; 2 Cor. 6:14–16.
16. 1 Cor. 5:6,7,13; 2 Thess. 3:6,14,15; Matt. 7:6.

The real but spiritual presence of Christ means only the worthy, only those who come through Christ, receive him. Unworthy participants are those who reject the way of faith. They spurn the grace and forgiveness won by Christ and hence add to their condemnation. Likely the words in 1 Corinthians 11:29 ('For anyone who eats and drinks without recognising the body of the Lord eats and drinks judgment on himself') have reference to one's attitude to other believers, fellow members of the church, the body of Christ. Certainly the selfish, spirit shown by some of the Corinthians is completely contrary to the meaning of the sacrament in which we confess our utter and equal dependence upon Christ for salvation.

This section also indicates the supervision of the table: only those are to be admitted who have a sufficient knowledge, who profess true faith and are living in an apparently godly way.

THOUGHTS FROM OTHER MINDS

'As you see, all that is spoken concerning the Sacrament is grounded and depends upon *faith*. If a man has faith, even if it is ever so little, he gets some hold of Christ, and some insight in the understanding of this Sacrament; but if he is without faith, even if a man takes trouble to make the Sacraments ever so clear, it is not possible for him to get any hold of Christ or any insight in Him. Without faith we cannot be Christians, nor can we see God or feel God in Christ without faith. Faith is the only thing which translates our souls out of the death and damnation in which we were born, and plants us into life. Thus all the study and endeavour of a Christian should be directed to this, to ask that the Lord in His mercy may enlighten his mind with the eye of faith, and kindle in his heart a love of faith, and work in his heart a thirst and desire for the object of faith, and more and more to thirst and hunger for the food of faith, that nourishes us to life eternal.'

Robert Bruce (1554–1631)[3]

FOR DISCUSSION

1. State and discuss the six purposes of the Supper noted in 29:1.

2. It has been said that the Supper speaks of commemoration, communion and consummation. Explain.

3. What is the distinctive doctrine of the Roman Catholic and Lutheran churches concerning the presence of Christ in the Supper? What flows from the respective views of these churches?

4. Who is a worthy receiver?

5. How does the preaching of the word relate to the Supper? What is suitable preparation for the Supper?

6. How should the Table be supervised by the elders? (1) By open invitation with decision according to individual conscience; (2) By invitation with limitation to members in good standing of Christ's church; (3) By limitation to members of the local congregation or other churches in the same denomination? (4) Some other way?

3. *The Mystery of the Lord's Supper: Sermons by Robert Bruce*, ed. T. F. Torrance (James Clarke, 1958), 137–138.

CHAPTER 30
CHURCH DISCIPLINE

ANALYSIS *WCF 30:1–4*
1. The distinct government in the church
2. The power of the keys
3. The aims of church discipline
4. The kinds of discipline

30.1 The distinct government in the church

The Lord Jesus, as King and Head of his church, has appointed a government in it, in the hands of church office-bearers, distinct from the civil rulers.[1]

1. Isa. 9:6,7; 1 Tim. 5:17; 1 Thess. 5:12; Acts 20:17,28; Heb. 13:7,17,24; 1 Cor. 12:28; Matt. 28:18–20.

According to Robert Baillie at the Assembly this section was expressly framed against Erastianism, the teaching that makes the civil power supreme and in effect makes the church a department of state. King James VI, who wanted to control the church through appointment of a few bishops, held that 'Presbytery agrees as well with a monarchy as God and the devil.' The statements expressed to him by Andrew Melville (1545–1622) in 1596 have sounded down the years. 'Sir, as diverse times before I have told you, so now again I must tell you,—there are two Kings and two Kingdoms in Scotland; there is King James, the head of the commonwealth, and there is Christ Jesus, the head of the church, whose subject King James VI is, and of whose kingdom he is not a King, nor a Lord, not a Head but a member.' In short, the Presbyterian view is to recognise the co-ordinate jurisdiction of both church and state, rather than placing one or other in the supreme place. Our service of God necessarily involves giving Caesar what belongs to him, but authority in the church is not among what belongs to him.

The Westminster Assembly had already drawn up a *Form of Presbyterial Church Government* in which they had dealt with church government and asserted the permanent officers of the church to be pastors, teachers, other church governors and deacons. There was a measure of compromise in the Form, particularly in the matter of the eldership where not all in England were prepared to accept that the ruling elder was a scriptural presbyter, hence the phrase in the Form: *other church governors*. The Scottish church accepted the Form by an Act of 10 February 1645 in a manner which did not undermine the principles of the *Second Book of Discipline* 1578, a book which enshrined the presbyter view of the eldership. No doubt the practical lesson of all this is that in matters of church government of lesser importance, if the end is achieved in practice some compromise on the theory may be tolerated.

30.2 The power of the keys

The keys of the kingdom of heaven are committed to these church office-bearers. They thus have power, as occasion requires, to declare sins forgiven or not; to shut the kingdom of heaven against the impenitent, both by the word and discipline; and to open it to penitent sinners, by the ministry of the gospel and by release from discipline.[2]

2. Matt. 16:19; Matt. 18:17,18; Jn 20:21–23; 2 Cor. 2:6–8.

The power of the keys belongs to the church (Matt 16:19), the power of the sword to the state (Rom. 13:4). The power of the keys is the power to exercise jurisdiction and authoritative control in the church and belongs exclusively to the church officers (cf. Q 83 of the Heidelberg Catechism).

The power of the keys is ministerial, that is, the power to administer the law of Christ in his word rather than to make law (cf. WCF 31:3).

In the preaching of the Gospel, in the administration of the sacraments and in the exercise of church discipline, sins are either forgiven the penitent or not forgiven the impenitent. The church does not absolve (no priest or minister on earth can do that) but the church pronounces absolution to the believing and pronounces doom to the unrepentant. Public prayer needs to affirm this.

30.3 The aims of church discipline

Church discipline is necessary for the reclaiming and regaining of offending believers, for deterring others from committing similar offences, for purging out the leaven which might infect the whole lump, for vindicating the honour of Christ and the holy profession of the gospel, and for preventing the wrath of God, which might justly fall upon the church, should it allow his covenant and its seals to be profaned by notorious and obstinate offenders.[3]

3. 1 Cor. 5; 1 Tim. 5:20; Matt. 7:6; 1 Tim. 1:20; 1 Cor. 11:27–34 with Jude 23.

Church discipline does not apply to every kind of sin but only to those sins which cause scandal or bring open reproach on the cause of Christ. Meddling with family concerns, or attempting to drag secret sins into the light, are not to be encouraged. Censurable offences may be public or private. Private offences do not include every breach of God's law, but are those which cause offence, bring reproach or mar edification, and are known to a few. In these cases the procedure in Matthew 18:5 applies. Public offences are of a more flagrant and open kind. The first object of discipline is to get at the truth, and the ultimate object is to lead the guilty to repentance by Scriptural means that he might be restored.

30.4 The kinds of discipline

To achieve these ends most effectively, the officer-bearers of the church are to proceed according to the nature of the offence and the degree of the offender's guilt to admonish the offender, to suspend the offender from the sacrament of the Lord's Supper for a period, or to excommunicate the offender from the church.[4]

4. 1 Thess. 5:12; 2 Thess. 3:6,14,15; 1 Cor. 5:4,5,13; Matt. 18:17; Titus 3:10.

Admonition consists in solemnly addressing the person found guilty, placing the person's sin before him, warning him of his danger, and exhorting him to greater circumspection. Admonition may take the stronger form of rebuke, that is, a solemn expression of reproof and censure in the name of the Lord Jesus.

Suspension or temporary depriving of church privileges or office is resorted to when the gravity of the offence demands it, or where admonition or rebuke have proved ineffective. Sometimes an offence is such that it requires a person holding office to be deposed from it while his membership in the congregation is unaffected.

Excommunication is usually divided into the lesser and the greater. The lesser excommunication amounts to a formal removal of the person from the membership roll and declaring him no longer a member of the church. It is usually applied when an offence, although proved, is obstinately denied. Excommunication in its highest sense (1 Cor.5:4–5; 1 Tim. 1:20) is for grave and flagrant sins and involves the public pronouncing of the sentence of excommunication upon the impenitent person, and public prayer for his repentance. Concerning such a person 'the people are to be warned that they hold that person to be cast out of the church, and that they shun all unnecessary converse with him or her; nevertheless, excommunication dissolves not the bonds of civil or natural relations, nor exempts from the duties belonging to them'.[1] The greater excommunication is relatively rare in Presbyterian circles, particularly in the 20th century. It is too rare.

A member who has been subject to discipline and is duly restored is entitled to be held in tender and brotherly regard by all his fellow members.

THOUGHTS FROM OTHER MINDS

'When I first entered upon the work of the ministry among you, I was exceedingly ignorant of the vast importance of church discipline. I thought that my great work and almost only work was to pray and preach. . . . But it pleased God, who teaches his servants in another way than man teaches, to bless some of the cases of discipline to the manifest and undeniable conversion of the souls of those under our care; and from that hour a new light broke into my mind, and I saw that if preaching be an ordinance of Christ, so is church discipline.'

R. M. McCheyne (1813–1843)[2]

FOR DISCUSSION

1. Is our sin without effect on others? What principle is suggested by the sin of Achan (Joshua 7)? by the sin of Jonah (Jonah 1)?

2. Are Christian love and discipline for offences compatible?

3. What is the difference between absolution by a priest as taught by Rome and absolution as taught in the Confession?

4. Compare excommunication in the highest sense as explained above with the practice of the Exclusive Brethren in breaking all social contact even within families.

---

1. *Form of Process*, viii 17; General Assembly of the Church of Scotland, 18 April 1707.
2. Andrew Bonar, *Life of Robert Murray McCheyne* (Banner of Truth, 1960), 87–88.

CHAPTER 31
SYNODS AND COUNCILS

ANALYSIS *WCF 31:1–5*
1. The right of wider assemblies
2. The right of calling assemblies
3. The functions of synods and their authority
4. The fallibility of synods and councils
5. The jurisdiction of synods and councils

31.1 The right of wider assemblies

For the better government and further edification of the church, there ought to be such assemblies as are commonly called synods or councils.[1]

1. Acts 15:2,4,6.

The right of assembly is here asserted. The term 'synod' is used in a wide sense for an assembly of church office-bearers beyond a single congregation, and so includes presbyteries, synods, general assemblies and special gatherings such as Westminster itself.

31.2 The right of calling church assemblies

In the case of churches not organised or constituted in government, ministers may meet synodically without commission from their churches, and civil rulers may lawfully call a synod of ministers and other fit persons to consult and advise about matters of religion.[2] In cases where the church is organised, a synod of ministers and elders delegated from their churches may meet as often as is necessary for the good of the church by exercising the inherent right to do so given by Christ, even if the civil authorities withhold or deny their consent.[3]

2. Isa. 49:23; 1 Tim. 2:1,2; 2 Chron. 19:8–11; 2 Chron. 29 & 30; Matt. 2:4,5; Prov. 11:14.
3. Acts 15:2,4,22,23,25.

This section in its original form was qualified in the Act of the Church of Scotland adopting the Confession in 1647 (see text in Appendix) and has thus been reworded in line with the explanation there given. The original wording stated (1) the lawfulness of the civil ruler calling a synod, and (2) the right of the church to hold synods if the civil ruler was an open enemy of the church. This wording was considered not sufficiently strong in its assertion of the liberties of the church under Christ. It was the view of Scottish Presbyterians in the Covenanting period that the liberty of calling religious assemblies and meeting in them was essential to the maintenance of the Gospel.

The American church early combined sections 1 and 2 into a statement generally in line with the Scottish qualification although without reference to the right of the civil ruler to call a synod in cases where the church was not organised.

31.3 The functions and authorities of synods

It belongs to the members of synods and councils, acting as servants of God, to decide controversies of faith and cases of conscience, to set down rules and directions for the better arranging of the public worship of God and the government of his church, and to receive and judge authoritatively on complaints in cases of maladministration in the church. These decisions and rulings, if in accordance with the word of God, are to be received with reverence and submission, not only because they agree with the word, but because God has given the authority in his word for synods and councils so to act.[4]

4. Acts 15:15,19,24,27–31; Acts 16:4; Matt. 18:17–20.

Church assemblies deal with doctrine, church order and review of geographically narrower assemblies. Biblical church courts administer the law of Christ in his word by applying and enforcing it and are not competent to make new law. This section rejects the Independent theory of church power which sees synods and councils as at best advisory but having no authority over congregations.

31.4 The fallibility of synods and councils

All synods or councils since the Apostles' times, whether general or particular, may err, and many have erred. Therefore they are not to be made the rule of faith or practice, but are to be used as a help in both.[5]

5. Eph. 2:20; Acts 17:11; 1 Cor. 2:5; 2 Cor. 1:24.

This statement is in agreement with the facts of history as different Councils have contradicted each other on very important issues. Still, Protestants do not despise the decisions of the General Councils to AD 451, and their doctrinal conclusions are embodied in the Westminster Confession. Since the First Vatican Council (1870) the Pope has been regarded by Rome as the final authority in matters of faith and morals, thus placing a General Council on a lesser level.

This section also applies to the Confession since it is not inspired or infallible but seeks simply to set forth the teaching of Scripture in concise form. It is not the final authority but Scripture is (cf. WCF 1: 2). It is a help to faith not the rule of faith, and that should be made evident in the resolution of controversies. Nevertheless, those who subscribe the Confession, voluntarily acknowledging its doctrine to be agreeable to Scripture, are not in a position to repudiate the doctrine and remain within the communion of which the Confession is the bond unless they have secured through the appropriate steps the necessary revision.

31.5 The jurisdiction of synods and councils

Synods and councils are to consider or decide nothing but ecclesiastical matters, and they are not to interfere with civil affairs which concern the commonwealth. However, a respectfully worded petition may be directed to the civil authorities in extraordinary cases, and, if requested by the civil authorities, advice to clear the conscience may be tendered.[6]

6. Luke 12:13,14; John 18:36.

This section very properly limits the bounds of church assemblies. 'Church and State may co-operate in the advancement of objects common to both; but each must be careful to act within its own proper sphere . . .'[1]

THOUGHTS FROM OTHER MINDS

'Let us not be led astray, therefore, by the modernist minister, lacking almost invariably anything approaching the Biblical knowledge or the mental capacity of the Westminster Divines, who as a substitute for the Gospel, hurls forth imperatives: "The Church must give a lead . . ." and the like.'

F. Maxwell Bradshaw (1910–1992)[2]

FOR DISCUSSION

1. Discuss the respective role of the Church and the Christian in politics (cf. WCF 23:2).

2. Critically assess 'liberation theology.'

1. Robert Shaw, *An Exposition of the Confession of Faith* (Blackie and Son, 1857), 314.
2. R. S. Ward, ed. *A Witness for Christ*, 415.

CHAPTER 32
THE STATE OF THE DEAD AND THE RESURRECTION

ANALYSIS *WCF 32:1–3*

1. Death and the intermediate state
- a. the death of the body
- b. the persistence of the soul
- c. the souls of the righteous in conscious bliss
- d. the souls of the wicked in conscious pain
- e. no place such as purgatory

2–3. The last day and the resurrection change
- a. those alive changed
- b. the dead raised bodily
- c. the different destinations

32.1 Death and the intermediate state

The bodies of human beings after death return to dust and decay,[1] but their souls neither die nor become unconscious, for they are inherently immortal and immediately return to God who gave them.[2] The souls of the righteous are perfected in holiness at death and are received into the highest heavens where they behold the face of God in light and glory while they wait for the full redemption of their bodies.[3] The souls of the wicked are thrown into hell, where they remain in torments and utter darkness, reserved for the judgment of the great day.[4] Scripture recognises no places for souls separated from their bodies other than these two.

1. Gen. 3:19; Acts 13:36.
2. Luke 23:43; Eccl. 12:7.
3. Heb. 12:23; 2 Cor. 5:1,6,8; Phil. 1:23 with Acts 3:21 and Eph. 4:10.
4. Luke 16:23,24; Acts 1:25; Jude 6,7; 1 Pet. 3:19.

In death there appears to be no distinction between believer and unbeliever: all die and all decay. However, physical death is the *last* enemy to be destroyed because God has purposed that there be a succession of generations and a world history. If believers were now exempt, that world history could not unfold.

As was noted on WCF 4:2, man is essentially an embodied spirit. Even though man's soul and body can be separated, this is not the normal situation but is part of the result of sin. The Greeks in New Testament times held that the body was a kind of prison for the soul, and that death meant the release of the soul to enter a higher existence with the gods. On this view (shared by many today) the body has no future. But this understanding is foreign to Scripture which thinks of the body and soul (or spirit) as mutually interdependent. This accounts for a number of passages, particularly in poetic contexts, which might seem to teach that physical death is the end of conscious existence (eg. Psalm 6:5). Biblically speaking, life is shadowy and unsubstantial if it is not embodied life in God's world, hence the emphasis on the resurrection, when what was made very good in the beginning will achieve its goal. Only God has immortality as being its fount and source, but the human person, once created, has an endless existence. The world to come is a place of embodied life and not an ethereal place of disembodied spirits.

Human physical death is one of the consequences of sin (Gen. 2:17; Rom. 5:12), but it cannot sever the spiritual union with Christ which the believer now enjoys. Jesus teaches that the body can be destroyed when the soul is safe (Matt 10:28). Paul can say that to depart and be with Christ is better for him (Phil. 1:23), for he has a closer fellowship with Christ than if he remains here. The believer is sometimes described as asleep in Jesus, for in the fulness of Christ's salvation his redemption will be perfected at the resurrection. The body is still cared for by Christ who died and rose again to save the whole person, not a disembodied person (cf. the beautiful words of *Shorter Catechism,* 37). 'If the Spirit of him who raised Jesus from the dead is living in you, he who raised Christ from the dead will also give life to your mortal bodies through his Spirit, who lives in you' (Rom. 8:11).

Jesus contrasts eternal life and eternal death (Matt 25:46), and speaks more of the fire of hell, the outer darkness and the endless destruction than anyone else. Such images are drawn from our own experience here but they speak of a reality worse than the images. They cannot be made to fit the teaching that the wicked will be annihilated so that immortality is conditional—for believers only. The truth is that we need to focus on the justice of God. We could not worship God if he was immoral, making no distinction between good and evil. He will punish the wicked, but the punishment is based strictly on the demerit of the individual not on some arbitrary standard. 'Not one soul will be in hell who does not deserve to be; and no one's hell will be deeper or darker than is right. God's wrath cannot be compromised by miscarriages of justice.'[1] At physical death the unbeliever knows the judgment of God for his sin, and at the resurrection this judgment is confirmed.

32.2 The last day and the resurrection change

Those living on earth at the last day will not die, but will be changed.[5] All the dead will be raised up with the same bodies they had previously, although with different qualities, and these will be united again to their souls for ever.[6]

5. 1 Thess. 4:17; 1 Cor. 15:51,52.
6. Job 19:26,27; 1 Cor. 15:42–44.

Instead of dying and experiencing the change in the resurrection, those alive on the last day of this world order will experience that change without death intervening. Resurrection is not reanimation to the same life, nor abandonment of the old body and exchanging it for a new one.

1. Macleod, *Behold Your God*, 105.

Resurrection means that there is an essential continuity between the present body and the body of the resurrection, but there is also difference so that the body is fitted for a new sphere of existence. The inability to conceptualise the difference is not an argument against the reality: even the natural world provides a parallel (1 Cor.15:35ff). Note Paul's exhortation about honouring God with the body (1 Cor.6:19–20): it has an eternal destiny.

32.3 The last day and the resurrection change

By the power of Christ the bodies of the unjust will be raised to dishonour. By his Spirit, Christ will raise the bodies of the just to honour, and make them like his own glorious body.[7]

7. Acts 24:15; Jn 5:28,29; 1 Cor. 15:43; Phil. 3:21.

There is little in Scripture on the resurrection of unbelievers, but what there is is clear enough. At the resurrection they are raised to be condemned. The sentence is confirmed and what Revelation 20:14 calls the second death occurs.

Christ's resurrection body is the pattern of the believer's resurrection body. His body was not non-material yet it possessed new qualities, being able to pass through closed doors, and being beyond the power of death. When Paul speaks of the *spiritual* body of the resurrection he contrasts it with the *natural* (Greek: *psychikos*) body. He means that the spiritual body is supernatural. The spiritual body is the body equipped and empowered by the Holy Spirit so that it is fitted for the world where righteousness has its home. There will be recognition in glory with each person's individuality contributing to the perfection of community in Christ.

THOUGHTS FROM OTHER MINDS

'Does it matter whether an evangelical is a conditionalist or not? I think it does: for a conditionalist's idea of God will miss out on the glory of divine justice, and his idea of worship will miss out on praise for God's judgements, and his idea of heaven will miss out on the thought that praise for God's judgements goes on (cf. Rev. 16:5–7; 19:1–5), and his idea of man will miss out on the awesome dignity of our having been made to last for eternity, and in his preaching of the gospel he will miss out on telling the unconverted that their prospects without Christ are as bad as they possibly could be—for on the conditionalist view they aren't! These, surely, are sad losses. Conditionalism, logically thought through, cannot but impoverish a Christian man, and limit his usefulness to the Lord.'

J. I. Packer (1926–2020)[2]

FOR DISCUSSION

1. Seventh-day Adventists, Christadelphians and Jehovah's Witnesses are among those teaching conditional immortality, but there are some influences now in evangelical circles. Discuss J. I. Packer's comment.

2. Scripture never idealises the disembodied state, yet there is a continuity between the experience in that state and the eternal state. Discuss.

3. What are some of the implications of the resurrection of the body (eg. is the world to come a world in space and time)?

---

2. *The Problem of Eternal Punishment,* Leon Morris Lecture, Melbourne, 31 August 1990.

CHAPTER 33
THE LAST JUDGMENT AND ETERNAL STATE

ANALYSIS *WCF 33:1–3*

1. The day of judgment of men and angels

a. appointed by God
b. committed to the Son
c. embracing men and angels
d. based on deeds

2. God's purpose in this judgment

a. to show his mercy
b. to show his justice

3. The present practical value of this doctrine

a. a. to deter from sin
b. b. to comfort the godly in their trials
c. c. to encourage a holy walk

33.1 The day of judgment of humans and angels

God has appointed a day in which he will judge the world in righteousness by Jesus Christ,[1] to whom all authority and right to judge has been given by the Father.[2] In that day not only the apostate angels will be judged,[3] but also all persons who have lived on the earth will appear before the tribunal of Christ to give an account of their thoughts, words, and deeds, and to receive according to what they have done in the body, whether good or evil.[4]

1. Acts 17:31.
2. John 5:22,27.
3. 1 Cor. 6:3; Jude 6; 2 Peter 2:4.
4. 2 Cor. 5:10; Eccl. 12:14; Rom. 2:16; Rom. 14:10,12; Matt. 12:36,37.

33.2 God's purpose in this judgement

God's purpose in appointing this day is to make known the glory of his mercy in the eternal salvation of the elect, and the glory of his justice in the damnation of the reprobate, who are wicked and disobedient. For in that day the righteous will go into everlasting life, and receive the fulness of joy and refreshing which comes from the presence of the Lord; but the wicked, who do not know God nor obey the gospel of Jesus Christ, will be thrown into eternal torments and punished with everlasting destruction from the presence of the Lord, and from the glory of his power.[5]

5. Matt. 25:31–46; Rom. 2:5,6; Rom. 9:22,23; Matt. 25:21; Acts 3:19; 2 Thess. 1:7–10.

The teaching of the Confession is that the last judgment follows on the general resurrection. Compare the express statement of the Larger Catechism Q.88: 'Immediately after the resurrection shall follow the general and final judgment of angels and men . . .' We read nothing of the *holy* angels being judged, but that the believers will judge (the fallen) angels is asserted in 1 Cor.6:3. All men will be judged at the same judgment on the basis of what they have done, since what we do reveals character and character shows our relationship to Christ, or lack of it. Believers look forward to the judgment as the day of public vindication in which the transforming power of saving faith will be evidenced and glory given to Christ. Their sins will not come into view because they are covered by Christ's righteousness. The unbeliever should dread the judgment day, for the sinfulness of sin and unbelief as its root will be revealed and condemned to the praise of God's justice.

33.3 The present practical value of this doctrine

To deter everyone from sin and for the greater comfort of the godly in their adversity, Christ would have us to be firmly persuaded that there will be a day of judgment.[6] He would also have us to be in ignorance of when that day shall be, so that we may shake off all unspiritual attitudes and be always watchful since we do not know at what hour the Lord will come, and so that we might always be prepared to say, 'Come, Lord Jesus, come quickly. Amen.'[7]

6. 2 Pet. 3:11,14; 2 Cor. 5:10,11; 2 Thess. 1:5–7; Luke 21:27,28; Rom. 8:23–25.

7. Matt. 24:36,42–44; Mark 13:35–37; Luke 12:35,36; Rev. 22:20.

Scripture teaches that the fact of the judgment to come has a bearing on present living: it deters some from evil and gives comfort to those who suffer injustice here and now. Scripture links indifference to the truth of Christ's coming in judgment to careless and evil conduct, while belief in this truth is a stimulus to godliness.

Jesus stated that he did not know the time of his return (Matt 24:36). As the Son of God he knows, but as the Mediator it was not given him to know and reveal it. How foolish for us to suppose we can know or even to say we cannot know the exact time but Scripture provides signs which indicate an approximate date.

Wars and rumours of war, famines, earthquakes, false prophets and false Christs are characteristic of the whole period before Christ's return, and do not provide specific time indications. Similarly, the fact that the gospel must be preached in the whole world and that there are to be many called from the Jewish people are not so clear in meaning that we can identify a fulfilment with dogmatism.

The major emphasis of the NT is the call to steadfastness in a hostile environment, the call to faithful service so that the coming of Christ will not mean loss but joy. Further, the Christian does not set his hope on some better day for the church before the end, however confident he may be that such days will come, for such days are not the fullness of glory. The horizon of the believer's hope is the return of Christ and the ushering in of a new heaven and a new earth where righteousness has its home.

THOUGHTS FROM OTHER MINDS

'To a believer, the mere possibility, or even absolute certainty, of ages being yet to elapse before the Lord comes again, ought no more to diminish the influence of that event on his mind and heart and conscience, than the fact that ages have elapsed since the Lord came at first lessens the moral weight of his constant vivid sight of Christ and him crucified. . . . Behind me Christ dying; before me Christ coming. Is it not thus, and only thus, that I live by the faith of him who loved me and gave himself for me; that I live also by the power of the world to come; enduring as seeing him who is invisible?'

Robert S. Candlish (1806–1873)[1]

1. *The Gospel of Forgiveness* (Adam and Charles Black, 1878), 445,455.

ADDENDUM: UNFULFILLED PROPHECY

At several periods of church history the view has been quite widely advocated that Christ returns to set up a millennial kingdom of 1,000 years based at Jerusalem, the end of which will be closed by an apostasy and the general resurrection and last judgment. The 1,000 years of Revelation 20 is identified with this earthly reign of Christ. This approach had some followers in the second century and later, in the 17th century (chiefly among the Fifth Monarchy men), and from about 1830 with the rise of the Brethren movement. Its roots lie in a literalistic approach to Scripture promises, and pessimism about the church in its present form. The Old Testament promises seem to have had inadequate fulfilment, and a future millennium is projected during which they will be fully and literally fulfilled.[1]

Difficulties in the common pre-millennial approach include:

1. A failure to grasp that the Old Testament kingdom was a prefiguring of the realities to come in Christ, just as were the sacrifices of the Mosaic law. The New Testament is emphatic that Jesus has succeeded to the true throne of David (Acts 2:30ff) which is in heaven, and that a rebuilding of earthly Jerusalem as the centre of Jesus' reign is not to be thought of, nor a restoration of the earthly temple and sacrificial system.

1. It is worth noting that the Westminster Confession does not quote Revelation 20 at any point, and teaches a general resurrection and last judgement of all.

2. Sundry disharmonious elements exist including, placing a cluster of events as chronological indicators near the end, when Jesus insists the day or hour of his return cannot be known by us; the necessity of a resurrection of some believers at the beginning of the millennium and others at the close, thus breaking up the general resurrection; the mingling of glorified saints and unglorified persons; and the problem of what actually is achieved during the millennium, and also the nature and basis of salvation during it.
3. In the form of dispensationalism, which had significant impact on American evangelicals from 1870 to 1970, including the "Left Behind" series of books by Tim La Haye more recently, many additional complications arise of which it is not necessary to speak here.

In reaction to the extreme futurism of the dispensational approach, an extreme *preterist* (past-fulfilment) school has arisen. It regards all the prophecies, including that of Christ's return, as fulfilled in the destruction of Jerusalem in AD 70. Although some passages of Scripture sometimes referred to the second coming do refer to the destruction of Jerusalem, the extreme preterist reaction is to be strongly rejected as not doing justice to the already/not yet tension concerning the kingdom of God. The transfiguration of Jesus, his resurrection, and the overthrow of Jerusalem are revelatory of Christ's glory and kingdom to be revealed in fullness at the consummation.

Two other approaches are known as post-millennialism and a-millennialism. Both recognize the continuity between OT Israel and the NT church as an expanded Israel embracing believers from all the nations.

Post millennialism means Christ comes *after* a future period (not necessarily a literal 1,000 years) during which period the church will know considerable blessing and revival. Post and pre-millennialists agree that the optimistic expectation of the Old Testament will be fulfilled, the former saying in and through the church by the ministry of the word and the power of God's Spirit in the conversion of multitudes, and the latter by positing an earthly kingdom of outward splendour, and having some pessimism about the value and function of the church (a view already criticized above).

A-millennialism accepts the passage in Revelation, but usually interprets it as the period between the ascension and the return of Christ, when Satan is bound sufficiently so as to ensure the spread of the gospel among the nations. It may be optimistic or pessimistic about the progress of the Gospel, and in the optimistic form is similar in many ways to post-millennialism. The a-millennial position is nowadays commonly somewhat pessimistic and does not expect a general conversion of mankind, and is also commonly *futurist* in orientation, putting the apostasy, tribulation, and man of sin just before the end rather than seeing these as operative throughout Christian history as was the older view.

Others explain the 1,000 years as a symbol of the blessedness of believers who have died and are reigning with Christ. This contrasts with the short time of suffering of the church still on earth, symbolically represented by terms elsewhere in Revelation, such as 42 months or a time, times and half a time. In the Westminster period the a- and post-millennial type positions of an optimistic kind was common (cf. Larger Catechism 191). A few in the Westminster Assembly, such as Dr. Twisse and Thomas Goodwin, influenced by the writings of J. H. Alsted and Joseph Mede, taught that the power of Papal antichrist would soon collapse and a literal millennium begin, marked by a glorious but *not* personal appearance of Christ for the resurrection of the martyrs and the conversion of the Jews. This is not classic pre-millennialism. The pre-millennial position proper was advocated by an Independent pastor, John Archer, who published

The Personal Reign of Christ Upon Earth in 1642. The Confession does not seem to allow for a true pre-millennial position, which was not only rejected by mainstream Puritans but was also discredited for the next 150 years by the excesses of the Fifth Monarchy Men.

I have not located any Scottish Presbyterian minister who was pre-millennial in the period 1560–1700. Nevertheless, some Scots ministers, such as the Bonar brothers, adopted pre-millennial views in the 1830s, but did not have them as the focus of their preaching, and again it was a passing phase. In America the situation was rather different, and a stream of pre-millennial opinion (its literalism reactive to modernism) remains in some parts of American Presbyterianism.

UNFULFILLED PROPHECY

The following principles, in part derived from a study of the significance of the parables of Matthew 13, embody a suggested approach.

1. The kingdom of God that was the subject of Old Testament promise and expectation has begun with the ministry of Jesus.
2. Jesus taught his disciples about the kingdom and equipped them so that they could bring out the old treasures (promises) as well as new (fulfilments), and told them to make known from the housetops what he had taught them in private. The post-resurrection data concerning the kingdom and the church cannot be regarded as other than the public proclamation and elucidation of that revealed in principle by Jesus.
3. Any interpretation of the Old Testament which disregards the disclosures made by Jesus cannot be correct. The Old Testament must be interpreted by the Gospel not the Gospel or the future by a reading of the Old Testament which bypasses the Gospel.
4. The present form of the kingdom is that state of affairs which arises from the Father giving authority to his Christ. It begins with the public ministry of Jesus and is to have a future world wide development to be climaxed by the return of Christ in glory to usher in the eternal kingdom.
5. The Old Testament promise and expectation is to find its fulfilment in and through the church as the realm where kingdom blessings are now experienced.
6. The devil will oppose the work of the kingdom but force is not to be resorted to gain conversions. The consummation will come

when the harvest is ready, but will be unexpected and unannounced. A gradual and steady progress cannot be safely inferred from the data, nor can we establish more than that evil will continue in greater or less degree until the consummation.

7. Christ's return will be personal, visible and bodily. It will not be on earth to be seen by a few, but in the heavens to be seen by all. It will be accompanied by the general resurrection, last judgment and the eternal kingdom embracing a new heavens and a new earth.
8. The watchword for the Christian is faithfulness in a hostile environment.

"Come Lord Jesus, come quickly."

ADDITIONAL CHAPTERS

In 1903 the Presbyterian Church in the United States of America (the 'Northern' Church) added two new chapters to the Confession, "Of the Holy Spirit" (#34) and 'Of the Gospel of the Love of God and Missions' (#35), with a view to more fully expressing its teaching. In 1942 the Presbyterian Church in the United States (the 'Southern' Church) also added these two chapters after chapter 8 with one verbal change ('these' to 'those' in section 4 of new chapter 9 and the omission of 'until it shall cover the earth' after 'increased' in this same section). The 1942 text is reproduced here without change other than the conforming of three old verbal forms to their modern equivalents in the chapter on 'The Gospel.'

GENERAL NOTE

People with little grasp of the Biblical and Calvinistic teaching might regard some of the statements in these extra chapters as inconsistent, and so regard them as contradicting the teaching of the saving love of God for his elect embodied in the rest of the Confession, thus allowing for the rejection of such teaching. However, if construed according to the words themselves apart from the motivations of the framers, there is nothing of weight to object to in the wording of the two chapters.[1]

It is certainly true that the changes were held as softening the distinctive Calvinism in the PCUSA after 1903 so that union with the explicitly

1. See also B.B.Warfield, "The Confession of Faith as Revised in 1903," in *Selected Shorter Writings* (P&R Publishing, 1973) 2:370–410.

Arminian *Cumberland Presbyterian Church* was facilitated in 1906. Similar changes in other churches at about this time reflect the same trend (eg. the Declaratory Act of the *United Presbyterian Church of Scotland* 1879 and the Declaratory Statement in The Basis of Union of *The Presbyterian Church of Australia* 1901). The motivation in Scotland in 1879 was even more obviously in the way of relaxing the Calvinistic position. Hence, strict subscribers to the Confession (such as the writer) are inclined to reject the additional chapter on the Gospel Call as unnecessary and as implying a false dichotomy as if to suggest that the Confession in theory and/or practice led to hyper-calvinism.

There is also a rationalising construction from within the Reformed camp found, for example, in Herman Hoeksema and the *Protestant Reformed Churches* in America, which resulted in the rejection of common grace in 1924. This construction, which in part is a reaction, denies that God has any favour to the non-elect (contrary to Matt. 5:44ff; Acts 14:17; Psalm 145:9 etc), and regards common grace as inconsistent with man's depravity and inability to do good (forgetting depravity is relative in degree not absolute, and that it is *spiritual* good that he is unable to do, not *any* good at all). The Arminian tendency denies the particularism of redemptive grace while the Hoeksema position denies the universality of common grace. Both must be held, and in their Biblical balance.

THE HOLY SPIRIT

The chapter on the Holy Spirit gathers together the teaching of the Confession and Catechisms and gives a positive expression to the doctrine of 'common grace' implied in them.[1]

ANALYSIS

1. The Person of the Holy Spirit
a. in relation to the Godhead
b. in relation to moral creatures

2–4. The Activities of the Holy Spirit
a. in relation to creation
b. in relation to mankind
c. in the giving of special revelation
d. in the spread of the gospel
e. in the application of redemption
f. in the church

1. The Holy Spirit, the third person in the Trinity, proceeding from the Father and the Son, of the same substance and equal in power and glory, is, together with the Father and the Son, to be believed in, loved, obeyed and worshipped throughout all ages.

2 Cor. 13:14; Jn 15:26; Mat 28:19; Mat 3:6; Luke 1:35; Eph. 4:30; Heb. 10:29; 1 Cor. 10:10,11; Rev. 22:17; Eph. 2:18–22; John 14:26; Jn 16:7; Gal. 4:6; Acts 5:3,4; Acts 16:6,7; Mark 3:29; Rom. 8:26,27; 1 Jn. 2:20–27. [This section combines teaching from 2:3 and 21:2.]

2. He is the Lord and Giver of life, everywhere present, and is the source of all good thoughts, pure desires, and holy counsels in men. By him the prophets were moved to speak the word of God, and all the writers

1. For a detailed study, see O. Palmer Robertson, "The Holy Spirit in the Westminster Confession," in *Westminster Confession in the 21st Century*, ed. Ligon Duncan (Mentor, 2004), 57–99.

of the Holy Scriptures inspired to record infallibly the mind and will of God. The dispensation of the gospel is especially committed to him. He prepares the way for it, accompanies it with his persuasive power, and urges its message upon the reason and conscience of men, so that they who reject its merciful offer are not only without excuse, but are also guilty of resisting the Holy Spirit.

Eph. 4:30; Eph. 5:9; Gen. 1:2; John 3:5,6,8; Acts 2:1–21; Gal. 5:22–25; John 16:8–11; 2 Pet. 1:21; 2 Tim. 3:16; 1 Cor. 2:10–14; 1 Pet. 1:11; Jn 16:13–15; 1 Cor. 2:10–14; Acts 7:51; 1 Thess. 5:19; Eph. 4:30; Psalm 104:30. [This section draws on WCF 1:1, 5:6, 10.4 and 16.7, and renders explicit the doctrine of 'common grace' implicit in the Confession. It provides the explanation of the blessings unbelievers enjoy, the good qualities they may display and the cultural attainments they may achieve, but is not intended to alter the truth of our inability to do spiritual good apart from regeneration.]

3. The Holy Spirit, whom the Father is ever willing to give to all who ask him, is the only efficient agent in the application of redemption. He regenerates men by his grace, convicts them of sin, moves them to repentance, and persuades and enables them to embrace Jesus Christ by faith. He unites all believers to Christ, dwells in them as their Comforter and Sanctifier, gives to them the spirit of Adoption and Prayer, and performs all those gracious offices by which they are sanctified and sealed to the day of redemption.

Jn 3:1–8; Acts 2:38; Luke 11:13; 1 Cor. 12:3; Jn 7:37–39; John 16:13; John 16:7–11; Rev. 22:17; Titus 3:5–7; 2 Thess. 2:13; Gal. 4:6; 1 Jn. 4:2; Rom. 8:14,17,26,27; Eph. 4:30; 1 Cor. 2:13–16. [This section summarises teaching concerning the Spirit found in WCF 7.3, 8.8 and chapters 10 to 18.]

4. By the indwelling of the Holy Spirit, all believers, being vitally united to Christ who is the Head, are thus united one to another in the church, which is his body. He calls and anoints ministers for their holy office, qualifies all other officers in the church for their special work, and imparts various gifts and graces to its members. He gives efficacy to the word and to the ordinances of the gospel. By him the church will be preserved, increased, purified, and at last made perfectly holy in the presence of God.

Eph. 2:14–18; Eph. 4:1–6; Eph. 5:18; Acts 2:4; Acts 13:2; 1 Cor. 12:2; 2 Pet. 1:19–21; 1 Thess. 1:5,6; Jn 20:22,23; Matt. 28: 19,20. [This section draws on WCF 26.1, 25.1, 25.3 and 24.1, with the last sentence providing a fitting summation and climax].

THE GOSPEL CALL

This chapter (entitled in the 1942 PCUS enactment 'Of the Gospel') is really a treatment of the external call. The gospel is to be preached to all because God commands it; moreover the atoning work of Christ is sufficient for all. It is not a lack in Christ nor is it the decree of election which prevents people coming to Christ. Rather, it is their own sinful unwillingness. There is nothing in this chapter at all inconsistent with the rest of the Confession, and its content may be paralleled in standard Calvinistic books of theology from the Westminster period as well as before and since (but see general note above).

ANALYSIS

1. **The free offer of the gospel**
2. **The content of the gospel**
3. **Response to the gospel**
4. **Furtherance of the gospel**

1. God, in infinite and perfect love, having provided in the covenant of grace, through the mediation of the Lord Jesus Christ, a way of life and salvation, sufficient for all and adapted to the whole lost race of man, freely offers this salvation to all men in the gospel.

Rev. 22:17; John 3:16; 1 Jn. 2:1,2; Acts 2:38,39; Matt. 11:28–30; 2 Cor. 5:14–19; Titus 2:11; Heb. 2:9; Luke 24:46,47.

2. In the gospel God declares his love for the world and his desire that all men should be saved; reveals fully and clearly the only way of salvation; promises eternal life to all who truly repent and believe in

Christ; invites and commands all to embrace the offered mercy; and by his Spirit accompanying the word pleads with men to accept his gracious invitation.

Matt. 28:19,20; Acts 4:12; John 6:37–40; John 17:3; Acts 16:31; Acts 2:38; Gal. 2:16–20; Rom. 1:16,17; Rom. 4:5; Acts 13:38,39,48; 2 Pet. 3:9; Matt. 11:28–30; Mark 1:14,15; Acts 17:30; Rev. 22:17; Ezek. 33:11; Isa. 1:18; Luke 13:34.

3. It is the duty and privilege of everyone who hears the gospel immediately to accept its merciful provisions; and they who continue in impenitence and unbelief incur aggravated guilt and perish by their own fault.

Heb. 2:3; Heb. 12:25; Acts 13:46; Matt. 10:32,33; Luke 12:47,48; Heb. 10:29.

"The good news is not that all men are saved, but if they come to Christ they will be saved. Every man - sinner, ungodly, impenitent, hypocrite, backslider—is to be invited and even pleaded with... If the offering love is spurned—if the suffering Christ is rejected—they are lost. Indeed, the very gravity of unbelief in the face of evangelism is precisely that it is a rejection of so great a love and so great a Saviour."[1]

4. Since there is no other way of salvation than that revealed in the gospel, and since in the divinely established and ordinary method of grace faith comes by hearing the word of God, Christ has commissioned his church to go into all the world and to make disciples of all nations. All believers are, therefore, under obligation to sustain the ordinances of the Christian religion where they are already established, and to contribute by their prayers, gifts, and personal efforts to the extension of the kingdom of Christ throughout the whole earth.

Acts 4:12; Matt. 28:19,20; Acts 1:8; Rom. 10:13–15; Heb. 10:19–25; Gal. 3:28; 1 Cor. 16:1,2; Matt. 9:36–38; Acts 13:2–4; Col. 3:16; Rev. 22:17; Col. 1:28,29.

1. Donald Macleod, *Behold your God* (Christian Focus, 1990), 153.

APPENDIX: SUBSCRIPTION TO THE CONFESSION IN HISTORY

At the beginning of this book the importance of Confessional Subscription has been outlined. If at the time of the Westminster Assembly there were some who did not think it necessary to require a Confession to be personally subscribed by church office-bearers, the general view in Scotland was overwhelmingly in favour of such a use, and it had also been the requirement in England in earlier times. A strict acceptance of the Confession was required by the (Presbyterian) Church of Scotland with gradual breaking down under the onslaught of critical views from about 1870. In other English-speaking lands (e.g. Ireland, North America), where the Presbyterian Church was not the established church, there tended to be a measure of informality in subscription in the 18th century which was tightened when fears of doctrinal error were abroad.

In the latter part of the 19th century something of a fall back to an evangelical consensus over against anti-supernaturalism occurred. A further fall back to liberal-evangelicalism was characteristic of the period about 1900: the supernatural facts at the heart of redemption were accepted but higher critical views of Scripture, and an Arminian or even moral influence theory of the atonement became common. In the period 1879–1904 many larger Presbyterian churches relaxed their subscription. A further tragic fall back to liberal theology from about 1920 was broken by neo-orthodoxy about 1948. A resurgence of the older Reformed theology of the Confession occurred from the mid 1960s.

This appendix provides outline details about the Scottish, Irish and American experiences with subscription. The subscription in the USA commonly allows for exceptions to be allowed by Presbyteries, something that is not part of the Scottish tradition, and includes direct subscription to the Catechisms. For thorough discussion see Rowland S. Ward, 'Subscription to the Confession' in *The Westminster Confession into the 21st Century*, Vol 3. 77–138.

SCOTLAND

Literature: As well as the Acts of the various Scottish Churches see the listing and commentary in *The Proceedings of the Second General Council of the Presbyterian Alliance* (Presbyterian Journal Co., 1880), 965–1036; also A.I.C. Heron (ed), *The Westminster Confession in the Church Today* (Saint Andrew Press, 1982), 17–27, 132–140 and Appendix; Kenneth R. Ross, *Church and Creed in Scotland: The Free Church Case 1900–1904 and its Origins* (Rutherford House, 1988); Ian Hamilton, *The Erosion of Calvinist Orthodoxy: Seceders and Subscription in Scottish Presbyterianism* (Rutherford House, 1990).

The Solemn League and Covenant was approved by the Assembly of the Church of Scotland in 1643 as also by the Westminster Assembly, and sought:

> 'the preservation of the reformed religion in the Church of Scotland, in doctrine, worship, discipline and government against our common enemies; the reformation of religion in the kingdoms of England and Ireland, in doctrine worship, discipline and government according to the word of God and the example of the best reformed Churches; and shall endeavour to bring the Churches of God in the three kingdoms to the nearest conjunction and uniformity in religion, confession of faith, form of church-government, directory for worship and catechising;

> that we and our posterity after us, may, as brethren, live in faith and love, and the Lord may delight to dwell in the midst of us.'

The Solemn League and Covenant was ratified by Parliament in 1644 and renewed by all ranks in 1648. The Westminster Standards were a major result of this Covenant.

The Assembly of the Church of Scotland adopted the *Westminster Confession of Faith* as agreeable to the word of God and in nothing contrary to the previously received doctrine of the Church. This adoption was as to "the truth of the matter," that is, it involved acceptance of the doctrines expressed by the language of the Confession. Certain qualifications on matters related to the power of the civil magistrate were made also.

Act approving the Confession of Faith [August 27, 1647]

> A confession of Faith for the Kirks of God in the three kingdoms, being the chiefest part of that uniformity in religion which, by the Solemn League and Covenant, we are bound to endeavour:
>
> And there being accordingly a Confession of Faith agreed upon by the Assembly of Divines sitting at Westminster, with the assistance of Commissioners from the Kirk of Scotland; which Confession was sent from our Commissioners at London to the Commissioners of the Kirk met at Edinburgh in January last, and hath been in this Assembly twice publicly read over, examined, and considered; copies thereof being also printed, that it might be particularly perused by all the members of this assembly, unto whom frequent intimation was publicly made, to put in their doubts and objections, if they had any:
>
> And the said Confession being, upon due examination thereof, found by the assembly to be most agreeable to the word of God, and in nothing contrary to the received doctrine, worship, discipline, and government of the Kirk.

And, lastly, It being so necessary, and so much longed for, that the said Confession be, with all possible diligence and expedition, approved and established in both kingdoms, as a principal part of the intended uniformity in religion, and as a special means for the more effectual suppressing of the many dangerous errors and heresies of these times;

THE GENERAL ASSEMBLY DOTH THEREFORE, after mature deliberation, agree unto, and approve the said Confession, as to the truth of the matter; (judging it to be most orthodox, and grounded upon the word of God;) and also, as to the point of uniformity, agreeing for our part, that it be a common Confession of Faith for the three kingdoms.

THE ASSEMBLY DOTH ALSO bless the Lord, and thankfully acknowledge his great mercy, in that so excellent a Confession of Faith is prepared, and thus far agreed upon in both kingdoms; which we look upon as a great strengthening of the true reformed religion against the common enemies thereof.

BUT, lest out intention and meaning be in some particulars misunderstood, it is hereby expressly declared and provided,

THAT the not mentioning in this Confession the several sorts of ecclesiastical officers and assemblies, shall be no prejudice to the truth of Christ in these particulars, to be expressed fully in the Directory of Government.

IT IS FURTHER DECLARED, That the Assembly understandeth some parts of the second article of the thirty-one chapter only of kirks not settled, or constituted in point of government: And that although, in such kirks, a synod of Ministers, and other fit persons, may be called by the Magistrate's authority and nomination, without any other call, to consult and advise with about matters of religion; and although, likewise, the Ministers of Christ, without delegation from their churches, may of themselves, and by virtue of their office, meet together synodically in such kirks not yet constituted, yet neither of these ought to be done in kirks constituted and settled; it being always

> free to the Magistrate to advise with synods of Ministers and Ruling Elders, meeting upon delegation from their churches, either ordinarily, or, being indicted by his authority, occasionally, and *pro re nata*; it being also free to assemble together synodically, as well *pro re nata* as at the ordinary times, upon delegation from the churches, by the intrinsical power received from Christ, as often as it is necessary for the good of the Church so to assemble, in case the Magistrate, to the detriment of the Church, withhold or deny his consent; the necessity of occasional assemblies being first remonstrate unto him by humble supplication.

The Revolution Settlement of the Scottish Church in 1690 meant that the obligation of the covenants fell away but the Confession of Faith was anew ratified by the Parliament as 'containing the sum and substance of the doctrine of the Reformed Churches.' This sum and substance is not a reference to some elements of the Confession's teaching, but to the total of the doctrine expressed by the words of the Confession. The 1690 Assembly also required that preachers and elders 'be obliged to subscribe their approbation of the Confession of Faith.' Parliament legislated for subscription by ministers and preachers in 1693 and the Assembly enacted legislation in the following year. From 1700 the formula was also subscribed by elders. School teachers were required to subscribe the Confession too. In 1711 prescribed questions and a formula rather more explicit of the commitment implied in the 1694 formula were introduced for ministers and the 1694 formula was retained for elders.

Formula, to be subscribed by all such as shall pass trials, in order to be licensed, and that shall be ordained ministers, or admitted to parishes [May 22, 1711]

I   do hereby declare, that I do sincerely own and believe the whole doctrine contained in the Confession of Faith, approved by the General Assemblies of this National Church, and ratified by law in the year 1690, and frequently confirmed by divers Acts of Parliament since that time, to be the truths of God; and I do own the same as the confession of my faith: As likewise, I do own the purity of worship presently authorised and practised in this Church, and also the Presbyterian government and discipline now so happily established therein; which doctrine, worship, and Church government, I am persuaded are founded on the Word of God, and agreeable thereto: And I promise, that, through the grace of God, I shall firmly and constantly adhere to the same, and to the utmost of my power, shall, in my station, assert, maintain, and defend the said doctrine, worship, discipline, and government of this Church, by Kirk-sessions, Presbyteries, Provincial Synods and General Assemblies; and that I shall in my practice conform myself to the said worship, and submit to the said discipline and government, and never endeavour, directly nor indirectly, the prejudice or subversion of the same; and I promise, that I shall follow no divisive courses from the present establishment in this Church; renouncing all doctrines, tenets, and opinions whatsoever, contrary to, or inconsistent with, the said doctrine worship, discipline, or government of this Church.

This 'whole doctrine' subscription is still maintained in the Free Church of Scotland and similar bodies, but in the Church of Scotland the current subscription is much weakened to unspecified 'fundamental doctrines of the Christian faith contained in the Confession of Faith of this Church'.

IRELAND

Literature: See J. M. Barkley, *The Westminster Formularies in Irish Presbyterianism* (Graham & Heslip, 1956) and A. W. Godfrey-Brown, et al., *Challenge and Conflict: Essays in Irish Presbyterian History and Doctrine* (W. & B. Baird, 1981). Code of the Presbyterian Church in Ireland, June 2020.

The first Presbytery in Ireland dates from 1642 at Carrickfergus, and was constituted by 5 chaplains and 4 elders belonging to Scottish regiments sent to quell the Irish rebellion of 1641. It does not appear that formal subscription was required in the early period, whether to the Scots Confession of 1560 or to the Westminster Confession from 1647. Although there is no doubt that it was adhered to, and there is evidence of verbal assent being required in the 1670s, it was not until 1698 that the General Synod of Ulster required subscription by licentiates. In areas outside the jurisdiction of this northern Synod formal subscription was still not required. Legal toleration was granted by the State in 1719 on the basis of the Westminster Confession, but some scrupled subscription. These non-subscribers in general were not notably unorthodox but they were influenced by the intellectual current of the time which favoured Arminianism and moderatism. They argued that creeds other than the Bible were inconsistent with the final authority of Scripture and with individual freedom. They tended to limit their adherence to the doctrines in the Confession which they judged essential, a subjective and highly unsatisfactory position. The non-subscribers were placed in the Presbytery of Antrim, which was then excluded from the Synod of Ulster in 1726, but inter-communion continued in the main.

Despite reaffirming subscription in 1784, practice was lax. The rise of Arianism (denial of Christ's deity) in the early 19th century led to Henry Cooke leading an effort to enforce subscription. This succeeded in 1829 and the 17 non-subscribers withdrew and formed the Remonstrant Synod. In 1835 the General Synod of Ulster made subscription compulsory for all ministers, licentiates and elders, and thus paved the way for reunion with the Secession Synod on July 10, 1840 to form the *Presbyterian Church in Ireland* with the Confession adopted by the Church of Scotland in 1647 as its basis. Having drifted, of recent years the PCI has made considerable progressing in recovering orthodoxy,

The current subscription in the PCI is: '*I believe the Westminster Confession of Faith as described in the Code, chapter 1, paragraphs 12–14, to be founded on and agreeable to the Word of God and as such I subscribe it as the Confession of my faith.*' The sections of the Code referred to are:

> **12. The Presbyterian Church in Ireland,** as a witness for Christ, has adopted subordinate standards. In these are found what the Church understands the Word of God to teach on certain important points of doctrine and worship. These subordinate standards are a testimony for truth and against error, and serve as a bond of union for members of the Church.
>
> **13. The Confession of Faith** (as approved by the Church of Scotland in her Act of 1647), and the Larger and Shorter Catechisms, prepared by the Westminster Assembly of Divines, are the subordinate standards of the Presbyterian Church in Ireland. Accepting these subordinate standards, the Church holds that civil rulers must be obedient to Christ in their own area of authority, yet they ought not to attempt, in any way, to constrain any person's religious beliefs or intrude upon their rights of conscience.
>
> **14. The Church alone** has the right to interpret and explain her standards, under the guidance of the Spirit of God.

The smaller *Reformed Presbyterian* and *Evangelical Presbyterian* bodies are quite strict in maintaining adherence to the Confession.

UNITED STATES OF AMERICA

Literature: See Charles Hodge, *The Constitutional History of the Presbyterian Church in the United States of America* (William S. Martein, 1851), 127–215; also his *The Church and its Polity* (Thomas Nelson, 1879), 317–342; Morton H. Smith, *Studies in Southern Presbyterian Theology* (P&R, 1987), 17–44; L.J. Trinterud, *The Forming of an American Tradition: A Re-examination of Colonial Presbyterianism* (Westminster Press, 1949, 1970); James R. Payton, Jr., 'The Background and Significance of the Adopting Act of 1729' in C. G. Dennison & R.C. Gamble, *Pressing Toward the Mark: Essays Commemorating Fifty Years of the Orthodox Presbyterian Church* (Committee for the Historian of the Orthodox Presbyterian Church, 1986), 131–145.

The earliest Presbyterian congregations in what is now the United States of America were established by English Puritans in the early decades of the 17th century. Scots-Irish settlers furthered development, and Francis Mackemie organised the first Presbytery in 1706. Formal subscription was not required in the early period, but the effects of erroneous tendencies in Scotland and Ireland furthered the desire for strict subscription. A few ministers doubted the propriety of subscription to a man-made document and were not sure orthodoxy could be preserved by such a means. However, on the morning of September 19, 1729 a *Preliminary Act* was passed by the Synod of Philadelphia as follows:

ALTHOUGH THE SYNOD do not claim or pretend to any authority of imposing our faith upon other men's consciences, but do profess our just dissatisfaction with, and abhorrence of such impositions, and do utterly disclaim all legislative power and authority in the Church, being willing to receive one another as Christ has received us to the glory of God, and admit to fellowship in sacred ordinances, all such as we have

God, and admit to fellowship in sacred ordinances, all such as we have grounds to believe Christ will at last admit to the kingdom of heaven, yet we are undoubtedly obliged to take care that the faith once delivered to the saints be kept pure and uncorrupt among us, and so handed down to our posterity; AND DO THEREFORE AGREE that all the ministers of this Synod, or that shall hereafter be admitted into this Synod, shall declare their agreement in, and approbation of, the Confession of Faith, with the Larger and Shorter Catechisms of the Assembly of Divines at Westminster, as being in all the essential and necessary articles, good forms of sound words and systems of Christian doctrine, and do also adopt the said Confession and Catechisms as the confession of our faith.

AND WE DO ALSO AGREE, that all the presbyteries within our bounds shall always take care not to admit any candidate of the ministry into the exercise of the sacred function but what declares his agreement in opinion with all the essential and necessary articles of said Confession, either by subscribing the said Confession of Faith and Catechisms, or by a verbal declaration of their assent thereto, as such minister or candidate shall think best.

AND IN CASE any minister of this Synod, or any candidate for the ministry, shall have any scruple with respect to any article or articles of said Confession or Catechisms, he shall at the time of his making said declaration declare his sentiments to the Presbytery or Synod, who shall, notwithstanding, admit him to the exercise of the ministry within our bounds, and to ministerial communion, if the Synod or Presbytery shall judge his scruple or mistake to be only about articles not essential and necessary in doctrine, worship, or government.

BUT IF THE SYNOD OR PRESBYTERY shall judge such ministers or candidates erroneous in essential and necessary articles of faith, the

Synod or Presbytery shall declare them uncapable of communion with them.

AND THE SYNOD DO SOLEMNLY AGREE, that none of us will traduce or use any opprobrious terms of those that differ from us in these extra-essential and not necessary points of doctrine, but treat them with the same friendship, kindness, and brotherly love, as if they had not differed from us in such sentiments.

In the afternoon of the same day this Act was applied by the ministers proposing their scruples. It was found possible to declare adherence unanimously to the WCF & Catechisms as:

> 'the confession of their faith, excepting some clauses in the twentieth and twenty-third chapters, concerning which clauses the Synod do unanimously declare, that they do not receive those articles in any such sense as to suppose the civil magistrate hath a controlling power over Synods with respect to the exercise of their ministerial authority; or power to persecute any for their religion, or in any sense contrary to the Protestant succession to the throne of Great Britain.'

For some years after there was debate within the church over the intent of what had been done. Some left for smaller Presbyterian bodies who held to every doctrinal point, while a few argued without success that all that was required was belief in the essential doctrines of Christianity rather than the essential and necessary articles of the Confession and Catechisms. The Synod had not contemplated significant departure from the whole doctrine of the Confession, and all the early ministers are known to have been strict Calvinists. Indeed, in 1730 and 1736 the Synod declared it did not intend such departure. In 1758, when a reunion of two Synods occurred, the first article read:

> 'Both Synods having always approved and received the Westminster Confession of Faith, Larger and Shorter Catechisms, as an orthodox and excellent system of doctrine, founded on the word of God; we do still receive the same as the confession of our faith . . . strictly enjoining it on all our ministers and probationers for the ministry, that they preach and teach according to the form of sound words in the said Confession and Catechisms, and avoid and oppose all errors contrary thereto.'

It has been plausibly argued that the intention in 1729 was that the ministers be committed to the Calvinistic or Reformed system of doctrine in the Confession as distinct from incidentals and sundry issues—whether the Pope is the Antichrist, whether marriage to a deceased wife's sister is lawful, the grounds of divorce. This was in fact the actual kind of adherence to the Confession which was general until late in the 19th century, and is defended by Charles Hodge. It is distinguished from adherence to every doctrinal proposition ('the whole doctrine' in Scottish parlance) and from the 'substance of doctrine,' theory which lacks definite meaning. It is generally known as the 'system of doctrine' position from the question to candidates for ordination from 1788: *'Do you receive and adopt the Confession of Faith of this Church as containing the system of doctrine taught in the Holy Scriptures?'*

It should be noted that the term 'system' was used in the 18th century to describe a work or writing containing a regularly arranged exposition of some subject, a systematic treatment, so the term may well have been virtually equivalent to the Scottish 'whole doctrine'. However, the Synod of 1729 had undoubtedly given Presbyteries the right to judge what was essential and necessary, and, as there was no explicit definition of such items, a broadening church could result. Thus, it has been argued that the move away from strict adherence to the Calvinistic system of doctrine in the Confession, is in continuity with the 1729 Adopting Act (so Trinterud,

Payton). The smaller American Presbyterian bodies have maintained a more strict subscription although generally also employing the term 'system of doctrine.' For Charles Hodge's exposition of this phrase see *The Church and its Polity* (New York 1879), 338–340.

A DRAFT MODERN SUBSCRIPTION

Here is an example of a modern subscription in the strict Scottish tradition. I have composed it in the light of historical experience so as to clarify the nature of subscription and the obligations of the subscriber, and in a manner that can be easily understood by the congregation before whom vows are taken.

1. I wholeheartedly and willingly acknowledge before God without mental reservation, that the Holy Scriptures, consisting of the Old and New Testaments, are the Word of God and the only rule of faith and conduct.
2. I further wholeheartedly and willingly acknowledge before God that I believe all the doctrines contained in the Westminster Confession of Faith received by the Church of Scotland in the year 1647, and interpreted in the Adopting Act of this Church in the year...., to be a faithful setting forth of the teaching of the Word of God. To all those doctrines, both major and minor, I subscribe without reservation, and confess them to be my own understanding of the teaching of the Word of God, which I will assert, maintain and defend against all doctrines and opinions contrary to or inconsistent with them.
3. I further pledge that I will teach the doctrines of the Christian faith with Biblical balance, giving a central place

to the person and work of Christ, and pressing on all who hear the obligation to repent and believe the Gospel.

4. In making this subscription I understand that the Westminster Confession is not on a level with the Word of God. Thus, I do not declare that the statements of doctrine in it are necessarily formulated in the best manner, or that they are exhaustive statements of the doctrines expressed, or that every teaching of Scripture is dealt with or every error condemned, or that mere allusions or incidental remarks are binding. Nevertheless, I subscribe as previously stated to all the teachings intentionally conveyed by the Confession because I believe them to be derived from the Holy Scriptures and in agreement with them.

5. Should at any time a question arise as to my understanding of any of the teachings of the Word of God that may seem to conflict with my subscription to the teaching of the Confession, I solemnly undertake not to act or teach independently but to bring such a matter before the relevant church assembly for clarification or resolution, including by final appeal to the Word of God.

6. I further acknowledge that the principles of Presbyterian government by elders duly met in congregational, regional and broader assemblies, as also the simplicity and spirituality of worship as practised by this Church, are soundly based on the Word of God. I acknowledge the authority of the Church to administer the teaching of the Word of God in subjection to that Word, and I promise to observe the Practice and Procedure of the Church in an orderly manner, and to uphold its worship, government and discipline. Should I

have cause in conscience to disagree with a lawful decision of the church, I recognise that I may clear my conscience by a formal dissent, but that I remain obligated to submit to my brothers in Church assembly and to promote the unity of the Church.

SELECTED BIBLIOGRAPHY

This bibliography generally lists titles in historical order. It is not exhaustive but will lead one to other material. It aims to give most major references directly referring to the study of the Confession by those friendly to its theology, and some that are not.

A. TEXTS OF THE CONFESSION

1. EARLIER STANDARD TEXT

Carruthers, S.W. *The Westminster Confession of Faith, Being an account of the Preparation and Printing of its Seven Leading Edition to which is appended a Critical Text of the Confession with notes thereon* (Manchester, 1937).

Most printed editions of the text contain punctuation and other errors (particularly at 20:2), as well as mistakes in the Biblical citations. The Carruthers' 1937 text is included in the cloth editions published by the Free Presbyterian Church of Scotland since 1994. An accurately printed edition of S. W. Carruthers' text (in parallel with the Savoy Declaration) may be found in Michael Owen (ed) *Witness of Faith: Historic Documents of the Uniting Church in Australia* (Melbourne 1984) 121–173.

NOTE: Dr. Carruthers also prepared a text from the handwritten manuscript of Cornelius Burges. It was printed by the Presbyterian Church of England in 1946 and adopted by the Orthodox Presbyterian Church (US) in 1956 and the Presbyterian Church in America in 1973.

It has a number of unimportant variations from the official text as noted in the Introduction to this book.

2. CURRENT STANDARD TEXT

Bower, John. *The Confession of Faith: A Critical Text and Introduction* (Grand Rapids: Reformation Heritage Books, 2020) A very thorough and scholarly production.

3. MODERN LANGUAGE TEXTS

The revival of interest in the Reformed faith has seen several modern language editions of the Westminster Confession. The first known to the writer is actually a rendering into modern English of the 1689 Baptist version of the Confession, variously known as the *Old London Confession* or the *Philadelphia Confession*. The work was done in a competent manner by Mr S. M. Houghton and was published by Carey Publications in England in 1975 under the title *A Faith to Confess*. It has been circulated widely.

Four other modernisations of the WCF originate with American Presbyterians:

In 1971 the Synod of the Reformed Presbyterian Church of North America (RPCNA) proposed that the language of the Confession be updated and a Committee from that church, the Orthodox Presbyterian Church (OPC) and the Reformed Presbyterian Church, Evangelical Synod, [since 1982 part of the Presbyterian Church in America (PCA)], worked on the project, completing a draft in 1980.

1. After some alterations were made, the resultant text was approved by the RPCNA in 1985 as a teaching aid, and an edition in parallel

with the original text was published in 1992 as the *Modern Language Revision*.

2. The OPC sent copies of the draft to lower courts only in 1989. It was pervasively revised and approved in 1993 by the OPC as a *Modern English Study Version*, and is available in an edition in parallel with the original. This is a very conservative revision.
3. Meanwhile, in 1979 Summertown Texts in Tennessee published a modernisation of the American text entitled *An Authentic Modern Version*. It was prepared with the involvement of Douglas Kelly, Hugh McClure and Philip Rollinson. Although it is not based on the best original text, it was subsequently adopted by the Evangelical Presbyterian Church, US. A second revised edition was issued in 1984. (A British edition of this text was published in Northern Ireland in 1990.)
4. The fourth modernised text was issued by Presby Press in 1988 as *A Contemporary Edition*, and was prepared by Donald Remillard of the PCA.

In 1992, I published a modernisation in conjunction with my commentary, *The Westminster Confession for the Church Today*, being then unaware of Remillard's work or the published RPCNA and OPC texts. My 1992 text, carefully revised was published in July 1996 with the two catechisms modernised on the same principles as *The Westminster Confession and Catechisms in Modern English.* It was reprinted in 2000, 2001 and 2007. (The Shorter Catechism had been first published in modern English in 1981 under the title *Learning the Christian Faith*.)

B. SOURCES FOR THE WESTMINSTER ASSEMBLY DEBATES

1. Lightfoot, John. 'Journal of the Proceedings of the Westminster Assembly of Divines: January 1, 1643 to December 31, 1644', and 'Letters to and from Dr. Lightfoot' in *Collected Works* (London 1824) Vol. 13.
2. Mitchell, Alex F. and Struthers, John, (eds). *Minutes of the Sessions of the Westminster Assembly of Divines* (Nov 1644 to March 1649) (Edinburgh 1874; most recent reprint, Edmonton, Canada 1991).
3. Baillie, Robert. *The Letters and Journal of Robert Baillie, MA, Principal of University of Glasgow* (ed D. Laing; Edinburgh 1841).
4. Gillespie, George. 'Notes of Debates and Proceedings of the Assembly of Divines and Other Commissioners at Westminster, February 1644 to January 1645' (ed D. Meek; Edinburgh 1846; reprinted in *The Works of George Gillespie* Vol 2 (Edmonton, Canada 1991).
5. *Van Dixhoorn, Chad (ed.). The Minutes and Papers of the Westminster Assembly* 5 volumes, 3200 pages (Oxford: OUP, 2012). Dr. Van Dixhoorn located nearly all the Assembly's papers and documents in 2002. This critical edition will be foundational for all future scholarly work in the field.

C. COMMENTARIES ON THE WESMINSTER CONFESSION

1. Dickson, David. *Truth's Victory Over Error* (Edinburgh, 1684; reprinted Glasgow, 1764). This is an unauthorised translation from the Latin class lectures by Dickson (c.1583–1662), Professor of Theology at Edinburgh. The first edition was issued under the name of George Sinclair, but the plagiarism was soon discovered leading to the couplet: 'No errors in this book I see,/ But G.S. where D.D. should be.' Dickson goes through the Confession propounding the assertions by

way of question, and providing answers that throw light on how he understood the Confession's teaching. Not of great use today.

2. Shaw, Robert. *Exposition of the Westminster Confession of Faith.* (Edinburgh, 1845). Shaw was minister of the Original Secession Church at Whitburn, Scotland. This competent exposition was reprinted in 1877 and reissued at Inverness in 1973 under the title *The Reformed Faith*, and more recently under its original title.

3. Hodge, A.A. *A Commentary on the Confession of Faith* (Philadelphia, 1869; reprinted by Banner of Truth Trust 1958 under the title *The Confession of Faith).* Analytical and theological.

4. Macpherson, John. *The Confession of Faith*, second edition (Edinburgh, 1882) A succinct exposition, well informed on historical theology, by a minister of the Free Church of Scotland; a fine work.

5. Beattie, Francis R. *The Presbyterian Standards: An Exposition of the Westminster Confession and Catechisms* (Richmond, Va. 1896) 431pp. Reprinted 1997.

6. Morris, Edward D. *Theology of the Westminster Symbols: A Commentary homiletical, doctrinal, practical on the Confession of Faith and Catechisms and the Related Formularies of the Presbyterian Church* (Columbus, Ohio. 1900) 857pp.

7. Green, J.B. *A Harmony of the Westminster Presbyterian Standards with explanatory notes* (Richmond, Va. 1951). The text of the Confession and Catechisms in parallel with analytical notes, largely based on F. R. Beattie. A useful volume.

8. Clark, G.H. *What Presbyterians Believe* (1955) revised and republished as *What Do Presbyterians Believe?* (Philadelphia, 1965). Originating as a series of popular articles, this is undoubtedly a Calvinistic

presentation but overall is uneven. Clark did not regard it as a formal commentary.

9. Hendry, George S. *The Westminster Confession for Today; a Contemporary Interpretation* (Richmond, Va. 1960). John Leith's assessment ('more a statement of Christian faith from the Barthian perspective than an effort to understand the Confession') is apt.

10. Williamson, G.I. *The Westminster Confession of Faith for Study Classes* (Philadelphia, 1964), 309pp. A theological and practical treatment.

11. Philip, James, *The Westminster Confession of Faith*. Published in two roneoed booklets 1966 and revised and enlarged 1983/1984, this is a practical treatment in a mid-week study class by the minister of Holyrood Church of Scotland, Edinburgh.

12. Wilkinson, T.L. *The Westminster Confession Now* (Melbourne, 1992). By a former Professor at the Reformed Theological College, Geelong; 224 pages A4 format, spiral bound; later edition in A5 format

13. Ward, Rowland S. *The Westminster Confession for the Church Today* (Presbyterian Church of Eastern Australia in Melbourne, 1992). The first edition of the book in your hands

6. 14. Van Dixhoorn, Chad, *Confessing the Faith – A reader's guide to the Westminster Confession of Faith* (Edinburgh: Banner of truth, 2014). A fine and accessible guide; includes historic text and OPC 1993 Modern text in parallel columns.

D. OTHER ASSESSMENTS

(a) General

1. Carson, J.L. & Hall, D.W. (eds). *To Glorify and Enjoy God: A Commemoration of the Westminster Assembly* (Edinburgh 1994). A

useful modern introduction. Note the bibliographical suggestions, 301–308.

2. Barker, William S. Puritan Profiles (Fearn 1996). Excellent profiles of 54 Puritan leaders at the time of the Westminster assembly.

3. Duncan, J. Ligon (ed). *The Westminster Confession into the 21st Century* (Vol 1 (2004), Vol 2 (2004), Vol 3 (2009)). An excellent series; some chapters in the first three volumes are referenced below under (d).

(b) History

1. Reid, James. *Memoirs of the Westminster Divines* (Paisley, 1811; reprinted Edinburgh, 1982) 390pp

2. Hetherington, W.M. *History of the Westminster Assembly of Divines* (Edinburgh 1843; fifth edition New York 1890); reprinted Still Waters 1993.

3. Mitchell, A. F. *The Westminster Assembly: Its History and its Standards* (London 1883); reprinted Still Waters 1992.

4. Beveridge, W. A *Short History of the Westminster Assembly* (Edinburgh, 1904) reprinted A Press 1991.

5. Warfield, B.B. *The Westminster Assembly and its Work* (Oxford, 1931). Reprinted from journal articles 1893–1908.

6. Carruthers, S.W. *The Everyday Work of the Westminster Assembly* (Philadelphia, 1943).

7. Leith, John H. *Assembly at Westminster: Reformed Theology in the Making* (Richmond, Va. 1973). Leith is not quite in the theological mould of Westminster but his writings are well worth reading.

8. Paul, Robert S. *The Assembly of the Lord* (Edinburgh, 1985). A full length treatment by a specialist in the period with special reference to church government.

10. Hall, David W. *Windows on Westminster* (Norcross, Ga., 1993).

11. Van Dixhoorn, Chad. 'The Westminster Assembly at Work' in *The Westminster Confession into the 21st Century*, Vol 3. 19–53.

12. Ward, Rowland S. *A Short Introduction to the Westminster Assembly and its Work* (Lansvale, NSW: Tulip Publishing, 2019)

(c) **Theology — General**

1. Walker, James. *The Theology and Theologians of Scotland 1560–1750* (second edition, Edinburgh, 1888; reprinted Edinburgh, 1982). A masterly coverage of views on predestination and providence, the atonement, the visible church and the headship of Christ in the church.

2. Briggs, C.A. *Whither? A theological question for our times* (1889; 3rd edition Edinburgh, 1900). Briggs was not truly sympathetic with Westminster theology and aimed to refute the Princeton position, but this critical overview of the content of the Confession is not without value in stimulating thought.

3. Shedd, W.G.T. *Calvinism: Pure and Mixed — A Defence of the Westminster Standards* (New York, 1893; reprinted Edinburgh, 1986). Deals with the issues under attack in the 1880s and 1890s. Valuable.

4. Macleod, Donald. 'The Westminster Confession Today' in *Banner of Truth Magazine*, # 101 (February, 1972) 15–26. Also see the superb overview by Macleod in the introductory essay in Fergusson, D. & Elliott, M.W., (eds.), *The History of Scottish Theology* Volume 2 *[The Early Enlightenment to the Late Victorian Era]* (Oxford: OUP, 2019).

5. Murray, John. 'The Theology of the Westminster Confession of Faith' in *Collected Writings* 4 (Edinburgh, 1982) 241–263.

6. Ferguson, Sinclair B. 'The Teaching of the Confession' in A.I.C.Heron (ed) *The Westminster Confession in the Church Today* (Edinburgh, 1982) 28–39. [Some other sections of this rather uneven volume are also worthwhile.]

7. Letham, Robert. *The Westminster Assembly – Reading its Theology in Historical Context* (Phillipsburg, NJ: P&R 2009).

8. Haykin, A. G., & Jones, Mark (eds.) *Drawn into Controversie: Reformed Theological Diversity and Debates within Seventeenth-Century British Puritanism* (Göttingen: Vandenhoek & Ruprecht, 2011). Twelve essays including on imputation of the active obedience of Christ, English hypothetic universalism, covenant theology, assurance etc..

9. Beeke, Joel R. & Jones, Mark. *A Puritan Theology – Doctrine for Life* (Grand Rapids: Reformation Heritage Books, 2012) A great resource.

10. Fesko, J. V. *The Theology of the Westminster Standards – Historical Context and Theological Insights* (Wheaton,Ill: Crossway, 2014).

11. Maceod, Donald. *Therefore the Truth I Speak – Scottish Theology 1500–1700* (Fearn: Mentor, 2020). A wonderful volume with authoritative and accessible material; particularly good coverage of Federal theology

(d) Special issues – a selection of significant material

Subscription

Ward, Rowland S. 'Subscription to the Confession' in *The Westminster Confession into the 21st Century,* Vol 3. 77–138.

Chapter 1 — Scripture

Fesko, J.V. & Richard, Guy M. 'Natural Theology and the Westminster Confession of Faith' in *The Westminster Confession into the 21st Century,* Vol. 3, 223–266.

Spear, Wayne R. 'The Westminster Assembly and Biblical Interpretation' in John H. White (ed) *The Book of Books: Essays on the Scriptures in Honor of Johanes G. Vos* (P&R, 1978), 45–54,56.

Silva, Moisés. 'Old Princeton, Westminster and Inerrancy' in *Westminster Theological Journal* 50 (1988), 65–80.

Muller, Richard A. *Reformed Dogmatics Vol. 2: Holy Scripture* (Grand Rapids 1993, 2003). This full-length historical study supersedes all others and effectively answers critics such as Karl Barth and J.B.Rogers.

Robertson, O.P. *The Final Word* (Edinburgh, 1993) provides helpful teaching on the finality of Scripture and the cessation of the revelatory gifts.

Curtis, Byron. ' "Private Spirits" in the Westminster Confession of Faith 1:10 and in Catholic-Protestant debate (1588–1652),' in *WThJ* 58 (1996), 257–299 and Garnet H. Milne's 'Response' in *WThJ* 61 (1999), 101–110.

Chapter 2 — God

Macleod, Donald. *Behold Your God* (Fearn, Ross-shire: Mentor, 1995).

Chapter 3 — Divine Decree

Shedd, W. G. T. *Calvinism: Pure and Mixed* [1893] (rep. 1986), 29–91.

Warfield, B. B. *The Westminster Assembly and Its Work*, 122–151.

MacGregor, James. 'The Free Offer in the Westminster Confession' [1890] in *Banner of Truth Magazine*, July/August 1970, 51–58.

Clark, R. Scott. 'Janus, the Well Meant Offer of the Gospel, and Westminster Theology' in David VanDrunen (ed), *The Pattern of Sound Doctrine* (Phillipsburg: P&R, 2004), 149–179.

Thomas, Derek W. H. 'The Westminster Consensus on the Decree: The Infra/Supra Lapsarian debate' in *The Westminster Confession into the 21st Century*, Vol 3 (2009), 267–289.

MacLeod, Donald. *Compel Them to Come In: Calvinism and the Free Offer of the Gospel* (Fearn: Christian Focus, 2020).

Chapter 7 — Covenant

Perkins, Harrison. *Catholicity and the Covenant of Works: James Ussher and the Reformed Tradition* (Oxford University Press, 2020). An important contribution.

Ward, Rowland S. *God and Adam: Reformed Theology & the Creation Covenant* (Melbourne, 2003; new edition Lansvale, NSW: Tulip Publishing, 2019)

Macleod, Donald. *Therefore the Truth I Speak* (Fearn: Mentor, 2020).

Chapter 8 — Christ the Mediator

Macleod, Donald. *The Person of Christ* (IVP 1998); also *Christ Crucified – Understanding the Atonement* (Nottingham: IVP, 2014).

Nicole, Roger. 'John Calvin's View of the Extent of the Atonement' *WThJ*, Vol. 47 (1985), 197–225.

Rouwendal, P. L. 'Calvin's Forgotten Classical Position on the Extent of the Atonement' in *WThJ*, Vol. 70 (2008), 317–335.

Chapter 9:3 — Human Freedom

Helm, Paul. 'Or to Prepare Himself Thereunto' in *Banner of Truth Magazine* #175 (April 1978), 20–22.

Chapter 12 — Adoption

Trumper, Tim J.R. 'The Theological History of Adoption' in *Scottish Bulletin of Evangelical Theology*, Vol 20.1 (2002), 4–28; Vol. 20.2, 177–202.

Beeke, Joel R. 'Transforming Power and Comfort: The Puritans on Adoption' in Anthony T. Selvaggio (ed), *The Faith Once Delivered* (Phillipsburg: P&R, 2007), 63–105.

Chapter 18 — Assurance

Beeke, Joel R. *Assurance of Faith: Calvin, English Puritanism and the Dutch Second Reformation* (New York, 1994), 534pp. A masterly study indispensable to future study of the doctrine.

Dever, Mark E. 'Calvin, Westminster & Assurance' in *The Westminster Confession into the 21st Century* Vol. 1 (2003), 303–341.

Chapter 19 — Law of God

Ferguson, Sinclair B. 'An Assembly of Theonomists? The Teaching of the Westminster Divines on the Law of God' in W.S.Barker & W.R.Godfrey (eds), *Theonomy: A Reformed Critique* (Grand Rapids 1990), 315–349.

Troxel, A. Craig & Wallace, Peter J. 'Men in Combat over the Civil Law: "General Equity" in WCF 19.4' in *WThJ* 64 (2002), 307–318.

Chapter 21 — Religious Worship & the Sabbath Day

Ward, Rowland S. *The Psalms in Christian Worship* (Melbourne, 1992).

Gaffin, R. B. 'Westminster and the Sabbath' in *The Westminster Confession into the 21st Century* Vol. 1, 123–144.

Gordon, T. David. 'The Westminster Assembly's Unworkable and Unscriptural View of Worship' – a review of R.J.Gore's *Covenantal Worship* in *WThJ* 65 (2003), 345–356.

Needham, Nick. 'Westminster & Worship: Psalms, Hymns? Musical Instruments?' in *The Westminster Confession into the 21st Century* Vol. 2, 223–306.

Chapter 23:3 — Church & State

Bradshaw, F.M. 'The Christian Attitude to Politics' in *A Witness for Christ: The Presbyterian Church of Eastern Australia 1846–1996* (1996), 411–415.

Cunningham, William. 'The Westminster Confession on the Relation Between Church and State' in *Discussions on Church Principles* (Edinburgh, 1863), 211–234

Kerr, A.G. 'On the Civil Magistrate' in W. J. Ham (ed) *Reformation Applied* (Strathpine North, 1983) [Presbyterian Reformed Church of Australia viewpoint.]

Graham, Clement. 'The Headship of Christ in a Pluralist Society' in *Crown Him Lord of All* (Edinburgh, 1993), 136–152.

Chapter 25 — Church

Macpherson, John. *The Doctrine of the Church in Scottish Theology* (Edinburgh 1903).

Avis, Paul D.L. ' "The True Church" in Reformation Theology' in *Scottish Journal of Theology* 30 (1977), 319–345.

Kyle, R.G. 'The Nature of the Church in the Thought of John Knox' in *Scottish Journal of Theology* 37 (1984), 485–501.

Ward, R.S. 'The Man of Sin' in *The Banner of Truth Magazine,* December 1977; 26–32.

Roberts, Maurice. 'Turretine on the Antichrist' in *The Banner of Truth Magazine* August/September 1991, 1–8.

Chapter 28 — Baptism

Wright, David, F. 'Baptism at the Westminster Assembly' in *The Westminster Confession into the 21st Century* Vol. 1, 161–186 but its claim of baptismal regeneration is not well founded.

Chapter 29 — The Lord's Supper

Duncan, J. Ligon. 'True Communion with Christ: Calvin, Westminster and Consensus on the Lord's Supper' in *The Westminster Confession into the 21st Century* Vol. 1, 429–476 and another view:

Spear, Wayne R. 'The Nature of the Lord's Supper according to Calvin and the Westminster Confession in *The Westminster Confession into the 21st Century,* Vol. 3, 355ff.

Chapter 31:2 — Synods and Councils

See under Chapter 23

Chapters 32/33 — Eschatology

Gribben, Crawford. *The Puritan Millennium: Literature and Theology, 1550–1682* (Four Courts Press, 2000).

Thomas, Derek W.H. 'The Eschatology of the Westminster Confession & Assembly', in *The Westminster Confession into the 21st Century* Vol. 2, 307–380.

Chapters 5:6; 9:3; 10:4; 16:7 Common grace (also see p.273.)

Shedd, W.G.T. *Calvinism Pure and Mixed*, 92–101

Macleod, Donald. *Behold Your God* (Fearn, Ross-shire 1990), 145–176.

American changes/additions

Robertson, O. Palmer. 'The Holy Spirit in the WCF' in *The Westminster Confession into the 21st Century* Vol. 1, 57–99.

Shedd, W.G.T. *Calvinism Pure and Unmixed*, 1–22.

Warfield, B.B. 'The Confession of Faith as Revised in 1903' in *Selected Shorter Writings* II (P&R Publishing, 1973), 370–410.

INDEX OF NAMES

Allen, Arthur, 228
Alsted, Johann Heinrich, 331
Ames, William, 44, 161
Amyraut, Moses, 82
Archer, John, 331
Arminius, 76, 138
Augustine, 18, 26, 93–94, 138, 142, 251

Baillie, Robert, 309
Barkley, J. M., 347
Barth, Karl, 73
Bavinck, Herman, 62, 67, 78, 86, 124, 181
Baxter, Richard, 50
Beauchamp, Paul, 92
Berkouwer, G. C., 290
Beza, Theodore, 291
Boettner, Loraine, 70
Bonhoeffer, Dietrich, 229
Boniface VIII, 269
Boston, Thomas, 117, 121
Bradshaw, F. M., 255, 318
Brown, A. J., 46
Brown, Dan, 28
Bruce, Robert, 292, 308
Bucan, William, 102
Bulkeley, Peter, 119
Bunyan, John, 197

Cajetan, 94
Calvin, John, 33, 55, 69, 72, 84, 94, 98, 174, 195, 277–78, 280
Cameron, John, 82
Candlish, Robert S., 328
Carruthers, Samuel William, 3
Chafer, Lewis Sperry, 123
Chillingworth, William, 58
Cicero, 103
Clement VIII, 40
Cooke, Henry, 347
Cunningham, William, 105, 156, 272, 275

Darby, J.N., 123
Dennison, C.G., 349
Denny, James, 285
Duncan, John, 158

Fee, Gordon, 266
Ferguson, Sinclair, 204
Finlayson, R. A., 74, 78, 84

Gamble, R. C., 349
Gardner, K. J., 150
Gillespie, George, 237
Godfrey-Brown, AW, 347
Goodwin, Thomas, 285, 331
Graham, Clement, 5
Green, James B., 5, 160, 189
Guthrie, William, 197

Hamilton, Ian, 342
Heron, A.I.C., 342
Hodge, A. A., 248
Hodge, Charles, 349, 352–53
Hoekema, A. A., 102, 170
Hoeksema, Herman, 336

Irenaeus, 27

James VI, 309
Jerome, 27, 44
Josephus, 22

La Haye, Tim, 330
Leo X, 269
Leo XII, 40
Lightfoot, John, 49, 94, 295
Luther, Martin, 44, 72, 134, 140, 155, 157, 209

Mackay, John L., 107
Mackemie, Francis, 349
Macleod, Donald, 56, 143, 321, 340
Macleod, John, 161
Macpherson, John, 12, 47, 64, 78, 104, 130, 135, 180, 187, 240, 273
McCheyne, Robert M., 313
McGrath, Alister, 68
Mede, Joseph, 331
Melville, Andrew, 309
Mitchell, Alex F., 219
Monod, Jacques, 90
Moss, C. B., 31
Muhammed, 27, 35–36
Muller, Richard, 55
Murray, Iain, 281
Murray, John, 33, 101, 125, 164, 170, 192, 267, 281

Owen, John, 45

Packer, J. I., 45, 56, 101, 323
Pareus, David, 96
Payton, James R., 349
Pinnock, Clark, 76
Pius IV, 40
Polanus, Amandus, 114
Poole, Matthew, 100
Poythress, Vern, 260

Ramm, Bernard, 173
Robertson, O. Palmer, 241, 337
Rollock, Robert, 49, 108, 114
Ross, Kenneth R., 342
Rous, Francis, 225
Rutherford, Samuel, 49, 117, 255

Sabellius, 67, 69
Scofield, C. I., 123
Shaw, Robert, 174
Shedd, W. G. T, 149
Sixtus V, 40
Smith, Joseph, 36
Smith, Morton H., 116, 349
Smith, T. Jollie, 91
Spurgeon, Charles H., 227

Tertullian, 58
Trinterud, L. J., 349, 352
Troxel, A. Craig, 206
Trueman, Carl R., 19, 229
Turretin, Francis, 19, 95, 98, 237
Twisse, William, 331

Waldron, Samuel, 191, 285, 302
Walker, James, 273
Wallace, Peter, 206
Warfield, B. B., 78, 100, 335

Webb, R. A., 86, 165
Wesley, John, 76, 111, 169
Whitaker, Jeremiah, 78
White, Ellen, 37
Williamson, G. I., 171, 292
Witsius, Herman, 116
Wollebius, Johannes, 211
Wright, N. T., 155

Young, E. J., 99

INDEX OF PROOFTEXTS

Genesis	WCF
1	4.2
1:2	4.1
1:26	4.2, 9.2; 19.1
1:27	4.2, 6.3, 19.1
1:28	4.2; 6.3
2:2,3	21.7
2:7	4.2
2:16	6.3, 9.2
2:17	4.2, 6.2, 6.3, 7.2, 9.2,19.1
2:18	24.2
2:24	24.1
3:6	4,2, 6.2, 9.2
3:7	6.2
3:8	4.2, 6.2
3:9-11	4.2
3:13	6.1
3:15	7.3, 8.6, 25.2
3:19	32.1
3:23	4.2
4:4	16.6
4:5	16.7
6:3	6.3
6:5	6.2, 6.4
8:21	6.4
8:22	5.2
17:1	2.1
17:7	25.2, 27.1, 28.4
17:9	28.4
17:10	27.1, 27.2
18:27	21.3
24:2-3	22.3
24:5-6	22.3
24:8-9	22.3
24:57-58	24.3
28:20	22.6
28:21-22	22.6
34:14	24.3, 27.1
45:7	5.1
49:10	19.4
50:20	5.4
Exodus	
3:14	2.1
4:24-26	28.5
7:3	5.6
8:15	5.6
8:32	5.6
12:48	27.1
16:23	21.8
16:25-26	21.8
16:29-30	21.8
20:4-6	21.1
20:7	22.1, 22.2, 22.3
20:8	21.7, 21.8
20:10-11	21.7
20:15	26.3
21:13	5.2
21	19.4
22:1-29	19.4
22:7-11	22.3
28:38	16.6
31:15-17	21.8
34:1	19.2
34:6-7	2.1
34:16	24.3
Leviticus	
18	24.4
18:24-28	24.4
19:12	22.1
20:19-21	24.4
24:16	23.3
26:1-14	19.6
Numbers	
5:19	22.3
5:21	22.3
30:5, 8,12-13	22.7
Deuteronomy	
2:30	5.6

4:15-16	2.1
4:15-20	21.1
5:32	19.2
6:4	2.1
6:6-7	21.6
6:13	21.5, 22.2
7:3-4	24.3
10:4	19.2
10:20	22.1
12:32	21.1
13:5-6	23.3
13:6-12	20.4
13:10	23.3
19:5	5.2
23:21-23	22.6
24:1-4	24.6
29:4	5.6
29:29	3.8
30:6	10.1
30:19	9.1

Joshua

7:19	15.6
9:18-19	22.4
24:14	21.1

Ruth

4:12	21.4

1 Samuel

1:11	22.6
2:25	7.1
15:21-23	16.1
23:11-12	3.2
25:22	22.4
25:32-34	22.4

2 Samuel

6:18, 20	21.6
7:29	21.4
11:27	17.3
12:14	17.3
12:21-23	21.4
16:10	5.4
21:1	22.4
23:3	23.2
24:1	5.4, 5.5

1 Kings

2:35	23.4
8:27	2.1
8:31	22.2
11:4	24.3
21:27, 29	16.7
22:22-23	5.4
22:28, 34	5.2

2 Kings

6:6	5.3
8:12-13	5.6
10:30-31	16.7
18:4	23.3
19.28	5.4
23:1-16	23.3
23:5-6, 9	20.4
23:20-21	20.4
23:25	15.2

1 Chronicles

10:4, 13, 14	5.4
13:1-9	23.3
21:1	5.4

2 Chronicles

6:22	22.1
15:12,13	20.4, 23.3
15:16	20.4
19:8-11	23.3, 31.2
26:18	23.3
29 & 30	23.3, 31.2
32:25-26	5.5
32:31	5.5
34:33	20.4, 23.3

Ezra

7:23, 25-28	20.4, 23.3
9:13-14	19.6
10:5	22.2

Nehemiah

5:12	22.3
9:32-33	2.1
10:29	21.5
13:15-19, 21	21.8
13:15, 17, 21, 22, 25, 30	20.4
13:22	16.2
13:25-27	24.3

Esther

4:16	21.5
9:22	21.5

Job

1:5	21.6
8:13-14	18.1
9:2-3	16:2
9:20	16.6
9:32-33	7.1
11:7-9	2.1
13:15	18.4
14:4	6.3
15:14	6.3
19:26-27	32.2
21:14-15	16.7
22:2-3	2.2, 7.1, 16.5

26:13	4.1
26:14	2.1
28:28	19.1
33:4	4.1
34:20	5.3
35:7-8	7.1, 16.5
38-41	5.1

Psalms

2:6	8.1
2.8	25.2
2:10-12	23.2
4:6-7	18.3
5:5-6	2.1
14:4	16.7
15:5	22.4
16:2	16.5
18:3	21.1
19:1-3	1.1
19:11	19.6
19:13	15.5
22:1	18.4
22:30	8.1
24:4	22.4
31:22	18.4
31:23	21.1
32:1	7.6
32:3,4	17.3
32:5	11.5, 15.6
32:6	15.6
33:5-6	4.1
33:10-11	5.1
34:12-16	19.6
36:3	16.7
37:11	19.6
40:7-8	8.4
45:7	8.3, 26.3
47:7	21.3
50:14	22.6
50:21	5.4
51 (title)	17.3
51	15.6
51:4	15.2, 15.6
51:5	6.3, 15.6
51.7	11.5, 15.6
51.8	11.5, 17.3, 18.4
51:9	11.5, 6
51:10	11.5, 17.3
51:11	11.5
51:12	11.5, 17.3, 18.4
51:14	15.6, 17.3, 18.4
61.8	22.5
62:8	21.1
65.2	21.3
66:13-14	22.5, 22.6
72:17	25.5
73	5.5
73:15	18.4
76:10	5.4
76:11	22.5
77:1-10	18.4
77:1-12	5.5, 18.3
81:11-12	5.6
82:3-4	23.2
88	18.3, 18.4
89:30	19.6
89:31-32	11.5, 17.3, 19.6
89:33	11.5, 19.6
89:34	19.6
90:2	2.1
94:8-11	5.1
100:2-3	7.1
102:28	25.5
103:13	12.1
104:24	4.1, 5.1
107	21:5
110	18.8
110:3	10.1
110:5-6	7.1
115:3	2.1
116:12-13	16.2
119:4-6	19.6
119:6	15.2
119:32	18.3
119:59	15.2
119:68	2.2, 21.1
119:71	20.1
119:101, 104	19.6
119:105	1.7
119:106	15.2
119:128	15.2, 19.6
119:130	1.7
122:9	23.3
130:3	16.5
130:4	18.3
132:2-6	22.6
135:6	5.1
143:2	16.5, 16.6
145:3	2.1
145:7	5.1
145:17	2.2, 5.1
147:6	2.2

Proverbs

1:20, 21, 24	21.6

2:17	24.1
8:15-16	23.2
8:34	21.6
11:14	31.2
14:26	12:1
15:3	5.1
16:4	2.1, 3.3
16:33	3.1
20:9	6.5
22:19-21	1.1
28:13	15.6

Ecclesiastes

5:1-2	21.3
5:4-5	21.5, 22.5
5:6	22.5
7:20	6.5
7.29	4.2, 6.2, 9.2, 19.1
12:7	4.2, 32.1
12:14	33.1

Song of Solomon

1:4	10.1
5:2, 3, 4, 6	17.3
5: 2, 3, 6	18.4

Isaiah

1:12	16.7
1:16-17	15:4
2:3	26:2
6:3	2.1
6:9-10	5.6
8:14	5.6
8:19-20	1.1
8:20	1.8, 20.2
9:6	30:1
9:7	25:2, 30.1
10:6-7	5.2, 5.4
10:12	5.4
19:21	21.5, 22.5
29:13	16.1
30:22	15.2
40:13-17	7.1
42:1	8.1
42:6	7.3
42:8	26.3
43:3-5, 14	5.7
49:23	20.4, 23.3, 31.2
50:10	18.3, 18.4
53:4-6	11.3
53:10	8.1
53:10-12	11:3
54:7-10	18.4
55:4-5	8.1
55:7	15.4
55:10-11	5.3
56:2, 4, 6, 7	21.7
56:6-7	21.6
58:13	21.8
59:21	1.5, 25.3
63:14	5.1
63:17	17.3
64:5	17.3
64:6	16.5
64:7	16.2, 17.3
64:9	17.3
65:16	22.2
66:2	14.2, 21.5

Jeremiah

4:2	22.3, 22.4
5:7	22.2
8:9	20.2
10:7	21.1
10:10	2.1
10:12	4.1
10:25	21.6
14:9	12.1
17:9	6.2
23:6	11.1
23:23-24	2.1
31:3	17.2
31:18-19	15.2
31:33	19.7
31:33-34	7.6
31:35	5.2
32:40	17.2, 18.4
44:25-26	22.5

Lamentations

3:31	12.1
3:39	6.6

Ezekiel

11:5	2.2
11:19	10.1
16:20-21	25.2
16:61-63	15.3
17:16,18,19	22:4
18:30-31	15.2
36:26	7.3, 10.1, 16.2
36.27	7.3, 10.1, 10.2, 16.2, 19.7
36.31	15.2, 15,3
36:32	15.3

Daniel

3:27	5.3
3:29	20.4

4:25 2.2
4:34 5.1
4:35 2.2, 5.1
9:24-25 8.5, 11.3
9:27 19.2

Hosea

1:4 16.7
1:7 5.3
2:21-22 5.3
5:11 20.2
14:2,4 15.3

Joel

2:12 15.2, 21.5
2:13 15.2

Amos

2:7 24.4
5:15 15.2
5:21-22 16.7
9:8-9 5.7

Micah

3:11 18.1
6:8 16.1
7:7-9 18.4

Nahum

1:2-3 2.1

Haggai

2:14 16.7

Zechariah

12:10 15.1
13:2-3 20.4

Malachi

1:11 21.6
2:11-12 24.3
2:15 24.2
3:6 2.1
4:2-3 8.8

NEW TESTAMENT

Matthew

1:18-20 24.5
2:4-5 23.3, 31.2
3:11 27.3, 28.2
3:15 8.4
3:16 2.3
3:17 2.3, 11.3
4:4 1.1, 5.3
4:7 1.1
4:9 21.1
4:10 1.1, 21.1, 21.2
5:5 19.6
5:16 16.2
5:17 8.4, 19.4, 19.5, 21.7
5:18 1.8, 19.5, 21.7
5:19 19.5
5:31-5.32 24.5
5:34, 37 22.2
5:38-39 19.4
6:2, 5 16:7
6:6, 11 21.6
6:12 11.5
6:12, 15, 16 21.3
6:16 16.7
6:30 12,1, 14.3
6:32 12.1
7:6 29.8, 30.3
7:22 10.4, 18.1
7:23 18.1
8:9 23.2
8:10 14.3, 23.2
9:15 21.5
10:28 4.2
10:29-31 5.1
11:21-23 3.2
11:25-26 3.7
12:1-13 21.8
12:25 30.4
12:36 15.4, 33.1
12:37 33.1
13:12 5.6
13:19 21.5
13:20-21 10.4
13:24-30 25.5
13:40-42 8.4
13:47 25.2., 25.5
15:9 16.1, 20.2, 21.1, 29.4
15:19 6.4
16:18 25.5
16:19 23.3; 30.2
17:12 3.1, 9.1
18:15, 16 20.4
18:17 20.4, 23.3, 30.2-3, 31.3
18:18 30.2, 31.3
18:19-20 31.3
19:5, 6, 8, 9 24.1
19:6 24.6
19:11-12 22.7
22:14 10.4
22:29, 31 1.1
22:37-40 19.2
23:8-10 20.2, 25.6
23:23 16.7
24:36-44 33.3
25.21 16.6, 33.2
25:23 16.6
25:29 5.6

25:31-45 33.2
25:41 3.3, 6.6, 16.7
25:42, 43, 45 16.7
26 8.4
26:26 29.2, 29.3, 29.5
26:27 27.2-3, 29.2,3,5, 29.5
26:28 27.2-3, 29.3,5
26:29 29.5
26:37-38 8.4
26:69-72 18.4
26:70, 72, 74 17.3
26:75 11.5
27 8.4
27:46 8.4
28:18 8.3, 30.1
28:19 2.3, 7.6, 21.5, 25.3, 25.5, 27.1, 27,3, 27.4, 28.1, 28.2, 28.4, 30.1
28:20 7.6, 25.3, 25.5, 27,3, 28.1, 28.2, 30.1

Mark

1:4 28.1
1:15 15.1
6:18 24.4
6:26 22.7
6:52 17.3
7:4 28.3
9:24 18.3
10:13-16 28.4
11:24 21.3
12:33 21.1
13:35-37 33.3
14:22-24 29.3
14:23 29.4
14:66-72 5.5
16:14 17.3
16:15-16 7.3, 28.4
16:19 8.4

Luke

1:3-4 1.1
1:6 15.2
1:20 11.5
1:27, 31, 35 8.2
1:33 8:1
1:74-75 20.3
3:14 23.2
4:16 21.6
7:30 28.5
10:20 3.8
12:13-14 31.5
12:35-36 33.3
13:3, 5 15.3
16:23-24 32.1
16:25-26 21.4
16:29, 31 1.2
17:3-4 15.6
17:5 14.1
17:10 7.1, 16.2, 16.5, 19.6
18:15 28.4
18.15-16 10.3
19:8 15.5
21:27-28 33.3
22:19 29.3
22:20 7.4, 7.6, 29.3
22:31 14.3
22:32 11.5, 14.3, 17.2, 18.4
22:44 8.4
23:43 4.2, 32.1
24:6 29.6
24:27 1.3
24:39 2.1, 29.6
24:44 1.3
24:47 15.1

John

1:1 8.2
1:2-3 4.1
1:12 11:2, 12.1, 14.2
1:14 2.3, 8.2, 8.3
1:16 26.1
1:18 2.3
1:33 28.2
3:3, 5, 8 10.3
3:5, 8 28.6
3:13 8.7
3:16 7.3, 8.1
3.34 8.3
4:21 21.6
4:22 10.4, 20.2
4:23 21.6
4:24 2.1, 21.6
4:42 14.2
5:22 8.3, 33.1
5:23 21.2

5:25	10.2
5:26	2.2
5:27	8.3., 33.1
5:28-29	32.3
5:39, 46	1.8
6:37	8.8, 10.1, 10.2
6:39	8.8
6:44	7.3, 9.3, 10.1
6:45	1.6, 7.3, 10.1
6:64	3.6, 10.4
6:65	3.6, 9.3, 10.4
6:66	10.4
7:38-39	20.1
8:24	10.4
8:34	9.4, 20.3
8:36	9.4
8:41	18.1
8:47	3.6
8:56	7.5
10:15-16	8.8
10:18	8.4
10:26	3.6
10:28	11.5, 17.1, 17.2
10:29	17.1
13:18	3.4
14:6	10.4, 21.2
14.13-14	21.3
14:16	17.2
14:26	8.8
14:17	17.2
15:4	16.2
15:5	9.3, 16.2
15:8	16.2
15:13, 15	8.8
15:26	2.3
16.2	16.1
16:13-14	1.5
17:2	8.5
17:3	10.4
17:6	8.1, 8.8
17:9	3.6
17:11	17.2
17:17	8.8, 13.1
17:20	21.4
17:24	17.2
18:36	31.5
19:11	3.1
20:20-23	30.2
20:25, 27	8.4
21:15-17	5.5

Acts

1:11	8.4
1:25	32.1
2:23	3.15, 2.5.4
2:23-27	8.4
2:36	8.3
2:38-39	10.3, 28.4
2:38	28.6
2.39	25.2
2:41	28.3, 28.6
2:42	21.5, 21.6, 26.2
2:44-45, 46	26.2
2:47	25.2
3:19	33.2
3:21	8.1
4:12	10.3, 10.4
4:19	20.2
4:27-28	3.1, 5.4
5:4	26.3
5:29	20.2
7:2	2.2
8:13, 23	28.5
8:37-38	28.4
10:1-2	23.2
10:2	21.6, 28.5
10:4, 22, 31	28.5
10:33	21.5
10:38	8.3
10:42	8.4
10:43	11.1
10:45, 47	28.5
11:18	15.1
11:29-30	26.2
13:36	32.1
13:37	8.4
13:38-39	11.1
13:39	19.6
13:42	21.6
14:11, 15	2.1
15:2, 4	31.1, 31.2
15:6	31.1
15:10-11	20.1
15:11	7.6, 14.2
15:15	1.8, 31.3
15:15-16	1.9
15:18	2.2, 3.2, 5.1
15:19	31.3
15:21	21.5
15:22, 23, 25	31.2
15:24, 25, 27-31	31.3

Reference	Section
16:4	31.3
16:31	14.2
16:33	28.3
17:24-25	2.2, 4.2, 7.1, 21.1
17:26	5.1, 6.3
17:28	5.1
17:30	15.3
17:31	8.1, 15.3, 33.1
20:7	21.7, 29.3
20:17	30.1
20:21	15.1
20:28	8.7, 30.1
20:32	13.1, 14.1
23:12, 14	22.7
24:14	14.2
24.15	32.3
25.9-11	23.4
26:6-7	16.2
26:18	10.1, 20.1
27:31, 44	5.3
28:25	1.10
28:26-27	5.6
Romans	
1:3-4	8.2
1:11, 12, 14	26.1
1:16-17	14.1
1:19-20	1.1
1:20	4.1, 21.1
1:24	5.6
1:24	5.6
1:25	21.2
1:26, 28	5.6
1:32	1.1, 20.4
2:1	1.1
2:5-6	33.2
2:14-15	1.1, 4.2, 19.1
2:15	6.6
2:16	33.1
2:28-29	27.3
3:2	1.3
3:10-19	6.2
3:9, 19	6.6
3:10-12	6.4
3:10, 12	9.3
3:20	7.3, 16.5, 19.6
3.21	7.3, 7.6
3:22	7.6, 11.1
3:23	6.2, 7.6
3:24	11.1, 11.3, 15.3
3:25-26	8.5, 11.1
3:7-28	11.1
3:28	11.2
3:30	7.6
3:31	19.5
4:2, 4	16.5
4:3	7.6
4:5-8	11.1
4:6	7.6, 16.5
4:11	7.5, 14.1, 27.1, 28.4 28.5
4:12	28.4
4:16-17	7.6
4:19-20	5.3, 14.3
4:21	5.3
4:22	11.6
4:23-24	7.6, 11.6
4:25	11.4
5:1	11.2,18.3, 20.1
5:2	12.1, 18.1, 18.3, 20.1
5:5	18.1, 18.3
5:6	6.4, 9.3
5:8-10, 19	11.3
5:12-20	7.2
5:12,15-19	6.3
5:17-18	11.1
5:19	8.5
6:1-2	18.3
6:3-4	27.1, 28.1
6:5	13.1, 26.1, 28.1
6.6	13.1, 26.1
6:9	8.4
6:12	19.6
6.6	13.1, 26.1
6:9	8.4
6:12	19.6
6:14	13.1, 13.2, 19.6, 20.1
6:16-17	10.1
6:18	9.4, 10.1
6:22	9.4, 16.2
6:23	6.6, 15.4
7:2-3	24.5
7:5, 7, 8	6.5
7:7,9	19.6
7:12	2.2, 19.6
7:14	6.5, 19.6
7:15	9.4, 16.5
7:17	6.5
7:18	6.4, 6.5, 9.4, 13.2, 16.5

7:19, 21	9.4
7:22	19.6
7:23	6.5, 9.4, 13.2
7:24	19.6
7:25	6.5, 19.6
8:1	15.4, 18.3, 19.6, 20.1
8:2	10.1
8:3	7.3, 19.6
8:4	19.6
8:7	6.4
8:9	8.8, 10.2, 10.3
8:12	18.3
8:13	13.1
8:14	8.8, 20.1
8:15	12.1, 18.2, 20.1
8:16	18.2
8:18	16.5
8:17	12.1
8:20	6.6
8:23-25	33.3
8:26	21.3
8:28-29	3.6
8:28	5.7, 20.1
8:30	3.5, 3.6, 10.1 11.1, 11.4
8:32	11.3
8:33-39	17.2
8:33	3.8
8:34	8.4, 8.8
9:5	2.2, 8.2
9:11	3.2, 3.5, 10.2
9:13	3.3, 3.5
9:15	3.1
9:16	3.2, 3.5, 16.7
9:17	3.7, 5.1
9:18	3.1, 3.2, 3.7
9:20	3.8
9:21	3.7
9:22	3.3, 3.7, 33.2
9:23	3.3, 33.2
10:2	16.1
10:5	7.2, 19.1
10:6,9	7.3
10:12	21.1
10:14	14.1
10:15	23.3
10:17	14.1, 20.2
11:3-4	25.4
11:5-6	3.8
11:7	5.6, 10.1
11:8	5.6
11:16	25:2
11:18-19	25.5
11:32	5.4, 6.1
11:33	2.2, 3.1, 3.8, 5.4
11:34	2.2, 5.4
11:36	2.1, 2.2
12:2	16.1
13:1-8	20.4
13:1	23.1-3
13:2	23.1, 23.2
13:3	20.4, 23.1
13:4	20.4, 23.1-3
13:5-7	23.4
13:8-9	19.2, 19.5
13:10	19.5
14:4	20.2
14:9	8.4
14:10	8.4, 33.1
14:12	33.1
14:17	18.3
14:23	20.2
15:4	1.1, 1.8
15:8	27.1
15:9-12	25.2
15:13	18.3
15:18-19	8.8
16:26	14.2
16:27	2.1

1 Corinthians

1:2	25.2
1:21	1.1
1:30	8.1, 11.1
1:31	11.1
2:5	31.4
2:9	1.6
2:10	1.5, 1.6, 10.1
2:11	1.5
2:12	1.5, 1.6, 10.1, 18.3
2:13	1.1
2:14	1.1, 9.3, 10.2
3:21-23	26.1
4:1	23.3, 27.4
4:2	23.3
5	30.3
5:1	20.4, 24.4
5:4	30:3

Reference	Sections
5:5	20.4, 30.3
5:6	25.4, 29.8
5:7	7.5, 19.2, 25.4, 29.8
5:11	20.4
5:13	20.4, 29.8, 30.3
6:3	33.1
6:11	13.1
7:2	22:7, 24:2
7:5	21.5
7:9	22.7, 24.2
7:14	25.2, 28.4
7:15	24.6
7:19	19.6
7:23	20.2, 22.7
7:36--39	24.3
8:4	2.1
8:6	2.1, 26.3
9:8-10	19.4
10:1-4	7.5, 27.5
10:16	27.1, 29.1, 29.4, 29.7
10:17	29.1
10:21	27.1, 29.1
11:13-4	1.6
11:20	26.2, 27.4, 29.3
11:23-29	21.5
11:23	7.6, 27.1, 27.4, 29.1, 29.3
11:24	7.6, 29.1, 29.3, 29.6
11:25	7.4, 7.6, 27.1, 29.1-4, 29.6
11:26	27.1, 29:1-4, 6
11:27-34	30.3
11:27	29.4-5, 29.8
11:28	29:4-5, 29.7-8
11:29	29.4, 29.8
11:30	11.5
11:32	11.5, 17.3
12:7	26.1
12:12	25.2
12:13	25.2, 27.3, 28.1, 29.1
12:28	23.3, 25.3, 30.1
12:29	23.3
13:3	16.7
13:12	25.5
14:6, 9, 11, 12, 14, 24, 26-28	1.8
14:14	21.3
14:26, 40	1.6
15:3-4	8.4
15:21-22	6.3
15:25-26	8.8
15:42-44	32.2
15:43	32.3
15:49	6.3
15:51-52	32.2
15:54-57	20.1
16:1-2	21.7
16:22	10.4

2 Corinthians

Reference	Sections
1:12	18.2
1:22-23	18:2
1:23	22.1, 22.2
1:24	20.2, 31.4
2:6-8	30.2
2:8	15.6
2:15-16	5.6
3:3	10.1
3:5	16.2
3:6-9	7.5
3:6	10.1
3:13, 17, 19	20.1
3:18	13.2
4:13	8.8, 14.1
5:1, 6, 8	32.1
5:10	33.1,33.3
5:11	33.3
5:19	11.1
5:21	11.1, 11.3
6:14	24.3,29.8
6:15	29.8
6:16	19.6, 29.8
6:17	19.2
6:18	12.1
7:1	13.1, 13.2, 18.3
7:11	15.2
8 Chapter	26.2
8:12	16.6
9 Chapter	26.2
9:2	16.2
11:3	6.1
12:7-9	5.5
13:14	2.3, 21.12

Galatians

Reference	Sections
1:4	20.1
1:6-7	10.4

1:8 1.6, 10.4
1:9 1.6
1:10 20.2
2:4-5 20.2
2:16 11.1, 11.4, 19.6
2:20 14:2
3:7 7.5
3:8 7.5, 11.4
3:9 7.5, 11.6, 20.1, 28.4
3:10 6.6, 7.2, 19.1
3:11 7.3
3:12 7.2, 19.1
3:13 11.6, 19.6, 20.1
3:14 7.5, 7.6, 11.6, 20.1, 28.4
3:16 7.6
3:21 7.3, 19.7
3:24 19.6
3:27 27.1, 28.1, 28.6
4:1-3 19.2, 20.1
4:4 8.1, 8.2, 8.4, 8.6, 11.4, 12.1, 19.6
4:5 8.6, 12.1, 19.6
4:7 20.1
5:1 20.1, 20.2
5.6 11.2
5:13 20.3
5:14, 16 19.6
5:17 6.5, 9.4, 13.2, 16.2, 16.5
5:18-21 19.6
5:22-23 16.5, 19.6
5:24 13.1
6.10 26.1

Ephesians

1:3 18.3
1:4 3.5,3.6,18.3
1:5 3.3,3.6,12.1
1:6 3.3, 3.5, 3.8, 16.6
1:7 8.8, 11.1, 11.3, 15.3
1:8 8.8
1:9 3.5, 8.8
1:10 10.1, 25.1
1:11 2.1, 3.1, 3.5, 5.1, 8.5, 10.1
1:12 3.5
1:13 18.2
1:14 8.5, 18.2
1:17-19 10.1, 14.1
1:22 25.1, 25.6
1:23 25.1
2:1 6.2, 9.3, 10.1
2:2 6.4, 9.3, 10.1
2:3 6.4, 6.6, 9.3, 10.1
2:4 9.3, 10.1, 10.2
2:5 9.3, 10.1, 10.2, 26.1
2:6 26.1
2:7 11.1, 11.3
2:8 10.2, 11.1, 14.1, 16.5
2:9 10.2, 16.5
2:10 3.6, 16.2
2:12 10.4
2:15-19 7.6
2:15, 16 19.2
2:18 21.2
2:19 25.2
2:20 1.2, 1.10, 31.4
3:10 5.1
3:12 12.1
3:15 25.2
3:13-19 13.1, 26.1
3:17-19 18.3
4:10 32.1
4:11-12 23.3, 25.3
4:13 9.5, 25.3
4:15-16 13.2, 26.1
4:18 6.6
4:24 4.2
4:28 22.7, 26.3
4:30 12.1, 17.3, 18.2, 18.4
4:31 18.4
5:2 8.5, 11.3
5:19 21.5
5:23 8.1, 25.1
5:25 28.6
5:26 13.1, 28.6
5:27, 32 25.1
6:2 19.5, 19.6
6:3 19.6
6:16 14.3
6:18 21.3, 21.6

Philippians

1:6 17.1
1:11 16.2
1:15, 16, 18 16:7
1:23 32.1
2:6 8.2
2:8 8.4
2:12 16.2
2:13 9.4, 10.1, 16.2
3:9 11.1
3:10 13.1, 26.1
3:12 13.2
3:21 32.3
4:6 21.3
4:13 16.2

Colossians

1:11 13.1
1:13 9.4, 20.1
1:16 4.2
1:18 25.1,25.6, 26.3
1:19 8.3, 8.5, 26.3
1:20 8.5
1:21 6.4, 11.4
1:22 11.4
2:2 14.3
2:3 8.3
2:9 8.2
2:11-12 7.5, 28.1, 28.4
2:13 9.3
2:14 19.2
2:15 8.8
2:16 19.2
2:17 7.6, 19.2
2:18 21.2
2:19 26.1
2:20, 22 20.2
2:23 20.2, 21.1
3:10 4.2
3:16 1.8, 21.5
3:17 21.2
4:2 21.3

1 Thessalonians

1:9 2.1
1:10 20.1
2:13 1.4, 14.2
4:17 32.2
5:9 3.5, 3.6
5:10 3.6
5:11, 14 26.1
5:12 30.1, 30.3
5:23 13.2

2 Thessalonians

1:5-7 33.3
1:7-10 33.2
1:9 6.6
2:2 1.6
2:3-4, 8-9 25.6
2:4 23:4
2:10-12 5.6
2:13 3.6, 10.1, 13.1
2:14 10.1
3:3 17.2
3:6, 15 29.8, 30.3
3:14 20.4, 29.8, 30.3

1 Timothy

1:13, 15 15.5
1:17 2.1
1:19 20.4
1:20 20.4, 30.3
2:1 21:4, 23.4, 31.2
2:2 30.4, 21.4, 23.2, 23.4, 31.2
2:5 8.1, 8.2, 11.3, 21.2
2:6 8.1, 11.3, 11.4
2:8 21.6
3:15 1.5
3:16 8.2
4:3 24.3
4:8 14.2
4:10 5.7
5:17 30.1
5:20 30.3
5:21 3.3
6:1 16.2
6:3-5 20.4
6:15 2.2, 26.3
6:16 26.3

2 Timothy

1.6 16.2
1:9 3.5, 10.1, 10.2
1:10 10.1
2:12 26.1
2:18 17.2
2:19 3:4, 3:7, 17.2

2:20	3.7
3:15	1.1, 1.6
3:16	1.2, 1.4, 1.6
3:17	1.6
4:2	21.5

Titus

1:10-11, 13	20.4
1:15	6.2, 16.7
2:5, 9-12	16.2
2:11, 12, 14	18.3
2:14	3.6, 20.1
3:1	23.4
3:3, 4, 5	9.3, 11.4
3:4,5	10.2
3:5	11.1, 16.5, 16.7, 27.2, 28.1, 28.6, 28.7
3:6, 7	11.4, 16.5
3:7	11.1,
3:10	20:4, 30:3

Hebrews

1:1	1.1
1:2	1.1, 4.1, 8.1
1:3	5.1
1:8-9	26.3
1:14	12.1
2:14, 16, 17	8.2
4:2	21.5
4:13	2.2
4:14,16	20.1
4:15	8.2
5:4	8.3, 23.3, 27.4
5.5	8.1, 8.3
5.6	8.1
5:13-14	14.3
6:4-5	10.4
6:10	16.6
6:11	14.3, 16.2, 18.2, 18.3
6:12	12.1, 14.3, 16.2, 18.3
6:16	22.2
6:17	3.1, 18.2
6:18,19	18.2
7:22	7.4, 8.3
7:23-24, 27	29.2
7:25	8.4, 17.2
7:26	8.3
8 chapter	7.5
8:10	19.7
9 chapter	7.5, 19.3
9:10	28.3
9:12-15	17.2
9.12, 14-16	8.5
9:14	8.7
9:15, 16, 17	7.4
9:19-22	28.3
9:22	29.2
9:24	8.4
9:25-28	29.2
10 chapter	7.5
10:1	19.2
10:5-12	8.4
10:10	11.3, 17.2
10:11, 12, 14, 18	29.2
10:14	8.5, 11.3, 11.5, 17.2
10:19-22	20.1
10:22	14.3
10:24	26.2
10:25	21.6, 26.2
10:39	14.1
11:3	4.2
11:4	16.6, 16.7
11:6	2.1, 16.7
11:13	7.5, 14.2
12:2	8.8, 14.3
12:6	12.1
12:14	13.1
12:22-28	7.6
12:23	9.5, 32.1
12:24	8.3
12:28	19.6, 21.3, 21.5
12:29	19.6
13:4	24.3
13:7	30.1
13:8	7.6, 8.6, 11.6
13:17	20.4, 30.1
13:20	16.6
13.21	16.1, 16.6, 17.2
13:24	30.1

James

1:6-7	21.3
1:13	3.1, 5.4
1:14	5.4, 6.4, 9.1
1:15	6.4
1:17	2.1, 3.1, 5.4
1:22	21.5
1:23-25	19.6
1:25	19.2

2:8,10	19.2, 19.5
2:11	19.2, 19.5, 19.6
2:12	19.2
2:17	11.2
2:18	16.2
2:22	11.2, 16.2
2.26	11.2
3:2	6.5
4:12	20.2
5:12	22.2
5:13	21.5
5:16	15.6

1 Peter

1:2	3.6, 11.4
1:3-4	12.1
1:5	3.6, 17.1
1:6	17.1
1:18	16.1
1:19-20	8.1, 11.4
2:2	14.1
2:5	16,6, 21.3
2:7	5.6
2:8	3.7, 5.6
2:9	16.2
2:11	13.2
2:13-14	19.4, 20.4, 23.1, 23.4
2:13	23.2
2:15	16.2
2:16	20.3, 20.4, 23.4
2:17	23.4
3:7	21.6
3:8-12	19.6
3:18	8.2, 8.7
3:19	32.1
3:21	27.3
4:2	22.7
5:7	12.1

2 Peter

1:3	16:2
1:4	18.2
1:5	16.2, 18.2
1:6-10	16.2
1:10	3.8, 17.1, 18.2, 18.3
1:11	18.2
1:19	1.1, 1.4
1:20	1.9
1:21	1.3, 1.4, 1.9
2:1	23.4
2:4	8.4, 33.1
2:8	3.7
2:10-11	23.4
2:19	30.3
3:11, 14	33.3
3:16	1.7
3:18	13.2

1 John

1:3	26.1
1:5	3.1
1:6	18.3
1:7	11.5, 18.3
1:8	6.5
1:9	11.5, 15.6
1:10	6.5, 13.2
2:1-2	8.8, 11.5, 18.3
2:3	16.2, 18.1, 18.2, 19.5
2:4	19.5
2:5	16.2
2:7-8	19.5
2:16	5.4
2:19	3.6, 17.2
2:20	1.5
2:27	1.5, 17.2
3:2	9.5, 18.3
3.3	18.3
3:4	6.6
3:9	17.1, 17.2, 18.4
3:14	18.1, 18.2
3:16	8.7, 26.1
3:17	26.1, 26.2
3:18	18.1, 26.1
3:19, 21, 24	18.1
4:8	2.1
4:13	18.3
4:16	2.1
4:18	20.1
5:4	13.2, 14.3
5:5	14.3
5:7	2.3
5:9	1.4
5:10	14.2
5:12	10.3
5:13	18.1, 18.3
5:14	21.3, 21.4
5:16	21.4
5:20	8.2

2 John

v9	10.4
v10-11	10.4, 20.4

Jude

v4	3.7
v6	8.4, 32.1, 33.1
v7	32.1
vv8-11	23.4
vv20-21	16.2
v23	19.2, 30.3
v24	9.5

Revelation

1:3	21.5
1:10	21.7
2 chapter	25.4, 25.5
2:2	20.4
2:4	17.3
2:14, 15, 20	20.4
3 chapter	25.4, 25.5
3.9	20.4
3:12	12.1
4:8	2.1
4:11	2.2
5:12-14	2.2
7:9	25.2
12:6, 14	25.4
13:6	25.6
13:8	8.6
13:12	20.2
13:15	23.4
13:16, 17	20.2, 23.4
14:13	21.4
17:12	20.41
17:14	23.2
17:16	20.4, 23.2
17:17	20.4
18:2	25.5
19:10	21.2
22:18-19	1.2
22:30	33.3

19:10	21.2
22:18-19	1.2
22:30	33.3
19:10	21.2
22:18-19	1.2
22:30	33.3

AN INDEX TO THE CONFESSION OF FAITH AND THE LARGER CATECHISM

References other than those prefixed LC (*Longer Catechism*) are to the Confession.

Acceptance. Believers are accepted as righteous in God's sight on the basis of the perfect obedience and full satisfaction of Christ alone (LC 70), which is credited to them by God and received by faith (CF 11:1, LC 70-72). How believers' good works are accepted in Christ (CF 16:6). Acceptance in prayer through Christ and his mediation (LC 180).

Access. No access without Mediator (CF 12; LC 39, 55, 181). Greater boldness of access in New Testament dispensation (CF 20:1).

Actions. God arranges and governs all things (CF 5:1; LC 18). See *Providence*.

Actual sins are fruit of corrupt nature (CF 6:4; LC 25). See *Sin*.

Admonition of offenders by the church (30:4). See *Discipline*.

Adoption, its nature and privileges (12; LC 74).

Adultery, a proper ground of divorce (24:5–6).

Amen, what it means (LC 196).

Angels, God's decree (3:3–4; LC 13); how created (LC 16). God's providence toward them (LC 19); what they do (LC 19); not to be worshipped (21:2; LC 105).

Antichrist and the Papacy (25:6).

Anxious and distracting cares forbidden (LC 105, 136, 142).

Apocrypha, not divinely inspired and of no authority in the church (1:3).

Ascension of Christ (8:4; LC 53).

Assemblies, Public, for the worship of God not to be neglected (20:6).

Assurance of grace and salvation may be had in this life (18:1–2; LC 80), without special revelation (8:3; LC 80). Its basis (3:8; 18:2; LC 80) and how it is strengthened through good works (16:2). Believers may lack it (18:3; LC 80; 172), find it variable or temporarily absent (11:5; 18:3–4; LC 81) but are never utterly deprived of the graces out of which it may be revived, and meantime are kept from utter despair (18:4; LC 81). All have duty to seek assurance (18:4) and to pray for it (LC 194). The fruits of assurance (18:3).

Atheism (LC 105).

Attributes of God (2:1–2; LC 7, 8, 101).

Bad company not to be kept (LC 139).

Baptism defined (28:1–2; LC 165); to continue to the end of the world (28:1; LC 176). Administration: by whom (27:4); not repeatable (28:7; LC 177); dipping not necessary but sprinkling right and proper (28:3). Baptism not essential to salvation but a sin to neglect it (28:5). Using our baptism to good effect (LC 167); comparison with Lord's Supper (LC 176–177).

Body of Christ, how present in the Lord's Supper (29:7; LC 170).

Body, mystical body of Christ. Comprised of true believers (29:1; LC 168), that is, the whole number of the elect united to Christ their head (25:1). What the union is (LC 66).

Bodies of believers after death and at the resurrection, and of the wicked (32:2–3; LC 86–87).

Books, lustful/provocative not to be read (LC 139).

Brothels, not to be allowed, tolerated, conducted or used (LC 139).

Calling (=vocation). It is a duty to have a lawful occupation and to be diligent in it (LC 141).

Capital punishment (LC 136).

Celibacy. Vows to singleness without the gift of God unlawful (22:7; LC 139).

Ceremonial law. See *Law*.

Chance. Ascribing the ultimate cause of anything to chance is sinful (LC 105 cf. 5:2).

Charity a duty (26:2; LC 141 cp 171).

Chastity (LC 138).

Children: how those who die in infancy are saved (10:3). The children of those professing the true religion belong to the visible church (25:2; LC 62) and are to be baptised (28:4; LC 166).

Christ. Why he is called this (LC 42). Is the only Mediator (8:1; LC 36); is truly God of one substance and equal with the Father (8:2; LC 11, 36) and in the fulness of time became man (8:2; LC 36–37). The necessity of his being God and man (LC 38–40). Appointed as Mediator by the Father (8:1), set apart and anointed by the Holy Spirit (8:3; LC 42), Christ undertook the office willingly (8:4). His perfect obedience and sacrifice of himself purchased reconciliation and eternal life for all the elect (8:5; LC 38), and the benefits of his mediation are effectively applied to them in every age (8:6,8; 3:6). Christ's office of a Prophet (LC 43), of a Priest (LC 44) and of a King (LC 45). See also *Ascension, Death of Christ, Exaltation of Christ, Resurrection of Christ, Trinity.*

Church: the object of God's special providence (5:7; LC 63). Christ its only head (8:1; 25:6). The catholic invisible church defined (25:1; LC 63); given to Christ from eternity (8:1); the benefits members enjoy (LC 65–66, 69, 82–83, 86, 90). The catholic visible church defined (25:2; *LC 62);* outside it no ordinary possibility of salvation (25:2); its privileges (25:3; LC 63); particular churches more or less pure (25:4) and the purest subject to impurity and error yet there will always be a church on earth (25:5).

Church government appointed by Christ in the hands of church officers distinct from the civil rulers (30:1; LC 45, 108), but they are not exempt from obedience to the civil rulers' lawful commands (23:4). Church officers have the power of the keys (30:2–4), and are not to be opposed in the lawful exercise of their authority on the plea of Christian liberty (20:4). Some circumstances concerning church government are to be arranged by human reason and Christian prudence in line with the general rules of Scripture (1:6).

Circumcision, one of the types and ordinances by which the covenant of grace was administered under the Old Testament (7:5; LC 34).

Civil rulers appointed by God (23:1) and have various duties (23:2; LC 129; 20:4). It is lawful for Christians to serve in public office (23:2). The duties of people, including church officers, toward civil rulers (23:4; LC 127); they are not to be opposed in the lawful exercise of their power on the plea of Christian liberty (20:4). Civil rulers may engage in war if there is just and necessary cause (23:2). Civil rulers' power in church matters stated (23:3). The sins of civil rulers (LC 130, 145), and the sins of people against them (LC 128). The Pope has no power over civil rulers or their people (23:4). Civil rulers to be obeyed even if of different religious beliefs (23:4).

Clothing, immodest, forbidden (LC 139).

Commandments, The Ten, summarise the moral law (19:2; LC 98) and are a perfect rule of righteousness (19:2). Rules for understanding them (LC 99). Exposition (LC 101–148). No person is able to keep them perfectly (LC 149).

Commercial practice. Unjust appropriations, unjust evictions, fraudulent dealing, lack of faithfulness in contracts etc. forbidden by eighth commandment (LC 142).

Communion of Saints, what it is (26:1–2); a privilege of the visible church (LC 63; 26:2); its relation to the Lord's Supper (29:1; LC 168); does not take away property rights (26:3).

Communion with Christ which the elect have (26:1); in this life (LC 69, 83); immediately after death (LC 86); at the resurrection and day of judgment (LC 87, 90). It results from their union with Christ (26:1), but does not maker them sharers of his deity or equal with him in any other way (26:3);is confirmed in the Lord's Supper (LC 168).

Condition. (1) perfect, personal and perpetual obedience required as the condition of the covenant of works (7:2; 19:1; LC 20). (2) God requires faith as the condition for a saving interest in Christ, and therefore graciously enables it (7:3; LC 32, 71).

Conduct. To be in righteousness and holiness corresponding to a holy profession (LC 112, 167).

Confession of sin. Always to be made to God in private with prayer (15:6; LC 178); sometimes to be made to others (15:6).

Conscience teaches us of God and duty (1:1; 21:1; LC 2) but is insufficient for salvation (1:1; 10:4; 21:1; LC 2, 60). Peace of conscience is a fruit of the sense of God's love (18:1,3; LC 83); believers may fall into sins which wound the conscience (17:3; 18:4); the wicked are punished with terrors of conscience (LC 28, 83).

Contentment. Submission to God is our duty (LC 104) and discontent at God's providence is sinful (LC 105). Contentment with our situation a duty (LC 147) and discontent with it sin (LC 148).

Controversies. Translations of Scripture from the original languages suffice for everyday purposes and for the main points related to salvation (1:7). It belongs to synods and councils, acting as servants of God, to decide controversies (31:3). The Hebrew and Greek texts of Scripture are that to which the church is finally to appeal (1:8). The Holy Spirit speaking in the Scripture is the supreme judge (1:10).

Corruption of nature. What it is (6:2,4; LC 25); actual sin a fruit of it (6:4; LC 25); how it is conveyed (6:3; LC 26. It remains in this life in the regenerate and it and its results are truly sin (6:5; 13:2; LC 78), but is pardoned and put to death through Christ (6:5).

Covenant. No enjoyment of God but by covenant (7:1). (1) Covenant of works (or of life) with condition (4:2; 7:2; 19:1; LC 20, 22). (2) Covenant of grace made with Christ as the second Adam and all the elect in him as his seed. (7:3; LC 30, 31, 32), Christ being the Mediator (8:1; LC 36). Faith in Christ required and graciously given (7:3; LC 32, 71). In what sense a testament (7:4). Administration under the Old Testament (7:5; LC 33, 34) and under the New (7:6; LC 35).

Councils (31)

Creation. Of the world (4:1; LC 15); of man (4:2; LC 17); of angels (LC 16).

Creatures. Rule over creatures given to mankind (4:2; LC 17); now cursed because of man's sin (LC 28); not to be worshipped (21:2; LC 105).

Curiosity. Bold and inquisitive searching into God's secrets forbidden (LC 105); prying or unprofitable questions forbidden (LC 113).

Curse. The wrath and curse of God is due to us for original and actual sin (6:6; LC 27); how to escape it (7:3; LC 153).

Cursing. All sinful cursing forbidden (LC 113).

Dancing. Lustful/provocative dancing forbidden (LC 139).

Dead. Prayers for the dead forbidden (21:4; LC 183).

Death in the human family is the wages of sin (6:6; LC 28, 84), and is appointed to all people (LC 84). How it is for the advantage of the righteous (LC 85). State of believers and of the wicked immediately after death (32:1; LC 86).

Death of Christ (8:4; LC 49). Christ experienced no decay in his death (8:4; LC 52). The divine nature sustained the human from sinking under death's power (LC 38). By his obedience and death Christ made a proper, real and full satisfaction to the justice of the Father (11:3; LC 71). Through the virtue of his death and resurrection believers are sanctified (13:1). Believers have fellowship with Christ in his death (26:1), and from his death and resurrection draw strength from the putting to death of sin and strengthening in grace (LC 167). The Lord's Supper is the memorial of Christ's death (29:1; LC 168); those who participate rightly meditate with love on his death and sufferings (LC 174), and receive and feed on all the benefits of his death (29:7).

Decrees of God. Their nature and extent (3:1–2; LC 12). How God carries out his decrees (LC 14). Predestination of the elect in Christ to everlasting glory includes all the means to the end (3:2–6); foreordination to everlasting death of the reprobate includes passing them by and ordaining to wrath because of their sin (3:2,7). How the doctrine of predestination is to be handled so as to be profitable (3:8). Inquisitive prying into God's decrees forbidden (LC 113).

Desertion. Deliberate desertion of a spouse unlawful (LC 139), but if it cannot be remedied by the church or the civil authorities, there is sufficient ground for divorce (24:6).

Despair, being the opposite of faith, is sinful (LC 105). Believers are kept from sinking into utter despair (18:4; LC 81).

Devil. All pacts and consulting with the devil are sinful (LC 105).

Diligence in our occupation is a duty (LC 141).

Dipping in baptism is not necessary (28:3).

Discipline of the church. Defined (30:2,4), its use (30:3), to whom applied (20:4; 29:8; 30:2) and how apportioned (30:4). Treatment of the penitent (30:2). Rash, harsh or biased judgments prohibited (LC 145).

Divorce lawful in case of adultery after marriage or deliberate desertion which cannot be remedied (24:5–6), but a public and orderly procedure is to be followed (24:6).

Doubting of being in Christ may exist with a true interest in him (17:3; 18:4; LC 81, 172).

Drunkenness forbidden (LC 139).

Effective calling. What it is (10:1; LC 67); it is from God's free grace not from anything foreseen in man (10:2; LC 67). All the elect, and them only, are effectively called (3:6; 10:1,4; LC 68).

Election flows solely from God's free grace from all eternity (3:5; LC 13). It includes the means as well as the end (3:6; LC 13). How elect infants and other elect persons incapable of being outwardly called by the word are saved (10:3). The value of the doctrine of election and how one may be assured of his election (4:8).

Eucharist (*see Lord's Supper*).

Exaltation of Christ (8:4; LC 51); in his resurrection (LC 52); in his sitting at the right hand of God (LC 54); in his coming to judge the world (LC 56).

Excommunication (30:2–4).

Expiation. Sin cannot be expiated except by the blood of Christ (LC 152).

Faith. What it is (14:2; LC 72). Faith in Christ all that is required of sinners for their justification. It is not the foundation of justification but the instrument by which Christ and his righteousness is received (12:2; LC 71). Faith is the work of the Spirit (14:1; LC 59, 72), ordinarily worked by the ministry of the word and strengthened by the word, sacraments and prayer (14:1). Often weak it always obtains the victory (14:3) and in many develops to full assurance (14:3; LC 80). Good works are the fruit and evidence of true faith (14:2; LC 52) which is never alone but is always accompanied by all other saving graces: it is not a dead faith but works by love (11:2; LC 73).

Fall of man. Its nature and effects (6; LC 21, 23, 25, 27–29); why permitted (6:1); how all mankind is involved in it (6:3; LC 22).

Family worship daily a duty required by God (21:6).

Fasting as a part of religious worship (LC 108; 21:5).

Foreknowledge. All things occur with certainty according to God's foreknowledge. (3:2)

Forgiveness (see *Sin*).

Fornication committed after a commitment to marry gives the innocent party just cause to withdraw from the agreement. (24:5)

Free-will. The will of man is neither forced nor by any necessity arising from within itself so as to be compelled to good or evil (3:1; 9:1). In the state of innocence man had freedom and power to do good (4:2; 9:2; LC 17). By the fall man lost all ability to will any spiritual good related to salvation (6:2,4; 9:3; LC 25, 192). The will is renewed in conversion and by God's grace set free to will and do what is spiritually good but imperfectly (9:4; 10:1; LC 67). Perseverance does not depend on free-will but rests on other grounds (17:2). The human will is made perfect and unchangeably free to will good and good alone only in glory (9:5).

Gambling, see *Wasteful recreations.*

Glory. Communion in glory with Christ which believers enjoy in this life (18:1–3; LC 83); immediately after death (32:1; LC 86); at the last day (32:3; 33:2; LC 87, 90).

Glory of God as the purpose of his decrees (3:3; LC 12); the glory of his grace as the aim of election (3:5; LC 18); the glory of his justice the aim of reprobation (3:7 LC 18); the glory of his eternal power, wisdom and goodness as the aim of creation (4:1); the revealing of the glory of his wisdom, power, goodness and mercy as the aim of all God's works of providence (5:1; LC 18), including the last judgment (32:10). To glorify God is the chief purpose for which man is made (LC 1). God is glorified by good works (16:2).

Gluttony a sin (LC 139).

God. The light of conscience and the works of God show that there is a God and our duty to him (1:1; 21:1; LC 2). There is only one God (2:1; LC 8). God's attributes or perfections (2:1–2; LC 7, 101). There are three co-equal persons in the Godhead distinguished by personal properties (2:3; LC 9–11). To God is due whatever worship, service or obedience he is pleased to require (2:2). Our duty to God (LC 104, 108, 112, 116) and what is opposite to it (LC 105, 109, 113, 119). Religious worship to be given to the Triune God alone and only in the mediation of Christ (21:2; LC 179, 181). God to be worshipped only in the way instituted in Scripture (21:1; LC 109). To glorify God and fully to enjoy him for ever is the chief purpose for which man is made (LC 1).

Good works. What they are and what they are not (16:1). They are the fruits and evidences of justifying faith (16:2); their purpose stated (16:2). Ability to do them is solely from the Spirit of Christ, but this is no excuse for carelessness on our part (16:3). We cannot do more than is required (16:4), nor can our best works merit pardon or eternal life (16:5), yet good works of believers are accepted by God in Christ and rewarded (16:6). The works of unregenerate people cannot please God although their neglect to do what God requires is more sinful (176:7). All persons will by judged bodily at the judgment day, and receive according to what they have done, whether good or evil (33:1).

Gospel. How the covenant of grace is administered under the gospel (7:6; LC 35); no salvation apart from the gospel (10:4; LC 60). In the gospel Christ does not lessen but strengthens our obligation to obey the moral law (19:5). Believers under the gospel have greater boldness of access to the throne of grace than was usual under the earlier dispensation (20:1).

Grace of God. Election flows solely from God's grace (3:5; LC 13); grace is revealed in the covenant of grace (7:3; LC 32). Effective calling is of God's free and special grace (10:2; LC 67). Justification is an act of God's free grace (11:3; LC 70-71) as is adoption (12; LC 74). The communion in grace which Christ has with believers stated (LC 69). All saving graces are the work of the Spirit (13–15; LC 32, 72, 75–77) and always accompany faith (11:2; LC 73). Perseverance in grace (17; LC 79); increase in it (13:1,3; LC 75). assurance of it (18; LC 80-81).

Guarantees. Unnecessary giving of guarantees to be avoided (LC 141).

Guarantor. Christ the Guarantor for believers (LC 71), he being fully equipped for this (8:3), and God accepts satisfaction accordingly (LC 71).

Hardening. Why and how sinners are hardened (5:6; LC 68). Believers may have their hearts hardened (17:3).

Headship of Christ. The elect are united to Christ as their head (25:1; 26:1; LC 64, 66). Christ is the only head of the church (25:6).

Hearing. What is required of those who hear the word preached (21:5; LC 160).

Heaven (32:1).

Hell (32:1; 33:2). The meaning of the expression in the Creed, 'he descended into hell' (LC 50).

Heretics to be rejected (LC 105).

Holiness. God is most holy in his purposes, works and commands (2:2). Man was created holy in God's image (4:2; LC 17), but by the fall became completed polluted (6:2). Believers are stimulated and strengthened by the sanctifying Spirit of God to the practice of holiness (13:1,3; LC 75) and are made perfectly holy in heaven (32:1; LC 86, 90). See also *Sanctification*.

Holy Spirit is equal with the Father (2:3; LC 11). In the covenant of grace he is promised to the elect (7:3; LC 32) and by him they are united to Christ (26:1), for by him the redemption purchased by Christ is applied to them (8:8; 11:4; LC 58–59); they are effectively called (10:1; LC 67), and have faith worked in their hearts (14:1; LC 59, 72). In adoption the Spirit is given to the elect (12; LC 74), and they are sanctified by the application of the death and resurrection of Christ to them (13:1; LC 75), having repentance and all other saving graces infused in them (13:1; LC 32, 75–77). Through the continual supply of strength from the Spirit, believers grow in grace (13:3; LC 75); the outward means are made effective by the Spirit to the elect for salvation (7:5–6; 25:3; LC 155, 161). Prayer is to be made by the Spirit's help (21:3; LC 182); ability to do good works is from him (16:3); assurance is attained through his testimony with our spirits that we are children of God (18:2; LC 80); by his abiding with believers they are secured from totally falling away, and are kept through faith to salvation (17:2; LC 79).

Hope. The hope of glory (18:1; LC 83). The hope of hypocrites (18:1).

Humiliation of Christ (8:2,4; LC 46); in his conception and birth (LC 47); in his life (LC 48); in his death (LC 49); after death (LC 50).

Hypocrisy. Profession of Christ in hypocrisy or for evil purposes is sinful (LC 113).

Idleness forbidden (LC 139, 142).

Idolatry of all kinds forbidden (LC 105, 109) and all representations of idolatry ought to be removed (LC 108).

Ignorant not to be admitted to the Lord's Table (29:8; LC 173).

Image of God. Man made in the image of God in knowledge, righteousness and holiness (4:2; LC 17), which image is renewed in sanctification (LC 75), fully perfected in heaven (32:1; LC 86, 90).

Image worship of all kinds forbidden (LC 109).

Imputation. The guilt of Adam's first sin is imputed to his descendants (6:3). The obedience righteousness and satisfaction of Christ is imputed to believers (11:1; LC 70-71, 77).

Incarnation of Christ (8:2; LC 37, 39).

Incest forbidden (LC 139). Incestuous marriages (24:4).

Increase of grace is from the sanctifying Spirit of Christ (13:1,3 (LC 75, 77).

Infants, how saved (10:3). Infants of one or both believing parents to be baptised (28:4; LC 166).

Inspiration. The books of the Old and New Testaments given by inspiration of God to be the rule of faith and life (1:1); they are the word of God written and thus not human writings as are uninspired books (1:3). God is their author (1:4) and they are immediately inspired by him in Hebrew and Greek (1:8), possessing entire perfection and infallible truth (1:5).

Intercession. Christ as our Priest (LC 44) makes intercession so that the redemption he has purchased may be applied to all believers (8:8; LC 55). The perseverance of believers depends on Christ's intercession.

Interest. Unjust interest forbidden (LC 142).

Jokes, perverting Scripture by godless jokes forbidden (LC 113).

Judge. Christ the judge of the world (8:1,4; 33:1). How he shall come at the last day (LC 56).

Judgments. God's judgments in sinners in this world (5:6; LC 28, 83). How believers may bring temporal judgments on themselves (17:3). God is just and awesome in his judgments (2:1).

Judgement, the last; what it is (33:1); appointed for angels and people (8:4; 33:1; LC 88); its purpose is to reveal God's mercy and justice (33:2). Christ shall be the judge (8:4; 33:1). How he shall come (LC 56). Why he would have us firmly persuaded of it (33:3). Why the time of it is concealed (33:3; LC 88). Judgment of the righteous (33:2; LC 90) and of the wicked (33:3; LC 89).

Judicial laws (see *Law*).

Justice of God fully satisfied by Christ's obedience and death (8:5; 11:3; LC 38, 71). God's justice revealed in works of providence (5:1); in the justification of sinners (11:3) and in the last judgment (33:2).

Justification. What it is (11:1; LC 70); is of God's free grace (11:3; LC 71); the meritorious ground is solely Christ and his righteousness (11:1–2; LC 73) the instrumental cause of justification is solely faith in Christ (11:1–2; LC 71) and the necessary evidence of justification is good works (LC 77). Only the elect are justified (3:6) but although decreed from eternity the elect are not justified until in time the Holy Spirit actually applies Christ to them (11:4). Justification the same under the Old Testament as the New (11:6). Justification and sanctification compared (LC 77). The results of justification (17:1; LC 77, 79). Remnants of corruption remain (6:5; 13:2; LC 78) and they fall into actual sin (17:3; LC 78) which God continues to forgive (11:5).

Keys. What the power of the keys is (30:2). Committed to church officers (30:2) and may not be assumed by civil rulers (30:3).

King. Christ the King of his church (30:1). How he carries out the office of a king (LC 45); what is meant by the coming of his kingdom (LC 191).

Knowledge. God's knowledge is infinite and infallible and does not depend on any created thing (2:2). The knowledge people have from conscience and the works of God (1:1; 21:1; LC 2). The Scriptures alone able to give knowledge of God and duty related to salvation (1:1; 21:1; LC 2).

Law. The *ceremonial* law defined (19:3); how the covenant of grace was administered under the Old Testament (7:5; 8:6; LC 34); the judicial law now discontinued (19:3; 20:1).

Law. The *judicial* law defined, no longer obligatory except to the extent of general principles of justice and right in it (19:4)

Law. The *moral* law defined (LC 93); was given to Adam with ability to keep it (4:2; 19:1; LC 92) and was restated in summary in the Ten Commandments (!9:2). Although believers are not under it as a covenant (19:6)) and are not able to keep it perfectly (LC 149), yet it continues to be a perfect rule of righteousness (19:2) binding all persons (19:5). The obligation of it is not lessened under the gospel but strengthened (19:5). No one can attain righteousness and life by the moral law which Christ alone has purchased for the elect by his perfect obedience (19:6; LC 94–95). The moral law has a 3-fold use: (1) as the standard for society; (2) as a rule of life leading to repentance; (3) as a rule of life for believers (19:6; LC 94–97).

Law-suits. Unnecessary lawsuits to be avoided (LC 141–142).

Liberty. Christian liberty is freedom from guilt, condemnation and curse, and free access to God and child-like obedience(20:1). While the same liberty was enjoyed under the Old Testament there was a relative restriction (20:1).

Liberty of Conscience. The obligation of conscience is to God alone (20:2); we are not obliged to any belief or practice contrary to Scripture (20:2) or anything additional to Scripture in matters of faith or worship (20:2); we have the responsibility to ensure Scripture informs the conscience, and to reject coercion of the conscience (20:2); in private life liberty is not to be perverted to licentiousness (20:3); in public life it is not to be perverted to individualism by opposing lawful church or civil authority (20:4).

Life. Eternal life was purchased by Christ's perfect obedience to the law (8:5). The tree of life was a pledge of the covenant of works (LC 20). The life of any person is not to be taken except for limited reasons (LC 136).

Lord's Day. All people know that a proper proportion of time should be set apart for the worship of God (21:7). In his word God has appointed one day in seven (21:7; LC 20, 116). The particular day in the different dispensations (21:7; LC 116). How to keep it holy (21:8; LC 117); how it is misused (LC 119); the reasons enforcing its observance (LC 120); why we are to remember it (LC 121). Direction to those with responsibility for others (LC 118).

Lord's Prayer (LC 186–196).

Lord's Supper. Its institution (29:1; LC 168), nature (29:2; LC 168), right administration (29:3; LC 169), rejection of certain abuses (29:4), relation of signs to things signified (29:5), rejection of transubstantiation (29:6), explanation of Christ's presence: it is spiritual to faith not physical (29:7; LC 170); unworthy recipients (29:8; LC 173). Preparation for the Supper (LC 171–172), attitude when participating (LC 174), and afterwards (LC 175). Comparison with Baptism (LC 176–177).

Lots. Lots to be used in a godly way (LC 112); sinful lots forbidden (LC 113).

Love. Election is of God's free love (3:5; LC 13), and is unchangeable (17:2; LC 79). The sense of God's love is may be enjoyed in this life (LC 83). Love to God is a duty (LC 104) which conscience shows (21:1); to love God with all is the sum of our duty to God (LC 102); love to God is necessary to acceptable prayer (21:3; LC 185); love to God and the brethren is necessary to proper participation in the Lord's Supper (LC 168, 171, 174). True believers are never utterly deprived of the love of Christ and other believers (18:4). Love is the sum of our duty to others (LC 122); love for neighbour described (LC 135, 141, 144, 147) and what is contrary to it (LC 136, 142, 145, 148).

Lying sinful (LC 145).

Marriage (24; LC 20, 139; 141) See also *Celibacy* and *Divorce*.

Mass. A detestable insult to Christ's one and only sacrifice (29:2).

Means. God uses means in his ordinary providence but is not bound by them (5:3). The outward and ordinary means of salvation under the Old Testament (7:5; LC 34), under the New (7:6; LC 35, 154). Diligent use of the prescribed means is required (LC 153) but they are not to be trusted in (LC 105). How they are made effective (25:3; LC 155, 161, 182). Unlawful means are not be used (LC 105).

Medicine to used soberly (LC 135).

Mercy. God's mercy (2:1; LC 7) is revealed in his providence (5:1). Its is of his mercy that the elect are delivered from sin and misery (LC 30); God is merciful to penitent sinners in Christ (15:2; LC 76; 180). Works of mercy are to be done, even on the Lord's Day (21:8; LC 117).

Merit. No merit in good works so far as pardon of sin or eternal life is concerned (16:5), nor can we merit the outward blessings of this life (LC 193), but we are to trust in the merits of Christ (LC 174) who appears in heaven in the merit of his obedience and sacrifice as our Priest (LC 55).

Messiah. The elect's object of faith in the Old Testament (7:5; 8:6; LC 34).

Ministry. Given by Christ (25:3) and its support a duty (LC 108). Qualifications of a minister (27:4; 28:2; LC 158); duties (27:4; 28:2; LC 156, 158–159, 169).

Moral Law (see *Law*).

Name of God. Oaths in God's name only (22:2). How the name of God ought to be used and how not (LC 112–114, 190).

Oaths. Lawful oaths and vows (22:1–4; LC 108, 113).

Obedience is due to God in whatever he commands (2:2; LC 104). Christ has rendered perfect obedience to the law in our nature (8:4; LC 38–39, 48, 97); his obedience is imputed or reckoned to believers (11:1; LC 70). How the sincere but imperfect obedience of believers is accepted and rewarded (16:6). Obedience due to the lawful commands of civil authorities (23:4; LC 127–128).

Occult practices forbidden (LC 113).

Offices of Christ. Prophet (LC 43); Priest (LC 44); and King (LC 45).

Ordinances (see *Sacraments*).

Original sin (see *Sin*).

Passover, one of the types and ordinances by which the covenant of grace was administered under the Old Testament (7:5; LC 34).

Patience. Patient bearing of the hand of God a duty, and also patient bearing and forgiving of injuries caused by others (LC 135).

Perseverance of the Saints. Although the believer may fall into serious sin (17:3; 18:4; LC 78), since salvation is of the Lord his endurance in it to the end is certain (17:1; LC 77, 79). The grounds for perseverance stated (17:2; LC 79). The means of recovery stated (11:5; 13:3).

Pornography forbidden (LC 139).

Polygamy unlawful (24:1; LC 139).

Pope has no jurisdiction over civil rulers or their people. He is not the head of the church (25:6).

Praise to be joined with prayer (LC 196).

Praise. The praise of any good we are, have or can do is not to be traced to chance, idols, ourselves or any other creature (LC 105).

Prayer. A duty of all (LC 178); to be made to God alone (21:2; LC 179), in the name of Christ by the help of his Spirit (21:3; LC 178). Praying in the name of Christ (LC 180) and why (LC 181). How the Spirit helps our prayers (LC 182). How prayer is to be offered (21:3; LC 185); for what and for whom we are to pray (21:4; LC 183–184). Prayer is not more acceptable now by being offered in or towards a particular place (21:6). The rule of prayer (LC 186).

Preaching of the word. Part of the ordinary worship of God (21:5); one of the means by which the covenant of grace is now administered (7:6; LC 35); a duty of properly appointed ministers of the gospel (LC 158). How ministers are to preach (LC 159); how hearers are to listen (LC 160).

Predestination (3:3–4; LC 13). How the doctrine is to be handled and used (3:8).

Private worship in families a daily duty (21:6; LC 156).

Providence (5:1; LC 34). God directs events to occur through the agency of secondary causes (3:1; 5:2), and ordinarily uses means but is not bound by them (5:3). Providence and sin in general (5:4); sin of believers (5:5); sin of the ungodly (5:6). Providence and angels (LC 19); man when created (LC 20); the care of the church (5:7; LC 43, 45, 63).

Public worship not to be neglected (21:6).

Punishment (see *Sin*).

Purgatory. Scripture recognises no such place (32:1).

Quarrelling (LC 113; 136).

Questions that are speculative or unprofitable to be avoided (LC 113).

Reading the Scriptures by oneself and in families (1:8; LC 156); in public worship (21:5); how to be read (21:5; LC 157). How made effective for salvation (LC 155). Perverting or misapplying sinful (LC 113).

Recreation to be moderate (LC 135–136) but not on the Lord's Day (21:8; LC 119).

Repentance. What it is (15:1–2; LC 75); not a satisfaction for sin but no pardon without it (15:3; LC 153), nor condemnation where it is (15:4,6). Repentance should be specific (15:5). The doctrine of repentance is to be preached by ministers (15:1). Repentance to be made to those offended (15:6).

Restitution (LC 141).

Resurrection of Christ (8:4; LC 52). An effect of Christ's power (LC 52), evidences his Divine Sonship, and satisfaction to divine justice (LC 52); assures believers of their resurrection (LC 52) in which they already share (26:1). They were justified by his resurrection (11:4; LC 52) and are being sanctified through the virtue of his death and resurrection (13:1; LC 75; 167).

Resurrection of the dead: just and unjust (32:2,3; LC 87).

Sabbath (see *Lord's Day*).

Sacraments in general (27:1–4; LC 161–164). See *Baptism* and the *Lord's Supper*.

Sacrifice. The covenant of grace was administered in the Old Testament by sacrifices which spoke of Christ to come (7:5; 8:6; LC 34). Christ has made a full satisfaction for sin by the sacrifice of himself (8:5; LC 44). There is no real sacrifice in the Lord's Supper (29:2) which is a lasting remembrance of Christ's once-for-all sacrifice (29:1).

Saints. All believers, not just eminent ones, are saints but none are to be worshipped (21:2; LC 105).

Salvation not possible for those who do not profess the Christian religion (10:4; LC 60), Christ being the only Saviour who has purchased salvation by his obedience and sacrifice (8:5; LC 83) for all the elect and them only (3:6) to whom the outward means are made effective for salvation by the Spirit (7:5–6; 25:3; LC 154–155, 161, 182) who works faith in Christ in their hearts (14:1; LC 72). Faith is necessarily required for their justification and salvation (7:3; 11:1; LC 32, 71). The Spirit works in them all other saving graces (13:1; LC 32, 75–77) which accompany faith (11:2; LC 73) and enables them to holiness —the way appointed them for salvation (13:1; LC 32). Elect infants dying in infancy are regenerated and saved by Christ through the Spirit (10:3).

Sanctification. What it is (13:1; LC 75); inseparably joined to justification from which it differs (LC 77). It is throughout the whole person but imperfect in this life (13:2; LC 75, 77). Progressive development through the Spirit (13:3), and at death perfected (32:1; LC 80) and at the day of judgment fully and for ever freed from all sin (LC 90).

Scripture. Why necessary (1:1); the identity and purpose of Scripture (1:2–3; LC 3,5) and its role as regards worship (21:1; LC 108–109); its authority derived from its Author (1:4); rational basis yet necessity of Spirit's witness to saving understanding (1:5; LC 4; 157); Scripture sufficient (1:6; LC 2, 5), clear on essential matters for ordinary people (1:7); original transmitted in purity and final appeal to Hebrew and Greek texts (1:8); translations to be made and sufficient for ordinary purposes (1:8: LC 156); interpretation grounded in grammatical meaning and Scripture interprets Scripture (1:9); the Spirit speaking in the Scripture the ultimate tribunal (1:10). See *Reading of Scripture*.

Self-examination (LC 171).

Sin, What it is (LC 24); original sin (LC 25); the sin of our first parents (6:1; LC 21) by which they fell from their original righteousness and communion with God and had their natures wholly corrupted (6:2; LC 25, 27); the guilt of this first sin imputed and the corruption conveyed to their descendants (6:3;; LC 22, 26), who are subject to the wrath of God and curse of the law (6:6; LC 27, 194). From the original corruption of nature all actual sins flow (6:4; LC 25) and they vary in degree of sinfulness according to circumstances (LC 150–151), but every sin deserves God's wrath and curse (6:6; LC 152). The punishments of sin in this world (5:5–6; 17:3; 18:4; LC 28, 83); in the world to come (32:1; 33:2; LC 29, 86, 89). Sin is pardoned for Christ's sake alone (11:1; 15:3; LC 70). The sin that leads to death (21:4; LC 183. Providence in regard to sin (5:4); why God permitted the first sin (6:1); why he leaves his children to fall into sin (5:5); why and how sinners are hardened (5:6; LC 68).

Sincerity. Believers love Christ sincerely (18:1); are never utterly without sincerity of heart (18:4). Ministers ought to preach sincerely (LC 159). We are to pray sincerely (LC 185). God is pleased to reward what is sincerely done by believers (16:6).

Singing psalms is part of religious worship (21:5). Singing of lustful songs is forbidden (LC 139).

Slandering sinful ((LC 145).

Soul of man is immortal (4:2; LC 17). State of soul when separated from body (32:1; LC 86).

Stage plays that are lustful forbidden (LC 139).

Sovereignty of God over his creation (2:2; 21:1); sovereignty to be ascribed to God alone (LC 196); prayer to give due recognition to God's sovereignty (LC 185, 189).

Speech that is ambiguous/equivocal to the prejudice of truth and justice forbidden (LC 145).

Superstition. Human ideas or inventions forbidden in worship (21:1; 109, 113).

Surety (see *Guarantor*).

Suspension from the Lord's Table (30:4).

Temptation. Why God leaves his children subject to temptations (5:5). The wicked given up to temptations (5:6). Temptation to be avoided (LC 99 [6], 135, 138). Praying against temptation (LC 195).

Toleration of false religion (LC 109)

Trinity. There is but one God; the Father the Son and the Holy Spirit is each God; the Father the Son and the Holy Spirit is each a distinct person co-equal and co-eternal with the others (2:2; LC 9–11); The second person became incarnate, uniting a human nature to his divine person, and by virtue of this personal union the proper works of each nature are accepted by God and relied on by believers as works of the whole person (7:7; LC 36–40).

War on specified grounds lawful (23:2).

Wasteful recreations are forbidden (LC 142).

Weights and measures, false, forbidden (LC 142).

Will of God. The purpose of God's will is most wise and holy (3:1; LC 12), unsearchable (3:7; LC 13), free and unchangeable (5:1; LC 14) and righteous (2:1). The will of God revealed in Scripture is the only rule of faith, worship and conduct. The whole will of God in all things concerning the edification and salvation of his people is revealed by Christ by his word and Spirit (LC 43). See also *Free-will.*

Work. Our work to be balanced and not excessive (LC 135, 136).

Worship is due to God (2:2) and conscience testifies to this (21:1), but God has instituted in the Scriptures the way he is to be worshipped (21:1; 1:6; LC 108–109. Worship to be given the Triune God alone in the mediation of Christ (21:2; LC 179, 181). The parts of religious worship (21:3–5); the places and times of worship (21:6); the special day of worship (21:7–8; LC 115–121).

Zeal for God required (LC 104); zeal which is corrupt, blind or indiscreet forbidden (LC 105).